T0267296

TUCUMCARI TONITE!

TUCUMCARI TONITE!

A Story of Railroads, Route 66,
and the Waning of a Western Town

DAVID H. STRATTON

University of New Mexico Press | Albuquerque

© 2022 by David H. Stratton
All rights reserved. Published 2022
Printed in the United States of America

ISBN 978-0-8263-6339-8 (paper)
ISBN 978-0-8263-6340-4 (electronic)
Library of Congress Control Number: 2021953099

Founded in 1889, the University of New Mexico sits on the
traditional homelands of the Pueblo of Sandia. The original peoples
of New Mexico—Pueblo, Navajo, and Apache—since time
immemorial have deep connections to the land and have made
significant contributions to the broader community statewide. We
honor the land itself and those who remain stewards of this land
throughout the generations and also acknowledge our committed
relationship to Indigenous peoples. We gratefully recognize our
history.

Cover illustration: (top) adapted from photograph by Mobilus in
Mobili, licensed under CC by 2.0; (bottom) courtesy of Le Deane
Studio.
Designed by Felicia Cedillos
Composed in Adobe Garamond Pro 10.25/14.25

To my children:

Nancy Stratton Hall, MEd, National Board-Certified Teacher

And to the memory of
Scott David Stratton, PhD
(1962–2014)

Michael J. Stratton, PhD
(1955–2016)

CONTENTS

PREFACE

Let's face it at the outset. A book about an author's hometown sounds fishy. But this is not an account of high school romances or youthful exploits on the gridiron. Various world religions require their converts to make pilgrimages, usually to an especially important place associated with that particular faith. The purpose is a renewal of individual spirituality or, more simply, to give the pilgrims a sense of fulfillment, a realization of who they are, and the meaning of life through a journey back to the source of holy beginnings. The following account, although it may fall short as a pilgrimage, is neither a definitive history of a town nor my own coming-of-age—or, in this case, old-age—memoir. For the most part it is a case study with scholarly intent of the influence of twentieth-century transportation development, largely of railroads and highways in the context of national trends, and its effects on one Western town. In short, besides railroads, the importance of early and modern roads, but particularly Route 66 and its successor Interstate 40, receive major attention.

Founded by the Rock Island Railroad in 1901, Tucumcari, New Mexico, became a regional rail center and division point where four lines converged and the Rock Island and the Southern Pacific met. Later, with the creation of the federal highway system in 1926, US Highway 66 ran through the middle of town. The period covered is mainly the twentieth century, although some parts run slightly beyond to give them a logical conclusion or for purposes of continuity. Tucumcari flourished as a railroad center and highway tourist mecca for most of the twentieth century, but it went into sharp decline as the century ended.

This account identifies, as the main interpretive explanation of Tucumcari's decline, the influence of powerful external forces that were at work, mainly those of a national technological and corporate industrial nature involving railroads as well as highway systems. On the other hand, largely to promote economic progress and offset external pressures, the town itself either employed certain internal forces or sanctioned outside initiatives that also contributed to the decline, particularly an urban renewal project that practically destroyed the original downtown business district. In short, Tucumcari's story is one that has been repeated countless times in small towns across the West and in other sections of the country as well.

It is important to note that I was born and raised two blocks south of US Highway 66, the fabled "Mother Road" and "Main Street of America," when it was still filled with tourists getting their "kicks" on the way from Chicago to Los Angeles. In fact, in his monumental novel *The Grapes of Wrath*, about the exodus to California during the Great Depression of the 1930s, John Steinbeck coined the term *mother road* on the same page that he mentioned "Tucumcari" as a town located on the legendary highway. Also, where I grew up on South Adams Street was close enough to the rail yards that I could hear, night and day, the harsh, banging, steel-on-steel sounds of freight cars being coupled together. And in bed at night, I went to sleep to the sweet music of steam locomotive whistles as the mighty engines passed through or did switching duty locally.

When starting to write this book, I had the firm determination to avoid slipping into some sort of emotional relationship with the subject, on the order of a worshipful biography, and making my hometown an idyllic place like those depicted by Hollywood in the old Andy Rooney movies of the 1930s. I must confess that along the way I fell under the classical spell, as described by Plato (with allowances for paraphrasing), that the city is the soul of its citizens writ large. As a result, I sometimes bestowed human qualities, both virtues and vices, on the town as if it were a person. In fact, toward the end of my scholarly efforts, while mulling over an analysis of Tucumcari history, I realized that, indeed, I did actually love the place, a sentiment that had once surfaced in an awkward, although sincere, expression of my feelings. I could imagine myself

Running across the grey prairie
Through yellow-beaned mesquite and squat prickly pear cactus
bearing scarlet fruit
Down ferrous-red arroyos and past purple-walled mesas

Up steep canyon slopes wrinkled like cowhide and dotted with
scrub junipers
Over the rocky Eyebrow
To the endless Llano stretching away over the horizon.

I have no excuses for my sentimental attachments to Tucumcari, past or present, nor do I intend to make any now. In fact, I believe that my personal involvement with the subject of this book has given me important insights that a more detached writer would lack. At the same time, I pledge that my emotions did not take the place of more sober scholarly judgments of my old hometown, even though there was always room for both.

The reader will notice a heavy reliance on local newspapers for source material in this account. This is the case because the subject has a large element of local history and also because, for most of the twentieth century, the Quay County newspapers recorded everything the editors considered as important in the community they served—and beyond. It is true that these publications almost always remained in a booster mode, which required careful interpretation, but by concentrating on reading between the lines, it was possible to ferret out the essential information. Otherwise, in dealing with an astute editor and colorful personality, like Paul Dodge of the *Tucumcari Daily News*, it was easy to trust most of his news and views as being reliable. Large segments are also told through the personal experiences of notable women, men, and ethnic and racial groups. Conventional source materials, such as government documents, manuscript collections, interviews, and memoirs, provide a large part of the information. Since my parents and grandparents came to the area soon after Tucumcari's founding, and I have always called it "my old hometown," their recollections, as well as my own, are a vital part of this book. Overall, it was my intent to write an informative narrative of a Western town's involvement with railroads and highways that brought less than happy results.

DAVID H. STRATTON
Olympia, Washington

ACKNOWLEDGMENTS

The problem with dragging out a research project—some twenty years in this case—comes in acknowledging the countless number of debts accumulated for help and essential advice. As a result, because of space limitations, I can only mention a few of those generous individuals and institutions that provided a helping hand along the way. LeRoy Ashby kindly read early drafts of the manuscript and made seasoned suggestions, as did Robert J. Seigel for later drafts. Individuals who provided important source material and/or information include Dale Martin, Gil Henshaw, Joe Bonem, Barton Jones, Lucy Nials, Jack R. Hanna, Jimmie and Dorothy Randals, Elwin Howard, and Fred S. Witty Jr. Of my former classmates at Tucumcari High School who gave me encouragement and helpful advice, I owe special thanks to Marian Farmer Knapp and Lynn Moncus. Richard D. Spence and Frank Kyle Turner graciously supplied lengthy manuscripts they had written from which I borrowed substantial information, as was the case with Joy Barrick Batson's correspondence during World War II. The following persons and their institutions were especially helpful in this project: Sue Shipman and the Washington State University Libraries, Claudia Rivers and the University of Texas at El Paso Libraries, and Michael S. Sweeney and the State Historical Society of Missouri, Research Center, Kansas City. For permission to use their photographs, I thank Glenn A. Gierzychi, Carol M. Highsmith, and Darel Greene. My appreciation also goes to Daryll DeWald, Dean, College of Arts and Sciences, Washington State University, for released time from classroom duties to do research and writing on this project. I am also indebted to Yetta Kohn Bidegain for her long-time contributions of crucial source material and kind encouragement, and to Veronica Mares and the Quay County Clerk's Office in Tucumcari for their cooperation in furnishing county records. For anyone I have left out, I apologize. However, I would be unforgivably remiss if I failed to acknowledge the many ways my former next-door neighbors, Tim and Linda Fisher, went out of their way to make life easier for me in the course of this project. They were the best darn neighbors an old coot could wish for. Last, but far from least, I am sure I could never have completed this project without the prolonged, tireless, devoted help in countless ways of my daughter, Nancy Stratton Hall. Bless you, dear one.

INTRODUCTION

Often depicted by Hollywood as uniformly statuesque and muscular, Plains Indians actually could be impressively tall, with many Sioux and Osage men standing well over six feet in height. Not so the Comanches, who dominated New Mexico's eastside tablelands and Canadian River corridor. Powerfully stocky but typically of squat build with stumpy legs, the Comanches seemed pathetic and clumsy. In fact, until they obtained horses originating from Spanish herds in New Mexico sometime before 1700 and moved onto the southern Great Plains, they had been confined to a humble, sedentary existence along the Rocky Mountain slopes north of the Arkansas River. There they had often faced hand-to-mouth hardship in their nomadic, short-range hunting forays afoot.[1] Once mounted on fleet horses, the Comanches, who afoot had been immobile and vulnerable, became unsurpassed buffalo slayers and the most feared raiders by both whites and other Indians of the Southern Plains. Like the later American craze to acquire automobiles, the obsession with horses among all the Plains tribes created a lucrative business for the Comanches. They excelled at both stealing and trading the animals, thereby making a major contribution to the spread of the horse culture across the entire Southwest. Significantly certain terms in their language, distinguished by its deep, robust quality and rolling *r*s, became the common trade patois understood by neighboring tribes.

The American West has experienced several transportation revolutions, but few could match the wondrous transformation of the Comanches from landlocked foot sloggers to "Cossacks" of the Plains or simply "the finest mounted warriors in North America." One other such revolution, however, did bring changes of even greater magnitude to the same remote southwestern prairies. For its sheer force to conquer the hinterlands, but even more so to create towns and mold individual lives, the railroad was unmatched in its effects. Moreover, from the 1870s to the late 1930s, according to a prominent railroad historian, "no private enterprise—not even the oil companies in the automobile age— occupied a position of similar power and influence."[2]

Many innocent passengers as well as depot bystanders, not to mention countless members of model railroad clubs, have been mesmerized by the mystic quality of trains. For some believers, like American world traveler Paul Theroux, it was a simple fascination punctuated by "I have seldom heard a train go by and not wished I was on it . . . [because] those whistles sing bewitchment." Others have undergone an equally intense baptism. In Nobel Prize–winner Yasunari Kawabata's novel *Snow Country* (1960), the main character is traveling on a passenger train at night looking out at the snow-covered landscape of northern Japan. Suddenly he feels the strange sensation of "watching a tableau in a dream," followed by the shadowy impression that the outside scenery, "dim in the gathering darkness," and his fellow passengers, "transparent and intangible," have become "melted together into a sort of symbolic world not of this world."[3] In a bygone-era passenger trains also crisscrossed every part of the United States, and several generations of Americans shared similar captivating experiences.

My own initiation into this eerie realm of hypnosis came at exactly 3:15 p.m. on July 31, 1935, in Tucumcari, New Mexico, when I was eight-and-a-half years old. On that hot summer day, the Rock Island's Number 11 passenger train came from the east and pulled slowly in front of the Tucumcari depot. Among those on board the steam-powered behemoth was the town's most prominent citizen. Arch Hurley was returning from Washington, DC, bearing the most important news in this southwestern community's relatively short history. As the climax of years of lobbying Congress and every influential national politician he could buttonhole, Hurley had finally succeeded in winning legislative approval for construction of Conchas Dam on the nearby Canadian River.[4]

A local newspaper hailed it as the culmination of "more than 25 years of dreaming and planning," and predicted that the dam's construction was sure to pump between $35 and $40 million into the town's Depression-stalled economy, doubling the population of 4,500 in the process. Local businessmen and Chamber of Commerce officials, in the exuberant spirit of frontier boosterism, had chipped in monthly amounts up to $25 apiece, a princely sum in those

Depression years, to finance Hurley's trips to the national capital.[5] Now they gathered at the depot as victors eager to claim the spoils. A throng of townspeople and country folks, so impressed by the occasion's significance that they came dressed in their Sunday-go-to-meeting best, rounded out the cheering crowd of 3,500 people. It was the largest assemblage yet in Quay County, even exceeding the horde of baseball fans which, a year earlier, had witnessed an impromptu major league exhibition game between the Chicago White Sox and the Pittsburgh Pirates, who had stopped off between trains.[6]

First, a respected barber led three cheers, the crowd sang "America" accompanied by a band, the barber's daughter directed the performance of a girls' chorus, and various and sundry dignitaries had their say. Then, Arch Hurley, a tall, dignified man who owned the local movie theater, climbed up on the back of a flatbed truck and gave his speech. He recounted the long struggle he had endured and the last-minute frustration just before the great triumph in Congress. Just when "all of those fighting for our dam were about ready to quit, but with their backs to the wall, [they] went at it again," he told them dramatically, "until finally President Roosevelt himself decided the matter by making the emphatic statement that the project was not to go into the waste basket, [but] was to be built." For Tucumcari, Hurley declared to thunderous applause, Conchas Dam would become the golden ladder out of the Great Depression and the gateway to endless future prosperity.[7]

All these grandiose pronouncements were lost on me. As Hurley's train slowly approached the depot before stopping—with whistles in the railroad yards and shops blowing, the town's fire siren blasting away, and all the church bells ringing—I was standing at the front of the crowd near the tracks. In the blink of an eye, I had the earthshaking transcendent sensation that I was moving and the train standing still, that I had been seized by a powerful force, and, held in its grip, had undergone an out-of-body experience. Although a physicist and some psychologists might prefer a more complicated scientific explanation, my phenomenon of trading motion with the train probably was a simple psychological illusion, a trick of the central nervous system common to railroad fans. Whatever the case, it was the beginning of my fascination with trains, but not as a devout railroad buff who memorizes ancient timetables, the grades on isolated stretches of tracks, and all the different models of locomotives. It was more like a restless sleeper who, lying in bed alone on a winter evening, cherishes the soothing sound of a bawdy steam locomotive whistle splitting the cold night air, and who can never forget the rising clickety-clack tempo of steel wheels on steel rails as a passenger coach pulls away from the depot into the exciting outside world. It was like music, at the same time soul soothing but also exciting, as if the clamor of an arriving train brought with it a new lease on life.

From its founding, the eastern New Mexico town of Tucumcari, if it had possessed human powers, might well have told of a comparable enthralling spell by railroads. Historically, a key influence in the town's development was its geographical location. It is situated in a broad east-west, canyon-like passageway along the Canadian River between a rugged riverine escarpment to the north and the high Llano Estacado (Staked Plain) on the south. This wide passageway, called the Canadian corridor in the following account, runs through eastern New Mexico and the Texas Panhandle, separating the Llano Estacado from the rest of the Great Plains. It was a favorite travel route for the early Plains people. Under Spanish and Mexican rule, the main trade connection for New Mexico was the Chihuahua Trail between Santa Fe and Chihuahua City in northern Mexico, a tributary link of the Camino Real (Royal Road) to Mexico City. With the annexation of New Mexico by the United States in 1848, however, this north-south transportation focus shifted to an east-west orientation, thereby enhancing the future prospects of the Canadian corridor for railway and highway projects. The east-west adaptation was soon solidified in the overland traffic of thousands of Forty-Niners to the California goldfields. Although the 35th parallel of latitude offered a favorable route through the Canadian corridor, it failed to gain federal approval for the first transcontinental railroad, which was built farther north in 1869. Later, the trajectory of Route 66, and especially Interstate 40, would more nearly approximate the 35th parallel route.

The town of Tucumcari was created from scratch on the open prairie, in 1901, by the arrival of the financially troubled Rock Island Railroad. This Chicago-based transportation giant had been building west to meet the regional El Paso and Northeastern Railroad at the Pecos River, thereby hoping to forge a link in its quest for a transcontinental connection. Later the Rock Island would have to settle for a subservient partnership role with the Southern Pacific in the Golden State Route between Chicago and Los Angeles. Branch tracks to the northern New Mexico coal mines at Dawson carried tons of coking coal through Tucumcari daily to the Arizona copper smelters of the giant Phelps,

Dodge and Company. The operational division point between the Southern Pacific and the Rock Island was moved from Santa Rosa to Tucumcari in 1907. In addition, the Tucumcari and Memphis Line, or T&M, an extension of the Choctaw, Oklahoma & Gulf Railroad between Memphis and Amarillo, Texas, reached Tucumcari in 1910. In less than a decade, then, four important lines converged on Tucumcari, making it a major regional railroad center. Under the magic wand of rails, the remote Western town, where buffalo, Comanche Indians, and Hispanic shepherds and traders had only lately roamed, was quickly transformed. It fast became a modern, booming industrial complex with steaming locomotives and speeding freight and passenger trains passing through. In the yards, a large roundhouse with spewing smokestacks and, elsewhere on the premises, several hundred skilled, unionized craftsmen, trainmen, and clerical staff members completed the picture.

About the same time Rock Island built its tracks through Tucumcari, the federal government encouraged homesteading on the public lands in eastern New Mexico. Thousands of eager settlers flocked in to claim the free land, and many hired railroad freight cars to transport themselves, their farm animals and equipment, and household goods. What certainly was that area's most pathetic story ensued when the earnest, hardworking homesteaders realized after a few years the impossibility of eking out a living on their marginal claims. They fled the stingy soil in droves. No matter how they had arrived, most of the first wave left by train if they could afford it. Later waves of dejected homesteaders pulled out, especially in the Dust Bowl of the 1930s but also during the Second World War and in the drought years of the 1950s. Now they left in cars and trucks, and many followed the "Okies" on Route 66 to California. Today across the abandoned countryside the network of roads, quickly etched into the landscape along section lines during the early homesteading days, has been largely erased, and the cattle guards replaced by the locked gates of big ranches. Needless to say, the exodus from the hinterlands dealt a serious blow to Tucumcari's economic well-being that was only partially alleviated by the opening of some forty thousand acres of adjacent irrigated farmlands watered from Conchas Dam.

One reason the twentieth century has been called the "American Century" is because of the nation's vibrant railroad system. But actually the "Golden Age of the Railroad in America" had started to wane in about 1916, shortly after the founding of Tucumcari, when the nation's track mileage reached a peak and began to shrink as the rails of deactivated branch lines were ripped up.[8] Automobiles, buses, and trucks, using the emerging national highway system, became increasingly strong competitors for passengers and freight, and airplanes started attracting passengers and taking over lucrative mail contracts. Nothing had more influence on the railroads, and Tucumcari itself, than the effects of ever-advancing technology, particularly the introduction of diesel locomotives that could run much longer distances without servicing or water than steam engines. Under such pressures the rail companies continually sought ways to economize and improve efficiency, which resulted in giant mergers and drastic reorganization of operational units. In one of these routine reorganizations, the Union Pacific, successor of the Southern Pacific, eliminated Tucumcari as a division operations center, inflicting a grievous wound that has never healed on the town.

As a result of these powerful outside forces, the railroad, which had created the town, stole away, abandoning its creation and leaving it like an orphan to fend for itself. In the past, four or five majestic passenger trains a day stopped at the local depot, innumerable chugging freights halted to discharge or take on cargoes, and yeoman switch engines hustled back and forth in the extensive sidetracks. These monumental machines plus the depot and its beanery (restaurant), the massive roundhouse, the long freight warehouse, the switching yards and tall coal chutes, the livestock holding pens, and other rail facilities had formed the nerve center of the town.

William Faulkner, in his novel *Light in August*, describes a place that might well have been Tucumcari:

> The town was a railroad division point. Even in mid-week there were many men about in the streets. The whole air of the place was masculine, transient; a population even whose husbands were at home only at intervals and on holidays—a population of men who led esoteric lives[,] whose actual scenes were removed and whose intermittent presence was pandered to like that of patrons in a theatre.[9]

In Tucumcari, day or night, standing only a block from the rail yards at a corner of Second and Main Street it was possible to feel, and see, the pulse of railroad life as the trains pulled in and out and "railroaders" walked the streets in their blue denim overalls and striped caps. In the town's railroad culture, train-operating crewmen—locomotive engineers, firemen, conductors, and brakemen—were conspicuous as the economic elite; they sent their kids to college and bought a new Oldsmobile or Buick every three years. Railroaders had their own jargon, which most townspeople also understood. And one thing was certain in this railroad town—life then was never dull even for teenagers. They could always go down to the depot and watch the world pass through.

Today there are no passenger trains in Tucumcari, having disappeared years ago, and the old business district around Second and Main looks like a ghost town. The remaining freights, bearing the Union Pacific logo, usually rip over the tracks in front of the depot, now a museum, at sixty miles an hour. The local folks are lucky to hear the engineer acknowledge their existence with the federally required blast of a diesel horn at Rock Island Street, the only land-level crossing in the town proper. (And unarguably a rasping diesel horn in no way matches the melodious salute from a steam locomotive whistle.) In short, Tucumcari got caught up and swept aside by the unrelenting change that characterizes industrialization.[10]

Meanwhile, in the railroad town's heyday from the 1920s to the 1960s, the economic benefits from the construction of Conchas Dam and the accompanying irrigation canal system also had far-reaching effects. College-educated engineers, large-scale contractors, top-level federal officials, highly skilled craftsmen, and specialized workers from all over the country poured in, making the town a relatively cosmopolitan place for its size. In addition, it enjoyed the stimulus of a burgeoning national tourist trade. The dark side of this flow of traffic, depicted in John Steinbeck's Depression-era novel, *The Grapes of Wrath*, in which he called Route 66 "the mother road," featured farm families displaced by the Dust Bowl passing through Tucumcari bound for the promised land of California.[11]

Steinbeck's novel developed a cult-following after it was produced as a Hollywood film in 1940, and Route 66 would be considered "the most famous road in America" as well as "the quintessential American highway." Such claims to fame became important to me personally because, again, I was born in 1927 two blocks south of Route 66 a year after it got that number officially, and I grew up with the highway as it increased in prominence. The surging line-up of cars—especially during the summer months—with so many different license plates from states I had only read about in school became an ingrained part of my young life. Growing up within sight of that stream of traffic was as much like Huck Finn's life on the Mississippi River as anything I can imagine.

On Route 66, W. A. Huggins, whose son Phares was my boyhood friend, built the acclaimed Blue Swallow Court (later changed to Motel) and he and his perky wife Mary Maud operated it for a few years. In fact, Maud Huggins named the Blue Swallow, wanting the title and the color of the gracefully swooping blue bird to suggest peaceful, soothing rest and sleep. William Archie "Arch" Huggins was one of the finest men I have ever known, a true specimen of moral rectitude and an exacting craftsman in his work in the building trade. Faithful in church attendance, calm in demeanor, he practiced his religion unobtrusively in everyday life. Although his complexion and stature suggested a large measure of American Indian lineage, his Oklahoma and Arkansas background remained a mystery that his family members never discussed publicly.[12]

I liked to hang out with Phares Huggins in the Blue Swallow's small lobby talking to the guests. Oklahoma-born Will Rogers had become a national celebrity as a Hollywood film star and America's most beloved humorist, as a syndicated newspaper columnist and radio commentator. Route 66 was named the "Will Rogers Highway" after he was killed in an Alaska plane crash in 1935. On one occasion at the Blue Swallow, I met a "genuine" Hollywood movie actor, Leon "Abner" Weaver of the hillbilly musical comedy group Weaver Brothers & Elviry. Renowned for playing the musical saw in films and vaudeville stage shows, Weaver reminisced about his movie role with singing cowboy Gene Autry, and then dropped his bombshell. He had actually known the great Will Rogers, told of visiting his Santa Monica ranch, and casually referred to him as "Bill." Then he scrawled "best Wishes to David—Abner Weaver, Weaver Bros Elviry Co" on a Blue Swallow business card and gave it to me. I was overwhelmed by this brush with celebrity greatness.[13]

At the Blue Swallow it was always tempting to read the postcards that departed guests had dropped in a basket for mailing. The touristy messages ranged from reports about staying overnight in this "crazy-named town" to a thwarted afternoon stroll out to Tucumcari Mountain. In the mirage of summer heat waves, the mountain seemed only a few city blocks away, but, as the exhausted tourist discovered, the distance was actually three miles and much too far for a leisurely walk—particularly with the temperature approaching 100 degrees.[14] And the

William Archie "Arch" and Mary
Maud Huggins. He built the
Blue Swallow Court (Motel) in
1939, and she named it. They
operated the Blue Swallow until
1943. Photo by the author.

Blue Swallow took on a special identity in community life as well. A man committed suicide in one of the rooms. During the travel restrictions and gasoline
rationing of World War II, my favorite high school teacher spent the first night of
her honeymoon at the Blue Swallow and then the next day boarded a train to El
Paso for a week's outing.

Young boys in Tucumcari often spent their slack hours on summer days
looking for excitement at the numerous gasoline filling stations along Route 66
in town. In front, these establishments had tall, brightly painted gas pumps
topped by round glass cylinder tanks with numbered lines measuring gallons.
The gas was pumped up to the glass tanks manually by laboriously pulling a
long-handled lever at the side back and forth. A hose dispensed by gravity the
specific gallons a tourist requested. Inside, the stations had inviting candy

counters and iced-down soda pop coolers. As a practical joke, a high-and-mighty attendant, perched authoritatively atop the big boxlike cooler, might send the kids on futile errands to a series of other Route 66 gas stations to borrow a "left-handed monkey wrench" for some mysterious mechanical problem. Or the gullible kids might be dispatched to obtain a "pie stretcher," supposedly for use on one of the small pecan pies in the display case, so it would be large enough to share. A kid could also fill his perpetually flat bicycle tires at the gas station and, while doing so, hear the attendant telling another adult about a racy incident with an attractive woman tourist. It seemed that he understood her to ask about getting the floorboard of her car swept out, and he had shouted back over his shoulder that he would just blow it out with the air hose to save time. Actually, she had been asking about using the restroom. On other summer days young boys killed time by sitting along the then-curbless highway watching the historic Dust Bowl caravan of cars and trucks pass by on its way to California. With youthful insensitivity they shared a tasteless joke of the day: "How do you tell a rich Okie from a poor one?" Answer: "The rich Okie has two mattresses tied on top of his car."

After World War II, during which the grown-up boys had been drafted for military service, the romance of the road lured multitudes of Americans in their cars over the two national highways that converged on Tucumcari, US 54 and US 66, and produced a myriad of motels, restaurants, service stations, convenience stores, and curio shops. A popular television series and a more popular song encouraged Americans to "get your kicks on Route 66," which was quickly dubbed the "Main Street of America."[15] As Tucumcari Tonite! advertising signs appeared along Route 66, the town became part of the fabled highway's lore. Most notably, the Blue Swallow Motel, which by then was touted as the "first modern local motel," and had long boasted in blazing neon lights, "100% Refrigerated Air," gained legendary status. In time, no television or other media presentation of the Mother Road (now capitalized) would seem authentic without an illustration featuring the celebrated swooping swallow.

Tucumcari had become more than a railroad center; it had taken on the trappings of a full-blown transportation mecca. Rail lines converged on the town from all four directions, and two major US highways, 66 and 54, plus principal state roads added to the network. Like the retreat of the railroads, the federal Interstate Highway Act of 1956 eventually helped sap local economic vitality by replacing Route 66 through town with Interstate 40 and its bypass around the southern outskirts. The original full-scale transportation system now became subservient to the I-40 freeway, whose bypasses created a townless highway.

Progress in transportation development, it seemed, had no mercy to spare on small towns. In the grand scheme of national industrialization, dot com technology, and globalization, the fate of Tucumcari is hardly unique because a multitude of other towns suffered similar calamities. But it is unique for the people living there because it happened to them. From now on they could no longer rely on the boundless optimism implicit in western boosterism for the solution of all ills, economic and social. In a way the isolated, remote town of Tucumcari became an exaggerated example of what had happened in the United States itself during the last decades of the twentieth century, as many Americans lost faith in inexorable progress. When the twenty-first century dawned, Tucumcari, proud of its past prominence, struggled on, with the lingering hope of a renaissance delivered by some new, as yet unidentified, wave of external economic or technological change.

A century earlier the Comanches experienced similar misfortune when the horse culture proved no match for the railroad, which transported army troops quickly to strategic points and brought throngs of settlers into what had been the Indian's private domain. Quanah Parker and his western Quahada, or Kwahada (Antelope) band, the fiercest, most aloof of all Comanches, had often ridden across the Llano Estacado and the Canadian Corridor on raids and knew every part by heart. The day of such exploits had ended, however, following the army's conquest of the Plains tribes in 1875. The Indians lost not only their homeland but their freedom as well.[16]

Some Comanches would plead for a reservation on the upper Canadian or Pecos Rivers but had to accept Fort Sill in Oklahoma instead. At Fort Sill, Quanah Parker, the son of an Indian father and a captive Texan mother, shrewdly walked a tightrope between the two cultures and, cooperating with federal officials, was made chief of all the Comanche bands. Now a national celebrity, who, as a friend of the president, attended Theodore Roosevelt's inauguration in 1905, he later hosted Teddy in Oklahoma for a wolf hunt. He built a ten-room house and installed one of the first home telephones in Oklahoma. At one time he was reportedly the wealthiest of all Native Americans through his ranching and business interests. But he stoutly resisted official pressures to abandon polygamous marriage (eight wives altogether, five at one time); accept Christianity, preferring the peyote cult; or cut off his traditional long braids. Even so, Quanah Parker, chief of all Comanches, those Cossacks of the Prairies who had revolutionized horse transportation on the Southern Plains, showed a keen understanding of the new industrial America. He helped promote and supposedly invested $40,000 (a princely sum at the time) in a Texas short-line railroad starting in the Texas town named for him—the Quanah, Acme, and Pacific Railway. It is said that he liked to climb aboard the railroad's locomotives, blow the whistle, and ring the bell. In this instance Quanah Parker of the Quahada band was riding the wave of the present, not the past, in transportation development.

Chapter 1

THE JEWISH FOUNDING FATHERS

bove the heavy, double, wooden doors of the Quay County district courtroom in Tucumcari a New Deal–era mural depicts a golden-armored Spanish conquistador sitting on a rock under a sparse tree with Tucumcari Mountain in the background. The inscription reads, "I, Francisco Vasquez [*sic*] de Coronado, have passed this way and left my mark." No ironclad proof exists that Coronado actually sat overlooking the future site of the "'Infant Wonder' of the Great Staked Plains," as early Tucumcari was called. On the other hand, it would be difficult to prove that he did not. The exact route of his expedition is a topic of heated controversy. However, Coronado probably did stop at or near Tucumcari Mountain with Tucumcari's location in sight toward the Canadian River to the north.

In the spring of 1541, the handsome, fair-haired, thirty-two-year-old Spaniard, left the Rio Grande Valley near today's Albuquerque to explore the Canadian River corridor and the Southern Plains in quest of the fabled land of Quivira and possible opportunities for trade and colonization. Any assumption that the numbers of this exploratory force compared with the 30-plus members of the later American Lewis and Cark Expedition must be immediately dismissed. Coronado's entrada, or expedition, to unexplored lands, had at least 1,500 people—a mix of Spaniards, Indians, French, Germans, Africans, one Scot, and others, including infantrymen and mounted troops, mule skinners, servants and attendants, slaves and porters, Indian allies, and Franciscan priests—not to mention, soldiers' wives and their children. The mass also included an immense herd of oxen, horses, mules, sheep, and other livestock as well as wheeled vehicles such as wagons and military carts. Somewhere on the west side of the Pecos River, probably upriver from today's Santa Rosa near Anton Chico, the conquistadors lashed together a floating platform of timbers that the people gingerly crossed single file followed by the animals and vehicles in their turn. This was the first bridge carrying traffic headed for the Canadian River corridor and the future site of Tucumcari. Amid the "constant bedlam of shouting and cursing by herdsmen and horse wranglers, mingled with the bellowing and bleating of the animals," the mob fanned out across the red-earth prairie as it marched toward Tucumcari Mountain. A billowing cloud of dust inevitably marked the path. Upon reaching the location of the mountain and gazing at the level landscape to the north, Coronado and his followers made up the largest human presence in the immediate area until Tucumcari itself arose more than 350 years later.

Over the years others stopped at the mountain or looked with approval on that locality as a place of habitation. At one time or another several generations of Plains people established campsites at the bottom of the mountain's north slope where the face had crumpled away, revealing, like streaks in a ham, its red, layered geological structure. In fact, for the next three hundred years travelers usually found an Indian encampment in the vicinity. In 1853 Lieutenant Amiel W. Whipple of the of the US Army, who was investigating a possible transcontinental railroad route along the 35th parallel of latitude, reported favorably on the "Tucumcari Hills" area. He thought that this site had "every facility for a large settlement" that in a short time might "become the centre of a flourishing State." To questions about an existing population base to support a railroad, Whipple readily replied that if one was built, people would come.[1] And that is what happened in the case of Tucumcari.

The immediate seedbeds for the founding of Tucumcari were the by-then-abandoned Fort Bascom, established about eight miles north of the town site on the Canadian River during the Civil War and its civilian outpost, the village of Liberty, five miles south of the fort. The actual groundwork for the establishment of Tucumcari began, however, on a snowy fall day in 1900 when a carriage of Chicago-based Rock Island Railroad officials stopped at Liberty. Given shelter by the Goldenberg family, local Jewish merchants, the strangers apparently confided that the railroad would soon lay tracks in the vicinity on its way to link up with the El Paso & Northeastern Railway at the Pecos River near Santa Rosa. At first the settlers at Liberty were skeptical, as the story goes, but their doubts soon vanished. Railroad surveyors appeared, saying a "strong possibility" existed that a good-sized town would arise somewhere nearby.[2]

Tucumcari Mountain, "The Lonely Sentinel on the Plain," a landmark guide for generations of explorers and travelers, gave a name to the town at its foot. Sheryl Savas / Alamy Stock Photo (Image ID: CW50J7).

Pyramid Mountain. Located a few miles southwest of Tucumcari, this 570-foot peak with exposed strata gained fame in the 1850s when used to support a geological theory that the general area had a Jurassic past. This idea set off a lengthy controversy that ended with only part of the peak recognized for Jurassic age. LeDeane Studio, Tucumcari.

Accordingly, with characteristic western enterprise, three Jewish entrepreneurs, Alexander Daniel Goldenberg, his brother Max Buchanan Goldenberg, and their brother-in-law Jacob Wertheim, spearheaded the formation of a real estate agency and prepared to cash in on the railroad's recent arrival. With a working capital of $10,000 (soon increased to $20,000 of "paid up stock"), the Tucumcari Townsite and Investment Company had as its mission "buying and selling real estate, laying off and establishing a townsite, selling town lots and doing anything necessary in conducting a general townsite business." The date was November 22, 1901, and this was the beginning of Tucumcari. The company's officers of record were Lee Kewen Smith, president; James Alexander "Alex" Street, vice president; Alex Goldenberg in the all-important financial post of treasurer; and Wertheim as secretary.[3] Although Max Goldenberg's name did not appear in this list, he nonetheless had an important role in the firm. All five were Tucumcari's founding fathers, but the Goldenbergs and Wertheim undoubtedly put up most of the money and, therefore, controlled the venture.[4]

The town's location and its christening also had railroad origins. Tucumcari Mountain, standing in a corridor created by the Canadian River between the Llano Estacado (Staked Plain) on the south and an elevated escarpment to the north, was the dominating feature of the landscape for miles around. A conveniently located water supply—a scarcity in that region—existed in springs at the foot of the mountain and in nearby creeks. The main reason for the location, however, must be credited to railroad builder Charles B. Eddy. He had decided that a convenient, although rough, passageway provided by Atarque Creek canyon north of this spot made the best link for a branch line between the Rock Island Railroad and coalfields he had recently acquired 132 miles away at Dawson.[5] "Tucumcari," the Comanche name for the mountain, had been recorded in 1788 and again in 1792 by Pierre (or "Pedro") Vial, a peripatetic French explorer who often worked for the Spanish. Although translation from Comanche is tricky, the best bet comes from *tukamukaru*, meaning "to lie in wait for someone or something to approach," or loosely interpreted, "lookout peak."[6]

Quite simply, the town's location in the beginning and its fate from then on was largely determined by a railroad. In turn, it was only logical to give the settlement the name of the dominant landmark. The christening itself occurred

Quay County, New
Mexico.

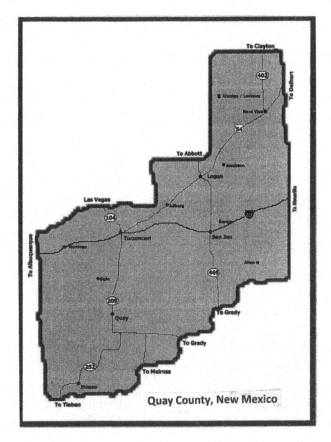

after the Rock Island tracks had arrived at the site. At first only a colony of tents
stood north of the town site in December 1901, even though the railroad construction crews had reached there more than a month earlier. Adding to the
bucolic scene, a herd of antelope often grazed peacefully nearby. But the railroad construction camp had no formal name, going by "Liberty Junction,"
"Douglas," "Six-Shooter Siding," and "Ragtown" (from the windblown laundry
left hanging on the surrounding thorny mesquite bushes).[7] A Rock Island construction engineer suggested it be named for the celebrated landmark, looming
up in the background. That name with a railroad origin stuck.[8]

According to local legend, the investment company's officers had been
uncertain of the exact location of the rail line and its depot. As insurance, they

had supposedly filed a straight north-south ribbon of homestead claims between the Canadian River and Tucumcari Mountain, thereby monopolizing any future town site. Although this story resembles the classic myth of frontier enterprise common in Hollywood Westerns, it is half wrong, and the other half is not quite right. First, it would have been impossible for only four or five claimants, each with the limitation of 160-acre homestead entries, to monopolize the twelve-mile expanse of land between the river and the mountain or any extensive swath of it. Moreover, the myth glosses over a more intriguing scenario of how Jewish entrepreneurs acquired the land they needed, became the main founding fathers of Tucumcari, and played a crucial role in the town's more than half-century of success as a commercial and transportation center.[9]

After the Civil War, a sizable contingent of predominantly German Jewish immigrants came to New Mexico, and many of them bypassed Santa Fe for opportunities east of the Pecos River at the trading outpost of Las Vegas. Until it was surpassed by Albuquerque around 1920, Las Vegas was the largest urban community, with the largest Jewish population—and first synagogue, Congregation Montefiore—in New Mexico for the roughly four decades following the arrival of the Atchison, Topeka & Santa Fe Railroad in 1879.[10] The Jewish patriarch of Las Vegas and architect of the territory's mercantile capitalism, Charles Ilfeld, had become wealthy and influential through his widespread merchandising, sheep ranching, money lending, and land interests.[11] A pattern emerged in which Jewish newcomers often worked first at the Ilfeld firm in Las Vegas or one of its several branches before striking out on their own as merchants, ranchers, or land dealers. It's not surprising that two Jewish entrepreneurs familiar with Ilfeld's success had turned up ninety miles to the east at Tucumcari.

Among the German Jewish immigrants who came to New Mexico after the Civil War, brothers Alex and Max Goldenberg, who married Henrietta and Emma, both sisters of Jacob Wertheim, usually teamed up with Wertheim in business affairs. Another brother, Hugo Goldenberg, chose a different path, eventually in ranching near Santa Rosa. Alex had skipped a hands-on apprenticeship with Charles Ilfeld, but Max and Hugo Goldenberg had both been associated with the Las Vegas patriarch in business affairs. In 1899 Alex Goldenberg turned up at Liberty where, probably financed by Max, he and Wertheim bought the Jarrell General Merchandise Store. Significantly the

Goldenbergs' cousin, Max Norhaus, was Ilfeld's budding partner and heir apparent. This family relationship gave the Goldenbergs a niche in a tight-knit, kinship-centered Jewish network that emphasized ethnicity, family loyalty, and a common Jewish heritage as well as a source to borrow funds.[12]

While the myth of Tucumcari's founding that involved a ribbon of homestead claims between the Canadian River and Tucumcari Mountain has its appeal, the real story starts at the future intersection of Main and Second Streets with the Joseph Israel Building, the Vorenberg Hotel, the First National Bank, and the Sands-Dorsey Drugstore at the corners. This important crossroads, which became the pulse of the downtown business district, lies only a block or so from the train depot where Second Street temporarily dead ends. In terms of strategic real estate investment and sales, the Goldenbergs and their associates had to gain control of the land adjacent to the hublike depot, around which they would plat their town site. In the beginning, however, the real estate cohorts did not know where the all-important depot would be built. In April and May 1901, six months before the Rock Island tracks reached the site of Tucumcari, Alex Goldenberg and Jacob Wertheim had entered 160-acre homestead claims straddling the prospective railroad route where they apparently thought the depot would be situated, but the claims proved to be too far west of the eventual location.[13] Despite the isolated prairie locale, and the difficulty of getting reliable advanced information, the determined Jewish-immigrant entrepreneurs were no country bumpkins. After learning the depot's real location, they took immediate steps to possess the adjacent area, which involved other, although not necessarily easier, ways than filing a row of homestead claims.

The methodical process that Alex Goldenberg used in obtaining the 120 acres comprising the original town site revealed both his sophisticated business acumen and, probably, his family's financial connections through the Ilfeld Company. Strangely enough, the trail to Goldenberg's acquisition of 80 acres south of the depot began with William H. Riley, an African American Civil War veteran living in Ocala, Florida, who had served in Company I, Forty-Fifth Regiment of the US Colored Infantry Volunteers. Riley never resided within a thousand miles of Tucumcari, but his military service entitled him to a Soldiers' Additional Homestead entry of approximately 80 acres of public land. He sold these rights in the form of a paper certificate, or scrip, with the location of the land itself left blank, to A. A. Thomas, a Washington attorney and land broker. In turn, Thomas sold the certificate to William E. Moses, a Denver lawyer specializing in scrip, who transferred the document, dated November 21, 1901, to Alex Goldenberg for $600. Goldenberg could use the paper form like a blank check to select any 80 acres he liked from the public domain available. Two days later at Clayton, in the legal process of ownership, Goldenberg paid a registration fee of $11.03 and used the scrip originating with Riley to purchase 80 acres of the public domain south of the future Second and Main intersection.[14]

In a similar transaction, Goldenberg had used land scrip to obtain the remaining 40 acres of the original 120-acre town site. This acquisition involved another Union Army veteran, William Kirkpatrick of Rockerville, Pennington County, South Dakota, who had exchanged his ownership of land in the Black Hills Forest Reserve, originating from his military service, for equivalent rights elsewhere. Ollin E. Smith, an enterprising lawyer who practiced in Tucumcari and Clayton, had somehow become Kirkpatrick's legal representative and sold some of his "lieu land scrip" for $600 to Goldenberg, who used it to acquire the 40 acres east of the depot.[15] The town founders needed to control the land around the all-important train station, and the 120-acre town site covered only three sides of it. Fortunately, Lee K. Smith had filed a 40-acre homestead claim adjoining the depot on the west, which meant that the town-site group, with control of a total 160 acres had that centerpiece of railroad activity completely surrounded. In effect, most of the essential parts of downtown Tucumcari around Main and Second Streets had been obtained by Alex Goldenberg's shrewd land deals stretching back through Denver; Washington, DC; Ocala, Florida; and the Black Hills of South Dakota. With all the pieces in place, the Goldenbergs and their business associates, as explained earlier, could now activate the Tucumcari Townsite and Investment Company and look forward to reaping the rewards bestowed by a railroad town.

Charles B. Eddy originally an Eastern investor—also became crucially important to Tucumcari. The husky, bearded, former New Yorker already had the reputation of a successful western promoter for his Pecos River Valley irrigation and railroad projects when he conceived a grander vision. He would establish towns and develop mines, resorts, and timberlands to the northeast of El Paso, with a railroad network binding everything together. As part of this plan, Eddy tried to interest the Rock Island in helping him construct tracks between its railhead at Liberal, Kansas, and his base of operations in El Paso. He was

Original Town Plat of
Tucumcari. Graphic design
by Chris Maple.

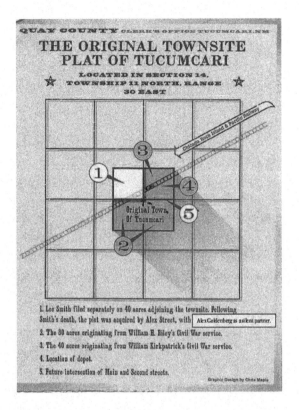

QUAY COUNTY CLERK'S OFFICE TUCUMCARI, NM

THE ORIGINAL TOWNSITE
PLAT OF TUCUMCARI
LOCATED IN SECTION 14,
☆ TOWNSHIP 11 NORTH, RANGE ☆
30 EAST

Chicago, Rock Island & Pacific Railway

③

①

④

Original Town
Of Tucumcari ⑤

②

1. Lee Smith filed separately on 40 acres adjoining the townsite. Following Smith's death, the plot was acquired by Alex Street, with | Alex Goldenberg as a silent partner.
2. The 80 acres originating from William H. Riley's Civil War service.
3. The 40 acres originating from William Kirkpatrick's Civil War service.
4. Location of depot.
5. Future intersection of Main and Second streets.

Graphic Design by Chris Maple

turned down. In his best swashbuckling style, Eddy proceeded anyway, laying
tracks north out of El Paso, founding the town of Alamogordo, and constructing one of the steepest western branch lines into the Sacramento Mountain
timberlands around Cloudcroft. The mainline of his rails beyond Alamogordo
toward the Pecos River had reached Carrizozo when Eddy faced the dilemma
of securing a reliable source of coal for his steam locomotives. Promising coal
prospects near Capitan proved unsatisfactory. At this point William Ashton
"W. A." Hawkins, Eddy's right-hand man and a skilled corporate attorney,
saved the day by outmaneuvering other bidders to gain an option on the rich
coal deposits in northern New Mexico owned by rancher John B. Dawson.[16]

Eddy, with his Dawson coalfield triumph in prospect and a functioning
railroad in operation, finally reached an agreement with the Rock Island for a
meeting of their rails on the west side of the Pecos River. Building from Liberal,

Rock Island crews of 2,500 workers set out to reach that juncture, accompanied by a corps of female camp followers and a smallpox epidemic that raced westward through the construction camps and left countless lonely graves behind. The workers, often laying 2.5 miles of track a day and more than 260 in about a year, had passed Tucumcari by early November 1901. An early tourist observed that thousands of laborers with picks and shovels and droves of mule skinners, hired to manage herds of mules and operate plows, scrapers, and Fresno scrapers, were hard at work west of the Tucumcari construction camp. In the rough country approaching Santa Rosa, the Rock Island's previous pace slowed perceptibly. To construct tracks at Los Tanos Canyon took forty-five tons of black powder, twenty-four tons of dynamite, and three tons of "Judson explosives" (gunpowder coated with nitroglycerine) to blast out four successive eighty-foot excavations in solid rock. On Christmas Day the tracklayers and a locomotive triumphantly entered Santa Rosa. At the same time Charles B. Eddy was pushing his crews working east from Carrizozo to meet the Rock Island at the Pecos River.[17]

The erection of the two largest bridges on the new line, over the Canadian River near present-day Logan and across the Pecos River at Santa Rosa, had presented time-consuming challenges. At Logan the single-track structure that measured 769 feet in length, 135 high, and stood on six steel piers took six months to complete. At Santa Rosa the steel bridge spanning the Pecos River closely resembled the Canadian River structure in general features. These were two of the highest bridges in the more than 8,000 miles of Rock Island lines. Rearing up in stark contrast among the rolling sand hills and prairie country, the two massive steel structures, with Tucumcari in between, displayed unmistakable reminders that the industrial age had arrived in the Canadian corridor.

At 9:30 a.m. on February 1, 1902, a small crowd consisting of Charles B. Eddy and some of his Eastern financial backers, as well as prominent residents of El Paso and other regional communities, shivered in the frosty morning air as they witnessed the last spike driven for the rails joining Eddy's El Paso & Northeastern Railway tracks with those of the Rock Island. Eddy "eagerly watched the closing work" and then crossed over the connected rails in his private railroad car, the Paso del Norte, accompanied by a few distinguished guests.[18] The Chicago, Rock Island and Pacific Railroad had long aspired to become a transcontinental line, and, in fact, had added "Pacific" to its original title for that reason. The celebratory event at the Pecos River marked the completion of the financially strapped Rock Island's latest desperate attempt to forge its own line to the Pacific Ocean, a quest it never satisfactorily achieved. Charles B. Eddy's El Paso & Northeastern Railway (EP&NE) had laid the tracks as far as Carrizozo when he organized a subsidiary company, the El Paso and Rock Island Railway, to complete the job to the Pecos River. Afterward, Rock Island officials denied having "any immediate intention" to build or acquire tracks west of El Paso. At the same time, however, they boasted of making "satisfactory traffic arrangements" with the Southern Pacific (SP) that would provide the Chicago-based railroad with "a fair and reasonable exchange of business" from California and Mexico and allow the SP to share markets in the Rock Island's territory. A prominent industry journal, the *Railway Age*, apparently influenced by such pronouncements, identified Eddy's EP&NE as "a division" of the Rock Island and also mistakenly declared that the latter had "added another line to the list of transcontinental roads."[19]

In more realistic terms, the Rock Island's hopes of becoming an authentic transcontinental railroad ended in the celebratory event at the Pecos River—actually 1,300 feet beyond the river. A recent authoritative study states that the cooperative arrangement, as "close partners," with the Southern Pacific for joint operation of Golden State passenger trains between Chicago and Los Angeles "fostered a large interchange of freight traffic on the same route."[20] This agreement, which lasted until 1968, began on March 1, 1902, when the Rock Island started passenger service on "its new El Paso line" by sending out of Chicago "a well-filled train of seven cars." Since the train passed through Tucumcari, it also ushered in passenger service for that new railroad town as well.[21]

Before completion of the Rock Island mainline, grading had started on both ends of the Dawson spur out of Tucumcari. By May 1902 the workers had graded fifty miles north of town, and by August 20 other rail employees were unloading construction material in the local yards, while another 225 were laying rails in both directions out of the railroad station of French, where the branch line crossed the Santa Fe tracks between Raton and Las Vegas. A threat that would have doomed Tucumcari seemed forgotten in all this feverish building activity. The eastern owners of the Bell Ranch had initially blocked a right of way across their domain, raising the possibility that the branch route would be shifted farther east to a junction with the Rock Island mainline at Logan.

Fortunately, condemnation proceedings in the courts nullified the ranching fiefdom's opposition, although this would not be the last time the Bell Ranch tried to block projects that benefitted Tucumcari. With the Dawson connection assured, one newspaper proclaimed that the small settlement of Tucumcari was destined to become "a great coal and rail center" with a roundhouse, coal chutes, switching yards, and all the other facilities necessary for a major "divisional and junctional point."[22]

Meanwhile, newly minted Tucumcari grew rapidly. The Goldenbergs' real estate company had platted town lots; laid out alleys and broad streets; and reserved spaces for parks, schools, churches, and public buildings. The firm's donations included an entire city block for a county courthouse, four lots for a Catholic church and priest's manse, property for a Baptist church, and later, west of town, the cemetery where several Goldenbergs are buried. With town lots priced at $50 to $250, sales had amounted "in the aggregate" to $1,000 in two hours. In August 1902 the *Pathfinder* stated that the town site had expanded to "about 200 acres, of which 50 have been sold." By 1905 the size of the town site had been increased to 500 acres.[23]

Among other early business firms, probably in late January 1902, the Goldenbergs had established their main merchandising branch at Tucumcari. Once transplanted from Liberty, the new M. B. Goldenberg & Co. was incorporated in 1903 with Max as president, Wertheim as vice president, and Alex as secretary-treasurer. The new company ran newspaper ads worthy of the Ilfeld firm in Las Vegas, boasting, "We carry a full and complete line of EVERYTHING." In fact, the Goldenbergs even found a market for the tough fiber of yucca, or bear grass, and shipped out of Quay County several carloads of the ubiquitous, spear-shaped plant in 1913 alone. Situated on the southeast corner of Main and Third Streets, it was for years, as one of its ads proclaimed, "'The Big, Busy Store' of Tucumcari," and the town's largest and most prestigious business establishment. The original building was remodeled, complete with a second-story façade, space for business offices, and a rope-geared elevator activated when a passenger pulled on the rope.[24]

From the beginning business was so good, in both real estate and merchandising, that as early as August 1902, the Goldenbergs' debt to the Charles Ilfeld Company, once above $11,000, had been paid off, and the account showed an interest-bearing credit exceeding $9,000. The Goldenbergs also shook off Ilfeld's domination in another important way. Ilfeld had controlled his trade territory with an iron hand because he was the only source of wholesale goods and credit for smaller merchants like the Goldenbergs. Once railroads sliced through eastern New Mexico, however, these firms could tap into national trade networks to fulfill their needs. An Ilfeld company executive readily conceded that the railroads had "cut us off" from Tucumcari and freed the Goldenbergs to purchase wholesale goods "wherever they pleased."[25]

The hard-driving Alex Goldenberg often appeared in public as the mastermind of the family's business affairs. It seemed that he was involved in every civic project and every new business venture. In fact, he even organized a brass band and led the fundraising drive to hire a band leader from Kansas. With Alex as the front man and Max always in the background, the M. B. Goldenberg and Company's mercantile business and the family's real estate and land operations, a sheep company, as well as other ventures, continued to prosper. In one notable instance, among several legal disputes between the Goldenbergs and the railroads, Alex took on the best combined legal talent of the El Paso & Southwestern and the Rock Island and won an important victory on the federally mandated width of the Rock Island's right of way through the original town site. The court decision supported Alex's contention of one hundred feet on either side of the tracks, not two hundred feet on each side nor two hundred on one side and one hundrd feet on the other, as the railroads claimed.[26]

In the early years everything had not always gone smoothly for the town-site company. The venture was hardly up and running before it received a violent jolt in the shooting death of Lee K. Smith, the nominal president. Smith and Alex Street, the vice president, had been partners in a bar at Liberty, which they moved to the new railroad settlement. Their Legal Tender Saloon's newspaper ads declared that it was "The Pioneer House of its Kind" in town, with "Everybody Welcome and Everybody Treated Right." Despite such friendly greetings, bad blood developed between the Legal Tender and James D. Eakin, junior partner in Melini and Eakin, a wholesale liquor distributor with headquarters in Albuquerque and branches in New Mexico and Arizona. Eakin had bought a business lot from the town-site company, supposedly with the understanding that he would operate only a wholesale business and not compete with the local retail saloons. The saloon owners, however, refused to buy their stock from Eakin, purchasing elsewhere. Eagan promptly announced that, in conjunction with his wholesale outlet, he would also open a regular retail concern called the Alvarado Club Bar. In addition, he pledged to serve a free hot lunch and undercut the prevailing price of twenty-five cents per drink by selling his for ten cents apiece. Led by Lee K. Smith, the other saloon owners responded by warning Eakin that they would run him out of town.[27]

About 11:30 p.m., on Saturday night, May 10, 1902, Smith, accompanied by Joe Stewart, a real estate agent and reputed gambler, entered the Alvarado Club carrying a holstered pistol and ordered drinks. When served, Smith commented "in a joking way" about the low price of the liquor, saying, "That's pretty cheap, ain't it?" To which Eakin replied, "Yes, and I propose to keep it so." At this point accounts differ on what happened next, but Smith may have slapped Eakin's face. Then, amid mixed signals on who was drawing weapons, Eakin quickly pulled a gun from under the counter and shot Smith dead. In the ensuing turmoil, as the crowd in the bar scattered, the Alvarado Club bartender, Louis Fonville, fatally wounded Smith's companion, Joe Stewart, with a double-barreled shotgun blast. Eakin, Fonville, and the bar's manager then barricaded themselves in the Alvarado Club, only allowing a delegation from the threatening crowd gathered outside to remove Smith's body and the dying Stewart. Tucumcari was still part of Guadalupe County, and the sheriff and a deputy arrived by train at 3:00 p.m. the next day to take command of the situation. In the meantime, there had been spasmodic shooting into the Alvarado Club, wounding Louis Fonville but not fatally. The sheriff, fearing lynch-mob action, promptly hustled Eakin and Fonville by the next train to Santa Rosa for safekeeping, and then to Las Vegas.[28]

Probably because Quay County was not formed until 1903, the prosecution of Eakin and Fonville was delayed for more than two years and "seemed to have dropped into oblivion." The two men were jailed briefly in Las Vegas and, pending grand jury action, released on bail. After the creation of Quay County with Tucumcari as the county seat, Eakin and Fonville were finally indicted for murder on June 30, 1904, and again released on bail. However, in a strange deal between the district attorney and Eakin's lawyer, the indictments were promptly transferred for trial to Alamogordo and the Otero County judicial district. There, the case apparently "fell through the cracks" and probably was dismissed for the lack of interest and doubts about Eakin and Fonville's criminal guilt.[29]

At about the same time as the Alvarado Club shooting, sketchy rumors and conflicting accounts of the early town's greatest slaughter began circulating. Supposedly, a Saturday night saloon brawl broke out between drunken cowboys fresh off the range and equally inebriated tracklayers when a railroad worker pulled a knife on a cowhand. In the ensuing chaos, the cowboys had reportedly responded by shooting and killing between nine and thirteen rail workers. Before the cowhands hurriedly got out of town, they either buried the bodies in an embankment or loaded some of them on a departing railroad boxcar, giving rise to vague reports that five bodies had turned up on a Kansas rail siding. Whatever happened, those involved either left town immediately or were sworn to ironclad secrecy.[30]

The main reason for Tucumcari's existence, it soon became apparent, was to serve as a rail junction between the Rock Island mainline and the 132-mile branch line running north to the Dawson coalfields. By all odds, Santa Rosa, an established village at the western end of the Rock Island's mainline, should have been the division point. And the place did boom for a while, as the Rock Island made it the first operational junction with Charles B. Eddy's El Paso & Northeastern and constructed maintenance facilities there, including shops and a roundhouse. Later, environmental circumstances may have favored Tucumcari when the division offices were moved from Santa Rosa. From the start, Eddy's EP&NE steam locomotives had experienced serious problems with mineral corrosion in their boilers, mainly from the high alkali and gypsum content of the water available along the railroad's route. Intense foaming and low motive power, followed by the sudden collapse of internal tubing, often resulted. Even new engines had suddenly shut down, delaying track construction to the junction with the Rock Island at the Pecos River. Santa Rosa had abundant water underground as well as in beautiful blue, "bottomless" lakes and the Pecos River, but supposedly most of this water contained the same corrosive minerals harmful to locomotive boilers.[31]

Anecdotal accounts say that concern for better water constituted the sole reason for transferring the division point to Tucumcari. However, this assertion claims too much. It is true that Tucumcari's water supply from deep wells, despite local opinion that it was "hard," may have been less corrosive. The importance of Dawson and its coal supply, however, suggested that, logically, the location of the division point should be at the busy branch junction with the Rock Island's main line, and this argument likely swung far more weight in the final decision. The prospect of a fourth rail connection for Tucumcari, the Rock Island's subsidiary Tucumcari and Memphis Line, also probably had some influence in the choice.[32]

Before the shift took place, Tucumcari had to face yet another threat of losing the all-important Dawson coal traffic. At the same time that Charles B. Eddy, with his various holdings in financial trouble, decided to sell the El Paso & Northeastern along with its Dawson coalfields, the Phelps Dodge Corporation badly needed to obtain its own source of fuel because of a Colorado coal strike. As the story goes, the price Eddy asked seemed laughably unreasonable to Phelps Dodge executives, who, in reply, told of their plans to acquire coal from the Four Corners area and build a new rail line from the Farmington vicinity to meet the Santa Fe Railroad at either Albuquerque or Gallup. Eddy listened politely until they finished, then dropped his bombshell. There was only one flaw in their plan, Eddy said dryly; he had investigated Four Corners coal and it would not produce coke for copper smelters. Phelps Dodge soon capitulated and paid Eddy's asking price of $16 million.[33] Following the sale, on July 1, 1905, the new owners, primarily interested in Dawson coke for their Arizona copper smelters, as well as coal for their steam locomotives, started planning to transfer the divisional operations to Tucumcari as soon as possible.

Despite an enhanced role in the regional railroad network, Tucumcari for years continued a tail-wagging-the-dog relationship with Dawson and its rich coal mines. In fact, the arrangement became more clearly defined as Phelps Dodge began investing substantial amounts to upgrade the branch line, buying new locomotives and coal cars, and expanding the facilities at Dawson, including the construction of larger furnaces to turn coal into coke. From its beginning Dawson had attracted a workforce of mixed nationalities—80 percent were foreign born—and now Phelps Dodge established a model company town. These facilities included subsidized homes and boarding accommodations as well as two churches; a school system with a high school; both a hospital and a dispensary; and a "completely modern" company store employing a staff of forty. For entertainment there was a combination auditorium, bowling alley, and pool hall, and even a golf course and a swimming pool. Significantly, the school buildings were constructed of brick, suggesting permanence for the town—a false assurance, as it turned out.[34]

Charles B. Eddy had shipped the first carload of coal from Dawson in May

1902. Under Phelps Dodge ownership, production increased significantly until, in 1910, the mines yielded more than 1 million tons, or nearly half of all the coal produced in New Mexico. Six years later the annual output had increased to 1.5 million tons. Phelps Dodge subsidiaries, known in succession as the Dawson Fuel Company; Stag Canyon Fuel Company; and Phelps Dodge Corporation, Stag Canon Branch, worked ten underground mines altogether. According to a Phelps Dodge history, "[The] continuous seam of low-sulfur coal . . . measured more than ten miles long, five miles wide, and often as much as eleven feet thick." Hundreds of coke ovens, "joined together in a chain," stood on the edge of the coal operations, pouring out smoke and fire. At night a glow above them was visible for miles. As early as 1905, when Phelps Dodge assumed ownership, the town of Dawson had already reached a population variously estimated between two thousand and four thousand people, and it continued to increase in size until it claimed nine thousand residents. All of this industrial might and concentration of skilled workers meant that Dawson was larger, and more important economically, than the aspiring rail hub of Tucumcari.[35]

Wielding its corporate might, Phelps Dodge solved the pesky problem of the sixty-mile "stub" of Rock Island tracks between the Dawson line's terminus at Tucumcari and Santa Rosa. The copper giant forced the Rock Island to accept a favorable leasing arrangement for the sixty miles of trackage that gave clear control of rail traffic from Dawson all the way through Tucumcari and El Paso to its western headquarters at Douglas, Arizona—and beyond to a complex of southwestern and Mexican copper mines, mills, and smelters.[36] In short, through the El Paso & Southwestern Railroad, Tucumcari had gained a direct connection with an industrial realm that residents of the budding metropolis could have only imagined previously. According to a local newspaper, it was the biggest thing yet in the town's short history. Two years later, in mid-summer of 1907, the newspaper reported, "Yes, Tucumcari is a division, or in other words where the Rock Island delivers the goods to the [El Paso &] Southwestern." As such, the newspaper fairly chortled, it was the "best town" on the two railroad lines between Liberal, Kansas, and El Paso, Texas.[37]

Construction had started locally on extensive sidetracks, a water supply system, and a machine shop and roundhouse with a big turntable to repair locomotives and fifteen stalls to house them. The roundhouse would employ two hundred workers. Ten additional clerical employees reported in at the depot the Rock Island built, and switch engines steamed busily around the local yards. About 300 rail cars loaded with coal and coke awaited transit at Tucumcari and another 1,100 were backed up on various sidings all the way to Dawson. All of these cars could expect reasonably quick shipment out, a newspaper report predicted, because, under EP&SW control of the sixty-mile segment of tracks to Santa Rosa, the flow of rail traffic had become smooth and steady, rather than spasmodic, as was the case in the uneasy relationship between Eddy's El Paso & Northeastern and the Rock Island.[38]

When the EP&SW moved the division point to Tucumcari, it literally changed the tempo of the town. Earlier, different systems of keeping time— usually by the position of the sun—had only led to confusion. In 1883 the major railroads cooperated in the creation of "standard time" (at first known as "Standard Railroad Time"), which was adjusted to fit four time zones and put the entire country on the same schedule. This significant change had the far-reaching effect of causing "the pulse" of involved communities, such as Tucumcari, to "beat in 'perfect time' with that of the railroad." The Call Board, with prioritized work assignments for operating crews, the around-the-clock shifts of shop and yard workers, and the arrivals and departures of freights and passenger trains also helped determine the pace of the entire community. As a direct result, in deference to the El Paso & Southwestern, which ran on Mountain Time, an hour behind the Rock Island's Central Time, the local post office, banks, and churches announced that they would turn their clocks back an hour, and the entire town followed suit. Generally, the New Mexico-Texas state line was the boundary between the two time zones, but for years, in deference to Rock Island operations, maps showed a small wedge-shaped slice of Central Time protruding from West Texas along the railroad tracks to the Tucumcari rail-yard limits. If shifting the division point to Tucumcari changed the tempo, it also affected the town's temperature. According to a local newspaper, "The pay roll of the railroad at Tucumcari is the city's business thermometer."[39]

Tucumcari's reputation as a railroad center got another boost when, in 1910, the long-delayed Tucumcari and Memphis Railway, an offshoot of the Chicago, Rock Island, & Choctaw Railway Company, made a junction with Rock Island tracks a mile east of town. This line, which ran from Memphis west to Oklahoma City, Amarillo, and ended at Tucumcari, had been started under another name as an independent endeavor but became part of the Rock Island in May

1902. When Rock Island trains finally rolled into town over this route in May 1910, Tucumcari could boast that it was now a full-fledged rail center with lines converging on it from all four directions. For the Rock Island, however, this was one more event signaling the end of the Chicago-based railroad's westward expansion and its hopes of becoming a real transcontinental line.[40]

The presence of the railroad industry acted as an explosive force, dramatically increasing the population of the town, but especially boosting the growth of Quay County by furnishing transportation for throngs of incoming homesteaders and thus creating several rural satellite villages around Tucumcari. From June 1906 to June 1907, in New Mexico Territory, twenty thousand homesteaders filed on nearly 2.5 million acres of land—an area about the size of Connecticut. Quay County alone registered 773,560 acres of entries, or more than a fourth of the homestead acreage in the territory for that period.[41]

When the homesteaders came in, they might have made the trip in various ways. In about 1905 or 1906, a caravan of twenty-six prairie schooners came from Ardmore, Oklahoma, to found the Jordan community on the Llano Estacado, and as late as May 1915, ten covered wagons were lined up on Main Street with occupants who had arrived to file homestead claims.[42] Others came on horseback, by passenger train, or, by the 1910s, in Model-T Fords. For long distances, however, the most comfortable way to make the trip was to load all the family's worldly possessions—household furnishings, farming equipment, horses and mules, milk cows, and pet dogs—into a rented railroad "Zulu Car" (immigrant freight car). Meals could be cooked on small wood-burning stoves, and lucky family members might ride in the passenger coaches away from the hubbub and stench of animal odors.[43]

On arrival in Tucumcari, the newcomers found special facilities awaiting them located next to the railroad yards. Their livestock and goods could be unloaded at the OK Wagon Yard or the Murray Wagon Yard, while the weary travelers slept on pallets nearby or checked into the Glenrock Hotel. A land agent would show up to conduct a tour, by horse and buggy or later in a Model-T Ford, of the areas still available for homesteading. Afterward, the newcomer would file a claim in the local federal land office, where, in July 1914, about 500,000 acres of public lands still remained unclaimed in the Tucumcari area. In February 1915 alone that office recorded 150 filings, and it seemed that the influx would continue at that level indefinitely. The Enlarged Homestead Act of 1909 had provided that new settlers could claim 320 acres, and the act made it possible for those who had already taken 160 acres to have that many more. Moreover, the Stock-Raising Homestead Act of 1916 allowed, under several restrictions, original 640-acre entries strictly for ranching, while also permitting established homesteaders to file an additional claim within a twenty-mile radius for the same purpose. The 1916 law, according to a newspaper report, made the Tucumcari land office temporarily "about the busiest place in New Mexico," with applicants lined up in the hallway waiting their turn.[44]

Among these throngs William Morland Lancaster stood out as an extraordinary homesteader, not because he was one of the many "lungers" with tuberculosis who came seeking a cure in the dry climate, which he was, but because of his main trade as a rural, traveling medical doctor. From his claim on the Caprock's rim north of the Plain community, and later a residence in Plain, Lancaster covered a seventy-mile expanse across the Llano Estacado between the Texas Panhandle and the Pecos River. Sometimes gone for several days, Dr. Lancaster at first traveled by horse and buggy, but ordered a motorcycle after only seeing a picture of one, and then paid $312 for a Model T. As an alternative in deep snow, he made his house calls riding inside a large wooden water barrel bolted to a sled with holes cut in the lid so he could see ahead and for the horse's reins to come through. For the return trip, if the call ran late into the night or early morning, as often happened in the delivery of babies, he would wrap himself with heavy bed clothing in the barrel, signal giddy-up to the horse, who knew the way back, and sleep all the way. Upon arrival at home, it was said, the horse was trained to kick the barrel and awaken him. In 1920, after eleven years of treating the sick and ailing across the Llano, Dr. Lancaster moved his family to Clovis, where he labored another forty years in more sedentary medical service.[45]

National events surfaced in Quay County when a Tucumcari publisher became alarmed about the potential effects of the Progressive Movement's conservation policy of withdrawing public lands for national forests and similar reserves. Convinced that "the rights of the people to take up and hold homesteads of 160 acres" were threatened, he took a stand in his newspaper against the conservationists, or "land grafters," as he labeled them. These enemies of the people, along with their allies in government, he said, were determined to exclude homesteaders and "illegally gobble up all the public domain and subject the same to run wild under the false pretense of water and reserve privileges." To show the publisher's dedication to the cause, he had already changed the name of his newspaper from the *Quay County Democrat* to the *Actual Settler*, a title more reflective of his sentiments. As the capstone, an Actual Settlers Club with substantial membership was organized in the newspaper office.[46]

No matter how or when they came, many sodbusters found survival on a 160-acre claim with stingy soil and meager rainfall too difficult to stay, even with the possible addition of a 320-acre enlarged homestead or a 640-acre ranching claim. Following a severe dry spell, in 1909–1912, they started leaving in droves. The winter of 1918–1919, with three-foot snow drifts and freezing temperatures that lasted until spring, took its toll on livestock as well as people. It became a common sight to see "large wagon loads of salted and dried cow hides [from frozen animals] on the road to town to be shipped to tanneries." In addition, the number of human deaths in the Spanish-flu epidemic at that time, along with the financial losses caused by the frigid weather, undoubtedly influenced some settlers to leave. Between 1910 and 1920 the population of Quay County plummeted by about 30 percent, from 14,912 to 10,444. Tucumcari managed to increase in population, but the diminishing rural consumer base became a serious problem for local businesses.[47]

At the same time as the influx of homesteaders, the Kohn family arrived at the railroad settlement of Montoya, but with decidedly different objectives from those of the sodbusters. The Kohns began by paying "a handsome figure" for the Henry K. Rountree and Company mercantile, land, and cattle interests. It was said that the owner wanted to sell out because he had become discouraged about business prospects by a prolonged drought. As a harbinger of the Kohns' financial success at Montoya, a big rain fell that very afternoon, ending the dry spell.[48] Montoya seemed an unlikely place to reap a fortune, but the Kohn family made the most of what they found there. As one newspaper editor later commented, "Starting out on a small scale, in what was then a desolate place, within a short period of ten years they became one of the richest firms in eastern New Mexico, making their money in the general merchandise, cattle and land business." In time, the youngest of three brothers, Charles, became a Republican power broker, heading the Republican county organization, serving as a member of the party's territorial and state central committees, and becoming an elected delegate to the state constitutional convention.[49] An older brother,

George, managed the Kohn Brothers General Store. Their widowed mother, Yetta Kohn, kept an eye on the family's affairs, but she increasingly passed most of the decision-making to the oldest son Howard.

Acclaimed locally as "the cattle king of the Montoya valley," Howard Kohn shipped mostly yearling steers, sometimes numbering 1,000 to 1,200 head, from the Montoya rail loading point. The Kohn daughter Belle and her husband, Albert Calisch, acquired a ranch in the Mesa Rica area. Calisch also became involved in county politics, but as a Democrat, later serving two terms in the state senate. He invested in the local newspaper, which began as the *Montoya Republican* but switched, as Calisch apparently did, to the *Montoya Democrat* when the voting pattern of the newly arrived homesteaders revealed an over-whelming majority of Democrats.[50] Of considerable importance, the Kohns had ready access to loans and advice from their uncle, Solomon Kohn, a wealthy New York City industrialist and financier.[51]

Members of the Kohn family also became involved in banking as well as ranching and the ownership of a hotel and several other local businesses. Amid these encouraging signs, however, came a series of tragic family losses. The cycle began on a happy note when Charles married at age forty-five on January 31, 1916. The bride was Hannah Bonem, daughter of Tucumcari Jewish merchant Herman Bonem. After the wedding the couple left by Rock Island passenger train for a honeymoon that abruptly turned to tragedy when Charles suddenly died of a massive tooth infection in Kansas City on the fourth day of the trip. Three days after Charles's death, his brother, George, died of a heart attack in Tucumcari's Vorenberg Hotel while awaiting the arrival by train of his brother's body. The stark chain of deaths did not stop there. In declining health after the passing of her two sons, Yetta Kohn died quietly about a year later.[52]

Following his mother's death, and with the impending move of the Calischs from Montoya to Tucumcari, and then to El Paso, Howard Kohn stood virtually alone. About this same time what had seemed like a bright future for Montoya was becoming an illusion because of the mass departure of homesteaders. Although this exodus foreshadowed doom for the mercantile trade at Montoya, it was hardly a total loss for Howard Kohn, who usually ended up with their land when the settlers could not repay loans to him or credit extended them at the Kohn Brothers store. Under these changing conditions, he made what was probably the most important business decision of his life when he traded the family's mercantile interests for Vidal Ortega's extensive ranch lands and cattle.[53] Now a full-fledged cattle king, his greatest need was someone to help keep an eye on his complex financial affairs.

Help came from an unexpected direction. Like so many lungers did then, the parents of Clara McGowan had moved to Montoya, hoping to find a cure for her father's tuberculosis. He took his own life in March 1919. Earlier Clara McGowan had visited her parents, who were living in a hotel owned by the Kohns. Clara had completed an accounting course in Indianapolis and had been making her own living in the office of a rough-and-tumble Mississippi lumber camp. Howard Kohn persuaded her to stay in Montoya as the bookkeeper for his business enterprises. A strikingly attractive blonde of twenty-three, she soon won the heart of her employer, thirty-nine years older. They married in January 1923. Despite the age difference, Kohn had found a mate well-qualified to help him manage his business accounts.[54]

Already well-known in Tucumcari, Howard Kohn moved his family, which now included an infant daughter, Yetta, to the town. The Kohns soon became familiar figures in local social and business circles. Later, apprehensive about the fatal kidnapping of Charles Lindbergh's baby son, Kohn parked his big blue Buick outside of his daughter's school every day and took her home safely. Howard Kohn died at his Tucumcari home November 2, 1933, at age seventy-two, after helping fight a prairie fire on his ranch and suffering a stroke. At his death Kohn was hailed for his influence in the phenomenal increase of cattle in Quay County, where, between 1912 and 1916 alone, the numbers had grown "by leaps and bounds" from 10,000 head to as many as a reputed 50,000. Kohn deserved special credit for upgrading the county's herds by the introduction of registered bulls.[55]

After her husband's death, Clara Kohn's accounting talents were put to the test in untangling Howard Kohn's maze of money lending, which approached commercial banking, and his *partido* contracts, the time-honored New Mexico system of loaning out livestock on the shares.[56] Clara Kohn eventually deciphered and reorganized these complex business interests. A few years after her marriage in 1938 to the town's most prominent physician and surgeon, Dr. Thomas B. Hoover, the Kohn ranch, the T-4, was doubled in size with a purchase of the 117,000-acre southwestern part of the Bell Ranch known as the "Mesa Rica Country." At the same time the Hoovers disposed of 20,000 acres of the T-4 south of US Highway

66. Howard Kohn had controlled 107,600 acres of land when he died, including 85,600 acres he owned outright and the rest in government and private leases. Today, the T-4 Cattle Company is owned by Howard Kohn's daughter Yetta Kohn Bidegain and her children and grandchildren; her husband, Phillip B. Bidegain, died in 2016.[57] The T-4 Ranch headquarters are still at Montoya, although that village is otherwise deserted, the livestock loading pens are gone, and the railroad no longer stops there to take on cattle shipments.[58]

Considering their influence on the town, Tucumcari never had many Jewish residents. By the First World War, the total Jewish population of New Mexico had grown slowly to about 860. At that time only 40—men, women, and children—of Tucumcari's 3,000 residents were Jewish.[59] The extended Goldenberg family—a total of 15 people—made up the greatest number. Over the years several other Jewish merchants, professionals, and business owners had also cast their lot in Tucumcari, some for the long haul, while others stayed only a few years. Jewish merchants in the West had a habit of moving on when serious setbacks occurred or if a new location offered prospects of greater profits.[60]

Of those who stayed put at Tucumcari, the Goldenberg clan was by far the most successful. In November 1926, however, M. B. Goldenberg and Company announced in a double-paged newspaper ad that it was quitting business. This news came as "something of a shock" to its many faithful customers, who had long regarded the store as the pillar of the local business community. About a year later, in January 1928, a local newspaper reported that the Goldenberg building would be remodeled into a new fifty-room hotel with all the latest conveniences. Experienced proprietor and former railroader W. A. Randle operated the Vorenberg and another hotel in Alamogordo. Six months later the local Goldenberg Electric Company, run by Alex's son Hugo, installed a big electric sign reading "Hotel Randle" atop the nearly remodeled structure. With fourteen-inch letters that glowed in red and green lights, it was the largest such sign in Tucumcari and could be noticed "for miles by tourists coming into town."[61]

The advent of the railroad in the Canadian corridor had first attracted the Goldenbergs and the Kohns to bet on the future of the Tucumcari area, and this gamble paid off handsomely. In turn, these Jewish entrepreneurs not only adapted to their surroundings and joined in promoting the common welfare but also backed these gestures with sizable monetary investments that raised the area's profile. Their ability in remote places like Tucumcari and Montoya to raise large sums whenever they chose, and to pour that money into area enterprises, is still a source of amazement. To state it plainly, probably no other Western town was influenced more by such a small band of Jewish entrepreneurs. These enterprising Jews founded the town, nurtured its early growth, and witnessed it become the urban trading center for surrounding rural communities.

Chapter 2

RAILROAD TOWN

n 1937 when Alex Street died in an Albuquerque hospital, his body was escorted 175 miles on Route 66 to Tucumcari by a motorcycle convoy of state policemen. A similar escort, headed by the chief of state police, representing Governor Clyde Tingley, and a bevy of state patrolmen and other lawmen from various towns, led the funeral procession to the local cemetery. An FBI agent, or "G-Man," representing his famous chief, J. Edgar Hoover, also joined the solemn parade. In addition, all traffic on nearby Route 66 and US 54 and trains on adjacent tracks were halted until the cortege passed by. At the funeral in the First Baptist Church, attended by a federal judge and other dignitaries, so many floral displays had banked the rostrum and "the mourners were so numerous that it took 30 minutes for them to view the body as it lay in state."[1]

State and national newspapers hailed Street's passing in heroic terms. His life had been one "well lived, crammed with adventure, replete with thrilling experiences, colorful to the extreme." As for his career in law enforcement: "He was just an ordinary cow-poke at the start . . . But because Alex Street had icy courage, a quick mind and a certain native honesty, he graduated from the ranks of the buckeroos and became one of the most famous peace officers of his time."[2] Born in Ripley, Mississippi, in 1868, James Alexander Street had dedicated most his life to law enforcement, including service as the first Quay County sheriff.[3] Street's friendly, disarming demeanor and distinctive small-town sheriff mannerisms, although in sharp contrast with the popular G-Man image of the day, conveniently masked keen sleuthing talents. He could look a suspect straight in the eyes, it was said, gain his confidence, "and make him cough up his past." At his death Alex Street was acclaimed as "the most respected and feared" FBI agent west of the Pecos River.[4]

Street's two most famous cases as a federal agent required some understanding of Native American cultures. In the 1920s, posing as a Fort Worth cattle
buyer—a trade he had pursued at Tucumcari—Special Agent Street headed the
"Cowboy" undercover detail of four Justice Department operatives on the
Osage Indian Reservation in Oklahoma involving a series of murders and
Indian oil rights. According to the *Kansas City Star*, Street had risked his life
"every minute of the months he worked on the case."[5] It was the new federal
agency's first high-profile murder case, and Director J. Edgar Hoover, that
"slender bundle of high-charged wires," wanted it to become a showcase for his
bureau. In fact, the successful solution gave a big boost to Hoover's budding
crime-fighting reputation and helped bring official designation of his agency as
the Federal Bureau of Investigation. A few years later, in another highly publicized assignment, Street singlehandedly brought to justice the killer of Henrietta Schmemler, a young Columbia University graduate student brutally
stabbed and beaten to death while conducting research on the White River
Apache Indian Reservation in Arizona. Although he probably never met them,
Street was cast in this dramatic case with three famous Columbia anthropolo-
gists—Franz Boas; Ruth Benedict, Schmemler's graduate advisor; and Margaret Mead—who were shocked by their young graduate student's murder and
kept up with the investigation.[6] Disguised as a sheepherder, Street obtained a
confession from the killer, who was convicted and sentenced to life imprisonment.[7] After Street resigned from the FBI, he served for a short time before his
death as a special investigator for the New Mexico state police.[8]

Earlier, in a much different role that involved industrialized America, not a
western Indian reservation, Special Agent Alex Street had made an unannounced, secretive trip to his old hometown during the National Railroad
Shopmen's Strike of 1922. He was under confidential orders from the Justice
Department and the White House in far-off Washington, DC. Obviously chosen because of his local popularity, Street likely had some second thoughts
about his present orders. Regardless, this would be Alex Street's last peace-
keeping assignment in Tucumcari.

During the First World War, the federal government had taken over the
nation's railroads and operated them for the duration. To manage this ambitious undertaking, the US Railroad Administration (USRA) was established
with Treasury Secretary William Gibbs McAdoo as its director general, or

"czar." Generally credited with success "in forming a unified railway system" to support the war effort, the USRA made concessions to the railroad workers, such as higher wages and increased bargaining power. At the same time, the USRA also ordered increases in freight rates and passenger fares so the railroads would have adequate revenue to cover the salary increases given to the railroaders. After the war a series of strikes plagued the United States, one of which was the National Railroad Shopmen's Strike of 1922. The "most far-reaching strikes" of the 1920s involved two essential national industries, coal and railroads. The grievances of the railroad workers resulted primarily from the wartime concessions made to labor organizations by the federal government, followed after the war by the union-busting tactics of railroad companies to reverse these advantages. Of all the strikes, the Great Railroad Strike of 1922 received the most publicity because of its magnitude, and, as such, the possibility that it would spread to other railway unions and brotherhoods and shut down the national transportation system. From July 1, when the shopmen across the country started walking out, until September and October, when most active signs ended, this strike claimed daily coverage in the press and attention at the highest levels of state and national government, including in the White House.[9]

As an important regional rail hub, Tucumcari became a storm center of the shopmen's strike. The local yards contained a large roundhouse as well as branch shops and similar facilities. These workers in Tucumcari were representative of the nationwide 400,000 men—no women[10]—who kept trains rolling by repairing and overhauling locomotives, freight cars, and passenger coaches. A diverse group with individual skills, the local workforce consisted of machinists, boilermakers, blacksmiths, electricians, sheet-metal craftsmen, coppersmiths, locomotive inspectors, and those who cared for the railway cars, called carmen. The 175 men at Tucumcari who practiced the various specialties, like their counterparts nationally, belonged to different unions or brotherhoods based on craft lines, but all were affiliated with the American Federation of Labor. Despite their separate craft affiliations, however, they usually worked together in teams or gangs and, thus, had a common group loyalty. The work of all the shopmen was constantly evaluated, and "Brownies" for mistakes and oversights, based on the Brown demerit system, might be assessed and entered in the worker's employment record. For most railroads, ninety or one hundred demerits could

Southern Pacific Round House Employees
1948   Tucumcari, NM

©LeDeane Studio
Tucumcari NM
3310

The Southern Pacific roundhouse provided work to many disappointed homesteaders. Custodial assignments to service railroad passenger cars were usually reserved for Hispanic employees. LeDeane Studio, Tucumcari.

lead to dismissal, at least prior to World War II. In short, Tucumcari was both a bustling industrial center and a hotbed of unionism.[11]

A watershed event for the town, the National Railroad Shopmen's Strike of 1922 fully initiated Tucumcari into the realities of the twentieth-century corporate world. It also revealed a great deal about the town's civic fiber, socioeconomic class structure, and, above all, its importance in the national transportation system. The strike began locally much as it did nationally. Nationwide, most shopmen, facing a 12.5 percent wage reduction decreed by the National Railroad Labor Board (from an average of seventy-two cents an hour to sixty-three cents), simply gathered up their tools and walked out with them on July 1. At Tucumcari the shopmen left their tools behind. Locally, groups of four to six strikers picketed morning and night near the roundhouse and other railroad property. Otherwise, things remained relatively quiet for the first few days.[12] An exception was the EP&SW's announcement on July 5 that those shopmen who walked out could not reclaim their jobs unless they returned to work by July 10.[13] This was an ultimatum, and the individual strikers had five days to decide what they would do.

Nationally, the shopmen's home communities and local police most often sided with the workers. In Tucumcari, where railroad paychecks were the bulwark of the local economy, the town backed the strikers, or at least voiced few objections. But on Saturday, July 18, the lid blew off. As the Rock Island Number 2 passenger train carrying the mail approached the depot from the west, a crowd of some seventy-five crossed in front of the locomotive and forced the engineer to stop before reaching the station. Then a sizable body of strikers boarded a passenger coach and attempted to capture six men who had been hired by the EP&SW as replacements in the shops. The situation became tense and explosive as the scabs were pushed around and threatened. At this point Special Agent Alex Street suddenly appeared on the scene as a one-man rescue squad. As some of the replacements tried to escape, Street promptly stepped up, stood off the attacking strikers, and calmed them down until he could whisk the replacements away to the safety of the roundhouse.[14]

Nor was this Street's only rescue mission that Saturday when the strike was turning violent. A much-publicized incident that same day involved two college-age youths who had been hired as replacements to fill the ice and water tanks of passenger coaches. Soon after the pair started working on the waiting train, thirty or forty strikers followed one of the young men into the icehouse and backed him against the wall. At the same time that someone in the crowd struck him with "a severe blow," another striker warned him, "Bud, this means that you get out of town." Defending himself with ice tongs, the youth dashed out of the icehouse with strikers in hot pursuit. At that moment who should suddenly appear to save the embattled lad but Special Agent Alex Street. Again, Street stood off the hostile shopmen, reasoned with them, and quickly escorted the youth to the roundhouse for protection.[15]

The young man's companion, captured by strikers and taken to the edge of town where he was badly beaten, finally fell into the hands of the county sheriff. This officer drove nine miles west of town and, in effect, kicked the youth out with the advice to catch a freight train and not return to Tucumcari. Farther west at Montoya two African American replacements had been intercepted earlier by a striker boarding party on a passenger train and were warned not to continue their trip. One of the two insisted he would go on to Tucumcari. The

Anglo leader of the boarding party replied, using several racial slurs: "I say you are going to get off, and you are going to get off. You know what they do to your people back down in Texas. That is what we are going to do to you here. We are going to swing you up." When the striker became distracted by a discussion with the conductor, the African American locked himself in the men's room of the passenger coach and stayed there most of the time until the next stop after Tucumcari. These hostile incidents against the replacements set the battle lines.[16]

As for Special Agent Street, who had mysteriously appeared in a town where he was respected as a founding father, he capped off his day with a stirring speech on the depot platform urging the strikers to cool their tempers. How and why Street happened to be on hand to assume a prominent role in the strike remained a mystery. In fact, his presence was part of carefully laid plans crafted by a master strategist and implemented in the White House with President Warren G. Harding's approval. This behind-the-scenes operative for the EP&SW was William Ashton Hawkins, the railroad's general counsel and head of its legal department at El Paso, who had earlier secured an option on the Dawson coalfields for Charles B. Eddy. Hawkins was widely respected as a skilled corporation lawyer and for his integrity and company loyalty. Of equal significance among his credentials, he had a direct pipeline to the White House and the Harding cabinet through his one-time law partner, Secretary of the Interior Albert B. Fall, a former US senator from New Mexico who would later become embroiled in the Teapot Dome scandal. In a loosely arranged law practice back in southern New Mexico, Fall had assisted Hawkins in the representation of railroads as well as mining companies, timber concerns, and large-scale land and water development enterprises. As members of the New Mexico territorial council, or senate, they had rammed through, over a gubernatorial veto, the Hawkins Act of 1903, which was roundly denounced as "the most remarkable piece of legislation ever enacted" and the handiwork of railroad executives. This restrictive measure forced injured railroad workers and passengers alike to try their cases only in New Mexico courts, notoriously favorable to corporations. Congress overturned the law, using its veto powers over territorial legislation.[17]

Now, as the EP&SW strategist, W. A. Hawkins saw in the railroad strike a "spirit of quasi-rebellion" and the reality of "a conspiracy with all of the secret and established resources of trained conspirators" that could well foster more "violent action." In this dire situation, as Hawkins perceived it, he relied on his connection with Secretary Fall and his own long experience in New Mexico politics to win a victory for the railroad. First, with Secretary Fall's backing, he arranged with Attorney General Harry M. Daugherty for Special Agent Street's assignment to Tucumcari. It was no accident, then, that Street had turned up unannounced to lend a hand in "maintaining law and order" for the EP&SW. But even though Hawkins applauded Street's one-man contributions thus far, he realized that more conventional force was necessary to break the shopmen's strike at Tucumcari.[18]

Hawkins next utilized his political connections in New Mexico to full advantage. He got the approval of Governor Merritt M. Mechem, a former district attorney in Quay County who had once shared an office with Sheriff Alex Street, for sending to Tucumcari a contingent of deputy US marshals backed by a federal court restraining order. Next, Hawkins's old law partner, Interior Secretary Albert B. Fall, quickly got an appointment with President Harding, made the plea for sending deputy US marshals to Tucumcari, and received Harding's approval. In fact, the president himself notified Attorney General Daugherty of his support for the Tucumcari strategy. Daugherty had already authorized the appointment of extra marshals in states affected by the strike, and he promptly approved the plan discussed by Hawkins and Governor Mechem for federal action at Tucumcari. In correspondence with his Rock Island legal counterpart in Chicago, Hawkins had received the draft of a court injunction and temporary restraining order used successfully by that railroad in Iowa. At Santa Fe, relying on this document as a model, Hawkins obtained a temporary restraining order from the US District Court of New Mexico against the various shopmen's unions and brotherhoods that listed by name 4 local union leaders and 118 workers. This decree prohibited those individuals from interfering with EP&SW operations in any way whatever, specifically in the use of intimidation, threats, violence, and picketing.[19]

Two days later, on July 24, a band of 25 fully armed deputy US marshals descended on the town of 3,500 population to present copies of the restraining order to the 122 individuals named and to remain and see that "the same is enforced and obeyed."[20] Unknown to the townspeople, the EP&SW was secretly paying most of the expenses for the marshals, who were federal employees, including round-trip transportation, meals, and incidental expenses. The railroad also bought and furnished the marshals with Colt revolvers, cartridge belts, holsters, and 1,250 rounds of ammunition. A Pullman sleeping car was sent to Tucumcari to provide lodging. After it became clear that the marshals would stay, W. A. Hawkins's undercover agent on the scene informed him of "an unusual sale of arms and ammunition" at Tucumcari in the past several days.[21]

While under siege by the deputy marshals, the strikers managed to eke out a victory, although a small one, by obtaining a temporary injunction that modified Hawkins's restraining order slightly.[22] Enforcement by the deputy marshals of Hawkins's mandate, even in a modified form, was almost enough to break the strike at Tucumcari. In addition, however, constant rumors that the shops would be moved back to Santa Rosa if the strike continued and the railroad's announcement that shopmen not at work by July 10 would lose their jobs had a devastating effect on the strikers' morale. In fact, this ultimatum had shattered support for the strike, especially for those with a family to feed, which most of them did.

Meanwhile, on the national scene, President Harding took a tougher stance in the railroad strike after he failed to broker a negotiated settlement. The stalemate was broken when Attorney General Daugherty went to Chicago, the location of the shopmen's national headquarters, and presented the government's case in federal district court. On September 1, Judge James H. Wilkerson, whose appointment Daugherty had recommended and who had recently sentenced the notorious Chicago crime boss Al Capone to prison, issued "the most sweeping injunction in American labor history." For instance, not only were the strikers forbidden from interfering with railroad operations in any way, they also were prohibited from discussing the strike in union meetings or speaking to the press about their cause. In effect, this temporary injunction doomed the National Railroad Shopmen's Strike of 1922, which was already dying a slow death at Tucumcari and nationwide anyway.[23]

Proud of his legal expertise, Interior Secretary Fall considered much of the Wilkerson decree unconstitutional and set off some fireworks in the next cabinet meeting when he openly criticized Attorney General Daugherty for the document.[24] W. A. Hawkins agreed with Fall generally on the Wilkerson injunction but came to a different conclusion. The Chicago decree applied to the whole country, which suggested that there was no longer a need for the New Mexico restraining order. Hawkins rejected this reasoning because, he said, certain features of the Wilkerson injunction left it wide open to be modified on appeal, but the New Mexico document "invites no such modification." In effect, the restrictions on the shopmen's strike at Tucumcari, Hawkins believed, were as effective and more legally sound than the provisions of the infamous, widely criticized Wilkerson injunction.[25] Thus Tucumcari had carved a niche for itself in American labor history.

The shopmen's strike at Tucumcari, according to the EP&SW bland annual report, ended on October 1, 1922, when the railroad signed an agreement with local shopmen, and "since which time the forces have been working on an efficient basis." It was hardly that simple. According to the EP&SW decree, those strikers who refused to meet the deadline and return to work by July 10 had lost their jobs and a reliable means to support their families. In fact, W. A. Hawkins declared that "not over twenty of the employees who struck have ever been taken back." The actual number was 21 of the 122 identified in the strike. For the ordinary workers who kept their jobs across the country, the nationwide shopmen's strike had similar results. They had to accept the wage reductions and would not see a significant raise in pay for almost twenty years.[26] As small consolation, the Railway Labor Act of 1926 for the first time guaranteed railroad employees the right to organize and bargain collectively. On the other hand, however, the shopmen's strike "drove a gap between management and labor that was never successfully bridged." It was 1949 before the shopmen and other non-operating crew workers at Tucumcari were placed on a five-day, forty-hour week for the same pay as a forty-eight-hour week.[27] Hard feelings remained even longer between the shopmen who managed to keep their jobs and the replacements hired at the time. At Tucumcari one railroad supervisor was still known behind his back as "Scabby" thirty years after the strike ended.

In the years before the National Railroad Shopmen's Strike of 1922 revealed the harsh realities of industrialization, the railroad presence had brought more pleasant benefits to Tucumcari. For instance, passenger train service, which began in 1902, had given the town more entertainment and religious as well as cultural advantages than most other places without such connections.[28] In 1917 the large traveling cast of the Gilbert and Sullivan hit musical *H.M.S. Pinafore* came to town for an engagement in the local Chautauqua series. The production, "direct from New York," brought with it by train "elaborate scenery, including a large ship . . . and every detail needed to produce an opera in a manner equal to its presentation in the largest cities." With a full-scale orchestra and a large chorus of young men and women, it was obvious that, as advertised, "no expense has been spared to make this the most elaborate [production] ever seen on any Chautauqua." Overall, more than one hundred people and eighteen different lecturers, actors, and companies of entertainers were involved in the Chautauqua series that season—all arriving by railroad. The popular play *Little Women* stood out among the other attractions.[29]

Likewise, three-time Democratic presidential nominee William Jennings Bryan, renowned for his historic "Cross of Gold" speech, made a Chautauqua appearance. The most famous speaker of the day, Bryan has been called the "Chautauqua itself," who often drew crowds of 30,000 and railroads ran special excursion trains to his appearances. His name on the billboard, it was said, was always good for "forty acres of parked Fords." Famed for his stand favoring prohibition, Bryan had resigned two years earlier as US secretary of state because of foreign policy differences with President Woodrow Wilson. Although Bryan's Chautauqua performances probably had a special appeal for small-town audiences, the presentation of popular theatrical productions such as *H.M.S. Pinafore* helped Tucumcari and other heartland towns identify with the urban industrial culture.[30]

In the early months of the First World War, the army made an appeal for railroaders to join special regiments being formed for the operation of railroads in France.[31] Locomotive engineer Thomas W. Hampton, later Tucumcari mayor, spent fourteen months in France with Company F, US Army Engineers. Lieutenant Isaac R. Kirkpatrick of the Quartermaster Corps, Motor Transport Division, died in a fatal accident the day before the Armistice ended the fighting. Ironically, he was killed in an automobile wreck while overseeing the delivery of supplies to the front. When his body was returned to Tucumcari for burial, the popular young man's cortege to the cemetery was a mile in length.[32]

Paris supposedly was saved during the war by the mobilization of thousands of automobiles, which were used in transporting French troops to stop the German army advancing on the city. With this example in mind, and in response to an urgent plea from Governor W. E. Lindsey, a sizable group of automobile owners met in Tucumcari at the county courthouse on the evening of September 6, 1917, formed the "Motor Minute Men of Quay County," and awaited further orders. Governor Lindsey had issued a statewide call to arms, stating that, along with two other new weapons of war—the airplane and the submarine—the automobile had become an integral part of a deadly air, sea, and land trio that might well be the determining factor in the present conflict. He continued: "There is a place for the automobile at home, as well as at the front. During these stressful times we never know when the emergency will arise here in New Mexico when the automobile will be imperatively needed." As a result, Governor Lindsey proposed the formation of a statewide organization of 1,500 automobile owners to be known as the "New Mexico Minute Men," who would "volunteer the use of their machines in the event of any war emergency." Under the command of the designated county "captain," Mayor M. R. James, the Tucumcari contingent went out in cars to the outlying communities and recruited other vehicle owners to the cause.[33] No record exists that the Motor Minute Men of Quay County were ever mobilized to turn back a foreign or domestic foe threatening Santa Fe. A detachment of the Texas National Guard, however, was dispatched to protect the railroad bridge over the Canadian River near Logan soon after the declaration of war.[34] With a minimum of fanfare, town leaders also organized a panel of "Four-Minute Men," in keeping with the nationwide wartime mandate of providing speakers in every community who stood up in public meetings and, in exactly the brief time their name indicated, extolled the war effort and promoted the sale of Liberty Bonds.[35]

Near the war's end, in October 1918, the Liberty Loan Special Train arrived in Tucumcari to support the latest Liberty Loan campaign. Known as the "Relic train," it displayed exhibits of war relics from overseas battlefields, mostly captured German weapons that "our boys are facing in France," the sight of which would make "all true red-blooded Americans see their duty to help win this war" by purchasing Liberty Bonds. At a public tour of the train, wounded "American heroes" fresh from the front gave rousing speeches about their war exploits. In addition, the local Liberty Loan Touring Committee returned home "tired but happy" after a successful train trip to neighboring communities to put Quay County "over the top" in the bond drive. In Tucumcari, according to a newspaper report, the town band and Liberty Chorus entertained at an open-air meeting while volunteers "worked the crowd" for pledges that brought the county closer to its goal in the sale of Liberty Bonds.[36]

The peak of building railroad trackage in the United States came about 1916. For New Mexico, the "Great Railroad-Building Era" ended with World War I when eleven rail corporations operated three thousand miles of tracks in the state. In Tucumcari, one newspaper correspondent observed that the town was the home station of some fifty-five railroad mail clerks, with six mail trains passing through daily. Forty miles of tracks crossed the local yards, which serviced the major livestock shipping point in eastern New Mexico, and also handled the most coal and coke cars in the Southwest. He also reported that the monthly railroad payroll amounted to $80,000 (approaching a million dollars in today's value). From that point on, the story was one of "persistent struggle" in the throes of corporate mergers and consolidation.[37] Although not an acquisition of additional tracks, Tucumcari gained an important new rail connection following the First World War and the shopmen's strike of 1922. In a major transitional event, Phelps Dodge sold the El Paso & Southwestern Railroad to the Southern Pacific in 1924. Copper was the firm's main business. After several boom-and-bust cycles in that market, a crippling downturn occurred in the early 1920s. As a result, Phelps Dodge realigned its holdings by disposing of some less valued subsidiaries and purchasing others that seemed to show more promise and fitted more logically into the new corporate configuration.[38] The EP&SW happened to be on the disposable list.

This new course by Phelps Dodge meant that Tucumcari would be part of a rail system that more nearly resembled a transcontinental line. Since 1902, in a cooperative arrangement, the SP and the Rock Island had operated Golden State passenger trains from Los Angeles to Chicago, with the Rock Island crews from Dalhart changing at Tucumcari. The Golden State Route still met the Rock Island at Tucumcari, but now the SP had control, not only of its original line from California to El Paso but also of alternate tracks from Tucson through El Paso to Tucumcari. In addition, the SP's longer Sunset Route, often considered a transcontinental, had reached New Orleans as early as 1883, and the acquisition in the 1930s of the Cotton Belt Route (the St. Louis Southwestern Railway) would open an SP connection to St. Louis. Significantly the SP's logo depicting the blazing rays of a sunset undoubtedly indicated that Tucumcari's Golden State Route was not only a more recent acquisition, but it also was considered less important than the Sunset Route in company circles. An obvious reason for this favoritism was that on the Golden State Route, although a shorter, more direct line, the SP had to share income with the Rock Island, while on the wholly owned Sunset Route to St. Louis, there was no such division of revenues. Besides these two routes, the SP's Shasta Route ran north to Portland, Oregon, while its Overland Route ended on the east at Ogden, Utah.[39]

The railroad—whether the Rock Island, the El Paso & Northeastern, the El Paso & Southwestern, and now the Southern Pacific—that owned the tracks and dominated rail traffic in and out of the local terminal cast its own distinctive spell over the town and its people. With the venerable "Espee" as master, railroad workers and Tucumcari itself got the benefits bestowed by a traditional, well-established railroad. Earlier lines had provided some medical services for employees through contracted physicians. As early as 1911, a local newspaper mentioned that Dr. M. J. Thomson, EP&SW and Rock Island surgeon, had built a modern hospital to treat his patients, and, in 1915, his partner, Dr. F. W. Noble, was appointed as the railroad surgeon in Tucumcari. Dr. O. E. Brown, who practiced locally for many years, probably arrived in the same capacity in 1919. Dr. James Mitchell Doughty, who became the town's most prominent physician, arrived under the auspices of the EP&SW in 1912. Doughty's wife contracted tuberculosis, and he decided to move to a warm, healing climate, perhaps Mexico City. In the process of doing so in 1910, he met an EP&SW official, who arranged for him to establish a small clinic for railroad use in Duran before going to Tucumcari. Once in Tucumcari, Doughty bought an interest in a private hospital used by the railroad, assisted company surgeon Dr. Noble in surgeries, and opened a general practice. His wife recovered from tuberculosis and lived to a ripe old age.[40]

For a town its size, then, Tucumcari had an unusual number of doctors and comparable medical facilities because of the physicians and surgeons the SP, as well as other railroads, had brought in under contract to care for their employees. These doctors usually opened a separate private practice and offered their services to the general public for everything from childbirth to major surgery. In short, the SP had established a superior system of contracted medical care long before it came to Tucumcari, and the town had immediate professional health benefits as a result. The Southern Pacific also offered more extensive coverage with worker health insurance, for one dollar a month, in 1927 and hospitalization as well. And the SP hospital in San Francisco, distinguished as the first established exclusively for railroad employees, covered an entire city block and housed the most recent medical services. Tucumcari newspapers frequently mentioned that railroad workers had gone to this well-staffed hospital for treatment or surgery. The SP also maintained a specialized sanatorium in Tucson and another hospital in Houston.[41]

Otherwise on the health scene, victims of tuberculosis, also known as the "white plague," frequently came to New Mexico by train from the humid zones in the Midwest or South for an indefinite stay, hoping to find a cure in the local dry, sunny climate. In the five-year period between 1885 and 1890, New Mexico attracted some 19,000 TB patients to an official population count of about 153,000. Since many of the health seekers possessed some wealth, their arrivals were "viewed as economic assets." In addition, since most were Anglos, their presence created an "anglicizing effect" that probably helped New Mexico achieve statehood in 1912. In short, their presence helped neutralize opposition to admission of a state whose people were, according to the *Chicago Tribune*, "not American, but 'Greaser,' persons ignorant of our laws, manners, customs, language, and institutions."[42] The influx of the afflicted continued until it assumed the proportions of a statewide industry in sanatoriums. Dr. John E. Manney, originally from Texas, was among the physicians who came to New Mexico to treat TB patients in specialized medical facilities. He established the Home Sanatorium in Tucumcari in 1907, and the next year built an annex to the sixteen-room center. Dr. Manney also proposed converting part of Tucumcari Mountain into a tuberculosis sanatorium, but his initiative failed to gain substantial support.[43] More often than not, the hopes of the TB patients who sought a cure in New Mexico went unfulfilled and their wasted bodies were shipped back home by train for burial. However, several prominent New Mexicans, including Clinton P. Anderson, US congressman, senator, and secretary of agriculture, and Bronson Cutting, publisher of the *Santa Fe New Mexican* and US senator, came to regain their health and stayed after they did so.[44]

Another distressed group had only a short distance to travel to fulfill their needs. Many sons and daughters of homesteaders realized before their parents did that life on a homestead claim offered no hope for the future, and they left the rural communities seeking greater opportunity. They often fled no farther than the county seat in their quest for a better life, and many of them found a measure of security that, in one way or another, involved the railroad. In 1907 Matthew M. Hanna and his wife Mary Jane moved from northwest Arkansas with their children, Hugh and Birdie, to a Plains wheat land homestead on the

Llano Estacado just east of Ragland. According to family history, Hanna "worked himself into an early grave" trying to make a living on the claim without success and died in the attempt. He was buried in a handmade wooden boxlike coffin, lined with only a bed sheet, in the little settlers' cemetery at Plain. Meanwhile his two children had left the homestead for Tucumcari where Hugh found a job with the El Paso & Southwestern Railroad and became a boilermaker in the roundhouse. Birdie got a job and a husband in the railroad town. She was employed in Louis Blitz's jewelry store at the Second and Main intersection, and she and Blitz later married.[45]

The daughter of another homesteader daughter, Mary Mabel Garrett, moved to Tucumcari where she married Hugh Hanna. By his own choice, Hanna worked the graveyard shift in the roundhouse from 11:00 p.m. to 7:00 a.m. for many years. Routinely, following eight hours sleep, he dressed, including a coat and tie, and walked the few blocks from his home on South Third Street to the downtown business district around the Main and Second intersection. There he chatted with acquaintances and drank coffee at Sands-Dorsey Drugstore with fellow railroaders.[46] In short, Hanna's railroad job let him enjoy this pleasant routine instead of plowing the dry, crusty earth on the family homestead, as might have been his fate.

For Hugh Hanna and many others, the railroad and Tucumcari as a railroad town acted as a safety valve for a failed homestead system of the early twentieth century.[47] The Dust Bowl of the 1930s was the legacy of this failed homestead system. The end results also demonstrate, however, the extent to which railroading affected countless individual lives not only in the local community but in surrounding rural areas as well.[48]

A locomotive engineer, when commenting on the dangers of railroad grade crossings, told a crew member morosely, "We always win."[49] It was an accident at a grade crossing in 1910 that profoundly influenced the life of Sarah D. Ulmer. Labeled "A Voice in the Wilderness," Sarah D. Ulmer was already a devout member of the Women's Christian Temperance Union and supported the Anti-Saloon League, both spearheads of the prohibition crusade. Then she rededicated and redoubled her efforts to achieve the goal of drying up Tucumcari as a memorial to her father's life after his sudden death at a railroad crossing. Born near Lima, Indiana, in 1855, the Reverend George Crowley Ulmer taught school and passed the bar examination before turning to the Methodist ministry and the role of unflinching prohibition advocate. Still totally dedicated to the dry cause, the Reverend Ulmer decided to get a fresh start on a homestead claim near Hudson in 1908. On the morning of June 13, 1910, in one of New Mexico's typical sandstorms, the peripatetic Reverend Ulmer reached the end of his travels. He had driven a wagon and two-horse team from his claim to the depot at Hudson for some barrels of water, arriving just as Rock Island passenger train No. 33 was passing through. Since Hudson was a flag station, meaning the train only stopped if flagged for a passenger to board, the engineer of the steam locomotive blew a customary blast of his whistle as an acknowledgment and continued at about fifteen miles an hour without stopping. Frightened by the steam whistle, the team of horses ran out of control along a county road paralleling the tracks, and when they reached the grade crossing, instead of shying away to the side, bolted in front of the train. Even at that slow speed, the impact of the massive engine killed both horses and Ulmer instantly. The locomotive backed up to the station, loaded on Ulmer's shattered body, and took it to Tucumcari.[50] Besides creating additional dedication to the prohibition cause for his daughter, the Reverend Ulmer's tragic death provided another example that railroads brought great social and economic benefits but not without certain costs.

For the next fifty years Sarah D. Ulmer was Quay County and Tucumcari's undisputed leading advocate of prohibition and best-known citizen of the homesteader community of Hudson. An intelligent, wiry, bundle of energy, Miss Sarah D. Ulmer—"Miss" usually preceded her name as if a part of it—was respected for her educational record as a graduate of Northwestern University, and was described as "one of the best posted and well read among the women in the state."[51] Miss Ulmer never married but instead became wedded to the prohibition movement. With the hard-drinking railroad town of Tucumcari, which tended to dominate Quay County on such issues, she faced a formidable challenge, although the town came within six ballots of voting itself dry in a 1915 local option election and approved the Eighteenth Amendment for national prohibition.[52] The only time Sarah D. Ulmer could rest came with the Eighteenth Amendment and national Prohibition from 1920 to 1933. And even then, the liquor forces eventually won with the Nineteenth Amendment, which ended Prohibition. That it was the only instance in American history a constitutional amendment had been repealed by another one offered little consolation to Sarah D. Ulmer.[53]

Unfortunately, weather conditions also greatly affected lives in the area. The local weather in Quay County, characterized by long droughts lasting months, if not years, and interspersed with summer deluges that caused previously dry creek beds to carry walls of water five or ten feet high, could cause great damage and deaths. In particular, the occasional torrential rains accompanied by flash floods often menaced, or halted, travel and caused wrecks. Monsoon rainfall during August 1933 was the second highest on record, and the night of August 28 was no exception, with three to four inches pelting down. Transcontinental & Western Air's Flight 31 out of Kansas City was cancelled because of bad weather but rescheduled to originate from Amarillo that night instead. The chances were "very good," official reports indicated, that the weather would "not remain open" by morning. As a result, the flight left for Albuquerque at 10:25 p.m. (Mountain Standard Time), two-and-a-half hours before the scheduled takeoff.[54] Besides the two pilots, only three passengers were onboard. Ralph and Beatrice Gore of Albuquerque had visited their son in Amarillo and invited their three-year-old granddaughter Evelyn to return with them for a brief stay. As a chief railway mail clerk, Ralph Gore undoubtedly knew that the airlines were taking over the transportation of mail and threatening his job. Ironically, the plane he was on carried two mail pouches.[55]

The Transcontinental & Western Air (T&WA) Ford 5-AT-05 Tri-Motor plane had an engine on each wing and the third one mounted on the nose of the fuselage directly in front of the pilots. By 11:28 p.m., with frequent static plaguing the electronic equipment of that day, only the words "Over Tucumcari" came through clearly from the pilot to the Amarillo airline agent. For most of the time from then until the crash at about 1:41 a.m., a period of two hours and thirteen minutes, the big Ford Tri-Motor plane apparently wandered around Quay County and beyond, with the pilot "attempting to skirt or surmount storms on the course [to Albuquerque]." The plane's "directional radio" was of little help. Somewhere southwest of Tucumcari, having lost his bearings in the cloudburst, he decided to return to Amarillo.

Rural residents along the Caprock at Ima heard the plane flying low in the storm. In the Quay community at the farm home of Marion and Edna Davis, the couple recalled that the plane, making an "awfully loud" noise, was flying so low when it passed nearby that it was momentarily blocked from their view by the farm's smokehouse. Then, as they watched the plane's flight through the worst storm they had seen in their twenty-eight years in Quay County, its lights barely visible, they heard an explosion and, for a few seconds, saw "a big pink flare of light" before it turned bright red. Making a call on the rural telephone lines, Edna Davis got word of the tragedy to the proprietor of the Quay store, Charlie Dunlap, who, as postmaster and deputy sheriff, was recognized as the community's majordomo. Dunlap promptly enlisted four neighbors, including Marion Davis and Davis's son-in-law, Jewel D. Stratton, to accompany him to the crash scene.[56]

Located about fifteen miles south of Tucumcari, the rough, remote Mesa Redonda (Round Table) has a flat top with steep cliff-like sides interspersed with deep canyons. While circling around trying to return to Amarillo, the pilots found themselves trapped in a box canyon along the slopes of Mesa Redonda, pulled up abruptly to gain altitude, and crashed into a solid sandstone canyon wall. The T&WA plane, with the nose engine at the front of the fuselage leading the way, had struck the dead-end canyon's south wall about five hundred feet below the mesa's rim, leaving a deep indentation to mark the exact spot. When the nose motor hit the cliff, it telescoped the cockpit, killing the two pilots instantly, and sent a shock wave that broke the fuselage apart in front of the passenger compartment. The two grandparents, still in their seats, were catapulted about thirty feet out of the wreckage. Ralph Gore's watch flew out of his pocket and landed several feet away. It had stopped at exactly 1:41. From the location of the bodies, the grandmother must have held the young granddaughter tightly in her lap since the child's body was found lying across her dead grandmother. Simultaneously the fuel tanks burst and set the remaining fuselage on fire. The nose engine had been "driven under a solid rock ledge" and burned so extensively that most of its identification numbers and marks were gone. Both wing motors and other wreckage were scattered down the canyon slope.

Meanwhile Deputy Sheriff Dunlap and his four companions had slowly made their way to the crash site where they "found all dead, the man, woman and baby passengers just a few yards from the plane, [and] the pilots in the plane, both burned to a crisp." They arranged to notify the airline of the crash by telephone from the Ragland store at the top of the Caprock. Meanwhile Edna Davis had sent some of her best bed sheets to cover the victims' bodies.[57] The assistant district attorney arrived later that day with undertakers from Clovis, who took charge of the bodies and personal belongings.

Between the crash site and Tucumcari, the bridges were out, the roads were under water, and the telephone lines down. Despite such travel difficulties, a crowd of curious onlookers as well as airline officials, including one who landed in a small plane on the surrounding prairie, soon gathered at Mesa Redonda. The assistant district attorney assembled a coroner's jury and held an inquest at the location with representatives of the airline in attendance. The airliner's speed at the time of impact was probably about eighty-five miles an hour, as determined by the short distance the fuselage skidded "in the direction of flight." One onlooker at the crash scene was impressed that the plane's engines as well as human body parts were scattered over such a large area. Bolstering the onlooker's impression that "the crash must have been terrific," he found a human heart lying on the ground at a considerable distance from the canyon wall.

At a later investigation held in Kansas City by the airline, the question of whether engine failure had any part in the crash became a major topic of discussion. The panel determined that a radio message from the pilot, garbled by static, had been interpreted as "Flying on two motors," but was actually "Flying between two cloud layers." In addition, the investigation concluded that the third motor on the fuselage nose was probably throttled down to improve the pilots' visibility but had not been turned off and was still running at the time it collided with the face of the cliff. If the plane had been flying on only two engines, the panel members agreed, the pilot would have landed at the Tucumcari airport instead of heading on for Albuquerque. In the board's opinion, responsibility for the crash should be charged "to error in the pilot's estimate of [the plane's] location complicated by severe weather conditions."[58]

At about the time of the plane crash, the most disastrous train wreck in the history of Tucumcari took place at the railroad bridge over Bluewater Creek five miles west of town. As previously mentioned, rainfall in the summer of 1933 had reached monsoon proportions. More than ten inches fell in forty-three days, beginning July 13. During the night of August 28, 1933, about four inches of rain had raised the waters of Bluewater Creek to more than ten feet in depth. Raging waters had undermined the railroad bridge's east pier and weakened the structure above. At dawn the deluxe Golden State passenger train, on its sixty-two-hour run from Los Angeles to Chicago, cautiously approached the bridge traveling about twenty miles an hour. The concrete and steel structure, built in 1914 and known locally as "Five-Mile Bridge," was about one hundred feet long. When the locomotive attempted to cross, the east end collapsed and the locomotive, baggage and mail cars, day coach, club car, and a tourist car and two standard sleepers plunged through. The engine fell with such force that the front end was buried in the eastern embankment well beyond the smokestack, while the day coach landed on the western bank, half in and half out the raging stream. The sleeper in which most of the injured were found crashed into the cars ahead of it, spun around, and came down with one end in the creek and the other resting on the baggage car. The mail car landed on top of the locomotive. Five Pullman coaches remained on the tracks above the wreck.[59]

Initially, seven passengers perished, as well as the engineer and the fireman, both Tucumcari residents, and forty-five were injured. Two more passengers died later in the local hospital, bringing the death toll to eleven. The scalded body of engineer C. J. Croft, with his head crushed and one foot missing as well as other injuries, indicated that he had died instantly. Croft's corpse had to be dug out from under the locomotive, as was the case with fireman James Randall, whose severed legs were found first and the rest of his body later. Randall's railroader watch was still running and keeping perfect time. Engineer Croft's missing foot was not found until after his body had been shipped to Colorado for burial, and it was sent separately. Some confusion arose about the number of fatalities when four other corpses, dislodged from their splintered coffins en route for burial, were discovered in the muddy waters around the baggage car. Paul D. Cook of El Paso, SP building and bridge inspector, was not only a passenger on the train but also among those killed when the bridge over Bluewater Creek collapsed. Ironically, SP officials had heard rumors about earlier erosion around the bridge's eastern pier and sent Cook on a special assignment to examine the structure. He was one day too late.[60]

Railroad officials declared that they were doing all "within our power" to care for the injured. H. S. Fairbank, superintendent of the SP's Rio Grande Division, flew in an airplane from his headquarters in El Paso to personally direct the recovery work. Several Tucumcari residents, who had rushed to the scene bringing first aid kits from home, volunteered as a rescue squad, wrapped the injured in blankets or laid them on planks, and carried them from the wrecked coaches up the hillside to safety. Later, these Good Samaritans and other townspeople welcomed some of the less injured passengers to stay in their homes. All the passengers able to travel left town on an eastbound special train late the next day after the wreck.

Immediately after the train wreck, SP Superintendent H. S. Fairbank and San Francisco officials of the railroad began an investigation of the Golden State disaster by appointing a board of inquiry. Members of the New Mexico State Corporation Commission from Santa Fe and representatives of the federal Interstate Commerce Commission were also on hand and participated in the hearings. Some fifty witnesses, including SP employees and former employees as well as other informed persons, testified before the board. Fairbank decided on closed sessions not open to the public. The inquiry concluded that the Golden State wreck had been caused by "unprecedented flood waters aggravated by the size and location of a highway bridge." In other words, it had become apparent during the investigation that the railroad officials wanted the hearings to show that the alignment of the concrete piers supporting the Route 66 structure, located immediately upstream to the south, had diverted the creek's natural flow so that it undermined the piers of the railroad bridge. A state highway engineer denied this argument, claiming that the Route 66 bridge actually protected the other structure by providing a buffer against flood waters. State corporation commission representatives pointed out that the support pilings under the railroad bridge were sticking up six to twelve feet above the creek bed, and not driven deep enough. Outraged by the SP's conduct of the investigation, J. D. Lamb, chairman of the state corporation commission and a former Tucumcari railroader and state representative, declared that the hearings had been a ruse to support the railroad's case in forthcoming damage suits brought by injured passengers and the families of those killed in the Golden State wreck. In announcing the corporation commission's separate findings, Lamb declared that the wreck was not an "act of God," but due to one thing—human negligence. The railroad had been warned about serious erosion in that part of Bluewater Creek, he said, and failed to monitor the bridge until it was too late. The SP's H. S. Fairbank in El Paso retorted that Lamb's claims were absurd, lacking any factual basis, and made for political purposes. Lamb reiterated his charges and called on Fairbank to release the transcripts of the Tucumcari hearings.[61] Further guilt or innocence remained to be argued in court during a series of damage suits for deaths and injuries incurred in the Golden State disaster.

As this wreck proved, and as a local newspaper declared in headlines,

Tucumcari was a "Railroad Town Thru and Thru." Railroads not only gave jobs to local folks but provided the town's prosperity and chief support as well. Although a small town and big national corporations were not always comfortable bedfellows, the editor continued, "Tucumcari, from necessity, must be for [the railroads] thru and thru." Regardless, a predestined role of greatness for the town seemed assured by the 1930 census returns. As pointed out earlier, the county had lost 30 percent of its rural population between 1910 and 1920, while Tucumcari had posted a gain of 600 persons. The most recent census, in 1930, had not only shown the rural population holding steady but also recorded a remarkable 33 percent increase for Tucumcari, bringing its population of 3,117 in 1920 to 4,143 in 1930. In its God-given partnership with railroads, local boosters had long believed, Tucumcari would surely become the most important city "between Kansas City and El Paso."[62]

Population numbers held no guarantee, of course, especially with the uncertainties of the Great Depression and World War II ahead. And as for the town-railroad partnership, airlines, trucks, buses, cars, a national interstate highway system, and, above all, the increasing number of diesel locomotives were lying in wait as spoilers. As the canny newspaper editor said, when a town's fate was tied to the railroad, some bad luck for the big business partner could quickly turn a town into "little less than a wide place in the cow trail." Perhaps a peek at the future came on Wednesday afternoon, September 25, 1929, when Buick dealer A. E. Rhode landed the shiny new Spartan airplane he had just bought in Tulsa at the airport east of town. It was "Tucumcari's first home-owned airplane."[63]

Chapter 3

HIGHWAYS AND BYWAYS

ny Hollywood producer casting an old-time, stereotypical newspaper editor would have to go no farther than Paul Dodge, who took over the *Tucumcari News* in 1923. Tucumcari was never the same again after the crusading, opinionated, worldly big-time journalist with a checkered background hit town, bought the leading newspaper, and made it his editorial bully pulpit. His picture, with an impish grin, cocked hat, and perpetual cigar, accompanied his "Man About Town" columns over the subtitle "He Sees; He Hears; He Comments." In these regular front-page forums, he assumed the persona of "Ole Mat" and gave a tongue lashing—or in his case, a pen lashing—to those he designated as the forces of evil, from the bosses of the local Democratic machine to the entire neighboring city of Amarillo, Texas. He saved his special displeasure for local merchants who failed to advertise in his newspaper and sent him bills on forms printed by out-of-town firms. In his editorials Dodge often became "Ye Pastor," philosophizing about the fallacies of humankind and offering his well-hewn views on whatever subject happened to be under consideration. Even in straight news articles, Ye Pastor often intruded to insert Dodge's take on the events or persons.

All these stances bordered on becoming offensive but were presented in such a pronounced spirit of personal good will that more often than not readers found themselves in agreement. Dodge was a genuine character. He knew it and worked constantly at keeping that image before his readers. As a special feature throughout the publication, Dodge adopted his own peculiar journalistic jargon of abbreviated words, such as "tho," "thru," "enuff," "colm" for column, and "Mrms" for Mr. and Mrs.; called Democrats "dimmycrats"; and invented nicknames for the two local railroads, "Sufferin' Pacific," or "Spee," and "Wrecked Island," or the "Big Rock on the Wreck Island." On the front-page masthead of each issue under the title, or elsewhere, there appeared exaggerated boasts claiming, for the paper itself, "Cussed by a Few—Discussed by Many—READ by ALL," or "Official Paper of the Common Herd," and, for the town, "Printed in the Biggest Little City in the World."

In a sense, Dodge's journalistic style, when boiled down, amounted to contrived entertainment for the unwashed masses, but he was dead serious about his editorial responsibility and his newspaper's importance in the community. And his style did attract readers and keep them interested, especially in local affairs—after they had caught up on the cartoon adventures of "Alley Oop" and "Out Our Way," or "The Bull of the Woods" and "Why Mothers Get Gray." No matter what dragons he was slaying at a given time, however, he remained dedicated to promoting the economic and cultural welfare, as he saw it, of the place where he had chosen to end his last days.

Paul Dodge took the editorial helm of the *Tucumcari News* on September 28, 1923. In announcing the sale, the former editor said that the weekly paper had been sold to Dodge and J. M. Brunworth of Hardin, Missouri, and he assured readers that both new owners were experienced newspapermen and "loyal Democrats" who would continue the publication's high standards. In fact, he said, Dodge had "been in the game for 25 years," had once lived in New Mexico, and wanted to get back. Dodge soon elaborated, but not much, on this sparse information about his background in an editorial and a separate double-columned statement that ran the entire length of the front page. He came to know the Southwest years ago by living "in various parts of it," and, Dodge continued in poetic terms unlike his usual brusque prose, he had especially loved the climate—"its soothing and satisfying sunshiny days and its wonderful, quiet and beautiful nights, with the myriad of stars twinkling above, appearing so close that one feels if he wished he could reach up and pluck them from their beautiful setting." Moreover, he had found the people of the Southwest to be free of "the aloofness, coldness, stiltedness and affectation that permeates all other parts of the country." In the Southwest, with its firm belief in progress, he declared, you are treated as a friend and brother and welcomed to stay and help improve the common good. That was why he had jumped at the opportunity to buy the newspaper and return "after an absence of more than 12 years." In fact, he had decided to settle down in Quay County only "after beating the highways, byways, and cowtrails of a number of states." Dodge also proudly described the additional advertising, cartoons, and national and international news the readers could expect to see with the new printing equipment that would enhance the paper's appearance.[1]

These sentiments provided little biographical information, but Dodge did clarify the new ownership's political orientation in the accompanying editorial column. Starting off with a southwestern affectation, "Howdy, People," he went on to explain, "Politically *The News* will remain Democratic, for the new owners were bred, born, nurtured, rocked and grew to manhood in the very cradle of Democracy—and to be other than Democrats would be treason to our forbears [*sic*]." The paper would be "aggressive and outspoken" on any issue concerning Quay County and would not "pussyfoot" on news the public needed to know, regardless of pressures to suppress the information. Nothing was said about the nature of the partnership of the two new owners—and later Dodge's name appeared as the sole owner—although J. E. Brunworth was at first listed on the masthead as business manager. Nor did he mention a "Mrs. Paul Dodge," whose name subsequently appeared on the masthead as "associate editor," and mysteriously disappeared after a couple of years. Later Dodge added some information about his sudden appearance in Tucumcari: "Ye pastor arrived in Quay county with a small pocketful of cash . . . [and] paid cash for the business he is now running." At that time Dodge had also invested more than $15,000 in cash (more than $200,000 in present-day dollars), he said, in improvements to the paper.[2] Details about his previous business and professional activities eventually came to public light in his obituary years later. Born on July 20, 1875, at Vandalia, Missouri, where his father was the respected editor of a Democratic newspaper, Paul Dodge graduated from the University of Missouri and for a while aspired to play big league baseball. But, as he recalled, "We didn't get there, bush league and semipro, as they call it today, was the limit." After working for a newspaper as a linotype operator, he became a traveling sales representative and machinist in the southern and western states for a linotype company, with headquarters in New Orleans, and was later employed at another printing equipment concern. Health problems led him to the more settled life of newspaper editor, first, on the *Ralls County Record* at New London, Missouri, and before coming to Tucumcari, the *Hardin News* at Hardin, Missouri, which he also owned. No mention was made in the obituary of a surviving wife, although a daughter and two brothers were listed.[3]

Dodge arrived at Tucumcari amid rapidly developing changes in the national transportation system, largely brought about by the increasing number of automobiles. Railroads had replaced wagon roads and now, it was said, railroads faced the same threat from national highways. The most obvious aspect of this revolution in mobility appeared when Americans exchanged their horses for cars. At the beginning of the twentieth century about twenty-five million horses took people around, while thirty years later roughly the same number of cars did the job. Like most crazes, the rising popularity of the automobile often faced skepticism and social condemnation as "rich men's toys," traveling houses of prostitution, and purveyors of disorder bearing ne'er-do-wells who played ukuleles and drank the devil's brew. In short, the first cars "seemed best suited to adventure" than for any practical use. But this old-fashioned ridicule soon faded away. Michigan farmer Henry Ford, who abandoned his farm horses to make 20-horsepower cars in Detroit, put it simply: "Everybody wants to be somewhere he ain't. As soon as he gets there he wants to go right back." The Ford Motor Company's Model T, or "Tin Lizzie," first marketed in 1908 and eventually priced at only $290, was largely responsible for making the exchange of horses for cars a reality. Since farmers outnumbered city folks, Ford made the Model T to be "the farmer's car," which explained its initial success. But, with the steadily declining rural population, this focus also spelled the Tin Lizzie's inevitable extinction. For farmers and city folks alike, however, one overwhelming advantage of automobiles over trains was that cars "freed travelers from the tyranny of the railroad timetables," allowing them, as their own conductor, to manage departure and arrival schedules as they pleased. In other words, the car placed "everyman in the driver's seat and let him choose his own destination."[4]

Until the 1920 census revealed officially for the first time that more people lived in town than in the country, America was a countrified nation of farmers living off the soil but looking for a convenient way to take their crops to market in town. Good roads, it was said, would "get the farmer out of the mud" and make rural life easier. That harbinger of good roads, the Rural Free Delivery of mail, had brought some benefits of the city to rural dwellers. What the farmer really wanted from cars and improved roads, however, was an escape from the drudgery of farming to the excitement of the city. Women who drove cars shared this male view. One federal official supposedly confronted a farmer's wife with statistics showing that only 12 percent of rural families had running water, while

60 percent owned a car, and asked why her family had a car but no bathtub? The woman answered easily, "Why, you can't go to town in a bathtub!"[5]

In fact, an important part of the automobile's popularity was the influence of women in their design, color, and comfort, accompanied by the increasing number of women drivers, who had also just won the right to vote nationally in the 1920 election. This circumstance, which resulted in "a rainbow of colors," doomed Henry Ford's insistence on "any color as long as it's black" for Model Ts. In turn, the revolution in style gave rise to General Motors more luxurious, variety-of-colors Chevrolet, which, by 1927–1928, outdistanced Ford in sales. By 1930 about one out of five Americans owned a car, which meant that—statistically at least—every man, woman, and child in the land could be riding in an automobile and enjoying a Sunday afternoon drive at the same time. And often that seemed the case for a people who had always been on the move but now had a new sense of motion through "automobility."[6]

As indicated, Henry Ford made the Model T as a farmer's car because at that time more Americans lived in the country than in cities and towns. Not surprisingly, then, the original emphasis in national road building was aimed at meeting the needs of the rural population. Indicative of this rural fixation, the Office of Public Roads, established in 1905, was placed in the Department of Agriculture, where the agency remained as the Bureau of Public Roads and other names for many years. As a result, the secretary of agriculture at first had administrative responsibility for federal involvement in the heated competition for funding that soon developed, and continued for years, between advocates of rural roads and those favoring national highways. In bureaucratic jargon this "raging controversy" became known as the "farm-to-market vs. trunk-line development question."[7]

However, the main problem in providing roads and highways to accommodate the burgeoning automobile traffic focused on who would build them. Once that thorny question was answered, the designation and numbering of national highways became a comparatively straightforward process. Previously the rough, rutted roads common in most parts of the country had been constructed locally, often by counties. The relatively wide travel range of cars, however, required longer roads that ran beyond a county, crossed state lines, and continued over several state boundaries. The matter of interstate traffic appeared to place the burden of developing a large-scale highway plan squarely on the federal government. But it was hardly that simple; the Constitution contained no explicit authority to do so. Finally, in the case *Wilson v. Shaw* (1907) the Supreme Court ruled that the interstate commerce clause allowed the federal government "to construct interstate highways." In 1916 Congress exercised this authority by appropriating $75 million in federal aid for highways, and ten years later federal routes were designated and numbered.[8]

Driving any distance before the establishment of an orderly highway marking system could be a real headache. By the 1920s long-distant travel had become only a little less difficult. At any main road intersection, telephone poles and fence posts, "like totem poles," displayed a confusing array of signs with arrows and instructions favoring this way or that. Guidebooks of the day could be of a little more help.[9] For example, driving from San Jon to Tucumcari, a distance of twenty-five miles or less, and using a guidebook with mileages beginning at Amarillo, could present some problems. Starting at San Jon, the driver was instructed to turn this way and that, and veer around canyons and Revuelta Creek until reaching a section line that pointed straight west more than five miles into Tucumcari. Along the way the driver would have encountered a jungle of signposts, numbered stakes, posted arrows, and stacks of rocks. Natural landmarks provided the most visible directional signage. Monument Rock, also known as "Stand Rock," and, because of its unusual el shape, "Apple Core Rock," was a tall, massive shale and sandstone pillar located about four miles west of San Jon. It served as both a road sign and tourist attraction until it collapsed well into the road-building era.[10]

As the designated federal administrative official in charge, Secretary of Agriculture Howard Gore appointed a twenty-one-member board from the nonfederal American Association of State Highway Officials to create the national highway system. After determining that the highways would be numbered, not named, the board approved eight primary east-west and ten north-south routes. Numbers were also given to fourteen secondary roads. In the allocation of double-digit numbers, the primary east-west routes ended in zero, and the primary north-south routes in one, while secondary north-south routes ended in five. As it turned out, north-south roadways ending in five became much more prevalent in the national highway system than those having one as a digit. In numbering the federal highways, the route between Chicago and Los Angeles was originally designated as US 60, but in an exchange, it ended up as US 66, which

Route 66 "Stand Rock," also called "Toadstool Rock" and "Apple Core Rock," marked the way of early routes such as the Ozark Trail and later became a tourist attraction. It collapsed soon after the establishment of Route 66 in 1926. US Army Drawing / Alamy Stock Photo (Image ID: 2CH3CBF).

would make a world of difference in popular culture, as explained later (chapter 8).[11] Significantly, Tucumcari just happened to become a host town for the brightest star in the Pegasus constellation of American highways—Route 66.

The availability of automobiles and the building of roads had quickly drawn the interest of Tucumcari. In New Mexico during the territorial period, a comprehensive state road system got little attention, although the ancient El Camino Real along the Rio Grande was designated as the main north-south route. In fact, so little regard had been paid to a road system that by the time of statehood, in 1912, it was still impossible to travel from most counties to the next with any certainty. Most of the road work was done by counties and had only local importance. When a state highway system was inaugurated in 1914, the new highway commission decided that 4,000 miles of roads would be more than ever needed. That mileage, however, was increased to 6,500 miles in 1917 and 10,000 miles by the 1950s. Significantly, in 1918, the first federally supported highway project in the state ran from Tucumcari to Montoya, eventually becoming a segment of Route 66. By the 1970s, with increased federal aid for highways, the New Mexico State Highway Department became the largest state agency.[12]

In the early 1900s the sudden influx of homesteaders into Quay County resulted in rough wagon roads being beaten out along section lines, many of which later became graded and maintained as county routes. This latter construction phase sometimes coincided with the appearance of automobiles. In 1907, at the same time that Roy Welch of the Quay community bought a "fine car" in Amarillo, work on roughing out a road from Tucumcari to Quay, a distance of about twenty miles, was progressing at a rapid pace. Welch had made the trip back from West Texas to Tucumcari, a distance of more than one hundred miles, in seven hours and thirty-nine minutes, which was, the *Tucumcari News* proclaimed, "the record to date." In a similar trip, between Tucumcari and Melrose, one E. A. Clem, known locally as the "Flying Dutchman" for his dare-devil speed in cars, drove the ninety-mile route of that day in a 16-horsepower Reo in two hours and forty-five minutes.[13]

In short order, a primitive bus line to Amarillo and the intervening communities (actually, the vehicle was a car) started service, and garages offering repair work as well as dealerships for the major brands opened for business. In 1913 a local newspaper heralded as a major event the arrival of a railroad carload of new Fords, including both four-door and two-door models at $700 or less, and also reported the formation of an automobile club in Quay County. Similar front-page attention was given to news that J. W. Corn would market a car made by the Dodge Brothers, who until a year ago had only turned out vehicle parts but now manufactured their own line of automobiles. Locals told of their experiences on extended trips across eastern New Mexico, including the difficulty of driving up the Caprock of the Llano Estacado to Ragland, and of tours to distant places like El Paso. In the spring of 1916, about thirty carloads of Tucumcari people made a "Booster Trip" with music and entertainment to several plains communities on the Llano Estacado, being joined along the way by additional cars. By 1920 Quay County, with a population of 10,444, had about 450 automobiles, or one car for every 30 persons, which was far below the national average of one car for every 14 persons.[14]

Various proposed and fulfilled plans for a national road network had been publicized before the federal system of 1926. The Good Roads Movement, which originated in 1870 with bicyclists who wanted better roads, peaked in the 1920s as a national political force for highway improvement. The Pikes Peak Ocean to Ocean Highway, the National Old Trails Road, the Atlantic and Pacific Highway, and the Lincoln Highway involved roads stretching between New York City and California. And the Interstate Postal Highway, or "Southwest Trail," that promised the shortest way to California, drew a great deal of local support.[15] Of the multitude of early byways, trails, roads, and similar endeavors, the Good Roads Movement and the Ozark Trail had the most direct effect on Tucumcari. The Ozark Trail, a patchwork of various existing roads, had several branches. As a general description, it ran from St. Louis through southwestern Missouri, into southwestern Oklahoma. From there, one branch headed across the Texas Panhandle to Tucumcari, stopping south of Las Vegas to join the National Old Trails Road the rest of the way to Los Angeles and San Francisco. Two other branches looped around to El Paso. The letters *OT* painted on posts and telephone poles indicated the various routes of the Ozark Trail. Thus, the combination beyond Tucumcari of the Ozark Trail and the National Old Trails Road came the closest to predating Route 66 as a link of the national highway system in that part of the Southwest.[16]

Largely a cooperative venture, the Ozark Trail was most often maintained by Good Roads committees in local communities and even by private individuals. Both Tucumcari and San Jon had Good Roads committees. Under an arrangement with the state highway agency, A. L. Flemister supervised a two-man crew that did maintenance work on the route between Tucumcari and the Texas line at Glenrio, much of it ungraded. Only the graded roadway between Tucumcari and Montoya was patrolled. Flemister and his crew did their work along the seventy-one miles between Montoya and Glenrio traveling in a truck loaded with their tools.[17] Established in 1913, the Ozark Trails Association erected a series of twenty-one obelisk monuments, located in city centers and bearing inscriptions of mileages to various places in the network. The obelisk in Tucumcari stood for years at the dead center of the Main and Second intersection. An Ozark Trail Garage and affiliated Ozark Trail Shop did business with that name "because the great auto road enters the business portion of the city right at the garage's door."[18]

Road construction itself was like the weather; everyone agreed on the need for roads, but nobody seemed to know what to do about it. The simple fact remained, however, that the countryside was filling up with homesteaders who wanted to buy goods in town, and merchants in town certainly wanted their business. The Quay County Road Board depended on the county road supervisor to collect a dedicated poll tax in the various precincts to augment its limited resources and sparse budget allocation from property taxes.[19] Instead of waiting for the county or state agencies to act, farmers and townspeople sometimes pitched in, or were drafted, to build or maintain rural roads. By 1914 a rough network of roads, some barely passable in bad weather, stretched out across Quay County. In truth, however, many of the connecting links were not roads at all but two parallel ruts hewn out across the prairies by wagons and Model Ts, always with enough undercarriage clearance between the ruts to avoid "high centering" a Ford.

The Good Roads Movement created the kind of enthusiasm associated with a religious revival meeting. When news reached Tucumcari that grain elevators in Melrose had paid eight cents more per bushel for plains wheat, it became a call to arms for town merchants. Putting it in a humorous light, the *News* reported:

> The good roads movement has finally struck Tucumcari with a vengeance and a number of her most influencial [*sic*] citizens are now engaged in the pleasant pastime of heaving rocks and dirt, dumping scrapers and cutting weeds along the line from here to Ragland. They went out yesterday and most of them are still on the job.
>
> Several of the merchants sent substitutes and while it was not expected to make a pike or boulevard in two days' time the road will be made passable for autos and loads of grain from the plains country.

About forty turned out from Tucumcari and worked south, while almost as many were working north to meet them. Similar Good Roads joint maintenance parties labored on the routes to Montoya and San Jon and on the steep road up the Caprock to Ragland. "Good roads do more for a county than any one other thing," the *News* article stated, "and everybody is directly benefited." This concern for good roads was doubly important because the town had just started getting a hint of the tourist trade, with "eleven foreign cars" seen on the streets during the weekend. Three carloads of Hill County, Texas, residents had also come to look at the countryside.[20]

In December 1916, the Chamber of Commerce called a meeting at the county courthouse, for the expressed purpose of finding "ways and means" of improving all Quay County roads. "This is indeed a subject of the hour," the chamber declared, "and one in which citizens residing in every section of the County are interested." The Good Roads evangelistic fervor had not worn off a week later when, in a standing-room-only meeting at the courthouse attended by representatives from all over the county, the assembled throng pledged a popular subscription bond issue of $160,000 for better roads, with funding promised to every precinct.[21]

Bridges also became an integral part of road building. At first this necessity involved only an improved way to cross streams, almost all of which had minimal flows except after big rains. About 150 yards long, the crossing at the Plaza Larga Creek on the way to Norton consisted of rock approaches from both sides and wooden railroad ties wired together in the streambed. Constructed at a cost of $350 donated by Tucumcari merchants, the completed job was considered "an excellent crossing for automobiles and wagons." Similar crossings were installed on the same road at Barancos Creek and elsewhere at a stream on future Route 66 near Endee. A few years later, in 1921, Tucumcari raised $6,000 in donations to build a bridge over the Plaza Larga on the road to Quay. The state-funded bridge over the Revuelta Creek between Tucumcari and San Jon presented a bigger challenge because of the stream's rocky gorge, but a state engineer pronounced the completed structure "one of the best ever done in the state."[22]

By 1920, when no less than forty-nine federal road projects had been authorized in New Mexico, the largesse flowing from Washington had become significant enough to include funding for the most expensive highway project yet in Quay County—a high bridge over the Canadian River near Logan. The early low-level bridge at this most dangerous river crossing in the county had washed out. As an alternative, it was possible for a Model T driver, after getting assurances of no approaching trains, to straddle the railroad bridge's rails and cross to the other side. In 1918 young William T. Pool, who lived with his parents north of the Canadian, had been badly trampled by a horse. With his father away in Oklahoma, Pool's mother borrowed a neighbor's Model T Ford, loaded in her injured son, and hurriedly crossed the railroad structure, which had no protective side guards, to medical treatment in Tucumcari. Or, farther down-stream where the river spread out and was relatively shallow, a team of horses for hire would pull cars across. The new highway bridge was reputedly the highest in the country until a similar one at the Arkansas River's Royal Gorge in Colorado claimed the record in 1929.[23]

The Canadian River highway bridge called for asphalt surfacing on its approaches, more than a third of a mile in length, at a cost of $128,216. The county's road allocation also included $112,575 to surface and gravel 21.8 miles west between Tucumcari and Montoya and $12,179 for 2.81 miles east toward San Jon. The state's share of the costs for all forty-nine projects required the passage of a special bond issue.[24] Except for the Canadian River bridge the future US 54, which ran from western Illinois through Tucumcari to the international border at El Paso, received relatively little attention, and long segments of it in New Mexico remained unpaved for years. Interestingly, US 54 paralleled the Rock Island Railroad route between Tucumcari and Pratt, Kansas, most of which was originally surveyed, or at least traveled, by Coronado four centuries earlier.[25]

The application of asphalt surfacing on the Canadian River bridge was a recent innovation since the extensive use of asphalt and concrete had not become a common practice yet. As a noted transportation historian says about early surfacing, "Even the best roads were paved mainly with good intentions." At Tucumcari, there were some false starts as well. In a harbinger of things to come, a model road project, financed with state funds, was constructed by a state highway engineer east of town in 1916 as part of the Ozark Trail. The roadbed, expertly graded to carry heavy loads and oiled partway, measured thirty-five feet wide for the first six miles, and thirty feet wide for the next five miles. Initiatives for paving most often began in town and spread later to include roads and highways in the country. When paving of the town's major streets came, it was usually done with asphalt instead of concrete.[26]

Road-building funds were always hard to obtain. Tucumcari bartered away its chances to get the location of today's Eastern New Mexico University at Portales in an exchange of legislative support for road funding.[27] Strangely enough, amid the local flurry over road construction and maintenance, the voters of Quay County rejected a bond issue for those purposes in 1915. The only explanation for this surprising outcome was the recent economic hard times.

One newspaper columnist contended that two hundred families that should be trading in Tucumcari were spending their money elsewhere because of better roads leading to those communities.[28]

Despite the pitfalls for a reformer, Paul Dodge, as the crusading editor of the *Tucumcari News*, was not about to avoid taking a stand and trying to mold public opinion on crucial issues such as priorities on roads. Dodge dispelled any previously held concepts about his role as an editor when he took a strident position on the rural versus national roads issue. Most of his attention on this subject concerned what he called the "South Road," that is, the road to Quay, up the Caprock to the Plains wheat-growing communities, and on toward Clovis. In this context Clovis became Tucumcari's natural competitor for the plains trade. Using some of his choice journalistic vitriol, Dodge took aim at this commercial enemy, targeting, in particular, the editor of the Clovis newspaper, who happened to be an old editorial foe. When the Clovis editor called Dodge "a wrecker rather than a builder" because of his lack of cooperation in promoting the economic growth of both towns, Dodge responded with a four-gun salute. "You old dryed up wart hog," he began, and also referred to his long-time adversary as "that long-nosed old she coyote over in Clovis" and "the Clovis hawk-eyed polecat," who had "a brain so small it rattled around like a pea in a large wash boiler." In between such colorful insults, Dodge made it plain that he would never cooperate in any publicity campaign that benefitted Clovis.[29]

Dodge did give unfailing support for the improvement of rural roads, and especially his South Road, repeatedly extolling the comparative economic advantages of country trade over profits from national highways. Although he backed the development of all the Tucumcari transportation arteries, he bemoaned the money spent on Route 66 and US 54 at the expense of the rural network and farmer trade.[30] He failed to foresee the effects of the rural population's continual erosion and the growing prospects of the burgeoning tourist trade, even though both were obviously happening before his eyes.

Dodge welcomed people of all pursuits into his editorial office, or "Ye pastor's sanctum sanctorum," as he called it, to talk about their experiences and listen to their complaints. And he usually recounted these impromptu interviews in his "Man About Town" column. For instance, Dodge commented that farmers from all over the county had been "pestering Ole Mat" about road-repair work, but he had decided to quit "bellyaching" about such matters—which he never did. In case the farmers really wanted good roads, he said, "they could do the bellyaching" from now on, and he would print their complaints. Soon afterward he was at it again, however, speaking for the farmers and questioning the county commissioners about when they were "going to start building a few roads toward the county seat instead of away from the county seat?" But he added the mock assurance, "Ole Mat isn't kicking, isn't complaining, nothing like that, atall, just wondering, thas all"—like the farmers were wondering.[31] Regardless, tourism was the wave of the future for Tucumcari, and the rural trade would continue to decline as homesteaders abandoned their farms and ranches.

Clovis remained a business competitor and enemy, but Dodge's special wrath was reserved for the city of Amarillo and its business leaders. Long after New Mexico paved its share of Route 66 to the state line, Amarillo seemed to ignore doing the same for its Route 66 segment in Texas. That stretch of Route 66 was graded but often lacked rudimentary improvements such as culverts in low dips that retained standing water after rains. If the water still flowed, several cars would be backed up at these places until the level subsided enough to avoid flooded-out motors. To add insult to injury, Dodge said, the Amarillo elite privately belittled the importance of Tucumcari. If that was not enough, differences had arisen over reports that Amarillo was routing tourists away from Tucumcari. These issues constituted the basis of the running no-holds-barred editorial battle that Dodge waged against Amarillo for almost fourteen years.

Not surprisingly, then, Paul Dodge almost came apart in print when learning, in August 1936, that the formal dedication of Route 66 in honor of the late Oklahoma-born Will Rogers would be held in Amarillo. "Now Ole Mat's asking you," Dodge told his readers, "ain't that one heck of a place to hold it, and after that Amarillo bunch and conglomerate mess of bull shooters and purveyors of hot air and broken promises have been yelling 'wolf' for 14 long years and haven't done one little bitathing [Dodge jargon] toward closing that gap between Amarillo and the New Mexico state line." Strangely enough, Dodge caustically observed, Amarillo boosters had "managed to get roads from every direction under the sun into Amarillo, except from the New Mexico line on Route 66."[32]

In an earlier exchange of editorial barbs, the *Amarillo Globe-News*, while expressing its deep concern over the paving problem, passed the buck by stating

Route 66 Signage. The division between Tucumcari and Amarillo on this sign was appropriate considering the heated newspaper editorial battle between the two over paving the highway in Texas. Gordon Steward / Alamy Stock Photo (Image ID: EXEW96).

that the city was blameless in the paving controversy because the Texas State Highway Department, not Amarillo, made decisions on highway improvements. The newspaper also revealed some undertones of the highway controversy. Dodge charged that Amarillo was stalling on the Route 66 project because its business community, fearing competition from Clovis, knew that US 60 running southwest to that hustling Plains city would also require paving if Route 66 became surfaced. The *Globe-News*, in a huff, claimed that Amarillo businesspeople were not "falling down on Highway 66 paving because they are afraid of Clovis," but instead were doing everything they could to get both highways surfaced appropriately. Dodge responded that he knew from personal experience that "Amarillo being afraid of Clovis" jokes had been standard fare for at least three years among delegates from New Mexico and Oklahoma at the annual Highway 66 Association meetings.[33]

By the summer of 1934, most of the western states reported that Route 66 would be paved inside their boundaries that year, but Amarillo expressed no hope of blacktopping its part of the highway until at least 1935.[34] Other issues, however, lay behind the paving controversy. When members of the local Kiwanis Club had visited Amarillo, according to Dodge, and gone around to several service stations innocently asking the best way west out of the city, they were invariably told to take US 60 instead of US 66. Moreover, Dodge, himself, had run the same test by inquiring in an Amarillo hotel lobby about the best route to California and had received US 60 as the answer, because US 66 was "Almost Impassable." Some of this reaction may have been an inferiority complex on the part of Tucumcari but strained economic relations between the two places undoubtedly had more validity. A recent Amarillo good will delegation 350 strong had come by train to Tucumcari, Dodge recalled, accepted local hospitality, "peddle[d] the bull," and then gone home "to laff at us suckers." Even worse, he said, Amarillo wholesalers had followed up on this good will tour by returning and under-biding local wholesalers. Then, Dodge got to the core of the ill will. Amarillo printing firms had also come in, cut their prices, and stolen away printing work that could have done in Tucumcari—obviously in a certain local newspaper's job printing plant. Dodge's editorial warfare, however, went beyond personal financial loss; he sincerely took offense for his town that "Amarillo is making a glaring grinning sucker of us." In fact, more than once he was ready to propose, but never actually did so, that Tucumcari merchants "should boycott every wholesale house in Amarillo until the Texas welchers and hot air sprayers make good on their promises." Texas finally paved its last segment of Route 66 shortly before Dodge's death in 1937.[35]

Dodge could hardly avoid taking notice of local and state politics, although he tried to make as few enemies as possible. As he observed, using his concocted journalistic jargon, "Polyticks in Quay county, especially in Tucumcari, is the outdoor, indoor, stove league, whittling club, tobacker chawing club, sport of sports." He criticized the county Democratic committee as a "machine," and as political "hangers-on" and "racketeers." He also enjoyed making fun of the factions as they competed in claiming who had the closest ties with the power structure in Santa Fe and the congressional delegation in Washington. Likewise, he gave limited approval to President Franklin D. Roosevelt's unsuccessful attempt to restructure the Supreme Court, and he commented at length on the ill will between Governor Clyde Tingley and the state's lone congressman, John J. Dempsey. He reserved special scorn for dominative Roy Smith, managing secretary of the Chamber of Commerce. In Dodge's opinion, Smith was "always up on his toes and stirring around like a hill of ants" if he could lead a local delegation to spend money in some other town instead of concentrating on bringing in outsiders to spend their money in Tucumcari. Dodge broke out of the Democratic fold when he quietly supported and voted for progressive Republican Bronson M. Cutting's reelection to the US Senate in 1934. When Cutting died in a plane crash shortly after the election, Dodge praised him as "the only real statesman" who had ever represented New Mexico in the nation's capital. Dodge's support of a Republican, albeit one of the Theodore Roosevelt stripe, was not that unusual since Cutting also carried Tucumcari—by four votes.[36]

If Dodge seemed to ignore the railroads that provided the life's blood for Tucumcari, it was because the improvement of rural roads always remained uppermost on his agenda. He was a realist, convinced that Tucumcari's continued existence depended on industrial trends, as interpreted by distant executives, and if the railroads ever pulled out, the town would become nothing more than "a wide place in the cow trail." One simple fact could not be avoided, he firmly believed, that "Tucumcari is a railway town," and people in both the town and the county should back the railroaders as well as their employers. Therefore, local events in the celebration of national Railroad Week, including a bull fight in the county stadium followed by "a mammoth street parade" led by two bands, got front-page coverage in Dodge's newspaper. Such special attention was only appropriate, he commented, "considering the taxes the railway companies pay, the wages the employees spend, [and that] just about one-third of the upkeep of everything in the West rides on their shoulders." As earlier evidence of the pervasive railroad influence, the *Daily News* had joined the Rock Island in sponsoring a special excursion to the Chicago World's Fair of 1934.[37]

From early visits to the Southwest, Dodge had learned that the Santa Fe Railroad had its way with the New Mexico state legislature, and after his arrival in Tucumcari, he realized that the Southern Pacific and the Rock Island were partners in this powerful railroad lobby. A trusted friend, Dodge reported in his "Man About Town" column, had made a trip to the state capital in Santa Fe, where a high-ranking legislator told the visitor that the Santa Fe Railroad controlled the legislative process there, and had gone to great lengths to do so.

For example, the corporate giant maintained an open tab for all house and senate members at "the best saloon in the state capital—the one handling the best
liquors" and gave "booze parties every night." As a result, any legislation the
Santa Fe did not like failed to be passed. It was safe bet, Dodge added wryly in
his column, that the Southern Pacific and the Rock Island were "standing their
share of the [saloon] expense."[38]

Even when he started out with criticism, however, he usually ended with
reminders of what railroads had done, and were continuing to do, for Quay
County and all of New Mexico. In fact, he declared as Ole Mat in his regular
"Man About Town" column that "the railways of this country are purty much
of a barometer on business conditions generally." When commenting on his
friend's trip to the state capital, Dodge had everything in place to lambast the
railroads, but shifted gears and went into a lengthy defense of the Santa Fe
Railroad for the development it brought to New Mexico, and then praised the
Southern Pacific and the Rock Island in the same way. "What would . . . [the
state] be today," he asked, "without our three railway systems?" Likewise, where
would the most important institutions of all—"our schools"—be without the
taxes paid by these transportation companies? "Every town in the state of 1,000
or more population, [and] many of the smaller ones," he wrote, "owe their
growth, development, [and] the growth and development of the country surrounding to the advent of the railways." Obviously, he said, without the railroads New Mexico would be a wilderness. As a parting shot, almost in the guise
of a public relations agent, he declared, "Foolish, foolish indeed, to even
remotely intimate the railway companies be denied any say whatever [in how]
. . . the taxes they pay the state and counties should be expended."[39]

Taking a different tact, Dodge came out in strong support of rail workers
and the differences they had with their corporate employers over pensions and
union rights. One role in his multilayered past, it so happened, had been as a
union organizer for the American Federation of Labor. Moreover, according to
his account, he had once gone head-to-head and won against nationally powerful Stone & Webster in an El Paso streetcar employees' strike.[40]

Dodge kept a close watch on emerging national patterns in the railroad
industry, especially those that affected Tucumcari, such as the decline in the
number of passengers riding trains and the increase of travel by automobile and
airplanes during the Great Depression. It seemed impossible, though, to predict

where issues concerning railroads would pop up next. When the Southern Pacific announced plans to terminate two passenger runs to California, Dodge determined that this action would reduce by one-third the passenger, mail, and railway express service to Tucumcari; would mean laying off three train crews plus their support contingents; and would do irreparable harm to local businesses. He encouraged town residents and civic organizations to mount a protest movement against the SP's plan. On another occasion, however, Dodge found an unexpected ally in the Rock Island for his perpetual concern over the improvement of rural roads. A visiting party of Rock Island freight officials complained bitterly that the roads around Tucumcari and the outlying communities were in such deplorable condition that farmers were hindered from transporting their crops to local railroad shipping points, thus having an adverse effect on Rock Island profits. One of the Rock Island officials threatened to propose to his superiors that the transportation corporation refuse "to pay further taxes in the county until the state quit building cross-state highways and built some farm to market roads."[41]

Later, in 1934, as if in response to the Rock Island official's complaint, grading and graveling began on the South Road from Tucumcari to the Plaza Larga Creek bridge, a stretch of about ten miles that had been "an eyesore for many years." This was only a small step in Dodge's goal of extending a good road up the Caprock to Ragland and on across the Plains wheat-farming district. These details about rural roads only suggest the painfully slow progress of Dodge's determined campaign to tap the Plains trade for Tucumcari. He never seemed to tire of preaching the economic virtues of the South Road over US Highways 54 and 66. Those routes had their advantages, he conceded, but "they are no where's near, no ways near, the asset our South Road is, even in its present condition." If the South Road was "blacktopped" to the Caprock, Dodge declared, it would bring more business to Tucumcari merchants "in a week's time than 54 and 66 will bring us in a month's time."[42]

Even though the Texas segment of Route 66 remained unpaved until the 1930s, it helped provide an important land transportation connection for Tucumcari. As long as the railroads offered frequent passenger service, Tucumcari's orientation toward bigger cities favored El Paso, not Albuquerque or Santa Fe. For medical purposes, however, Amarillo had become a regional health center with outstanding hospital facilities and a corps of specialized physicians and surgeons that served eastern New Mexico and the panhandles of Texas and Oklahoma. The problem arose in getting to that medical center quickly and safely. In one notable instance, though, the "mountain came to Mohammad," or more correctly, one of Amarillo's most skilled surgeons came to Tucumcari on newly designated Route 66 to perform emergency surgery on a five-year-old boy near death with a ruptured appendix. At the pleading of the boy's aunt, who was a nurse in an Amarillo hospital, the surgeon packed up his Model T Ford with medical gear, loaded in a skilled surgical nurse, and made the bumpy 110-mile trip to Tucumcari. Once there, he quickly cleared out the room, sterilized and arranged his instruments nearby, and performed a life-saving appendectomy for the boy on the family's kitchen table. Needless to say, the "kitchen table operation" took on a life of its own as the story was told and retold countless times. And the tale pretty well summed up travel on Route 66 at that time—as well as the difference between modern medical practice and what was possible then.

Chapter 4

A BIG DAM IN
THE MIDDLE OF NOWHERE

The most obvious feature in the construction of Conchas Dam was its remote, isolated location twenty-seven miles northwest of Tucumcari. After World War II, the Bell Ranch built an extensive network of roads and maintained them full-time with a mechanized grader. At the time Conchas Dam was constructed, however, the ranch contained "practically no passable roads" except the one to ranch headquarters, and no railroad nor improved public roadway ran within twenty-five miles of the dam site.[1] For that reason, early plans to develop water supply and irrigation projects around Tucumcari involved other sources. In fact, most early proposals usually focused on Pajarito Creek, a major tributary of the Canadian River. Attorney Royal A. Prentice added a touch of celebrity to the quest by taking General George W. Goethals, who had headed construction of the Panama Canal, on a tour of the Canadian River, investigating potential dam sites. Goethals designated the future location of Conchas Dam, just below the confluence of the Conchas River with the Canadian, as the ideal spot for such a project.[2]

The principal figure in securing Conchas Dam, however, was theater owner Arch Hurley, who virtually stumbled into a leadership role in 1922, after which the dam project became his obsession for the next fourteen years. Born in St. Paul, Minnesota, in 1880, Hurley spent his early years in Wichita Falls, Texas, and the coalfields of McAlester, Oklahoma. In 1913 he headed west and wound up owning the Princess Theater—and the Odeon in 1936 as well as a later drive-in theater on Route 66—a few years before silent pictures were replaced by the talkies.[3] He had only a passing interest in water development issues, according to local legend, until other town business leaders encouraged him to combine a trip to Cleveland for a motion picture–owners conference with a stopover in Chicago, whose mayor was rallying support for an ambitious western irrigation endeavor. From that time on, as the story goes, Hurley was hooked on locating the appropriate site for a major dam. In 1929, "still obsessed with the dream," he took a tour on horseback that ended where the Conchas River joins the Canadian. Just below this juncture, bluffs on either side rose more than five hundred feet above a chasm one thousand feet wide. At this point, by his own account, Hurley chose the same location as General Goethals had done ten years before and scribbled on a rock with chalk the prophetic inscription "dam site." He rode back to Tucumcari and boarded a train for Washington to fulfill his duties as a flood control commissioner—and undoubtedly to do some lobbying as well.[4]

Altogether, Arch Hurley made thirty-four rail trips to Washington, and also, as a member of various flood control and conservancy bodies, he attended meetings in Chicago, Memphis, New Orleans, Tulsa, Salt Lake City, and elsewhere, traveling a total of fifty thousand miles, or a distance equal to twice around the world. In these travels he spent an estimated $10,000 (more than $165,000 today) of his own money, and local boosters donated far more to support his lobbying activities.[5] The disastrous floods of the Mississippi Valley in 1927 quickened national interest in flood control for the river's drainage system, of which the Canadian River was a tributary after its northern and southern branches joined and made a juncture with the Arkansas River. In the Herculean struggle to obtain the dam, however, one thing was clear from the beginning. As one historian puts it, "appropriation," was the key word, not "authorization." The difference was obvious: "At various stages in the game, formal approval for the project did not equate with funding. If the money was in a bill, formal approval was not much of a worry. If the money was in jeopardy, having an approval in hand was cold comfort."[6] It was the political version of the children's game Blind Man's Bluff.

Hurley experienced both stages of this process. Congress might be on the verge of authorization, with favorable prospects for an appropriation, but Secretary of the Interior Harold L. Ickes, also director of the Public Works Administration, would become a roadblock. Ickes wielded great influence in the funding of public works projects, and he questioned the necessity of

Conchas Dam. Finally, President Franklin D. Roosevelt signed the Emergency Relief Act of 1935, which approved the project and virtually guaranteed its funding based on both flood control and work relief. According to firsthand witnesses, Roosevelt exclaimed at one point, "Now those poor people in that dry area will have some water."[7] After completion of Conchas Dam, the system of irrigation canals surrounding Tucumcari was named the Arch Hurley Conservancy District in Hurley's honor, reportedly the first time such a federally constructed project had been given the name of a person.[8]

Although Conchas Dam dwarfed any other New Deal project affecting Tucumcari, several other federal endeavors aimed at solving or relieving the Great Depression had significant benefits, and they deserve consideration before returning to construction of the dam. Paul Dodge not only kept a watchful eye on all these programs in progress but also constantly challenged his readers to support more progress. Probably with Depression-era problems in mind, Dodge wrote a front-page article asserting that towns as well as people could commit suicide, and he posed the question of whether Tucumcari might do so. His personal response to this question was surprising. In 1932, at the depths of the Great Depression with advertising at an all-time low, Dodge expanded his newspaper from a weekly to a six-day-a-week publication but continued to publish a weekly edition made up of material from the dailies. It started out as tabloid-sized and four to six pages but was larger if an oversized ad required more space. The subscription rate was 10 cents a week for home delivery and $2.50 a year by mail. At the beginning of the new edition, the combined mailing list numbered 2,600, all in Quay County. By regularly appealing for new subscribers and scolding local merchants for not advertising with him as well as hiring their job printing done elsewhere, he managed to eke out an existence for his newspaper and himself during the worst Depression years.

Dodge issued regular rallying appeals for everyone to forget past differences and work together to move the town ahead.[9] He indicated what needed to be done with his own shopping list of New Deal projects that would benefit Tucumcari. Zeroing in on the plums of President Franklin D. Roosevelt's economic recovery program of public works, he pressured county and city leaders to lobby for them. Dodge asked the county commissioners to get busy on replacing the "antiquated courthouse," pointing out that President Roosevelt was preparing to launch a major federal program for the construction of public

Main Street West
Tucumcari, New Mexico
August 1959

Tucumcari Main Street, looking west at the Main and Second Streets intersection, the heart of the old business district. LeDeane Studio, Tucumcari.

buildings. He liked the idea that Tucumcari should get the federal government to establish a Civilian Conservation Corps camp or unit that would build a large public park. Besides a new courthouse and the park, Tucumcari also needed a post office building, a public library, a city hall, a municipal lighting and power plant, a swimming pool, public playgrounds, "and many things that other towns are going after." To accomplish these important goals, Dodge called for public action "that will bring some of this government gravy to Tucumcari and Quay county."[10]

Dodge's shopping list enjoyed an impressive record of fulfillment. In fact, by the end of the New Deal's pump-priming initiatives almost all the objectives had been obtained. The federal government had already authorized the operation of four transient camps in New Mexico at Albuquerque, Raton, Las Cruces, and Tucumcari. The announced objective was to put the wanderers to work so they could make enough money to move on. At first the unit at Tucumcari was situated in the old Central School building. Later it was relocated to a newly constructed forty-acre compound on the northwestern outskirts of town.

As pointed out earlier, migrants entering town on the railroads and highways were directed to this facility, which opened in April 1933. In its first year in Central School, 4,200 men, at one time or another, registered as transients and 37,560 meals were served there. All the supplies had been purchased in town or from area farmers, thus stimulating the local economy. A seventy-year-old member of the McCoy family, noted for his participation in Kentucky's Hatfield-McCoy feud—and for his fathering of twenty-three children—was the most "famous" of those seeking a bed and hot meals at the transient camp.[11]

The City of Tucumcari provided forty acres for the new camp and arranged to make forty additional acres available for the transients to farm and graze milk cows. Plans called for the construction of five buildings on the original acreage, including a dormitory to house three hundred men, a mess hall, office building, commissary, and storeroom. Until completion of the dormitory, the camp's supervisor had several box tents installed and also stocked a rented downtown building with double-deck bunks to care for the overflow from Central School. Some locals complained bitterly that they could not feed their families, while the federal government handed out three square meals a day to the transients, and even gave them free medical attention.[12] The protests hardly subsided when the critics awakened to the well-known fact that Peggy's Place, an already established house of ill repute, offered its services within a stone's throw of the camp.[13] Paul Dodge editorialized in a negative vein. The transient camps were, he declared, undoubtedly the biggest flop of all the New Deal programs. It was true, he said, that these facilities had relieved railroad division points, such as Tucumcari, from "the horde of bums," but the program was creating a permanent class of hoboes by making that way of life easier and more attractive.[14]

As the last of the transients moved from Central School, a new, more important use was found for the camp, and the migrants were gradually transferred to other locations. The large Metropolitan Park, or "Five Mile Park," constructed by a Civilian Conservation Corps detachment, would surely have met with Paul Dodge's hearty approval, although he did not live to see its completion.[15] In November 1935, the first contingent of an eventual two hundred "CCC boys," as they were called locally, arrived to take over the transient camp, whose facilities were expanded to accommodate them.[16] Generally regarded as the New Deal's most popular work relief program, the CCC originally recruited young men between eighteen and twenty-three in age (later expanded to seventeen through twenty-eight) from impoverished families and put them to work as unskilled laborers. The projects had to be related to the conservation of natural resources, most typically reforestation, prevention of soil erosion, flood control, and similar endeavors. Enrollees were provided with housing, food, and other necessities. They were paid $30 a month but had to send $25 to their families, keeping only $5 for themselves, which might suggest that Peggy's Place had to look elsewhere than the cash-limited CCCs for most of its paying customers. The enrollees were issued military-style green clothing; their camps were administered by the army, with reserve officers as some of the supervisors; and they lived under a form of military discipline, although not given military training. Such conditions aroused widespread suspicion. Critics charged that President Roosevelt, contrary to overwhelming isolationist sentiment of the day, had the ulterior motive in the CCC of creating an undercover army. Whether true or not, former CCCs were customarily appointed as corporals and sergeants in the expanded draftee army of the Second World War.[17]

The name of Metropolitan Park originated in the program's bureaucratic authorization that directed the CCC, among other assignments, to engage in natural resources development of government-owned rural lands, which could include the construction of recreational parks and campgrounds for metropolitan centers. To meet the requirement of government ownership, the metropolitan City of Tucumcari levied a 1-cent-a-gallon city tax on gasoline to raise approximately $5,000 to purchase Sheriff Fred White's ranch and three adjoining acreages five miles west of town. Likewise, naming it Metropolitan Park established its kinship with Tucumcari, the nearest urban center, and helped allay any doubts about the fulfillment of federal requirements for such parks. The four hundred-acre plot was then presented as government-owned rural land suitable for development by the CCC.[18] It was a beautiful location enhanced by spring-fed Bluewater Creek, which flowed through it. The ambitious project, originally scheduled for two years, but taking about twice that time, called for one large dam impounding a sizable lake, and two smaller dams as well; picnic tables and fireplaces in several places; extensive graded roads and paths; and a swimming pool and bathhouse. When finished, the "simply magnificent" swimming pool lined with natural greenish flat flagstone quarried nearby was reputedly the largest in the state. Walkways of the native stone surrounded the pool and provided flooring for the veranda of the bathhouse-pavilion, a large adobe structure designed by noted architect Trent Thomas in the mode of the La Fonda Hotel in Santa Fe. One CCC enrollee who worked on the Metropolitan Park project recalled that "seemingly endless" truck convoys hauled in the flagstone, and the young men "dug the pool with picks and shovels, mixing cement in a mixer no larger than a washing machine." Since the park was a work relief project, WPA employees also had a role in the overall endeavor.[19]

In short, Metropolitan Park would have done credit to El Paso or Albuquerque, and it was undoubtedly the New Deal's most significant social legacy for Tucumcari. The swimming pool was a favorite recreational and meeting place for teenagers and young adults, while the pavilion, suitable for sizable gatherings, was popular for old-timers' reunions and similar get-togethers. The CCCs themselves contributed a distinctively different cultural outlook when mixing with the local southwestern population. The first contingents came from nearby CCC installations, but later enrollees, arriving straight from Philadelphia and other Eastern urban centers, had no reluctance to share their big-city views.[20] Besides its local importance, the reputation of the park's majestic swimming pool, along with the conveniently located picnicking and recreational areas, soon spread. Metropolitan Park became a major tourist attraction, especially for travelers on Route 66, which ran along its northern edge. As a result, the highway not only provided a convenient entryway for the people of Tucumcari but easy access to the park for tourists as well.

It was against his bulldog nature for Paul Dodge to sit back, relax, and revel in the victories his town had won in the last year or two. The closest he probably ever came to such a state of bliss occurred when the two biggest New Deal projects so far for Tucumcari were "in the bag." In the guise of "Mat" ("Man About Town") he wrote in the summer of 1935 that, with the approval of the CCC facility and Conchas Dam, "Mat sees Old Man depression leaving here so fast a game of checkers can be played on his coat tail."[21] Most of the other objectives on his shopping list were falling into place as well or would be shortly. A county courthouse and a city hall were built in the late 1930s; the City of Tucumcari bought out the privately owned utility company and housed the plant in a new structure; and a swimming pool and park were packaged together and delivered by the CCC. New post office and library buildings had to wait for years, while the nebulous objective of public playgrounds apparently failed to fit in the New Deal agenda. However, a stately yellow brick high school of two floors and a basement level, with a grassy athletic field, had already been completed with a public bond issue in 1930, and the New Deal financed an adobe junior high addition to the old high school as well as various improvements in that structure, including lowering the gym floor. One of the federal program's most important contributions was building the Tucumcari General Hospital, the town's first modern public hospital. A railroad overpass at the town's northern outskirts helped minimize a dangerous section of US Highway 54. And the WPA completed several projects benefitting the county's rural communities, particularly the construction or remodeling of school buildings.[22]

Because of its mythic reputation, Route 66 is usually not recognized for its part among public works projects during the Great Depression. As indicated, that highway in New Mexico originated as a patchwork of existing roads, primarily parts of another makeshift system, the Ozark Trail. This combination had then joined still another piecemeal route, the National Old Trails Road, to form a connection running the rest of the way to Los Angeles and San Francisco. Essentially a linkage of all these disparate parts, newly established Route 66 badly needed improvements, particularly several large-scale realignments, in its nearly 2,500-mile route from Chicago to Los Angeles. As a result, the New Deal gave considerable attention to the needs of the highway.

An earlier realignment in New Mexico, which still required major work, had been the personal project of Democratic Governor Arthur T. Hannett. Previously a Gallup lawyer who had championed union workers in a coal strike, Hannett took office shortly before the designation of Route 66 as a national highway in 1926. The original route looped up north from Santa Rosa to Romero near Las Vegas, where it joined US Highway 85, and then, in a circuitous way, ran through Santa Fe and then to Albuquerque. Hannett had become interested in "the possibilities of a transcontinental road" while serving on the state highway commission. As governor, he called a meeting of state highway engineers, and with a ruler he drew a straight line on a map from Santa Rosa to Albuquerque, declaring, "Gentlemen, this will be our new highway." With his two-year term ending, and the new, shorter route not even started, Hannett ordered the district highway engineer to complete construction of the sixty-nine-mile link from Santa Rosa toward Albuquerque before he left office. In an amazing feat requiring double work shifts, the job was done in thirty-one days.[23]

Heralded as "Hannett's Joke"—an accusation he dismissed—the shortcut had supposedly resulted from Hannett's conviction that the elitist economic and political establishment of Santa Fe had engineered his reelection defeat, and he contrived a bypass of the capital city as his revenge. Together with another realignment in the Santa Rosa vicinity, the new route, although still needing repairs, shortened the driving distance between Tucumcari and Albuquerque by about ninety miles and provided more of a straight shot west to California. In addition, by 1938, Route 66 had been paved in its entire length.

Early realignments and paving, such as Hannett's shortcut, helped, but plenty of work remained on the narrow, potholed roadway with no center dividing stripe in many stretches, much less companion warning stripes on the sides. In New Mexico, where scornful references were often made to that nine-foot-wide "sidewalk highway," Route 66 was more renowned for its narrow width than any prospects of legendary status. It was said that "only six inches" and a roll-your-own cigarette paper stood "between you and death on 66." During the New Deal era, Works Projects Administration (WPA) unskilled laborers on relief did many pick-and-shovel road repairs and improvements, such as straightening life-threatening curves and eliminating other dangerous problems going back to the rutted-route origins of the national highway system. The more skilled Public Works Administration (PWA) employees, hired under the auspices of private contractors, took on the major construction projects. The narrow width of Route 66 in New Mexico, however, remained a problem for years. In the 1960s Damon Kvols, president of the local Chamber of Commerce, had taken a leading role in lobbying and badgering state and federal highway agencies to widen the road and make it safer. On a business trip to Amarillo, he was killed on Route 66's "Death Alley" east of town in a head-on collision with a fully loaded semitruck and trailer carrying automobiles.[24]

With the work of both the WPA and the PWA underway, some 210,000 migrants fleeing the Dust Bowl of the Southwest and hard times in the Midwest and South traveled Route 66 on their way to California. The highway now began to assume its fabled image. John Steinbeck's Depression-era novel, *The Grapes of Wrath*, which developed a cult following after it became a Hollywood film in 1940, depicted weary Dust Bowl refugees passing through Tucumcari and stopping at Santa Rosa as they headed in their broken-down, overloaded truck to the Promised Land of California. Steinbeck mentioned Tucumcari as part of the trip on the same page that he called Route 66 "the mother road." For him, it was also "the road of light" and that "great cross-country highway" of escape and hope, "waving gently up and down on the map" from the Mississippi River to the Pacific Coast. The most-overlooked point in this saga, however, is that the increased heavy traffic of the westward-bound Dust Bowl refugees, not to mention the disillusioned flocks of returnees, caused damages that had to be repaired. Along with other public roadwork, there was "a viable alternative" in jobs that kept some prospective migrants employed at home, and not on the way to California.[25]

The list of WPA programs benefitting Tucumcari, such as the construction of sewers and sidewalks as well as the sponsorship of art exhibits, seemed almost endless. For example, any compilation of the WPA initiatives that provided employment for local residents would be incomplete without mentioning the "Privy Brigade." The small crew of this federally authorized sanitation project traveled regularly out of Tucumcari in a single flatbed truck loaded with tools, lumber, and preformed concrete bases for pit privies, and built sturdy new outhouses for farms and ranches across the countryside.

In another unusual example, the Agricultural Adjustment Act of 1933 aided drought-stricken ranchers by authorizing the federal government to buy their cattle, then either market or kill the livestock, thus alleviating a glutted beef market and, theoretically, raising prices. In short, as one historian puts it, "No one had ever seen anything like the drought of 1934–1935," and the New Deal had to find some way to help the beleaguered ranchers survive. By August 1934 exactly 1,388,077 cattle had been purchased in this program nationwide and $18,960,282 paid to the owners, about $13 and $14 per head. At about that same time, New Mexico reported that of its total 1,700,000 cattle, the federal government had bought 95,713, with about an equal number shot as shipped to market—47,533 and 48,180 respectively. By mid-August 1934, the cattle shot in Quay County numbered 6,686, while 8,240 had been purchased for shipment. The 420 head shot on the late Howard Kohn's T-4 Ranch was the largest number killed at one location in Quay County. This slaughter took place in a canyon and the carcasses remained there to rot. It is interesting that in seeking a way to defeat the Dust Bowl drought, both the T-4 and Bell Ranches shipped cattle en mass by rail to lush pastures in northern Mexico, where they grazed for about a year.[26]

The dark side of the much-criticized New Deal program of buying and killing cattle inevitably focused on the federally hired riflemen who shot the livestock. Paul Dodge wondered how these shooters, most stock growers themselves, "could pull the trigger" daily, especially on young calves. He interviewed several of the gunmen and found that some of them had nightmares from the experience. Dodge added as a personal note, "You know, when you think of doing a thing like that—shooting down hundreds of little calves, gentle old milk cows and even range cows every day, it is something to think of, and the old Mat is just so chicken-hearted he couldn't do anything like that."[27] One Tucumcari boy of nine shared Dodge's views after accompanying his father to a neighboring plains farm to witness such an occasion. He vividly recalled the rest of his life a scene in which the cattle seemed lined up as if facing execution by a firing squad, the executioner calmly firing his rifle with the spent shells rhythmically popping out to the side, and the doomed animals collapsing at the knees and falling to the ground like wet sacks of flour. Afterward, farm neighbors quickly skinned and butchered a few of the cattle, only cutting off choice hind quarters, which federal regulations permitted if the meat was not marketed or sold.

As the drought receded and market prices improved, the cattle industry made a comeback in Quay County. The railroad had erected livestock holding pens conveniently located adjacent to the train tracks to facilitate the loading and unloading of freight cars. Later the separately owned Tucumcari Livestock Sales ring began operations as a marketplace for buying and selling cattle, attracting buyers from Texas and Oklahoma as well as local dealers. By early 1941, with both the stockyards and the sales ring in full swing, the Tucumcari district led New Mexico in cattle shipments, marketing in one month 3,188 of the state's monthly total of 26,787 head.[28]

Although not on Dodge's list, the biggest dollop of New Deal gravy by far, with a separate lobbying effort, was the proposed construction of a multimillion-dollar federal dam on the nearby Canadian River. In the seemingly endless battle for Conchas Dam, a final hurdle remained. Congress had approved the project, but the contractors and workers had no legal right to enter Bell Ranch land and start work. The imperialist New England ranch owners had no intention of submitting meekly to this upstart invasion cloaked in the greater common good, and they mounted an obstructionist response. New Mexico sued in the State District

Court at Las Vegas for 1,100 acres of Bell Ranch property comprising the Conchas Dam town site, a right of way for the main road from Newkirk and easements for other roads, and a right of way for the dam site itself. The state had to pay for all these concessions but did not have enough money to do so. Governor Clyde Tingley, a devout New Deal Democrat on friendly terms with President Roosevelt, solved this problem by the bold action of going straight to the president for help. Roosevelt was attending the dedication of Boulder Dam (later renamed Hoover Dam) on the Colorado River. After spending more than an hour pleading his cause in Roosevelt's private railroad car, Tingley came away with the president's support, although not the immediate cash, for the purchase of the rights of way and easements.[29]

Meanwhile, public sentiment against the Bell Ranch in the region adjoining the dam site, mainly over the threatened loss of thousands of jobs, had been "aroused to a fever heat."[30] Regular attacks by Paul Dodge's *Daily News* keynoted the anxiety. In time, the temperature in this caldron was only increased by the political activity of Bell Ranch manager Albert K. Mitchell. A Republican stalwart who had served in the state legislature, Mitchell ran for governor in 1938 and for the US Senate in 1940, both times unsuccessfully. In fact, he had the double handicap in these campaigns of defending his ranch employer while trying to win election in solid Democratic New Mexico of the New Deal era. Born at Clayton, the son of a prominent northeastern New Mexico rancher, Mitchell obtained an Ivy League education at Cornell University, which offered an outstanding animal husbandry degree but less preparation for thorny political battles. In 1933, at age thirty-eight and already experienced in the cattle business, Mitchell was hired as manager of the Bell Ranch. A workaholic who not only managed the Bell Ranch but his family spread as well, he often made business trips and political junkets in a private airplane.[31]

Particularly in his campaign for governor in 1938, he had to walk a political tightrope in Tucumcari, where "the greatest interest" was a road "to Las Vegas by way of Conchas Dam." Mitchell promised that if elected governor "a good road will be provided to Conchas Dam," adding that he also favored paving State Road 18, Paul Dodge's South Road to the Plains. In a much-publicized, purloined telegram, dated a year earlier, he had, however, apparently asked a state senator to block legislation for a Conchas Dam road. As a historical account puts it, "Undoubtedly the most discouraging thing Mitchell had to deal with while he managed the Bell was representing the company's interests in the planning of Conchas Dam." In fact, later pressure by the Tucumcari Chamber of Commerce for the Conchas Dam highway and access to the dam's lake became so heated that Mitchell publicly invited that group, "individually and collectively," to go jump in newly created Conchas Lake.[32]

For the Bell Ranch itself and the absentee directors of the Red River Valley Company, it was like a Hollywood cowboy movie in which the good townsfolk always won and the big, scheming ranch barons always lost. Encroaching home-steaders had ended the reign of the cattle kings on the open range, and now the mighty Bell Ranch, always a closed range operation shielded by indisputable ancient land grants, faced a similar fate at the hands of a rapidly increasing, automobile-crazed urban population on the ranch's borders.[33] This was why the Red River Valley owners had opposed the dam from the beginning, because they saw the "domino effect" it would create.[34] It had been a losing battle since the arrival of the Rock Island Railroad thirty-five years before, followed by the unsuccessful efforts to keep the Dawson branch line from crossing Bell Ranch property. Or, to put it in a humorous vein, one day while on his rounds, a vet-eran Bell Ranch cowboy who had ridden all of its different ranges for many years, happened to drop in the Conchas town site's drug store soon after con-struction of the dam began. Leaning on the counter, he exclaimed, "Darned if I ever thought I'd get a malted milk in the middle of the south pasture."[35]

And so, disappointed also by an adverse ruling of the New Mexico State Supreme Court on their legal attempts to hold off progress, the Red River Val-ley directors chose to make a strategic retreat. They accepted $165,000 for 18,164.86 acres of land and damages as well as 2,500-acre-feet of Conchas Lake water annually, conducted in nine-inch piping to adjacent irrigated land called the Bell Farm. The company owners had put up a determined fight but one they could not win in the twentieth century. For the time being, peace had been declared with the signing of an agreement on November 13, 1935, in which Bell Ranch manager Albert K. Mitchell granted permission for Captain Hans Kramer, commanding the US Army Corps of Engineers (CE), Tucumcari Dis-trict, to enter the project area and begin construction of Conchas Dam.[36]

The newly created Tucumcari District, which constituted the beginning of similar CE work in New Mexico, had established temporary headquarters in the old Central School building and moved to the dam site later. Before actual construction began, however, the private contractors spent about a million dollars on a tramway system two miles long that stretched across the Canadian River to sand and gravel pits to supply a concrete mixing plant. Massive towers supported heavy-duty conveyor lines for the eighty buckets weighing more than five thousand pounds each that carried a cubic yard of sand and gravel or concrete. This aerial system only suggested the perplexing transportation problems that had to be overcome. For instance, a six-inch pipeline thirty miles long had to be dug from Tucumcari to supply natural gas to the dam site before serious operations got underway.[37]

As already indicated, no road existed between Tucumcari and the dam project. Survey crews soon determined that Newkirk, about thirty-five miles west on Route 66, and the Southern Pacific Railroad siding there would be the "jumping-off place" where tons of materials and equipment would be delivered, and then hauled by fleets of trucks the rest of the way. Most conspicuously, Newkirk soon had a gigantic holding tank where bulk cement was unloaded before shipment to the dam site. On April 12, 1937, a small ceremony at the site marked the laying of the first concrete on the dam, which would eventually consume 750,000 cubic yards of it. Newkirk became a miniature boomtown with temporary boarding houses, saloons, stores, and service stations. Only beer was permitted at the dam's town site, so the workers drove to Newkirk on Saturday nights for "payday whoopee," as they called it. Now virtually abandoned, this railroad siding then offered entertainment for the workers at the popular Hillcrest Dance Hall and, reportedly, other pleasures in houses of ill repute.[38]

At first, Route 66 from Tucumcari to Newkirk was only graveled, with the blacktop ending at the city limits. It was after survey work began at the dam site that the state issued contracts to pave the two gaps, to Montoya and from there to Newkirk.[39] This meant that the crews establishing the onsite survey camp had to make a hot dusty drive of 35 miles from Tucumcari to Newkirk— which was the easy part—and then an additional 26 miles on rough, rutted routes through more than a dozen ranch fence lines, each with a limp barbed-wire gate to open and close. At first the surveyors made the 120-mile round trip daily but then obtained army tents and set up a permanent camp at the project. A graded, graveled highway soon displaced the barbed-wire gates and provided a relatively fast, although dusty, route to the dam site.[40] Today, this road, once shrouded in dust mixed with the exhaust fumes of endless truck convoys hauling loads from Newkirk, has become paved State Highway 129 and part of Mesalands Scenic Byway, one of twenty-five such scenic drives in New Mexico.

Between August 1935, when workers arrived to build housing at the town site, and November 1939, when Captain Kramer and his Army Corps of Engineers staff left for another assignment, 3,000 workers constructed a dam regarded as "an engineering masterpiece." Costing $15.5 million, it stood 235 high and 1,250 feet long, and had the potential to retain a lake holding 550,000-acre-feet of water. With the accompanying earthen dikes, the project extended four miles across the flood plain. As New Mexico's biggest public works project of the day, Conchas Dam became a prime example of "New Deal multiagency cooperation." With the Corps of Engineers in charge, the workforce consisted of a mixture of WPA unskilled laborers on relief and PWA employees of the main private contractors, Bent Brothers and the Griffin Company of Los Angeles. The PWA workforce was more likely to be skilled and hired on the open market with less regard for poverty status. Later the CCC constructed facilities at the Conchas State Park. Since the dam was a work relief project, the enabling federal authorization specified that 90 percent must be WPA employees, with 80 percent of those from New Mexico and 20 percent from West Texas. In addition, 60 percent of the workers were Hispanics from New Mexico. The National Reemployment Service in Tucumcari, a New Deal affiliate of the US Department of Labor, had reached an early agreement with the Corps of Engineers to screen and provide all the WPA unskilled workers on the dam. This commitment, and the construction of Conchas Dam itself, began unceremoniously when Sam H. Stratton of the local Reemployment Service dispatched the first truck from Tucumcari to start work related to the dam. The lone truck was loaded with WPA laborers and their supplies, picks, and shovels, and similar basic equipment to begin digging by hand the Newkirk-Conchas Dam road.[41]

The decade of the 1930s, when Conchas Dam was constructed, is inextricably bound with the Dust Bowl and images of gaunt cattle, whirling tumble weeds piled against barbed-wire fence lines, and blinding sandstorms. To accompany the withering sand-laden winds, rainfall fell off for the decade of the 1930s. The average annual precipitation for Quay County is almost 16 inches—15.91 inches, to be exact—but the average for the 1930s was below the norm at 13.77 inches. In fact, the worst all-time annual precipitation for the county—6.13 inches—was set in 1934.[42]

First WPA workers sent from Tucumcari to Newkirk to start building a road to the Conchas Dam site. Sam H. Stratton of the US Reemployment Service in Tucumcari, who hired the workers, saw them off. Author's personal photo collection.

Many knowledgeable locals expressed doubt that the watershed would ever fill the reservoir and that the massive concrete dam would not hold water anyway. These fears proved to be ill-founded when the dam held fast against major leakage and the precipitation set an all-time annual record of 34.96 inches— more than twice the usual yearly amount—rapidly filling the lake in 1941. In fact, three inches of water flowed over the spillway that year, and 7.5 feet ran over for three days in 1943. That year some wags proposed rechristening the so-called Dust Bowl and calling it the Rain Bowl instead.[43]

Undoubtedly, besides the advent of the railroad and Route 66, Conchas Dam and an irrigation system were the greatest thing that ever happened to Tucumcari. The two projects were separate endeavors under two different federal agencies—the dam by the Corps of Engineers and irrigation by the Bureau of Reclamation—but they were, in some ways, companion undertakings. Irrigation had been given consideration in the early planning stages for the dam. A canal outlet was included in the dam's construction and the two federal agencies cooperated in planning allocations of the reservoir's 566,200 acre-feet storage capacity that reserved 98,800 for dead storage, 196,000 for flood control, and the greatest portion, 271,400 acre-feet, for irrigation. In the end the Corps operated and maintained the canal outlet structure, and Reclamation had charge of building and maintaining the canal system until the local irrigation district took control of it on January 1, 1954.[44]

Despite original estimates that 45,000 acres would be irrigated, no more than 34,000 acres of farmland, according to a consultant's report, have ever received water from Conchas Dam.[45] And drought conditions have frequently limited the amount, if any, available to farmers. The reservoir was full at the first water delivery in 1946, but "short water years" followed. In 1953 pumps were installed at the canal outlet because of Conchas Lake's low level, and the next two years were little better. Even worse, for, three years, starting in 2011 through 2013, no irrigation water flowed to the fields around Tucumcari because the lake failed to rise high enough to permit allocations in the project. Seepage of water from the canals and laterals was also a serious problem.[46] In any evaluation, at least of Conchas Dam, it must be remembered that it was authorized primarily for flood control with work relief as a component, not as a profit-making venture. Moreover, the tourist bonanza for Tucumcari provided by Conchas Lake and the irrigation project's stimulus to the local economy can hardly be overlooked.

With the dam well underway and congressional approval of the canal system, the Tucumcari City Council formed the Arch Hurley Conservancy District, which, in 1938, contracted with the Bureau of Reclamation for construction of the Tucumcari Project. The original agreement included a forty-year installment plan to repay the $5,655,000 construction debt. As it turned out, the conservancy district could not pay the first installment, and its financial situation hardly improved in the following years. As a result, the contract with the federal government was amended to ease the schedule of installment payments.[47] However, difficulties lay ahead: construction of the irrigation project was delayed by World War II.

After the completion of Conchas Dam in 1940, the Bell Ranch tried to keep most of the lake's shoreline, which led to another heated legal battle over public access and use of the body of water itself. Lengthy acrimonious exchanges between New Mexico officials and the Red River Valley Company ensued until the State Supreme Court authorized public access to Conchas Lake for fishing and boating.[48] The Bell Ranch owners had lost again. They had no time to lick their wounds, however, because they were already embroiled in yet another ferocious battle over a threatened intrusion into their crumbling empire. The "crusade" (in this case, an apt term) to construct the future State Highway 104 from Tucumcari to the lake and on through to Las Vegas was delayed temporarily until after the Second World War.

Tucumcari was abuzz with celebrations in 1940 and 1941. First came the year-long Coronado Cuarto Centennial celebration commemorating the four hundredth anniversary of the Spanish conquistador's probing of the Southwest. Under the auspices of the US Coronado Exposition Commission, with Clinton P. Anderson as New Mexico's managing director, each of the six states traversed by the Spaniard in 1840–1841 formed a Cuarto Centennial Commission and staged a spectacular drama called the Coronado Entrada (journey into unexplored territory). Each of the state bodies also published books and pamphlets, promoted the establishment and development of museums, and organized traditional cultural events. A series of professionally scripted and directed outdoor pageants with large local casts in period costumes were staged across New Mexico in eleven cities and towns. Specially trained workers disassembled and moved the huge steel-framed stage and props from place to place.[49]

Presented at night in the Tucumcari Stadium, more than 250 locals performed in various roles with some wearing armor and bearing weapons while riding on the twenty horses in the production. In fact, in his role as Coronado, City Clerk Jim Stark, red-haired like the explorer, broke an arm when his horse stumbled and fell, pinning him underneath the animal. The *Daily News* published a big special edition on the Coronado Expedition and the local Entrada ran a series of articles preceding the three nightly dramatic performances. An editorial claimed that the Entrada had put Tucumcari on the national tourist map, pointing out that one out of three cars entering the stadium area had out-of-state license plates.[50]

Even though the Coronado extravaganza was impressive for its scale and grandeur, it could not match the enthusiastic public response to the opening of Conchas Lake. In short, the court decision to that effect paved the way for the biggest celebration in Tucumcari's history until that time. Water in Conchas Lake stood at the dam's spillway, and on July 1, 1941, the lake was at last officially opened for the first fishing season. To add to this momentous event, Tucumcari also welcomed the national Highway 66 Association annual convention to town the same week. Plans called for delegates coming all the way from Chicago, where 66 began at the Great Lakes, to Santa Monica, California, where it ended at the Pacific Ocean, to receive royal treatment in an Old West motif. They would eat western barbeque, witness individual rodeo-style performances, and join in the town's biggest parade ever, led by the event's guest of honor, Governor John E. Miles, who had started his political career in Quay County. The delegates were also given an opportunity to see Conchas Dam and its lake for themselves.[51]

Arch Hurley was hailed nonstop as the "Daddy" of Conchas Dam. Likewise, Route 66 received frequent attention as the Mother Road and as the Will Rogers Memorial Highway. The same week as the Route 66 festivities, another throng converged on the town headed for outings at the newly opened lake.[52] The two simultaneous events gave Tucumcari an ideal opportunity to boast of its importance as a link in Route 66 and to publicize its big new tourist attraction in the monumental dam and the fishing and boating available on its lake. The Second World War started five months later, and this was the last carefree celebration for a long time.

Paul Dodge did not live to write sage comments as Mat in his "Man About Town" column on the opening of Conchas Lake or Tucumcari's distinction in hosting the national Highway 66 Association convention. While still young, he was told at the Mayo Clinic that he had only six months to live because of a heart condition.[53] He lasted long enough to see construction begin on Conchas Dam but died, with still undiminished will, from a weakened heart on June 8, 1937, at age sixty-one. He had written his own valedictory a few months earlier when reflecting on his time in Tucumcari and his role as editor of the "World's Greatest Tabloid Daily":

> I have had a good time, enjoyed every year of it, month, week, hour, minute, second of it—fact is, have enjoyed my stay here more than I ever enjoyed any stay any place, any time. If Ole Mat lives, he will be here Johnny on the spot, for another 13 years. Many friends we have made, fact is, have enjoyed my stay here more than I ever enjoyed any stay any place, any time. If Ole Mat lives he will be here Johnny on the spot, for another 13 years. Many friends we have made, every one appreciated and highly valued, a few enemies we have made, every one of them duly appreciated and highly prized—might say, we even love them. Ole Mat thinks he has given you a good newspaper for the past 13 years, hopes you also think so—at least I have done the best I know how.[54]

Pauline Sartain, wife of railroader Claude Sartain, began working for the *Tucumcari News* by chance in 1927. At that time Paul Dodge, who had arranged for room and board with the Sartains, happened to mention that he needed someone to replace an employee who had just quit. He asked Pauline Sartain if she would take the job, and she agreed to do so only until a permanent worker was hired. That was the beginning of her career in the newspaper business. Later, she became listed on the masthead as "Assistant," helping in editorial chores and otherwise, even soliciting advertising temporarily on one occasion. When Dodge's health started declining, she assumed the journalistic persona of "Pat" and often substituted her "Polly About Town" for his daily column. Paul Dodge left the *Tucumcari Daily News* to Pauline Sartain, who continued as its publisher until it was purchased by Clovis newspapermen Richard Hindley and Earl Grau in February 1940.[55]

The *Daily News* sponsored an annual fireworks display, collecting pennies and dollars from kids and adults alike to pay for the event. As that time approached, Dodge frequently commented that "the old ticker is sledge-hammering." Under the headline "Ticker Doesn't Tick As It Should Be Ticking," he wrote that he was "floored again this morning, put flat on his back in bed, for another period of recuperation." Then, from a sickbed shortly before his death, he wrote that he hoped "the kiddies" would get a fireworks display "as big as Ye Pastor wanted it to be." And it was the grandest fireworks extravaganza Tucumcari had witnessed until that time. Staged as a memorial to Dodge, the display attracted the largest crowd ever gathered in Quay County, estimated at 5,000 to 6,000 people, who filed into the local stadium on a warm summer night. So many cars were parked nearby that it took more than an hour to clear the area.[56] As a finale, with the stadium lights turned off, blazing fireworks spelled out Paul Dodge's name in memoriam on a large panel and a bugler somewhere in the darkness played "Taps."

Paul Dodge's importance and legacy are easily stated. He was certainly one of the most influential people and undoubtedly the single most colorful character of prominence in Tucumcari history. For the fourteen years between 1923 when he took over the *Tucumcari News* until his death in 1937, Paul Dodge embodied the town of Tucumcari, as much as one person can do, and his newspaper was its voice.

Chapter 5

THE HOMETOWN OF BILLY WALTERS

The local American Legion post was named for him, and he is listed among the more than one thousand sailors and Marines still entombed aboard the sunken US battleship *Arizona* at Pearl Harbor. Billy Walters was an unforgettable young man, remembered by those his age as a "good guy" and by older people as the "hard-working kind." To recall him as industrious or hard working became easy. It was the classic Horatio Alger story of a youth's struggle to overcome near poverty suitable for a Hollywood movie script of that day starring Andy Rooney. His single mother, working to feed and clothe a family of six children, ran the Star Rooming House, located near the railroad yards. As the oldest child and mainstay son, Billy Walters took odd jobs to bring in extra income, including chores at the secondhand store owned by his maternal grandfather. At loose ends after three years in town and graduation from Tucumcari High School in the spring of 1940, Billy Walters happened to see a poster inviting him to join the navy and see the world, and he believed it. With his family situation, college was hardly an option. That is why Billy Walters was seeing the world, or at least Hawaii, as a member of the *Arizona*'s fire-control gunnery contingent when shortly after eight o'clock on Sunday morning, December 7, 1941, Japanese bombers scored direct hits on the docked vessel. It started sinking immediately.[1]

Later investigations concluded that four bombs hit the *Arizona* and three fell in the water nearby. Earlier reports had claimed that a bomb went down the funnel, or smokestack, which might have accounted for the unusual number of casualties, but that theory was disproved, as the metal grating across the funnel's opening remained intact. In fact, most of the deaths resulted from a single 1,800-pound armor-piercing bomb that penetrated the polished teakwood deck, pierced two steel decks below, and ignited tons of munitions in the forward magazines. Like an exploding paper sack, the *Arizona*'s sides were blown out, causing the funnel to collapse inward and ripping the ship apart from bow to stern. The blast set off a gigantic column of fire and debris hundreds of feet high, knocked navy personnel on nearby vessels overboard, and jolted civilians in their Honolulu homes. High above, the Japanese air commander's bomber "trembled like a leaf," and he later wrote: "Suddenly a colossal explosion occurred [below]. A huge column of dark red smoke rose to 1,000 feet and a stiff shock wave reached our plane."[2] Hundreds of sailors and Marines onboard the exploding ship, including the entire band, were killed instantly in the blinding inferno. The *Arizona*'s captain and the admiral commanding the battleship division were vaporized on the bridge. Although doomed sailors trapped inside other ships at Pearl Harbor may have tapped out rescue messages in vain, no creditable evidence exists of this happening on the *Arizona*.[3] In any case, how and where Billy Walters died cannot be pinpointed.

Another *Arizona* crew member, Lieutenant Kleber S. Masterson, who was born in a homesteader half-dugout near San Jon in 1908 and graduated from the US Naval Academy in 1930, narrowly escaped becoming a casualty at Pearl Harbor. Instead of staying on board for the weekend, he had taken regular shore leave to be at home in Honolulu with his wife and two young sons. According to his later account, this was "the only reason" he lived to tell about his actions that day. Had he been at or near his fire-control battle station, Masterson undoubtedly would have suffered the same fate as Billy Walters. Hearing of the attack on the radio at home, he hurriedly drove to Pearl Harbor, as Japanese planes strafed the road ahead and behind him. He and another officer commandeered a motor launch and cautiously approached the stricken *Arizona*, where, as Masterson recalled: "We went over to the burning hulk of our ship, what was left of it, and hauled down the American Flag. It was the big Sunday ensign flying from [a jack staff on] the stern, and it was dragging in the water and getting all messed up with oil. So, just at sunset, we took the flag down." Although the two officers could still walk across the rear deck to retrieve the flag, the *Arizona* continued to sink into the mud until that section, too, became submerged within a few days. Because of his shore leave at home that weekend, Kleber S. Masterson lived to retire from the navy as a vice admiral in 1969.[4]

As for Billy Walters, a solemn memorial service in Tucumcari at the Center Street Methodist Church was conducted for that hapless young sailor, just short of his twentieth birthday when he died. It was attended by a large crowd that included his mother, grandfather, younger brother Dick, and four young sisters. The local unit of a national organization renamed itself the Billy Walters Navy Mothers Club, and the American Legion post would honor him in the same way. A few months later, young Dick Walters enlisted in the navy "to avenge the death of his brother."[5] The *Arizona* had just filled its fuel tanks the day before the attack. It is said that of the 500,000 gallons of oil still in the underwater wreckage, nine quarts seep out to the surface every day. At that rate, in terminology coined by surviving crew members, those oily "Black Tears" will continue to flow for the next six hundred years as a reminder of the first person from Tucumcari killed in World War II—William Spurgeon Walters Jr., Fire Controlman 3rd Class, United States Navy.

In a stroke of good luck, outdated maps apparently caused Japanese pilots to ignore the adjoining oil depot—with its plainly visible storage tanks hastily built above ground to save time and money—that supplied fuel for the Pacific Fleet. If the attack had destroyed this depot, it would have forced the fleet to obtain fuel on the California coast, more than 2,500 miles away.[6] The crew of the *Arizona* was not as fortunate. Of all the 2,403 people killed or missing that day, almost half of them perished on the ship or in the surrounding water where Billy Walters happened to draw an assignment. Only 335 officers and crew members of the big battleship survived. Walters was one of the 1,177, in a total of 1,512 present at the time, who lost their lives while serving aboard the USS *Arizona*, on what President Franklin D. Roosevelt told Congress was "a date that will live in infamy."[7]

A few months before Pearl Harbor, Sarah D. Ulmer, who, since the repeal of the Eighteenth Amendment had renewed her efforts to fight "demon rum," enjoyed the most spirited and promising local option election on prohibition the hard-drinking railroad and tourist town of Tucumcari would ever know. The catalyst for this campaign to make all of Quay County dry was the in-town traffic death of a popular high school student, James Riley Watson Jr., with teenage drinking as the well-known cause. Moreover, the fatal accident was the result of a teenage culture in which the automobile became a social symbol, a compact meeting place on Saturday night where high school boys and girls gathered separately in small bands, loaded into the family car, and cruised around town on exact, mapped-out routes. Laughing and exchanging gossip about current romantic pairings and rumored sexual adventures, they dragged Main Street regularly and spent equal time up and down the growing strip of cafes, service stations, and motels on Route 66. Sometimes the carloads of boys and girls would stop together at the city limits, get out, and have lively group conversations before continuing their scheduled routes. Often the carloads became mixed, but only temporarily, as female riders in one vehicle exchanged places with male counterparts in another car. At about midnight or later the boys would go to the Flag Ranch Café on Main Street, which stayed open all night to catch the railroader trade, for a Coke and hamburger and more talk. Under strict parental orders, most of the girls obediently went home and to bed.

Virtually every high school student, as well as most adults, knew by heart the essential details of the accident that took the life of the joke-cracking Junior Watson. He was acclaimed for his nervous energy, clever sayings, and creative invention of nonsensical terms, such as the frequent, rhythmic repetition of his code words, "Her-de-her, Her-de-her." On a Friday night in February 1940, a carload of five teenage boys looking for a good time paid an adult five dollars to buy them a bottle of whiskey, which they passed around and quickly consumed. Then, in high spirits, they sped off from the business district south on Third Street. As they approached the intersection with Route 66, the car crashed into another vehicle driven by Eula Sands, wife of druggist Leon Sands and stepdaughter of Alex Street, and turned over several times. Only one other boy was badly injured besides Junior Watson. Junior had been sitting in the middle of the front seat with the old-fashioned, floorboard gear shift sticking up directly in front of him and was struck in the stomach by the shift's knob. He died of a ruptured spleen and uncontrollable internal bleeding shortly afterward in the local hospital during surgery.[8] Perhaps it was as much the freakish nature of the accident as the death itself of a well-known classmate that caused severe, widespread emotional distress among the high school students—a trauma that soon struck their parents and across town as well. With both high school and junior high classes dismissed for Junior Watson's funeral in the Church of Christ sanctuary, the customary religious ceremony also became a civic protest against the deadly, and dastardly, "liquor traffic."

In a practical sense, Sarah D. Ulmer saw this tragic accident as an opportunity to promote the prohibition cause in Tucumcari and Quay County. When a politically savvy high school senior, Fred S. Witty Jr., visited her rural home near Hudson, expressing his concern about Junior Watson's death and the problem of teenage drinking generally, the result was the rough plan for a youth movement against liquor consumption. From that point on Ulmer did everything in her power to encourage the involvement of high school–age youths to work together in forming an organization that would bring a local option election on prohibition. Sometimes she stood on the sidelines urging them on, at other times she was in the middle of the fray. Witty Jr. also continued as a decisive force in organizing the youth movement, and later in obtaining funds and overseeing the collection of signatures on the petitions required to call a special election. At this crucial point, Dr. C. R. Barrick, who had recently arrived in town as pastor of the First Baptist Church, took an active role in directing and encouraging the formal establishment of a youth group.[9]

In March 1940, glaring boldfaced, front-page newspaper headlines reported that 250 high school–age boys and girls had met in the Presbyterian Church to answer the "'Call for Youth' to unite in the fight against 'liquor and the source of liquor'" and bring about a local option election on prohibition. Popular high school junior Francis Ball was elected as the president of the movement, and he promptly urged the assembled youths to bring their parents along to a mass meeting scheduled in the new county courthouse. At the mass meeting, which led to the formation of the Quay County Youth Organization, Ball included in his extended comments an obvious reference to Junior Watson's death in February: "For several months—many of our high school students have been seriously concerned about the freedom of the accessibility of liquor to the youth of our town and the growing consumption of liquor by the adults of our community. It's liquor, liquor everywhere and plenty to drink." The mass meeting was followed, until the election in early June, by youth rallies that recruited new members, marshaled forces to collect signatures on election petitions, and gathered support in the community.[10] This emotion-driven campaign, with strong overtones of a religious crusade, drew most of its moral and financial support from local churches, and many of its youthful advocates were undoubtedly motivated by their religious convictions.

The idealistic young people, backed by high-minded adults, probably did not anticipate the bruising, no-holds-barred fight ahead of them, but a battle of competing full-page newspaper ads soon revealed the tactics of the opposition. Oddly enough, both sides made frequent references to the recent enforcement of nationwide Prohibition, carefully choosing points that favored their cause. In fact, the strategy of the pro-liquor Quay County Citizens Committee, as revealed in a typical ad, played almost entirely on the alleged mistakes of the Prohibition era. The ad began with a capitalized statement by Abraham Lincoln in the Illinois State Legislature in 1840: "Prohibition Will Work A Great Injury To the Cause of Temperance." From that point on, the Citizens Committee made no attempt to deny that alcohol was a problem but claimed repeatedly that prohibition failed to provide an answer. The ad contended that "True Temperance," which meant drinking in moderation, could only be achieved through "Education" and "Supervision, control and taxation of licensed outlets." Otherwise, bone-dry prohibition would mean a return to "THE 'PROHIBITION' YEARS' . . . [which] saw our nation engulfed in a wave of crime, lawlessness . . . Saw the bootlegging gangs grow rich, defy the law, corrupt morals of our youth." In short, the ad appealed to the voters of Quay County not "to go backward to the days of bootlegging and the speakeasy."[11]

The Youth Organization's typical ad presented its case to voters by saying: "WE ARE ASKING you to vote against the legal and illegal sale of alcoholic beverages, against saloons, 'bootleggers, speakeasies, moonshiners, racketeers, Blind-Tigers, Gangsters'—against the sale of alcoholic beverages and the attending vices." Then came a moralistic and religious appeal: "WE ARE ASKING you to vote for law, order and decency—morality, culture, education and religion." Significantly, considering reported warnings of retaliation made to some merchants, the ad encouraged voters "not to be intimidated" by threats from the opposition of a "trade boycott or economic persecution." The rest of the printed appeal was devoted, for the most part, to a list of nine statements that either supported the dry cause or refuted claims made by the opposition. The issue, at least as represented in the competitive ads, boiled down to a choice between a completely dry town and county or an emphasis on temperance in the educated moderation of drinking alcoholic beverages.[12]

It seemed that an emotion-packed campaign led by the town's high school boys and girls, like the Children's Crusade to the Holy Land of the Middle Ages, was the precise formula needed to crack even hard-drinking Tucumcari and make it dry.[13] Like the abortive, disastrous failure of the Children's Crusade, however, the special local option election was no real contest, as the wet vote totaled almost two-to-one over the dry ballots, for a count of 2,191 to 1,261.

Tucumcari voted overwhelmingly for the wet cause, 1,251 to 479. In fact, the election had brought an impressive turnout in Tucumcari, with 1,730 total votes cast, while a comparatively light vote of 1,722 ballots was registered in the county.[14] These results sent a clear message that the railroad town of Tucumcari and its outlying rural communities were going to remain wet for now and for a long time to come.

Reliable reports seemed to substantiate charges by the Youth Organization that some downtown business owners, who gave early support to the dry crusade, had been threatened with economic reprisals by members of the wet Citizens Committee. On the other hand, the county's liquor dealers floated the idea after the election of calling a conference of city officials, licensed dealers, the clergy, and various interested organizations "to discuss the future operations of their establishments." The announced plan was aimed at eliminating misunderstandings and maintaining "the present high standards of the liquor industry." Although the proposal initially met "with considerable favor from all factions," the heated differences of the election continued afterward and apparently the conference never materialized.[15]

Never at a loss to get in the last word, Sarah D. Ulmer used her bylined newspaper column announcing a regular meeting of the Woman's Christian Temperance Union to insert a parting shot at the liquor traffic: "They say we lost the election. Well, we did not browbeat, bludgeon, or threaten anybody who did not agree with us. And that's more than this terrible, well-organized, liquor traffic can say. They tried to intimidate, and seem to have succeeded admirably . . . [with] every one who would listen to them." By early June 1940, when the election occurred, the Second World War in Europe was going badly for the Allies, with the British evacuating their troops from the continent at Dunkirk and France about to capitulate to Germany.[16] In that vein Ulmer used a widely held extremist view to castigate her own enemies, indicating in the process how much the election loss had pained her:

> Do you know that Adolf Hitler expects to gain possession of this country through the German brewers and distillers in America? Well he does, and you who voted with that gang betrayed your country into their hands, whether you intended to or not. Thank God I am no traitor, and I do not herd with a gang of traitors. I am no bully, and I do not run with bullies. I

am no coward, and according to the election figures, there are twelve hundred and sixty other souls in Quay County who cannot be bought or frightened by threats, either.

She concluded by saying that the recent election represented "only the first skirmish" and that the dry forces had learned how to deal the next time with those who would sell out their country for a profit.[17] Actually, although she continued the fight for prohibition, this was Sarah D. Ulmer's last hurrah, and she would never again have an influential role in a local option election on the issue.

The Western novelist and historian Larry McMurtry observed, "Though car wrecks happen everywhere, in the West death on the highway is as much a part of the culture as rodeos."[18] Junior Watson's death resulting from a car wreck within the city limits was unusual, although not unheard of, but the carnage on Route 66 beyond the town was another matter. In the years immediately before Pearl Harbor and the wartime restrictions that reduced tourist travel to a trickle, the highway death toll was already approaching slaughterhouse proportions—even before the postwar tidal wave of tourists bound for Disneyland. The sixty-mile stretch of Route 66 between Tucumcari and Santa Rosa, known as "death road," became infamous at this time for the number of casualties, with "Sure Death Bridge" near Newkirk the scene of several fatalities. Before tubeless pneumatic tires became the accepted equipment for cars, blowouts of inner tubes, standard accessories at that time, caused many of the wrecks. Throughout the 1930s the refugees fleeing the Dust Bowl for California contributed to increased travel on Route 66. Likewise, two World Fairs in 1939 and 1940, the Golden Gate International Exposition at San Francisco and the New York World's Fair, had a similar effect.[19]

In April 1940 one group of five tourists escaped death but suffered serious injuries at Sure Death Bridge when their car hit loose gravel and skidded, crashing into the bridge itself instead of overturning in the adjoining borrow ditch. The driver said he saw no signs warning him to slow down or drive with caution. In August 1941 two separate accidents, one a head-on collision at the bridge and another in the vicinity, brought sixteen people to the Tucumcari hospital for treatment. The next day four tourists were killed and two injured after their car hurtled off the highway near the fatal bridge. Two weeks later two people died when the car in which they were riding became involved in a three-car pileup and turned over several times eleven miles east of Santa Rosa. Three people died and four more were hospitalized from a head-on collision near Newkirk in December. With the war across the Atlantic in mind, the *Tucumcari Daily News* editor commented, "The slaughter raging in Europe has nothing on the American drama—'Murder on the Highways'—that shows every day in the year from coast to coast."[20]

Tucumcari soon got the reputation as the "city of many highway accidents." The *Daily News* editor, bemoaning that Tucumcari was saddled with such a reputation, declared that this label had resulted from "a false impression" of the actual circumstances. More accidents occurred near Santa Rosa, the editor said, but because that town had inadequate medical facilities, the highway victims were almost always brought to the local hospital. And since reports of the tragedies came from here, especially if the injured persons died, Tucumcari got the blame. Whatever the case, enough automobile accidents happened to go around on death road between Tucumcari and Santa Rosa. At a cost of $86,000, more than half furnished by the WPA, Tucumcari had recently acquired a new, up-to-date hospital on a five-acre plot at the town's southern outskirts where the increasing flow of highway victims could receive treatment. Those injured in railroad accidents, either on the job or in wrecks, also received medical attention at the local hospital. In December 1941, four seriously injured passengers and twenty-five more aboard a westbound Rock Island passenger train that derailed near Logan were brought to the hospital for treatment or checkups.[21]

The First World War had convinced Americans to avoid European wars. As World War II unfolded overseas, the United States launched a military buildup, announced as preparedness to stay out of the conflict in Europe. As a result, Tucumcari acquired its own "Little Army." Company C, 104th Anti-Tank Regiment, composed of about ninety local men, was officially mustered into the New Mexico National Guard, October 9, 1940, and inducted into active service, January 6, 1941. Less than two weeks later, the troops departed by train for training at Fort Sam Houston in San Antonio. Captain James A. Daily, who held a reserve commission and had managed a local auto parts store but now ran a local bar, commanded the company. A second unit, the Medical Detachment, 104th Anti-Tank Regiment, was commanded by Captain Thomas B. Hoover, the town's leading surgeon and husband of Clara Kohn Hoover.

Numbered among the other officers as well as enlisted personnel were many of the community's best-known young men, who had been high school classmates and played together on the Rattler teams. The company's recruitment process came to resemble a spirited brotherhood invitation to join up with your friends in a noble cause—all in the spirit of a Boy Scout weekend camping trip.

While waiting for their uniforms, weapons, and equipment to arrive, the troops, already under military discipline and routines, stayed in a temporary armory, remodeled from an existing building at Main and Third Streets. The scene at the railroad depot on that chilly winter night when the company departed for Fort Sam Houston brought both tears of apprehension and back-slapping encouragement as the young men, most of whom had grown up in Tucumcari, now soldiers in uniforms, went off to unknown battles and adventures. When Captain Daily, in his brand-new uniform with shiny silver bars on the collar, pulled up in a jeep with his driver, the commotion died down and the troops lined up in ranks. Then, in military order, Tucumcari's Little Army boarded the waiting train and left. The men had enlisted in the National Guard for three years and expected to return home after a year of active duty, but most of them were gone until the war ended in 1945.[22]

The war with its restrictions on civilian travel by automobile practically killed the tourist trade. But the conflict increased railroad activity to a fever pitch as troop-laden passenger trains and overloaded freights bearing military supplies passed through night and day. The social costs of the war were sometimes high. "In ninth grade came Pearl Harbor," Joy Louise Barrick recalled years later, adding, "It changed all of our lives."[23] A honey-blonde teenager with lively green eyes, Joy lived with her parents in Tucumcari where her father, Dr. C. R. Barrick, was pastor of the First Baptist Church. Soon after Pearl Harbor, Dr. Barrick volunteered to enter the army as a chaplain, causing the family to face the painful prospect of separation. After her father left for his army assignment, Joy expressed the distressing situation experienced by many Tucumcari families and millions of other Americans: "I would dream about him every night and he'd be around the house doing what he was always doing. Then I'd wake up and realize he wouldn't be there and my heart just sank."[24] As it turned out, Joy and her mother moved to southwestern towns near the army bases where her father was stationed until he was ordered to Europe in the last year of the war.

Joy Louise Barrick Batson, who, as a teenager, experienced the stresses and apprehension of the World II War home front and recorded them in her correspondence. Author's personal photo collection.

Countless other Americans also had the normal pattern of their lives disrupted as fathers, sons, brothers, or relatives entered the armed services or the family moved away for one or both parents to find work in the wartime industries of California or elsewhere. Joy Barrick's high school graduating class of 1945 at Tucumcari numbered fewer than forty, whereas classes in previous years and after the war were usually much larger. Wartime conditions, especially the shortage of gasoline and restrictions on travel, disrupted many high school activities such as senior class trips and particularly team sports. Several New Mexico high schools abandoned interscholastic sports "for the duration," with football, which involved large travel squads, as the main victim. Tucumcari High School continued both football and basketball but found it impossible to fill full schedules. Even the Clovis Wildcats, traditional rivals of Tucumcari's Rattlers, only managed to muster a basketball squad. As a result of such wartime conditions, the local football Rattlers played some existing teams twice in seasons shortened by a lack of opponents. In fact, football games during the 1943 and 1944 seasons included the House Cowboys. Strangely enough, the small plains community of House only fielded an eleven-member high school football team during the war years. The previous season the Rattlers had defeated a Cowboy team by a score of 47–0. But in the fall of 1944, House fielded a team looking for revenge, whose players appeared to be more mature, well-muscled young men—perhaps not high school students at all but graduates in past years and now exempted from the military draft to work on farms and ranches. Tucumcari school officials had apparently arranged with their counterparts at House to stage a football game between the two communities without regard to high school enrollment of the players. Such were the difficulties of travel restrictions and sports scheduling during the Second World War, and the Tucumcari high school team was glad to eke out a 6–0 victory over its bruising, muscular opponents from House in 1944.

Uprooting and mass migration during the war often resulted in heart-wrenching emotional pain, especially for children and teenagers. "Sometimes I want to be there so much," Joy Barrick said of her hometown, "it just hurts deep down in my chest." Travel to alleviate such distress or for other personal reasons was difficult, if not impossible. Automobile tires and gasoline were rationed and a ban on pleasure driving strictly enforced. A nationwide "Victory Speed" limit of 35 miles per hour made an ordeal of travel between Tucumcari and usually distant neighboring towns. As a result, the speed limit was customarily ignored. The area's farmers, considered "Soldiers without Uniforms" for their production of crops essential to the war effort, received special allowances of relatively cheap gasoline, colored purple to indicate that the cost did not include a state highway-use tax. The purple gas, authorized only for nonhighway farm machinery, operated just as well in cars as in tractors, and created many lawbreakers among rural citizens usually loyal to the war effort. In fact, one Tucumcari High School teenager burned purple gas regularly in his 1931 Model A Ford when driving back and forth on weekends to plow his father's wheat field near Forrest as well as around town. On one such trip to plow, in a hurry to return to town for a Saturday night date, he found when repeatedly hand-cranking the old Model A—whose foot pedal starters notoriously failed after the first couple of years—that the motor would not catch. In desperation, the young man knelt on his knees in the wheat field beside the car and prayed to God that if it would start, he would never misuse purple gas again. Model As had their moods, but they did obey heavenly commands. On the next turn of the crank, the motor kicked off immediately. The teenager made his date in town on time—and kept his promise about forsaking purple gas. Otherwise, ration books were issued for gasoline, with the average driver receiving an A card, good for only three to four gallons per week.[25] Much concerned about these restrictions on travel, Joy Barrick hoped her family could save up their A-card rations for several months and take a trip back to Tucumcari but discovered that this practice was not allowed.

Other previously plentiful goods were also rationed, such as sugar, butter, meat, coffee, cigarettes, and canned goods. Like girls and women everywhere, Joy and her mother learned to improvise with innovative new recipes.

Unrationed chicken was often substituted for beef or pork. At a school banquet, Joy reported, the "meat dish" was a combination of chicken, spaghetti, cheese, and onions. The rest of the menu consisted of a fresh vegetable salad, hot rolls (with butter, otherwise rationed, brought by a farmer's daughter), and fruit in Jell-O. By the end of the war, despite rationing, Americans were eating better and spending more money on food than ever before. Civilians on the home front were encouraged to forget scarcities and travel restrictions by giving blood at the Red Cross. Joy remarked after she and several high school girl friends had wrapped Red Cross bandages that it gave her "a good feeling deep down inside" to know that she was "helping a little bit in the war."

It would be difficult to exaggerate the importance of the radio in bringing war news and entertainment into virtually every American home during World War II. Newspapers, the mail, and movie newsreels conveyed wartime images and news, but none had the immediacy of the radio. The same was true for entertainment, such as music or dramatic and comedy shows. As one keen observer puts it, "Radio was World War II America's connection to the nation and the world." In short, before the pleasures of television images, the powers of imagination were equally effective as families huddled around a radio most nights to hear the most popular dramatic series of the time, the *Lux Radio Theatre*, hosted by Hollywood film producer Cecil B. DeMille, or the top comedy shows, such as the Bob Hope, Red Skelton, and Fred Allen Shows. Then, for amusement as well as news, the stentorian voice of Walter Winchell would fill the room with his opening lines: "Hello, Mr. and Mrs. America and all the ships at sea." Or, the trusted war news commentator Edward R. Murrow would report direct from Europe with precise intonations on every syllable. The first announcements of the Pearl Harbor attack and dropping the A-bombs came by radio as well as the addresses and "Fireside Chats" of President Franklin D. Roosevelt.[26]

At Tucumcari the Princess and Odeon Theaters provided nightly movies and Saturday and Sunday afternoon matinees, as well as regular battleground newsreels, to distract audiences from wartime deprivations. Hollywood produced 1,500 films during the war, about 375 of which depicted combat. By the middle of the war, Hollywood moguls understood that the public wanted more escapist musicals and comedies and fewer war films.[27] Joy Barrick and her high school friends reflected this national mood by preferring *George Washington*

Slept Here with Jack Benny; *My Friend, Flicka*, a coming-of-age drama about a boy's experiences raising a colt; and similar lighthearted fare. She also enjoyed more serious and subtle films such as *Random Harvest* and Charlie Chaplin's classic, *The Great Dictator*.[28] Saturday night in Tucumcari, as well as in other towns large and small during the Second World War, found capacity crowds attending, in the local vernacular, "the picture show."

Otherwise, during the war, a work order, issued in February 1940, authorized construction to begin on the first twenty-five miles of the canal system that supposedly would surround Tucumcari with more than forty thousand acres of irrigated fields. Harold W. Mutch, US Bureau of Reclamation project engineer, also announced that the federal agency and some WPA laborers would build twelve additional miles of the main canal and a distribution facility, where subsidiary canals would spread out into the Arch Hurley Conservancy District.[29] After Pearl Harbor, construction on the canals and tunnels proceeded spasmodically, depending on the exigencies of the war effort and the effectiveness of lobbying in Washington by Arch Hurley and other town civic and business leaders. Elsewhere in New Mexico, it was a different story. During World War II, New Mexico attracted a multitude of military installations, most notably air bases. Except for Tucumcari, it seemed that every town or village of any size had been given a US Army Air Corps airfield with all the accompanying economic and business advantages. In fact, New Mexico contained a "strategic web" of eight such aerial training bases, most located at existing municipal airports. Beginning at Albuquerque, this web spread out across the state to Alamogordo, Clovis, Roswell, Carlsbad, Fort Sumner, Deming, and Hobbs.[30]

That Tucumcari had been left out of this federal allocation was not overlooked. The *Daily News*, bemoaning the oversight, commented:

Seven months after Pearl Harbor—and Tucumcari still remains the stepchild of New Mexico—the town the Powers That Be forgot. In cities and towns all around us—both small and large—are humming war plants and projects, which are bringing new life and prosperity, insuring survival through these critical times of all small and large business institutions alike. But Tucumcari has been overlooked—completely neglected. While many much smaller towns in this immediate area are booming and enjoying the lush fruits of life-saving projects of one type or another, Tucumcari is sitting dejectedly on the outer fringe of this "select circle," helpless to do anything about the situation except to indulge in spasms of wishful thinking.[31]

There seemed to be no explanation for this obvious, painful oversight.

Yet the Tucumcari Airport east of town seemed like the ideal location for a military installation. It had received the second-largest federal prewar grant among six New Mexico cities to extend its runways and make other improvements. This grant, which reportedly made it "one of the most modern airports in the Southwest," would result in the construction of two "mammoth runways," nearly a mile long, two hundred feet wide, and paved with asphalt. The project also included adjacent taxiways about a mile and a half long and a beacon light. With announcement of the grant, a *Daily News* editorial declared, "At last Tucumcari has taken its rightful place along with several other state cities in aviation progress." In fact, the local grant was more than the awards received by either Clovis or Hobbs, both recipients of prized army airfields. Two months later, the same editor wrote that the "most important civic problem" facing Tucumcari at the time was the future of the landing field, especially as part of the war effort.[32]

The city council begged the state's congressional delegation for some kind of military installation, with the mayor adding, "We have been left without any consideration at all for too long." A *Daily News* editorial, while pointing out the virtues of the local airport, declared that Tucumcari "would not want any project for purely selfish reasons unless it would contribute something worthwhile toward winning the war." But Fort Sumner, which had no permanent airport, the editor complained, had acquired one of the prized Army Air Corps training bases. For a while, town boosters considered making a bid for a Relocation Center to house some of the 120,000 people of Japanese descent, most of them born in this country, and therefore American citizens, who were removed from the West Coast to compounds in the interior. In an open meeting, those in attendance continually used the term *aliens*, seeming to misunderstand that most of the relocated people were American citizens, not captured prisoners of war. As a result, even though a center would undoubtedly stimulate the local economy and provide jobs, the boosters decided to abandon plans for making a bid. Opinions expressed in the open meeting, replete with sentiments of nativism common at the time, made it clear that the proposal lacked any substantial support. In fact, the common belief was voiced that the "aliens" might want to stay in the community after their confinement, and although they could never assimilate with the local population, "we never would get rid of them."[33]

The best Tucumcari could obtain was a relatively small army pre-glider pilot training unit, which had been stationed at Clovis but was moved out as the airfield there became a full-fledged wartime Army Air Corps base. About 200 would-be glider pilots and their officers as well as 50 civilian instructors and accompanying maintenance crews, a total of about 350 personnel, started arriving in town in early September 1942.[34] The Vorenberg Hotel served as their barracks, a downtown restaurant as a mess hall, and the city airport as the training base. Since this was a pre-glider pilot program, the men's training consisted primarily of learning to fly light planes. The Glider School at Tucumcari Municipal Airport was operated under a special contract with a private company, the Cutter Carr Flying Service of Albuquerque. The makeshift arrangement at Tucumcari lasted only briefly, until March 1943, shortly before integration of the glider flying program into another part of the Army Air Corps later in the year.[35] The explanation of this federal neglect, especially after the phenomenal local lobbying success in obtaining Conchas Dam and the irrigation project, was apparently a simple matter of the political spoils system. The unrecorded final response to Tucumcari's pleas, according to the local rumor mill and widely believed, came straight from Washington. In effect, the state's congressional delegation supposedly communicated these facts of political life to the town's boosters, as follows: Tucumcari had received more than its share of the federal largesse in Conchas Dam and the irrigation project and, therefore, should stop complaining and shut up about an air base or any other big federal military bequest. And so, Tucumcari had to be satisfied during the Second World War with its small-fry, short-lived glider detachment and spasmodic construction of its emerging irrigation project—but without a major military installation. At the same time, it was surrounded by nearby wartime bases and facilities all over New Mexico as well as army airfields in adjacent West Texas at Amarillo, Lubbock, Pampa, and Dalhart.

The people of Tucumcari did get a close look at an aircraft larger than a glider in October 1944. Lieutenant Daylon Chafin, known locally as "Dayly Bread" for his unfailing hook shots while starring on the high school basketball team, piloted his four-engine B-17 Flying Fortress bomber with a full crew aboard on several tree-top passes over his hometown. In the plane above, crew members prostrated themselves with hands over their eyes, too apprehensive to look outside. Below on the ground, during the protracted flight pattern, housewives stood in the streets waving bed sheets, and men and boys, jumping up and down and shouting excitedly, waved both arms overhead—all thoroughly enjoying the spectacle. A dutiful state policeman, however, took a different view of Lieutenant Chafin's flight and reported it to military authorities. Chafin was court-martialed and dismissed from flying service.[36]

During World War II, which emphasized unanimity and concentration on the war effort, local politics, nevertheless, hit a fever pitch, caused heated divisions, and drew an unusual amount of public attention. Before Paul Dodge dominated the local press, a previous editor commented that the railroad corporations took little notice of local politics and devoted their energy to higher levels of governmental affairs that had importance.[37] Actually this assertion was hardly true for railroad corporations, particularly in matters of taxation and special levies. And besides the railroads themselves, the interests of the railroad labor unions always figured in local affairs. For instance, a union officer pointed out shortly before Pearl Harbor that, during the depths of the Great Depression, rail employees had willingly accepted a 10 percent wage reduction to aid the economically distressed railroads. Now that their employers were enjoying bountiful profits because of the defense buildup, however, the railroads had turned a deaf ear to union requests for wage increases to meet the rising costs of living.[38] In effect, the union leader's statement was another plea to the community for support—and, as usual, was accorded a sympathetic hearing by many residents.

The municipal election of 1944 was in many respects a power struggle— almost in the style of a Western gunfighter showdown—between the railroaders as workingmen and the local business elite. Previously the railroad presence had been obvious in the relatively large number of railroaders who took prominent roles in political affairs. Two Southern Pacific locomotive engineers, Thomas W. Hampton and W. D. "Spike" Ellison, regularly joined in the thick of local partisan battles. In the period following World War I when the status of ex-serviceman carried extraordinary weight, Ellison was elected secretary-treasurer of the Quay County Democratic Committee and headed the powerful county Democratic Veterans organization as well. In both positions, but particularly in the latter post, he had decisive influence on who got jobs on New Deal projects and in other matters concerning war veterans.[39] Also an ex-serviceman, the cigar-chomping Hampton, a self-proclaimed independent in politics, and something of a firebrand, operated on a broader scale. He ran unsuccessfully for county clerk and, with the same results, campaigned for appointment as postmaster, but gained election for successive terms on the city council. On the side, in addition to his railroad job, he owned and operated Hampton's Camp, or motel, on Route 66 in town and ran an attached gas station and small convenience store. The *Daily News* commented on his city council victory in 1936, "That the voters appreciate the services of Councilman Hampton—up for re-election for the third time—was shown by the vote he received, 689, leading the ticket." He was sometimes described as "fiery" as well as "popular with railroaders." As a matter of fact, five other railroaders were in the running for council seats, with two besides Hampton being elected.[40] By the time of Pearl Harbor, with more than ten years of partisan experience under his belt, Tom Hampton was ready to take on bigger challenges.

As a council member, Hampton had stirred up some excitement in that body by initiating cancellation of the local WPA-built hospital's lease to a private individual. His efforts led to the new hospital becoming "a city owned and city operated" medical facility.[41] Two years later, he made a bid for mayor, heading a Democratic Ticket of council candidates. In a field of three different tickets, packed with railroaders, Hampton handily defeated his main opponent, incumbent mayor Henry R. Priddy, and swept his slate of candidates into office with him.[42] This campaign had seen some mudslinging, but it could hardly match the "bare-knuckles" barrage of charges and accusations when Priddy, seeking revenge for his defeat in 1942, took on Hampton again two years later.

Back in 1942, the *Daily News* asked for a public airing of the city's financial affairs, charging that the "Priddy clique" had violated state law that prohibited municipal officials from selling goods to the city.[43] In all likelihood, in 1944, Tom Hampton took his cue from the newspaper's earlier entreaties. Now, in the current election, the Hampton Ticket Campaign Committee, in a series of lengthy newspaper ads, raised penetrating questions and made charges about previous misdeeds in city government operations. It was readily apparent that these potentially damaging assertions were based on extensive research in official records. Or, as the *Daily News*, which endorsed the Hampton ticket, put it bluntly: "This campaign more than any other in recent years saw the issues of the election placed squarely before the people," adding accusingly that these issues "had heretofore remained hidden in the background."[44]

Water and a reliable source of it also became an issue in the campaign. One ad reminded readers that in the summer of 1941 some sections of town had experienced a noticeable shortage of water for domestic use. As part of the supply problem, the city made a contract to deliver water to "the big railroad tank" at ten cents per thousand gallons, which was allegedly below cost. The Hampton administration had initiated negotiations, now in progress, with the railroads for an adjustment of the rate that would cover the expense of production. An investigation had also been conducted to see if the city could obtain water from Conchas Dam, but, according to the newspaper ads, an agency headed by Henry Priddy interfered with and sabotaged those efforts. Moreover, the ads claimed, the Priddy administration had floated bond issues at excessive interest rates to drill wells at Metropolitan Park—without expert geological consultation—and the water level had dropped, causing the pumps to deliver less volume than expected. In contrast, under Mayor Hampton, a new well had been drilled in a more favorable location, without another bond issue but with savings out of city revenues. However, an adequate water supply that would satisfy the needs of both the railroads and the city continued to be a problem.[45]

When Priddy was mayor, the city had bought the local electric light and power plant from a private utility company for $397,260. Of that amount, $349,175 represented the book value of the assets purchased, leaving the sum of $48,085, identified in available records as a "Utility Plant Acquisition adjustment." To the Hampton committee, this mysterious entry smelled like graft, even after an auditor, who readily understood the description, explained that the city had paid the private company for its "Goodwill." Almost hooting in disbelief, the Hampton group commented in one of its ads: "In other words, the City paid $48,084.83 for which they received absolutely nothing. Goodwill might be an asset in an old established mercantile firm, but whoever heard of goodwill being an asset to a public utility operating in a community without competition." The publicity committee, concluding that "it looks like Mr. Priddy was a mighty poor trader," demanded an explanation of what the city had received for almost $50,000. But that hardly ended the controversy over the utility purchase. A state auditor decided that a total of $21,828 paid to a Denver bond-buying concern as a part of this transaction was illegal under state law and should be recovered by the city. The firm had been dissolved, however, and its successor was not responsible for any previous liabilities.[46]

The publicity committee ads pointed out the Hampton administration's accomplishments and made additional charges concerning city affairs, but probably its most telling criticism involved the adversarial approach the Tucumcari business community had taken in negotiations with the Bell Ranch regarding Conchas Dam. In a novel interpretation, one ad asked: "Do you remember how the little group trespassed upon the Bell property, laid out rights of way, fixed the value of the land and at the same time proceeded to take over the land that would be covered by its [the lake's] waters? . . . Had we worked with the Bell's [*sic*] instead of antagonizing them, don't you believe we would now be fishing on the Canadian [anywhere we pleased]?" In this view of building the dam, it was a simple matter of dealing diplomatically, and therefore successfully, with a powerful neighbor. The Red River Valley Company, as owner of the Bell Ranch, was much more powerful "than all of us put together, [and] that being true, as has been amply demonstrated, why not try and work with them for our own good?"[47] This last question not only scolded the local business community for its tactics in acquiring Conchas Dam, but it also clearly bore implied advice on how to realize the much-discussed direct highway between Tucumcari and Conchas Lake.

For its part, the Greater Tucumcari Ticket of Henry R. Priddy usually took a kinder, gentler approach, running shorter newspaper ads with less wordy messages, publishing its own newsletter, and, at the end of the campaign, going on the air at the local radio station, KTNM. Tom Hampton had also reserved five minutes of airtime on KTNM but cancelled it after he heard the opposition broadcast. He told the station manager, Hampton said, to play some music instead because two political harangues in the same week were more than the listeners could tolerate. Reflecting what Tom Hampton derisively called the "Live and Love Priddy Platform," the Priddy ticket clothed its newspaper ads with an idealistic, and sometimes a moralistic, appeal to voters. For example, one ad with sparse wording otherwise, targeted the Hampton no-holds-barred strategy, saying: "The way an election campaign is conducted is often an indication of the kind of administration to follow. The Greater Tucumcari Ticket is conducting its campaign, not on the demerits of the opposition, but on its own merits." Another ad in the same vein declared, "If the operations and finances of the City of Tucumcari had been one-tenth as bad under the Priddy administration as the opposition claims, then Priddy and his entire Council would be behind bars."[48]

As a finale for the campaign, Tom Hampton published a long, chatty open letter in the *Daily News* addressed to the Priddy camp, in which he critiqued the opposition's radio broadcast, saying that he hoped there would be no hard feelings after the election.[49] The dramatic results of the vote count on April 4, 1944, dashed any hope that this wish would, in fact, be fulfilled. In the closest municipal election in Tucumcari's history, Henry R. Priddy defeated Thomas W. Hampton by only three votes (724 to 721 ballots), while three Priddy candidates and two from the Hampton ticket won city council seats. An official recanvas involving an examination of the poll books in comparison with the figures turned in by the election judges held three days later showed the same results. Both a district judge and the New Mexico Supreme Court ordered an actual recount of the ballots, but the outcome did not change.[50]

Otherwise, this hotly contested municipal election of 1944 had exposed a significant societal crack in the local community structure. The Hampton publicity committee contended that a societal and political division between railroaders and the local business community did not exist but, to the contrary, continually implied that such a split was a reality. In fact, one ad accused the opposition of mistakenly portraying the election as a power struggle between the railroaders as workingmen and the local business elite but afterward continued to imply that such a division did indeed exist. A "little group of so-called 'Businessmen,'" threatened with losing their grip on city affairs, had spread the rumor that "the Railroad Men were trying to run the town." Moreover, this "Termite Gang of Six" had proclaimed that the railroaders were "against the businessmen and that they must be eliminated from the picture if we are going to have a 'GREATER TUCUMCARI.'" As a result of such malicious rumor mongering, the ad stated, businessmen were told that they "must band together against the Workingmen and defeat them at the coming City election." Although shying away from publicly endorsing a railroader-business division, the Hampton group clearly believed it existed. This conviction lacked sociological or scientific support, but the intensity of the personal accusations during the campaign undoubtedly did reveal distinctive group differences.[51]

The election was over, but one issue aired during the campaign—the water supply the city shared with the railroad—continued to cause problems for several years. Steam locomotives had a huge appetite for both water and coal. The Dawson mines could furnish plenty of coal for the big machines, but quenching their thirst was not as easily done. Some of the largest locomotives, while burning 500 pounds of coal per mile, could evaporate between 100 and 250 gallons of water in the same distance. This rate of water consumption meant that sizable and reliable supplies had to be available at relatively short intervals to keep the trains moving. Division operations had been shifted to Tucumcari, in part, because of popular belief that Santa Rosa's water had corrosive effects on locomotive boilers. Both the city and the SP drilled wells at Tucumcari or nearby, and the municipal government contracted to share its supply with the railroad. The agreement involved millions of gallons of the precious liquid. In midsummer 1947, for example, the SP advised the Tucumcari city manager that, because of the current drought, the railroad's surface water supply from Bonito Lake and reservoir, near Ruidoso, which connected with a pipeline running along the rail line from Carrizozo to Pastura, was falling short of its expected production. The railroad company was pumping all of its wells at Tucumcari at full volume in order to reduce its contracted consumption of city water from 13 million to 7.5 million gallons per month. The SP, anticipating that the total supply would soon fall short of its needs, requested an additional 250,000 gallons a day from the city. This water would have to be treated before its use in locomotive boilers, and the railroad company would do so, after moving the necessary equipment to Tucumcari. Following the Second World War, the SP changed over to diesel locomotives, which used comparatively little water, and this nagging concern faded away.[52]

The nation's railroads experienced what has been called their "finest hour" in World War II. In 1942, the first year of the war, they handled the greatest volume of freight and the most passenger traffic ever, and "with fewer locomotives, fewer cars, and fewer men than they had on their lines in 1929." A new federal agency, the Office of Defense Transportation—and indirectly the War Production Board—maintained strict supervision of all forms of transportation. By pledging to dedicate their resources to the war effort, however, the Southern Pacific and other railroads avoided a federal takeover, as had happened in the First World War. A. T. Mercier, the SP president, stated the case plainly in a widely published newspaper ad: "With America at war, the armed forces and war industries must have first call on transportation. This means not only that troop trains must be given right of way but also that the freight trains carrying [war] materials and supplies must be handled with the same dispatch." Although civilian passenger traffic to find jobs in West Coast war industries increased tenfold, train seating space became reserved for "Uncle Sam's boys first," and others were simply advised to stay at home unless travel was absolutely necessary. In fact, the SP implemented a reservation system that issued boarding passes, with military personnel under orders given the highest priority and others taking what was left. As a result, by 1944 the SP was obtaining 65 percent of its passenger revenue from such sources as military trains and entire coaches reserved for service personnel, not to mention those soldiers and sailors who traveled individually under orders on trains.[53] Under these circumstances, a railroad trip during the Second World War could be an ordeal. Children had to sit on their mothers' laps for long distances.[54] One Tucumcari teenager, who could board a California-bound passenger coach only because he was accompanying a sailor brother returning from leave, found no seat available. It was standing room only in the aisles all the way to Los Angeles. Fortunately, the youth had brought his clothes in a large, old-fashioned metal suitcase, which he and the brother took turns sitting on. Long lines formed outside the restrooms, so it was necessary to time visits there well ahead. Getting a meal in a dining car was out of the question because SP trains, because of wartime restrictions, usually had only one diner, if any, no matter the number of passengers on board. Buying food at a scheduled stop or catching an infrequent food vendor who shoved his way through the human mass were about the only ways to get a sandwich or box lunch.

Railroad employees, particularly train operating crews, could be given draft deferments as workers essential to the war effort. Both occasional conscriptions and enlistments, however, claimed many SP employees, causing a persistent labor shortage for the railroads at a time when their services were in more demand than ever. "Of all the problems faced by the Southern Pacific during World War II," a noted historian declares, "none was greater than meeting its employment needs." Various remedies were tried to meet this challenge. Shops went on ten-hour shifts, office forces worked two shifts a day, and more women were hired, even for track repair gangs previously the exclusive domain of men.

After some difficulty dealing with immigration restrictions, the SP also imported about 5,000 Mexican nationals as contract laborers.[55]

As a railroad division point, Tucumcari operated on a bustling wartime basis during World War II. Train operating crews of engineers, firemen, brakemen, and conductors made extra runs; those responsible for maintaining the water supply available to steam locomotives worked overtime; clerical staffs, as mentioned, put in double shifts; and shopmen worked longer days and nights. The SP's problem of keeping a workforce became an advantage for several individuals in Tucumcari, who found employment or better jobs with the railroad. James Harland "Jim" Stiles usually designed commercial signage, including the famous swooping Blue Swallow, and would later light up Route 66 across New Mexico with his many neon creations. He was hired by the SP as a security agent on passenger trains.[56]

In a different vein, some SP employees volunteered for active duty in the Army Military Railway Service's specialized railway operating and shop battalions, some of which had received training on the Santa Fe line out of Clovis. These specialized units matched the organization of a typical army battalion but with a civilian railroad division's various functions, such as dispatching, track repair, signal equipment, train operating crews, and so on, superimposed on the military structure of platoons and companies. At the top a Grand Division—in fact, seven of them by the war's end—represented something like a commercial rail corporation. Below, a total of twenty-four operating battalions, seven shop battalions, and support units made up the subsidiary parts of the organizational chart. Different railroads sponsored units of the Military Railway Service. The 705th Railway Grand Division, adopted by the Southern Pacific Company, ran military railroads in India and Burma. Battalion commanders, equivalent to division superintendents in the civilian world, held the rank of lieutenant colonel.[57]

William B. Sharp Jr., trainmaster for the SP's Rio Grande Division from Tucumcari to Carrizozo and Dawson, answered the call for experienced railroaders and was assigned to the Military Railway Service in Europe. He obtained the rank of colonel before returning to his prewar position at Tucumcari in July 1947. Dealing with antiquated French railroad rolling stock, he managed to move a steady stream of troop replacements as well as thousands of tons of supplies and equipment, including shipments to General George S. Patton's rapidly advancing

Third Army during the Battle of the Bulge. At the historic Compiegne armistice site of the First World War, Sharp commanded an MRS unit that operated the upscale, fresco-walled army canteen at the railroad station, often visited by General Dwight D. Eisenhower and other distinguished guests. Stationed for more than two years at Rheims and LeHavre, he had charge of some forty thousand German prisoners of war, whom he had to feed and clothe as well as manage their repatriation. After returning to the United States in early 1947, he briefly commanded the 765th Railroad Shop Battalion at Fort Eustis, Virginia, before leaving active duty. Colonel Sharp died in 1954 after his retirement as an SP trainmaster at Tucumcari.[58] Harold H. Sharpe, another Tucumcari railroader who left an SP management position for duty in the Military Railway Service, returned to his job briefly after the war, but then left again during the Korean conflict for a career in the army. Sharpe's military-style tombstone in the Tucumcari cemetery bears little evidence of his distinguished railroading for Uncle Sam, reading simply: "Lt Col—US Army—World War II—Korea."[59]

At the end of the Second World War, Tucumcari seemed to be on the brink of unprecedented progress and economic growth. A *Daily News* editor pointed out the prospects offered by the railroads. Many had considered railroads as "an obsolete form of transportation," and predicted that "ships, trucks, buses, and planes would supersede them." The role of the railroads in hauling "the crushing loads" of wartime military equipment and personnel had disposed of that idea and assured their importance for Tucumcari and the postwar world generally. More than 500 wartime workers had been employed at Tucumcari by the Southern Pacific, with a payroll of $120,000 a month (double the prewar amount). The continued postwar railroad presence would undoubtedly bring increased dividends. The irrigation project furnished another promising indication of future prosperity. Work was proceeding on the canal system, and the Bureau of Reclamation jobs had increased the town's population by some 475 persons, including contractors, laborers, and skilled workers, not to mention the federal agency's employees already in residence. Then there was the certainty of a renewed tourist trade, which had remained practically dormant during the war.[60]

But Tucumcari could not relax and rely on these prospects alone; action was required. The year 1940 had been the most prosperous time in Tucumcari history, and "from a prophetic viewpoint," according to a *Daily News* editorial, "even greater gains on the profit side of the ledger," could be expected in the future. That rosy prophesy of continual progress had been interrupted by the war. Now that the war was over, one local businessman declared, Tucumcari needed to restore its prewar momentum, "outgrow the cowtown stage," and improve its image. In fact, the Chamber of Commerce already had an open-ended wish list of close to twenty possible objectives. The top-targeted items under consideration included an adequate city water supply, a veterans hospital, a road to Conchas Dam, improvement of the local airport, construction of the proposed Ute Creek dam, and paving of US Highway 54. One objective also on the list, the improvement of rural roads in the county, brought up a sore point. Meager rainfall in 1945 had created the worst drought conditions since the Dust Bowl year of 1934—and that was the worst year on record. This meant that the erosion of rural population, already pronounced during the war, would probably continue. Such worries were cast aside, however, in the celebration following the dropping of two A-bombs that ended the war. County road crews would soon replace the wartime speed limit signs of 35 miles per hour and a local dealer would advertise "Ration Free" tires.[61]

Chapter 6

THE TOWNLESS HIGHWAY

T he postwar world hardly turned out as Tucumcari boosters had expected. On the international scene America had won a smashing victory in World War II, but tensions of the Cold War, which began in Europe before the fighting ended in the Pacific, made everyone nervous. Local economic conditions were also disturbing. The prospects of profitable mining for uranium ore nearby fizzled, and the campaign to obtain a state reformatory in town failed. An air force survey to locate the site of a new base likewise had no favorable result for Tucumcari.[1]

Moreover, in the two decades ahead, the country's railroads would face unprecedented challenges and make drastic adjustments that shook Tucumcari to its foundations. One vision that did materialize and thrive—for a time at least—was the booming tourist trade. The elimination of passenger trains by railroad companies and the expense of air travel caused the tourist industry to focus attention on the family automobile. According to a recent assessment of this momentous change:

> Few technological breakthroughs have had the social and economic impact
> of the automobile. It changed America's geography, spawning suburbs,
> shopping malls and [urban] sprawl as far as the eye could see. It redefined
> how we work and play, from the daily commute to the weekend trek to the
> beach. It expanded the heavy industry—steel-making, car production—that
> made the Midwest the economy's epicenter for decades. And, finally, but
> not least, the car became the quintessential symbol of American mobility,
> status, and independence.[2]

In fact, the automobile industry had become the biggest component of the

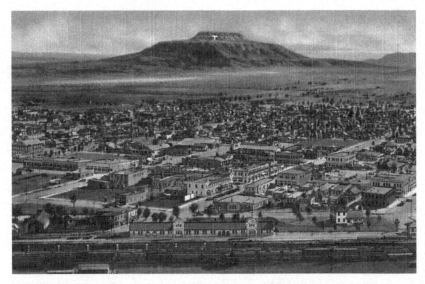

Tucumcari and the dominating presence three miles to the south—Tucumcari Mountain. Chronicle / Alamy Stock Photo (Image ID: G3CN2Y).

American industrial system, the biggest concentration of manufacturing might ever created and bigger than all other similar manufacturing on the rest of the globe combined. One of every six American workers was employed in some way in making cars. During the 1950s, American factories produced and marketed 58 million cars, enough that, statistically, about one of every three persons in a US population of more than 179 million might have bought a new vehicle in that decade.[3]

For the typical American owner, possession of the right car—not just any car—had become the premier badge of success and an indication of a certain degree of affluence, with a higher priority than a pricey home or a fashionable wardrobe. In fact, speculation about the influence of the automobile in the social realm knows no bounds. One wag even suggested that the make and model of car people drove became more important than the political party they belonged to. Or the father of a prospective bride might ask her suitor if he was a "Chevy man" or a "Ford man" before giving approval of the marriage. And a scholar who studied birth control proclaimed that, in most cases, when people had to make a choice between either a car or children, they took the automobile.[4] It is virtually impossible today to realize that in a small town like Tucumcari many people had no car until after the Second World War and the late 1940s. They could walk anywhere in town and take a train or bus for trips. A similar situation existed in large cities where street cars and buses were readily available.

By the 1950s it was a fact of life that cars had taken the place of trains as the most popular way to travel on trips, simply because an automobile and the open road were a more flexible means of covering long distances. Tourists were not limited to a set of fixed railroad tracks.[5] For young American families along Route 66, owning a late model car and the luxury of taking a vacation road trip to see Disneyland and other Southern California wonders became a routine part of life. Travel by car also got a boost by the concerted improvement of Route 66 and other existing highways and even more so in the new federal interstate highway system. A focal point of the rising tide of highway traffic, regardless of the destination involved, was overnight lodging conveniently located and reasonably priced.

The distinction of coining and using the combination of "mo" for motor and "tel" from hotel apparently belonged to one Arthur Heineman, who established Heineman's Milestone Motel on US Highway 101 at San Obispo, California, in 1926. But the entrepreneur who made the concept a reality for tourists, as "a home away from home," was undoubtedly Kemmons Wilson, who became "The Nation's Innkeeper" with his Holiday Inn chain of motels. Quite simply, Holiday Inn led the way for the motel industry's change from independent local businesses, perhaps loosely affiliated with similar enterprises, to a series of tightly organized lodgings owned by international corporations. In accomplishing a real consolidation, Wilson formed "what became the single largest lodging chain in the United States within only a matter of years." In fact, scholarly specialists say, "Holiday Inn became the motel of America."[6] And it all began when Wilson took his wife and five children on a vacation trip by car from Memphis to Washington, DC, in the summer of 1951. This family outing changed the face of the American tourist industry.

On the trip, Wilson found that staying in motels was expensive, especially since there was usually an extra charge for each of the five children, even though the whole family slept in the same room. By the time the family returned home, Wilson had in mind the plan for building a chain of motels that had a special appeal to families with children by charging only by the room, no matter how many slept there. Each motel would have, as attractions for kids, a swimming pool, a restaurant, as well as other special features. A series of such motels across the country, Wilson reasoned, would encourage customer loyalty by promising that each stop on a family trip would offer the same amenities. This feature also led Wilson to establish a unique computer network for advanced reservations called the "Holidex," at the time "the world's largest commercial computerized communication system." Other lodging chains soon followed this example for reservations, as they also did with his innovative arrangement of franchising new sites.[7]

When Wilson's skeptical wife asked how many motels he planned to build, he quickly calculated the dimensions of the United States and answered, "Oh, about 400 ought to do it." At that time no lodging chain or similar association could claim four hundred facilities, but thirty years later nearly two thousand of Wilson's motels had been opened in fifty different countries. In 1952, when Wilson built the first unit in Memphis, the draftsman for the project, who had just seen the Hollywood film musical *Holiday Inn*, nonchalantly scribbled "Holiday Inn" across his drawings, and the name stuck.[8] Wilson's timing for such an ambitious undertaking was just right, considering the lure of the nationwide automobile culture and the forthcoming interstate highway system.

At Tucumcari the one hundred-room Holiday Inn, franchised by the development firm of Allen Green and Associates of Memphis, opened in 1964. Located on Route 66 at the eastern city limits, it offered all the amenities Kemmons Wilson had envisioned—and more. The management surprised different guests every morning with their name on a Guest of the Day plaque and a bag of goodies. Inviting baskets of fresh apples were available in the lobby. Throughout the lobby and the Branding Iron Restaurant the décor featured the "Southwest/Western spirit of New Mexico" with rawhide upholstered furniture and photographs of nearby ranches. For kids, the motel had a large outdoor swimming pool and a policy of allowing pets. The Holiday Express chain was introduced later by the British brewing firm Bass PLC, which bought out the Holiday Inn chain and some of its subsidiaries in two purchases, one in 1988 for $475 million and another in 1990 for $2.23 billion. In 2007 a Holiday Inn Express opened in Tucumcari on the I-40 Bypass, and the original Holiday Inn on east Route 66 became a Quality Inn.[9]

In Tucumcari, modern motels like the Holiday Inn had evolved from the

Murray Wagon Yard where weary homesteaders, arriving in a "Zulu" railroad freight car with all their belongings, could unload and bed down on a pallet. Or they might take lodging at the adjacent Glenrock Hotel or other nearby hostelries. Later, besides the downtown Vorenberg and Randle Hotels, an open-air tourist camp had existed for a while on First Street, a few blocks south of the business district. Complexes of plain multiple structures called "cabin camps," like "Hampton's Camp" owned by future mayor Tom Hampton at the intersection of Third Street and Route 66, appeared when the highway became a thoroughfare. The heyday of the Route 66 tourist trade ushered in the more luxurious tourist court or inn and motel.[10]

Referring to this evolution of lodgings, local historian Gil Hinshaw sums up the importance of George J. Lins and his family by saying, "I rather think they made the tourism industry what it was in Tucumcari."[11] Lins was undoubtedly the only Tucumcari resident who played football for Notre Dame and graduated from that university—class of 1902, in his case. A big man with a hearty manner who sported a Van Dyke beard, Lins started making trips to town from the Midwest as a broomcorn buyer in the late 1920s. Still engaging in that trade, he moved to Tucumcari in 1928, where he established the Lins Broom Corn Company, sold the seed, and manufactured brooms. He then bought some tourist cabins, a restaurant, and a service station with a convenience store. The nine-unit motel became known as the Lins Motor Lodge. At the Lins Café he hauled in some large, petrified columns of rock and assembled a petrified garden. He designated one of the petrified rocks as the "New Mexico Blarney Stone" and charged tourists twenty-five cents to kiss it. By the time of Lins's death in 1952, his son, Thomas J. Lins, had joined his father in the family businesses, and later a daughter, Mary Elizabeth "Bettie" Ditto, enlarged the Lins complex until it became a major tourist facility.[12]

In this process of expansion, Bettie Ditto showed a keen business sense and unusual promotional ability at a time when national motel chains with virtually unlimited financial resources were moving into Tucumcari and locally owned lodgings of any size were an oddity. A single mother with two children, Ditto arrived in Tucumcari from Chicago in the middle of a blinding sandstorm in 1955 and fully intended to return home as soon as possible. She had inherited the nine-unit Lins Motor Court from her father's estate but could find no buyers for the property.

Bettie Ditto opened the Lazy L Motel—formerly the Lins Motor Lodge— which was later enlarged and renamed the Congress Inn. In 1959 John Farrell, an Amarillo lumber-company owner and construction financier, recognized Ditto's potential. They formed a highly successful business partnership that lasted for thirty-four years and extended to several other lodging projects else- where in New Mexico. From that point on, Bettie Ditto's ventures in the hos- pitality industry took off like a rocket to produce a conglomerate, the Pow Wow Industries, that occupied a six-acre plot and had from thirty to fifty employees. Ditto had adopted the Pow Wow trademark when she chose an affiliation with the Best Western system, which had evolved from a loose association of lodg- ings in the 1930s, called a "referral group." The name came from Ditto's habit of giving frequent parties that were dubbed "pow wows." The new trade con- nection required her to change the name of the Congress Inn because of an identity conflict with the holdings of another association member.

What became the largest lodging complex of its kind in Tucumcari grew from nine rooms to the ninety-two-unit Pow Wow Inn and three Pow Wow apartments as well as a restaurant and lounge and a gift shop. Ditto and John Farrell sold their Pow Wow interests twice but had to repossess the properties both times and rebuild the business. Farrell also backed construction of another major lodging, the Palomino Motel, as well as thirty new homes in town. A flexible leasing policy was one reason for Pow Wow's success. Before the Inter- state 40 Bypass, the Pow Wow usually had a 97 percent occupancy rate, par- tially because of contracts with Southern Pacific and Rock Island operating crews laying over in Tucumcari between runs. Even after the I-40 Bypass slowed down the tourist trade in the 1980s, the Pow Wow maintained a satisfactory capacity by making short-term rental agreements with groups of railroad employees, truckers, construction workers, and other transitory types.[13]

None of the Pow Wow developments would have been possible without the tireless work and brainy planning of Bettie Ditto. With the Pow Wow empire— motel, restaurant, lounge, gift shop, and apartments—under her direct supervi- sion, she displayed an exemplary hands-on management style. Attractive and petite, always fashionably dressed, Bettie Ditto most evenings circulated through the restaurant and lounge greeting guests as if she were the proprietor and hostess of an upscale Chicago night club. And perhaps now and then, businesslike but politely, she would encourage a patron to order another drink.[14]

Bettie Ditto got awards and honors from several outside agencies, but the local recognition she received probably indicated her importance more accurately. She became the first Chamber of Commerce woman board member, accepted the key to the city on her seventy-seventh birthday, and won election to the city commission when she was eighty-five years old. As an even greater honor, locals referred to her as "Mrs. Tucumcari" and the town's "matriarch of hospitality." Upon her death at age ninety-one in 2008, a local businessman characterized her precisely: "Bettie Ditto was the way Tucumcari should be: Upbeat, motivated, always looking at the half-full, not the half-empty [glass]. . . . We lost our ambassador for this city, and we will miss her more than we'll ever know."[15]

The most nationally famous lodging place on Route 66 in Tucumcari began about the same time as George Lins bought the tourist cabins that evolved into the Pow Wow complex. At first named the Blue Swallow Court, it later adopted the motel designation. Built by local contractor William Archie "Arch" Huggins in 1939, just before World War II, the motel was named by Huggins's wife Maud, who wanted the title and the color of the gracefully swooping blue bird

Famed Blue Swallow Motel with its renowned swooping blue swallow and 100% Refrigerated Air signage. Photo by Nancy Stratton Hall.

The Blue Swallow Motel's fan-shaped decorations of bright red, green, and yellow hues on its exterior plastered walls were an added artistic touch of master craftsman W. A. Huggins, who built the motel and whose specialty was plastering. yardbirdstock.com / Alamy Stock Photo (2AC2PME).

to suggest peaceful, soothing rest and sleep. A master craftsman with plastering and stuccoing as his specialty, Huggins laid the hollow tile walls, stuccoed them outside and plastered them inside, adding his own distinctive touch on the exterior. Using his hand trowel like an artist's brush, he fashioned in the stucco across the structure's upper facade, spreading out below a series of small multi-colored, fan-shaped ornamentations in rainbow hues of green, yellow, and brick red. In keeping with the custom for early lodging places, each of the original ten units had a smallish garage with overhead wooden doors between them. Two more units were added, in about 1948, on the northeastern end of the L-shaped structure. The Blue Swallow was listed in the National Register of Historic Places in 1993.[16]

W. A. Huggins and his energetic wife Maud operated the Blue Swallow for a few years, but with the restrictions on travel during World War II, they found that the motel business had become a losing proposition. For a short time, with the same economic disappointment, Maud Huggins and her daughter, Lela Chapman, had run a café in the back of the motel office building that boasted the distinction of serving the only foot-long hot dogs in town. In December 1943, Arch Huggins sold the Blue Swallow, at a loss on his investment, for $13,000.[17] Unwilling to give up on motels, however, he built two more after the war—and sold or traded both with more profitable results. The larger Townhouse Inn stood on Route 66 across the street just east of the Blue Swallow, and the Travelers Paradise Motor Lodge, also on Route 66 at the town's western outskirts. Arch and Maud Huggins operated the Paradise Lodge and the adjoining restaurant and service station for a few years before disposing of it in a deal that included other real estate.[18]

Huggins had sold the Blue Swallow to Wyley Stuart of Tucumcari, who sold it to Ted F. Jones, who died following a heart attack in 1954.[19] A series of individuals and real estate agencies owned the Blue Swallow, and it was closed for seven or eight months in 1960–1961. Floyd Redman, who grew up with the town, had slowly acquired and traded downtown property, including the Travelers Inn auto camp and the venerable Vorenberg Hotel. When business opportunities arose along Route 66, he bought the Bonanza Court motel, some retail venues, and the Blue Swallow Motel. In 1964 he gave the Blue Swallow to his fiancée, Lillian Leigon, as an engagement gift. They spent their wedding night there and made it their home until he died in 1973.[20] From 1964 on, for more than thirty years, the garrulous Lillian Redman held court daily, and nightly, at the Blue Swallow's front desk until advanced age forced her retirement in 1997. She and her "magical cat" Smoky moved to a little house close by the Blue Swallow so she could keep an eye on it. Even then, she returned periodically to the scene of her triumphal stand for brief visits and chats with the tourists.[21]

Lillian Leigon had come to town with her parents in 1922 when her father took a railroad job at Tucumcari. She discovered the outside world when she became a Harvey Girl, as the waitresses in Harvey House restaurants were called. These hotels and restaurants were usually allied with the Santa Fe Railroad. In that occupation she reportedly worked in El Tovar Hotel on the rim of the Grand Canyon, established as a Harvey House in conjunction with the Santa Fe. This internationally famous hostelry had quickly become a favorite vacation destination for the world's socially elite after it opened in 1905.[22]

As proprietor of the Blue Swallow, the seasoned and worldly-wise Lillian

Redman thoroughly enjoyed running her own lodging place and chatting with the tourists who stayed there. She often included a pep talk about the attractions of Tucumcari and the surrounding countryside. With her experience at Harvey House, she had no difficulty conversing with foreigners, including the many German and British visitors drawn by Route 66 lore and the motel's international reputation. She tried to help travelers who were broke but also considered the Blue Swallow rates as always reasonable. When she took over in 1964, the nightly rate was $2.50; thirty years later it was $10. At the end of her career, a local newspaper quoted her on such business practices: "We just raised the price enough to cover the cost of making a living. We weren't trying to get rich or anything. You can't put it all in your pocket. You have to help your customers. Lots of people come through Tucumcari that . . . [don't] have the price of a room, and they need a place to stay. It has to be reasonable." The Blue Swallow did not have its famous sign yet. To Lillian Redman, signage was the most obvious kind of advertising, and she quoted her husband as saying, "You're gonna have to have something with a lot of light that people can see down the road so they can find a place to stay." Neon signs were relatively expensive at the time, Lillian Redman recalled, and it was difficult to bend the glass just right for the figure of an authentic swooping blue swallow. Addition of the early boast "100% Refrigerated Air" caused no problem and has remained part of the neon signage to this day.[23]

Picnic tables and grills at the back as well as patio chairs placed on both sides of the office building added a welcoming gesture to the motel's personality. In March 1986, the *Smithsonian Magazine* declared that the Blue Swallow might be "the last, best and friendliest of the old-time motels" and the remnant of a "classic American institution," the locally owned Ma-and-Pa lodging operation. On the stormy night of the Smithsonian representative's visit, the motel was so crowded that its two suites had been divided to make a total of fourteen separate rooms. The article began by depicting a winter scene at the motel: "The snow had been falling in the West for days, choking the highways, and before long there were 14 trucks at the Blue Swallow Motel in Tucumcari, New Mexico, and 14 drivers in the motel's 14 rooms. The poker game went on around the clock. Mrs. Lillian Redman, who owns the Blue Swallow, kept the coffeepot boiling. Every now and then she got a hand in herself."[24] In short, it was Lillian Redman's long, engaging presence at the Blue Swallow's front desk that brought lodgers back again and again. Tourism was her life, and as she said, "Tourism is what's kept Tucumcari on the map." In 1998, after her retirement, she was inducted into the New Mexico Tourism Hall of Fame, although unfortunately she could not attend the ceremony because of poor health. Lillian Redman died a few months later in February 1999.[25]

With her long reign at the Blue Swallow, Redman herself as well as the motel became essential parts of the Route 66 legend. Few descriptive articles or historical accounts about the mythical highway, then or afterward, would pass muster without paying tribute to the acclaimed presiding matriarch as well as the swooping blue bird on one of Route 66's most celebrated neon signs. As for her own attachment, Lillian Redman recalled: "Route 66 had a definite feel to it. It made you feel warm all over. When it closed, I felt just like I lost an old friend."[26]

Tucumcari was renowned for its array of neon signs. In fact, as the Route 66 legend developed, nothing else in Tucumcari drew more attention from tourists than the neon Blue Swallow signage. It became "a beacon along historic Route

1953 Blue Swallow Court. This drawing shows the extent of the motel's facilities and grounds at a relatively early time. Courtesy of Le Deane Studio.

Tee Pee Curio Shop, a classic example of the many curio stores on Route 66. Located across old Route 66 from the Blue Swallow Motel, the Tee Pee has become as much of a tourist attraction as the famous motel. Lee Rentz / Alamy Stock Photo (Image ID: 2AT6JE9).

66 for more than seven decades, beckoning to road-weary travelers motoring between Chicago and Los Angeles." A contender, however, is located just across the road. The famous neon Blue Swallow is often paired in guidebooks with another aged survivor from Route 66's glory days, the teepee-shaped neon sign of the Tee Pee Curio Shop, which opened in 1944. "And as long as Americans get in their cars and motor west, they could," one well-informed journalist concludes, "count on Tucumcari's neon signs to light the way."[27]

The fighting in the Second World War had barely ended before highway fever struck Tucumcari again. Automobile tire rationing was set to end January 1, 1946, but boosters from Tucumcari and other communities along US Highway 54 decided to take immediate action. With the battle cry of "54 in 46," they met in Santa Fe with state officials and called for surfacing of the road's nineteen-mile unpaved segment in New Mexico. The state highway engineer promised that it would be done as soon as possible, as part of the state's postwar road construction program. Despite such promises, however,

Highway 54 remained for years a "stepchild" in New Mexico's highway program, and the final strip of paving near Carrizozo was not completed until 1954.[28] But the local highway fever continued, reaching its peak in the renewed demand for a road to Conchas Dam and Lake.[29]

The New England–based Red River Valley Company, owner of the Bell Ranch, had staged a series of strategic retreats against invasions of its closed-range ranch domain, which until well into the twentieth century had been protected by two ancient land grants and well-guarded barbed-wire fences. Having lost the court battle over the building of Conchas Dam and then the legal action over public access to Conchas Lake, the Bell Ranch proprietors could now be expected to resist the renewal of the public crusade for a road from Tucumcari to the dam and on to Las Vegas. This latest onslaught had been only temporarily interrupted by World War II. The New England company remained steadfast when, during the war, it had rejected Governor John J. Dempsey's request to open the Canadian River for public fishing.[30] Strangely enough, however, after the war ended the company decided to surrender and put up no further resistance to construction of the Conchas Dam Road. In short, unable and unwilling to withstand the forces of disintegration any longer, the Red River Valley Company sold its Bell Ranch holdings to manager Albert K. Mitchell and two other middlemen, who made the purchase solely for resale purposes. The new owners promptly liquidated the company, divided the property into six parts, and sold off each portion separately. By the end of July 1947, the sales process was completed. Both the original Bell Ranch and the River Valley Company, which had owned it since 1898, were no more.[31]

But the campaign for the Conchas Road had not ended. The Bell Ranch as the main barrier had been surmounted, only to be replaced by the State of New Mexico. For the next ten years, starting before the end of the Second World War in 1945, Tucumcari boosters alternately pleaded with and cajoled the state highway agency to start and then complete improvement and paving of the project. They badgered the state legislature and the congressional delegation with endless individual solicitations, group petitions, and threats—all with sympathetic hearings but meager results. One difficulty that hindered Tucumcari's cause was the location of the route's proposed 110-mile length to Las Vegas. Obviously, Tucumcari might benefit more from the project, since it was only 32 miles away from Conchas Lake, as compared with 78 miles for Las

Vegas. But, although seemingly a minor concern, only about 5.5 miles of the route lay in Quay County, while most of it was in San Miguel County. This geographical situation caused problems, particularly because most of the construction costs would come from the state highway funds allocated to San Miguel County, which had other priorities for road building and highway improvements. This circumstance also made it difficult to harmonize lobbying with state agencies and the legislature.[32]

Local efforts, although still unflagging, were energized by an address to the Chamber of Commerce made by Colonel Charles H. McNutt, Army Corps of Engineers district engineer in Albuquerque, who emphasized that Tucumcari was sitting on a tourist goldmine at nearby Conchas Lake. Only an "all-weather road" was needed, McNutt said, to cash in on this recreational bonanza. In what was music to the ears of his listeners, the colonel recounted the numerous times the state had committed itself in writing to construct "an asphalt-top road to Conchas." Further intriguing the audience, he pointed out that the Corps of Engineers had granted a twenty-five-year lease for Conchas State Park, with the condition that the park's recreational resources would be fully developed. Colonel McNutt, although holding out the possibility of cancellation as a bargaining chip with the state, declined to predict if such an extreme measure might be used.[33]

Construction on the 5.5 miles of the Conchas Road in Quay County—State Road 104, as it was numbered—had started in the summer of 1944 before the war ended and continued haphazardly thereafter. By the time of Colonel McNutt's address in spring 1950, the portion from Tucumcari to Conchas Lake existed but was described as "a mess right now," and so "pitted and rutted" that cars traveling that route would likely be damaged in some way. The segment from the lake to Las Vegas was "all but impassable." Nevertheless, there were already signs that other eastern New Mexico communities shared the *Daily News* editor's interest in cooperative action. Several neighboring counties had gone on record as giving "unanimous backing" for the road to Conchas Lake. Tucumcari boosters welcomed any backing they could get, although still accepting major responsibility for the project's completion.[34]

It became an emotional as well as an economic matter. In fact, various civic and business groups had formed 104 committees and literally dozens of individuals had not only contributed a total of $15,000 but also oversubscribed that amount by $3,000 to purchase rights of way to the San Miguel County line and on to Conchas Lake. This kind of enthusiasm prompted the *Daily News* to ask in a bold headline, "They Paid the Money; Where's the Road?"[35] Even after the Conchas Road was graded and graveled adequately, the struggle continued several years for blacktopping. Again, since 104 was not a federal highway, the "Knotty Problem" persisted that San Miguel County would have to pay for most of the paving out of its limited state road allocation, which it was reluctant to do. Finally, in the late 1950s, after short stretches were paved occasionally, the state stepped up and completed Tucumcari's long-sought modern highway to the recreational pleasures and tourist "cash crop" of Conchas Lake. About the same time, blacktopping began on the part between the dam and Las Vegas.[36] The package of Conchas Dam, the Arch Hurley irrigation project, and the direct highway connection with Conchas Lake was now tied together in a neat bundle. And the amazing question remained of how the huge, multimillion-dollar dam was ever built in the middle of nowhere, miles away from a railroad or improved roadway.

The pre–Second World War "blood bath" from automobile accidents grew exponentially after the war with the increased number of cars and the burgeoning traffic on Route 66. In 1956 the National Guard was called out in New Mexico to set up roadblocks, warn motorists of highway hazards, and help prevent the record of traffic deaths from being "written in blood-red ink." The stretch of two-lane highway east of Tucumcari to San Jon justly earned national attention as "Bloody 66," "Slaughter Alley," and "Suicide Road" because of frequent fatal automobile accidents, which had "reached epidemic numbers" by 1968. Referring to the nationwide traffic death toll at this time, an Associated Press article declared that the automobile was more deadly than war. On one Sunday in the summer of 1969, the traffic count of vehicles on Route 66 in New Mexico reached 10,247, and in one hour that morning 742 vehicles entered the state, or one every 4.8 seconds. Between January 1968 and August 1969, a total of seventy-six accidents had occurred and seventeen persons had died as a result. By the time the freeway was in full use in 1981, the state health agency released statistics showing that, along with suicide and homicides, violent death in traffic accidents was New Mexico's number one violent death problem.[37]

In truth, the famous highway became a virtual bloodbath for much of its 2,451-mile length between Chicago and Los Angeles.[38] New Mexico has traditionally recorded an unusually high rate of traffic deaths attributed to drunken drivers, which on occasion has reached "epidemic proportions" and run 50 percent above the national average. Narrow bridges also contributed to the highway death toll in New Mexico. In 1972 close to twenty people died when a Texas church bus loaded with youths on their way to a skiing vacation collided with a jackknifed cattle truck on a US Highways 60 and 84 bridge near Fort Sumner.[39]

A kindred evil in highway fatalities was the scandalous construction of shoddy roads in New Mexico, which inevitably contributed to the highway death toll. Graft and corruption in the state's pervasive political spoils system were not uncommon, not only involving contractors but sometimes highway commissioners, agency staff, and members of the state legislature as well. Highway scandals made top news in 1961 and drew a congressional subcommittee investigation. In these hearings, the highway morass in New Mexico was characterized as a "sickening, sorry mess of petty pandering, festering sores, appalling gall, two-timing public employe[es], creeping national sickness."[40] All too often, it seemed, paving had just been completed when it began to deteriorate. In one case involving an eight-mile stretch of Route 66 east of Tucumcari, the job had been finished only two months when it developed "pre-mature wrinkles" at one place and "washboards buckling up here and there." Even before new I-40's formal opening, two-inch-deep ruts began to appear in an 18.5-mile segment between Tucumcari and San Jon. While admitting that mistakes were made in the original construction, the state highway agency excused the damage as caused mainly by increased truck traffic. Curiously, however, the portion east between San Jon and Glenrio showed no signs of serious rutting. The only smooth roads among the "battered and bruised New Mexico highways," one critic complained, were the brand-new ones. In fact, a 4.8-mile segment of US Highways 70 and 80 through Lordsburg failed before it was finished.[41]

Speed traps, or sometimes called "booby traps," seem to have originated with the automobile. Reliable reports indicated as early as 1952 that Tucumcari was becoming known as a speed trap on Route 66 within the city limits, causing tourists to bypass the town. A concerned Chamber of Commerce assigned a special committee to plead with the city police for more courtesy and fewer tickets to tourists driving through town. The city took this problem seriously and launched Operation Coffee, gaining nationwide attention in doing so.

Instead of giving an out-of-state motorist a ticket for speeding, a smiling city police officer would approach the stopped car and write out an order for all the occupants to receive a free cup of coffee at any local restaurant, service station, or drugstore.[42]

The outlying stretches of Route 66 had gained such an unfavorable reputation among tourists that the prestigious American Automobile Association accused local authorities of approving "shotgun justice" with speed traps. New Mexico, whose official state nickname was the "Land of Enchantment," became widely known as the "Land of Entrapment." In 1964 a truck owner erected this sign along Route 66: "New Mexico the Fine State / Watch out the Gestapo Will Get You." Two years later, complaints had become so frequent that the district judge convened a grand jury to consider the outcries but with few remedial results. At that time in New Mexico, justices of the peace profited personally from speed traps since a significant part of their income was derived from the fines they levied for traffic violations.[43]

And still the highway troubles continued, most notably at the San Jon port of entry where the entire nine-member crew was suspended "due to irregularities and alleged short-changing of one or two motor carriers." At about the same time, an Albuquerque television reporter badmouthed Tucumcari, which would, he said, "clip every tourist who comes thru town." One woman tourist, in recounting "an incident of harassment" by a local police officer, concluded her emotional letter of complaint with the wry comment, "I hope all the people in your town are not like this officer."[44]

In the early days of Route 66, some states had long segments called "sidewalk highway" because of the wafer-thin width of only nine feet. Looking back, old-timers said of those narrow, pot-holed stretches that there was "only six inches and a [roll-your-own] cigarette paper between you and death on 66." As stated earlier, the president of the local Chamber of Commerce had championed highway safety on Route 66 and had implored both federal and state transportation agencies to do something about the width of the highway. Unfortunately, the forty-eight-year-old Damon Kvols died, having become another victim of "Slaughter Alley" when his car collided with a semitruck and trailer transporting automobiles.[45]

As it happened, 1964 became the most important year in Tucumcari history. At that time the location of an interstate highway bypass was determined, and the railroad presence began disappearing. Thirty-five years earlier an article had appeared in the prestigious periodical *New Republic* that reflected a scholarly, idealistic movement in urban planning popular among intellectuals of that day. The article called for what it dubbed the "The Townless Highway," which would "avoid each larger town and city by means of a bypass around it." These controlled-access express routes, the article said, should have "the double-tracking of the highway so as to make two separate parallel one-way roads at varying distances apart." Such a nationwide system should be constructed solely "for the motorist and kept free from every encroachment, except the filling stations and restaurants necessary for his convenience." The term *Townless Highway* held a special foreboding for Tucumcari and other small towns with a significant stake in the tourist trade. True, the prophetic article had mentioned provision for "side-lane approaches," or entrance and exit ramps off the primary roadway. From the beginning, however, it seemed reasonable to assume that these off-ramps would have minimal influence in staunching the economic bloodletting caused by the diversion of main-stem traffic previously through the towns but shifted to the *freeways*—a term in use as early as the 1930s.[46] The interstates would prove this assumption true for Tucumcari and hundreds of other towns and villages across America. Also, in apparent contradiction of the Townless Highway movement's lofty idealism, the interstates usually knifed straight across the map with little regard for features of the landscape, while Route 66 often curved, dipped, and looped, adapting itself to contours of the natural environment.

Dwight D. Eisenhower probably knew little about the futuristic urban-planning movement of the 1930s and its concept of highways. From personal experience, however, he had started even earlier developing his own view of transcontinental thoroughfares. In 1919, soon after the First World War, Lieutenant Colonel Eisenhower was one of 15 military observers who accompanied the US Army's First Transcontinental Motor Convoy on its overland trip of 3,251 miles from Washington, DC, to San Francisco. Comprised of 282 regularly assigned army personnel and 79 military vehicles, including heavy and light trucks, motorcycles, cars, and auxiliaries such as machine and blacksmith shops, the convoy's objectives were to test specialized vehicles actually used in the war, and others still untested. In this process, the special unit had to determine "the problems involved in moving an army across the continent," when the normal means of transportation were "damaged or destroyed by agents of an Asiatic enemy." Participants on the trip saw this "first motor convoy to cross the American Continent, [as] comparable to the first ox-team prairie-schooner trek" or later original crossings by other forms of transportation. The sixty-two-day journey, from July 7 to September 6, 1919, followed the route of the proposed Lincoln Highway, approximating today's Interstate 80, but then existing "largely in the imagination." At that time the route consisted mostly of a series of dirt roads, rough pathways, mountain trails, sandy deserts, and alkali flats. At its finish the convoy's undertaking was proclaimed a success for beginning "a new epoch in the long-distance operation of heavy motor transport." The military project also inevitably stirred public interest in the need to construct transcontinental highways.[47]

In Eisenhower's separate report, he paid particular attention to the performance of the various types and brands of vehicles, but he did observe that "some of the good roads are too narrow," causing one vehicle meeting another to pull off to the side. Eisenhower's experience on the cross-country trip undoubtedly had some influence in his determination, as president, to authorize the interstate highway system. In addition, as supreme allied commander in Europe during World War II, he so admired the German Autobahn system that it, too, figured prominently in his presidential decision making.[48]

Not that the idealistic urban planners of the 1930s or Eisenhower were the only ones with ideas for a grand scheme of national highways. It seemed that anyone who had ever given the subject passing attention had a suggestion. When Eisenhower became the thirty-fourth president in 1953, however, he had the determination and prestige to make the idea become a reality. As he had learned in the army, Eisenhower simply gave the command to staff members to draw up and implement a "dramatic plan" for a superhighway network. He believed the massive program essential for the nation's growth and prosperity, as well as for national defense, but specified that the entire system must be "self-liquidating" and avoid adding to the national debt. Otherwise, in military style, he left the details for the staff to work out and paid little attention to their efforts in the process. When his proposal stalled in Congress with substitute bills, however, he did come to its defense by emphasizing the need for a "modern interstate highway system" in his 1956 State of the Union Address. On June 29, 1956, while a patient in Walter Reed Army Hospital recovering from surgery for ileitis, President Eisenhower signed the National Interstate and Defense

Highway Act of 1956. The act authorized the biggest and most costly public works project in the nation's history. Estimated to cost about $40 billion, the completed highway system of 48,440 miles in length actually cost nearly three times as much, or $114,000 billion. Congress stipulated that additional federal taxes, primarily on gasoline, diesel, and tires, would be deposited in a special Highway Trust Fund earmarked to pay for 90 percent of the expense, with the states responsible for the other 10 percent.[49]

The measure Eisenhower signed created the new US Interstate Highway System. Like numbering of the older highways, a committee of the nonfederal American Association of State Highway Officials also did the job for the new network. Numbers for the interstates appeared on distinctive pear-shaped red and blue markers with white numbers, in contrast with the white shields and black numbers of the signs for the previous US highways. The designation "Interstate" at the top indicated the newer routes, while the particular state's name had graced the top of the older federal signage. Like the older system, east-west routes were assigned even numbers and north-south ones given odd numbers, with the ending numerals of 0 and 5 for major interstates. However, to minimize confusion with the previous system, the lowest numbered interstates were in the South and West and the highest in the North and East. Main interstates were given two digits, while shorter routes had three digits, with the last two numbers matching the parent highway—as in US 95 and US 195. The large green exit signs with white lettering indicating towns and adjacent roads met some opposition from federal highway administrator Betram Tallamy, who wanted dark blue backgrounds. Tallamy lost in a competitive viewing contest, and, as it turned out, he was actually color blind. Interstate 40, as one of the sixty-seven primary east-west interstate highways, had the distinction of fulfilling the dream of a transcontinental passageway along the 35th parallel of latitude, envisioned a century before as a wagon and railroad route.[50]

The Interstate 40 Bypass around Tucumcari had been foreshadowed for several years by rumors as well as a major adjustment of Route 66 through town. On the eve of the Second World War, an authoritative analysis of the national highway system and the requirements for future civilian and military use found that the main drawback of existing roadways was the clogging buildup of traffic at urban centers. The obvious solution was bypasses around these bottlenecks.[51] Also, before the war, gossip about changes of Route 66 away from

Route 66 through Tucumcari. The four-laned version of the highway, intended to speed up traffic through town, preceded construction of the Interstate 40 Bypass around the city limits. Heritage Image Partnership Ltd. / Alamy Stock Photo (Image ID: BHG8PG).

Tucumcari had surfaced occasionally, and this speculation became more frequent as hostilities drew to a close. Governor John J. Dempsey squelched a report that Route 66 would be changed from its current location, adding that the state would build roads to bring tourists into cities, "not to detour them around." The state highway engineer reinforced the governor's assertion by flatly stating that he would not recommend the building of any highway bypassing cities. Despite such protestations, however, a new four-lane superhighway in the Tucumcari vicinity seemed to be a certainty after the war ended.[52]

The most important adjustment, and hint of the future I-40, came in 1949 when Tucumcari became the first city in New Mexico to take advantage of the state's program of widening highways through urban centers to increase the free flow of traffic.[53] At Tucumcari, Route 66 was widened to four lanes inside the city limits. Local residents, alarmed by the dangers to school children crossing through the heavy traffic, demanded a traffic light on the highway but got only pedestrian crosswalks twelve feet wide painted yellow on the pavement with signs requiring drivers to stop when the walkways were occupied. Even without traffic lights, however, the crosswalks tended to defeat the objective of a free-flowing roadway.[54] During the widening construction work itself, tourists on Route 66 were sometimes advised in Amarillo to take Route 60 to Clovis and avoid any delays at Tucumcari. Until discredited by state officials, a wild rumor made the rounds locally that the detour would become permanent and significantly reduce travel on the Route 66 link to Tucumcari.

Amid such concerns, the town marked the fiftieth anniversary of its founding with a three-day Jubilee Celebration, highlighted by a rodeo and an unusually long parade.[55] At least briefly, locals could forget the constant stream of rumors and misleading reports that made Tucumcari officials nervous for years wondering about their highway future—and more specifically, the prospect of a bypass. They could not foresee, of course, that once the broad, four-lane (and in some areas, six-lane) interstates started becoming a reality, Detroit would manufacture bigger automobiles shaped and powered like rocket ships. These celestial vehicles demanded more space than the confining, newly constructed Route 66 through Tucumcari. Small-town concerns had relatively little importance in the modern world of "bigness." The emerging, wide-open freeways and the huge 1960s Cadillac Eldorado convertible that "took on the appearance of the Batmobile" complete with tail fins were perfectly matched for each other.[56]

Previous federal highways, like Route 66, had passed unobtrusively through the center of cities and towns in neat lanes, often on the designated Main Street itself, thus inviting tourists to come in and providing the locals with a ready access to the outside world. In effect, this kind of highway made an investment in the community and in its prosperity. On the other hand, the new interstates did not necessarily avoid large cities, often bludgeoning through the inner parts. In such cases these freeways might attempt to funnel traffic through as quickly as possible by carving out large chunks of valuable real estate for four to six lanes of traffic. It was possible to fight the unbending interstate system, and win—if you were big enough. San Francisco battled Interstate 280, the Embarcadero Freeway, to a standstill and demolished the parts already built. In Seattle, Interstate 5 knifed through the heart of the main business district, artificially separating historically connected downtown sections. For small towns like Tucumcari, however, the new system had only one intent—to bypass them.[57]

Surveying and construction of Interstate 40 in New Mexico started soon after President Eisenhower approved the Federal Interstate Highway Act of 1956, and a small section of the freeway west of Tucumcari had been completed by 1960. State officials told concerned residents not to worry, citing studies that bypasses helped a town by diverting big trucks and speeding automobiles, which did not stop in smaller places anyway. Moreover, the officials said, it would be years before the building of a bypass at Tucumcari.[58] Construction of I-40 in New Mexico proceeded gradually, not as a sudden, sweeping attack but starting in the rural, thinly populated areas, leaving bypasses around cities and larger towns until later. The schedule of construction in rural areas first gave Tucumcari time to prepare a strategy for delaying its bypass as long as possible. It was in this context that serious negotiations on the location of the Interstate 40 Bypass around the town began in 1959. Five years of intense controversy went by before there was any kind of resolution.

During that time, Tucumcari and Santa Rosa organized and led a statewide anti-bypass movement that challenged both state and federal highway agencies on their power to unilaterally impose interstate bypasses on communities without their consent. Quay County's state senator, backed by local sentiment as well as statewide business and civic opposition to bypasses, successfully cosponsored a bill in the legislature that probably had no equal elsewhere at the time. From the beginning, western states complained that standards suitable for the location of bypasses in the thickly populated East made no sense in those sparsely settled parts of the West with small, isolated towns struggling to stay alive. The anti-bypass measure stated that no state funds would be expended on highway projects "diverting traffic and commerce" from an existing route without "the express approval" of the affected community. Caught off guard by this effrontery from a pipsqueak state, the lordly federal Bureau of Public Roads (BPR) blustered about cutting off all federal highway funding in New Mexico. This was no trivial threat and involved big stakes. Interstate 40 crossed the state east to west, while Interstate 25 ran the entire length north and south, and Interstate 10 entered the southwestern corner for short distance. Other lesser federal roads were also covered by the anti-bypass legislation. In fact, a total of twenty highway contracts, most of them individual segments of I-40 and I-25, were in the planning stage for New Mexico.[59]

By September 1963, the two towns had spearheaded the formation of the New Mexico Communities By-Pass Association with elected officers, a board of directors, headquarters at Santa Rosa, twenty-two member organizations in other towns, and a bulletin published by the *Tucumcari Daily News*. Rallies were staged throughout the state to drum up support, recruit new members, and raise funds. The association's philosophy did not condemn all bypasses but, in harmony with state law, criticized as unrealistic the federal Bureau of Public Roads practice of applying the same policy "to small, isolated southwestern towns that they do to large, industrialized cities in the more congested areas of our country." Instead, every community should have a voice in establishing bypasses that determined their economic destiny and survival, and not be forced to accept them. State Senator Emmett Hart, who cosponsored the anti-bypass bill, wanted Tucumcari's new route to go through the city, not with fenced-in corridors but, as had been done in Texas, with curbs and medians that diverted traffic off the freeway into town. Or, as an alternative, he proposed the clearing of two city blocks to create space for a major exit and interchange complex. To provide more off-ramps, a local resident suggested splitting the bypass so that one side ran around the north part of town and the other on the southern fringe.[60] The anti-bypass association, however, was more of a stalling strategy than a solution. And the anti-bypass movement itself, although well-intentioned and realistically forecasting the destructive effects the bypasses would bring, had no chance of stopping or substantially altering the national interstate construction program. The New Mexico anti-bypass law, enacted in 1963 and subjected to combined attacks and incessant sniping by state and federal highway agencies, was repealed in 1966.[61]

Before repeal of the law, Tucumcari made a strategic retreat that changed the warfare from guerilla tactics to direct confrontation on a conventional battlefield. After eighteen months of enduring threats and bullying negotiations, Tucumcari became the first major town or city in New Mexico to make an agreement with state officials on the location of an I-40 Bypass. The momentous date was September 25, 1964.[62] At that time the New Mexico State Highway Commission accepted the Tucumcari City Commission's proposal for the bypass to skim along the southern city limits, not three or four miles beyond. Undoubtedly because of the anti-bypass movement, the town had acquired the clout to stand up against a powerful state agency, backed by the more powerful federal government, and make a deal. And the agreement, although having the appearance of a surrender rather than a strategic retreat, was another stage of stalling tactics. Tucumcari officials had not signed a carte blanche treaty but a document including ten binding conditions that were subject to prolonged interpretation as well as amendments, thus delaying completion of the bypass for years. In addition, a State District Court ruled that the state highway agency could not officially open the local bypass to traffic until completion of the entire route, which included the I-40 segment between Tucumcari and San Jon—a crucial issue in the stalling process. As a result, it would take nearly twenty years from the time Tucumcari made an agreement with the state highway commission until the I-40 Bypass officially opened around the town and traffic flowed uninterrupted across the entire state on the freeway.[63]

Besides continual haggling over the conditions in the agreement, Tucumcari officials developed a highly effective lobbying campaign with the state legislature and the state's congressional delegation. Thomas G. Morris of Tucumcari, who first served as a state representative and then as New Mexico's lone congressman from 1959 to 1969, took special interest in the location and progress of I-40, often using his influence to sway state and federal agencies.[64] In the US Senate, Tucumcari boosters also won the support of influential senator Dennis Chavez. Then, beginning in 1964, at the time of the fateful agreement, the town's cause gained a special champion in Chavez's successor, Senator Joseph M. Montoya, whose clout as a member of both the Public Works and the Appropriations Committees always got the attention of politically sensitive highway officials.

The political situation surrounding the I-40 Bypass also involved the Horatio Alger rise to prominence of Tucumcari mayor, and later state senator, Kenneth M. Schlientz, who had grown up in town showing few indications of his later accomplishments. As a high school student, he had started working at a service station in the days when an employee routinely rushed out to fill the customer's gas tank and test the tire pressure and check the engine oil. From that beginning he continued in the trade until he ran his own service station in town, as well as another one in San Jon, and became the wholesale bulk distributor for the Exxon Company.[65]

Bettie Ditto's brother Tom Lins had served on the city commission, and in 1967, briefly as mayor, until he lost a recall election. Kenneth Schlientz was appointed to fill the Lins vacancy, and, in a surprise decision, the two remaining commission members, who had barely survived in the recall election, chose the newcomer as mayor.[66] Young and eager, Schlientz took to the job like an experienced professional politician, managing to get the ear of Senator Montoya, as well as other state and federal power brokers. When any problem arose in Tucumcari with the bypass, Schlientz was not reluctant to call on his powerful political connections for help. After five years as mayor, and election to the state senate as a Republican, he shifted his base of operations to Santa Fe, a move that brought greater advantages for him to monitor the interstate highway program. In short, Kenneth Schlientz became the point man in Tucumcari's I-40 Bypass delaying tactics.[67]

In 1978, after the highway agency failed to meet the conditions in its agreement with Tucumcari, Senator Schlientz led a group that obtained a court order forcing compliance by the state. As a result, the agreement was amended to include another ten conditions. The most troublesome issue was the number and location of exit ramps.[68] Campaigning at Tucumcari for reelection in 1976, US Senator Montoya had declared that the five exits planned locally for I-40 were more per capita than for any other place of that size in the state. Montoya credited his clout in the Senate for this accomplishment, telling the crowd at a local Democratic dinner rally: "You wanted two interchanges here in Tucumcari, and little by little you started asking me for three. I got three. Then you asked me for four and I got four. Then you asked me for five and I got five." After an appropriate pause to let his remarks sink in, the senator said: "That's too many for a city like Tucumcari, but you got them." He then added for effect, "Now please don't ask me for a helicopter wing to pick up the tourists and drop them in the business district." In local terminology the comparatively large number of exit ramps at Tucumcari was described as something like "holes in a boot," since Interstate 25 had only three for Santa Fe.[69]

At one time the I-40 Bypass had stood for several months with only the western half finished around Tucumcari, and with a big vacant gap for the eastern half serving as recognition of Senator Schlientz's lobbying against the concrete monstrosity. On the other hand, the state highway agency used the excuse that a cash flow problem caused the delay, which may have had some validity. The federal Highway Trust Fund, which financed construction of the interstates, did experience shortfalls.[70] Once it sank in that a full-fledged freeway would arrive someday, however, locals accepted the prospect with indifference or dismay. Facing the inevitable declining number of tourists, one motel owner came up with a novel suggestion, based on federal subsidies to farmers for withholding land from production. It was only fair, he said, that the government should pay motel owners on Route 66 to leave a specified number of rooms vacant each night. In four Town Hall Meetings with outside panelists and funded by a federal grant, a learned economist and a high-ranking state official chose not to deliver the disturbing news that freeways were quickly becoming "the new Main Streets of America" and adversely altering and reshaping every "once-virginal town" they penetrated. A young girl foresaw the dangers ahead when she expressed the fear in her letter to Santa Claus that he would bypass her home like the new highway was going to do.[71]

By the time I-40 was formally dedicated in New Mexico, it had been in full use at Tucumcari for more than a month. On Thursday, June 25, 1981, following a scheduled meeting of the State Highway Commission at the Holiday Inn in Tucumcari, Highway Commissioner Carlos Gallegos cut a ribbon on I-40 and officially opened the interstate to traffic all the way across the state. Completion of the twenty-seven-mile stretch between Tucumcari and San Jon had delayed the inauguration until now. At first, in a test of basic democracy, the small village's tenacious opposition to a proposed bypass five miles away to the north had stymied the bureaucracy. The federal Bureau of Public Roads had chosen the northern route as a more direct continuation of I-40, while the state highway agency had come to favor San Jon's case, which involved a longer distance. In 1969 Senator Montoya revealed at a Senate subcommittee meeting conducted in Tucumcari that he had brokered a deal with the BPR on the I-40 alignment to the Texas state line, including the new location of the San Jon bypass. As Senator Montoya explained basic "highway politics," the BPR as a federal agency "plays no politics," while the state paid attention to the pleas of voters. The specifications for the new site, however, called for only one traffic interchange instead of the original two, and such construction details caused the village to continue its stalling resistance. Finally, San Jon won the battle involving completion of the last segment of I-40 in New Mexico, and the bypass was completed at the village's northern outskirts less than a month before the freeway's formal dedication. The I-40 Bypass had occupied center stage at Tucumcari for twenty years. With settlement of the San Jon issue and a few minor details, such as the local bypass lighting system, the long ordeal and its stalling tactics came to an end, and traffic was at last flowing uninterrupted across the entire state.[72]

The impact of the interstate system, according to its supporters, "had more influence on the shape and development" of America than any other "initiative of the middle third of the twentieth century." Or, as another assessment put it, the interstate highway system contributed more than any other factor to "an unprecedented democratization of mobility" among Americans. The interstates influenced the location of labor markets; the shift of population from the cities to the suburbs; and a similar movement of retail stores, wholesale outlets, warehouses, and factories. In addition, the freeways also created shopping centers and malls and founded or destroyed entire industries, for example, the shifting of meatpacking from large cities to small-town plants. In the nation's heartland, however, it was a different story. Small cities and towns feared that "like counterparts bypassed by railroads in the last century, they will wither and die." In fact, according to one assessment, for many small towns like Tucumcari, located on but bypassed by an interstate, their residents would heartily agree that, if the American people "had realized the sheer magnitude of the interests affected by this road system," it would never have been built.[73]

Undoubtedly a national interstate freeway system should have been built by the federal government. In fact, it was inevitable, given the transcontinental expanse of the United States and the popularity of automobiles among Americans. But if built, it should have been more protective of established tourist centers like Tucumcari. After all, at one fell swoop countless owners of motels, restaurants, service stations, and stores had seen the powerful federal government construct a web of interstates across the land that destroyed their livelihoods in the name of the "greater good" and national interest. Yet these Americans had not lost a war nor been conquered and subjugated like Southerners in the Civil War and Reconstruction, and they deserved better treatment. For instance, at major tourist centers, motorists might have encountered well-advertised, plainly marked exits to leave the interstate and get the same kicks as their parents and grandparents before them, by driving on the remnants of Route 66 or other historic routes or visiting scenic and local attractions. At Tucumcari a near perfect example of this option would have been a diversion off Interstate 40 that included travel along the historic "Main Street of America" through urban Tucumcari and beyond, east or west on long stretches of old Route 66. This option or similar ones, perhaps professionally managed and promoted like national monuments with interpretive centers, but more effectively structured than exit ramps alone, would have helped save millions of dollars in financial losses and avoided enormous ill will.

Chapter 7

RAILROAD BLUES

n that fateful year of 1964, when the city signed off on the I-40 Bypass, a "fire bell in the night" warned of yet another threat that would bring Tucumcari's demise as a railroad town. Only a few years earlier a newspaper editor, when discussing the town's economic base, had characterized the substantial railroad payroll as "an unfailing source of income." Like other optimistic predictions of that day, this pronouncement turned out to be a false hope. In reality, the railroads faced an altered world after the Second World War. Henry M. Goldenberg, who worked for the Southern Pacific Railroad most of his life, spoke from long firsthand experience when he recalled, "In 1964 they [the railroads] started to move out, and it just about killed the town."[1]

Giving a more complete account, also from firsthand observation, Frances McDaniel Prentice, wife of longtime railroad telegrapher Sylvester Prentice, told this story of Tucumcari's decline as a rail center:

> Traffic continued to decline. The mail contract was given to the trucks. Passenger service was dropped. Freight pick-up and delivery at the local depot was limited to car loads. Work was being transferred to El Paso. The machine shops were closed and the roundhouse was razed. RI [Rock Island] took bankruptcy and the [Tucumcari and Memphis] line to Amarillo abandoned. The train crews had their runs changed from Carrizozo to El Paso, and hundreds of families moved out of Tucumcari. A big payroll went with them, and the economy of the town suffered.

Tucumcari had been an important regional rail center and the junction point of the Southern Pacific and two Rock Island lines, as well as the Dawson branch. This past distinction, however, was meager compensation for the damaged town left behind.[2]

The reasons for this devastating result were obvious. On the national scene in the fateful year of 1964, Jervis Longdon Jr., board chairman of the Rock Island, had reported a "gloomy picture" to the company's stockholders. The railroad's passenger service had continued to lose riders, and it appeared "impossible to make it pay." For both business and personal travel people were using the airlines, and cheaper transportation was readily available in buses "on the ever-expanding and improving interstate highway system built by Uncle Sam." Then the board chairman got "to the heart of Rock Island's special problem." Besides wage increases and an inflationary economy, there was "the subnormal level of revenues," which was another way of saying, "The Rock Island must have more freight business."[3] Although the perpetually troubled Rock Island was hardly typical, the concerns Longdon mentioned were challenging the entire industry as well after World War II. The main competition for the SP, even more formidable than the pressure from other railroads, was the challenge of trucks, which were taking over the hauling of freight. In fact, President Eisenhower's spacious four-lane, divided interstate highways, inaugurated in 1956, would give trucking concerns a green light to expand their operations. Independent truckers, or "gypsies," which were virtually unregulated, posed a special problem because they could pick and choose their rates and win lucrative freight contracts in competition with regulated railroads. Competitors took away more business on every side, including shipping in coastal waters as well as in inland rivers, the larger lakes, and the Panama Canal.[4] To meet these challenges, as well as economize and operate more efficiently, the railroads routinely replaced steam locomotives with diesels in the 1940s. By the 1950s, with dieselization almost complete and the retirement of steamers virtually finalized, the industry concentrated on finding advanced models of diesels.[5] Next, in the 1960s and 1970s, to meet new challenges and remain financially solvent, mergers became the order of the day.[6] The Rock Island jumped into the alternate non-steam, diesel-electric field fairly early, in the 1920s, and began the shift to diesels in earnest in 1937. In 1936 the Rock Island still had more than 1,100 steamers in service, but by 1947 only half that many were still operating.

The Southern Pacific started dieselization later than the Rock Island. For years the Dawson mines supplied more than enough coal for SP locomotive boilers as well as the region's other needs. This was especially true after 1924 when the SP acquired the El Paso & Southwestern Railroad with a fleet of coal-fired engines. These locomotives, for which additional coal chutes were built where needed, continued to operate for years on the Rio Grande Division and as far west of Tucumcari as Tucson. But in one important way the SP had kept up with the Rock Island in innovative fuel usage. In the early 1900s it started to switch from coal to oil as fuel for steamers and by purchasing mostly oil-burning locomotives.

Edward L. Doheny, who opened both the California and Mexican petroleum industries, also led the transition from the "Kerosene Age," which featured lighting by oil lamps to the "Fuel-oil Age," for industrial uses. Doheny and a partner convinced the Santa Fe Railroad that oil was feasible and more economical than coal as fuel to burn in steam engines. Other California railroads, including the Southern Pacific, followed the Santa Fe example. By late 1901 the SP was burning 75,000 gallons of oil a month compared with 100,000 gallons by the Santa Fe.[7] The SP's post–World War II master plan called for replacing all steamers with diesels by 1960. Actually, the SP deactivated its last steam locomotive in December 1956, except for excursion runs, celebratory occasions, and those operating regularly in Mexico, and declared itself fully dieselized the next year.[8]

Even the casual observer noticed the difference between steam and diesel locomotives; the steamers were usually painted a dreary black while most of the diesels sported bright, attractive colors. At Tucumcari, by the spring of 1953, all freight runs to and from El Paso had been changed to diesels, and one diesel locomotive was in local switching duty. Passenger trains coming into town were still steam powered but would soon be converted to dieselization. As a result, the roundhouse crew had already been reduced by about twenty workers, and another ten faced the same fate in the near future. The introduction of the less thirsty diesels also drastically reduced the SP's reliance on the city's water supply.[9] The operational differences between the Rock Island's steam locomotives used in the one hundred-mile run from Dalhart to Tucumcari and the Southern Pacific's coal-burning engines had necessitated changing the engines on incoming and outgoing trains in the local yards. Switching took time and extra workers. On the other hand, the diesels introduced by the two lines were similar, which minimized the switching process, although the crews still changed at Tucumcari. Mainly, however, the diesels could travel farther with fewer stops

Former railroad depot, now, under local MainStreet organization's auspices, the Tucumcari Railroad Museum. Photo by Nancy Stratton Hall.

for water or labor-intensive maintenance. This fact, coupled with the wave of railroad mergers and reorganizations of the 1960s and 1970s, resulted in the relocation of administrative centers, partially to accommodate the operational range of diesels. It was only the beginning of trouble when, in one of the realignments, Tucumcari lost the designation as a division point.[10]

On a trip back to his hometown, Frank Kile Turner made it a point to visit the old railroad depot, which had been the "center of activity" for him when he was growing up in Tucumcari during the 1940s and 1950s.[11] As Turner recalled:

> I thought this place was the absolute center of the universe. Tucumcari was a true railroad town. So many of us were "railroad families" which meant a lot of family trips began and ended at the depot. If you weren't a railroad family, chances were pretty good that some part of your family income was tied in some way to the railroad. The depot was where a lot of its citizens left town to go to war, to college, to visit family and friends near and far, to find new work, and some just left.

At Christmastime eager children and their parents gathered at the depot to meet Santa Claus, who reportedly arrived on a special passenger train "straight from the North Pole." Like the town square in the East, the Tucumcari train station was a public space, the gathering place "to get the latest news and hear the freshest gossip[,] . . . to check the time, inquire about the arrival of the new Sears catalogue, and argue politics or the weather." Some depots of that day, with the addition of a pulpit and pews, could have easily passed as a church. The Tucumcari depot, built in prevalent Southwestern mission-style architecture, lacked the serene atmosphere of a church but still provided boarding passengers with a "civilized transition" from the quiet stability at home to the clickety-clack of a speeding train.[12] Even without a saintly configuration, the Tucumcari station remained the town's focal point, as the first depot had been when the Founding Fathers struggled to acquire the surrounding acreage for the original town site.

At mid-twentieth century, during Tucumcari's heyday as a railroad center, its companion terminals were Dawson, Carrizozo, and El Paso, with Carrizozo being the intermediate place for crew changes. Eight passenger trains and ten to twelve freights arrived and departed from the depot daily. Three days a week—Monday, Wednesday, and Friday—a mixed passenger and freight train called the "Polly" left on the branch line to Dawson and returned the next day. In addition, a regular flow of coal and coke cars from Dawson passed through Tucumcari until the mines were closed in 1950. Each day three Rock Island passenger trains either arrived from or departed to Chicago by way of Kansas City, and two came from or went on the Tucumcari and Memphis line to Memphis via Amarillo and Oklahoma City. And every day three Southern Pacific trains followed similar schedules to and from Los Angeles by way of El Paso, Tucson, and Phoenix. The first arrival of the day, Train #44 at 5:15 a.m. from Los Angeles, was actually a mail train with ten to twelve baggage and mail cars and only two coaches. It picked up passengers on the way at isolated stops such as Corona, Vaughn, Santa Rosa, Newkirk, Cuervo, and Montoya, and on its eastern leg at Logan and Nara Visa. The more prestigious passenger trains, such as the *Imperial* from Los Angeles to Chicago and the *Cherokee* to Memphis featured sleeping cars, coaches, diners, and lounges. The T&M's *Cherokee* also acted as a local, or commuter, stopping for passengers to board at Glenrio, Endee, Bard, and San Jon. Among the nation's famous streamliners, or upscale passenger trains of the day, the *Golden State* from Los Angeles to Chicago was, as previously explained, jointly operated by the Rock Island and the Southern Pacific.[13]

Passenger trains stopped over in Tucumcari from ten to thirty minutes or longer, depending on the need to transfer passengers, change crews, trade SP for Rock Island locomotives, load and unload mail and baggage as well as express items, take on water and ice, undergo some custodial cleaning, and switch cars from one line to another.[14] These layovers let passengers listen to the latest hit music coming from Two Gun Harry's short-order café located east of the depot just off railroad property. Harry Garrison, owner of the small eatery, first became a legend in his own mind, and then a real one. "Flamboyant, colorful and ebullient," as he has been described, "Harry was a gregarious man and Tucumcari's self-appointed ambassador to the world." Garrison put on an impressive show when he met incoming trains and escorted alighting passengers to his café. Dressed like a Hollywood singing cowboy, he wore all-white Western regalia and carried a fake pearl-handled six-gun on each hip. Garrison had a chance to actually fight crime, bare-fisted, when he "grappled for about 10 minutes" with a robber in his cafe before the burglar fled. It was the third time he had thwarted a burglary on the premises.[15]

It so happened that singer Dorothy Shay, "the Park Avenue Hillbillie," spent most of a half-hour stopover at Harry's café and later wrote a hit song about a cowboy named Two-Gun Harry and a place called Tucumcari. Although it never got to the top of *Billboard*'s ratings, Shay's rendition was a popular jukebox selection in 1948. Long afterward, many still identified the town with the song and the rhyming title, "Two Gun Harry from Tucumcari."[16] If not enticed to Harry's, passengers could stretch their legs by strolling a couple of blocks to the downtown business section at Main and Second Streets and grabbing a bite to eat at the Sands-Dorsey Drugstore fountain or at the Waffle House, Flag Ranch, Liberty, or Home Cafes. Or they could whet their thirsts at one of the watering holes in that neighborhood. If they were staying overnight, the Vorenberg and Randle Hotels were close by.

The most obvious choice for a real meal, of course, was the restaurant inside the depot. Although lacking the reputation of Harvey Houses with the glamour of the Harvey Girls as waitresses, which were regular features along the Santa Fe line, the local eatery had a distinguished background. Known formally as the Interstate, or popularly as the "Beanery," the restaurant concession was originally held by the Van Noy Interstate Company of Kansas City, which specialized in railroad dining establishments. Most of the waitresses were recruited from Kansas City and stayed in a dormitory near the rail yards. The Beanery could serve forty customers at its lunch counter and sixty more in a formal dining room, which featured table linen and silver service. Open twenty-four hours, the restaurant attracted railroad workers and local customers, as well as passengers, for meals and often scheduled banquets and other community social events. After about 1937, local contractors obtained the concession and operated the restaurant.[17]

The Beanery as well as the depot and adjoining rail yards bustled with activity during the passenger train arrivals and departures. However, what Frank Kyle Turner recalled as the "real train convention," or "an event," began in the early evening when three passenger trains—the westbound mail, the westbound Cherokee and the eastbound *Imperial*—arrived between 5:00 and 9:30. That was when the most locals came out to watch the trains arrive and depart, hoping to see a Hollywood movie star or, in springtime, a famous baseball player. During the Christmas season extra sections or specials were sometimes added, which produced an even larger local crowd of people-watchers. Some looked particularly for college football stars featured prominently on the sports pages who were bound for the Rose Bowl in Pasadena.[18] The last passenger train of the day to leave Tucumcari, the westbound mail that departed at 10:45 p.m., rolled out with little fanfare, often carrying several railroaders to section stations such as Montoya.

For railroad employees, who got free passes for themselves and their families, passenger service had a special meaning. As a boy, Henry C. Goldenberg, son of Southern Pacific car inspector Henry M. Goldenberg, always looked forward to the school year's end because his father often took the family to Los Angeles for a visit with grandparents and other relatives. Young Henry's mother always packed plenty of food for the trip, but sometimes as a special treat the family would pay to eat in the dining car with beautiful china and silverware and be served by dignified, white-coated black waiters. Young Henry got equal pleasure from the rare occasions when his father paid extra for the son to sleep in a Pullman car's luxurious berth with crisp white sheets and oversized pillows.[19] It was always a trip to anticipate—and to remember.

Frank Kile Turner, as a teenager busy with school activities, had no way of knowing that the end of an era for railroads at Tucumcari was beginning in the 1950s. Nor was it conceivable to other locals, as well as a host of middle-aged Americans, that it would soon be impossible to travel by passenger train across the vast prairies and canyon country beyond the Mississippi, following "the big circle route, the one that threw a steel lariat around the West."[20] The Southern Pacific was a leading advocate of ending passenger service. In 1966 the SP went on record officially, stating: "The long-haul passenger train has outlived its usefulness." In fact, the SP was accused of practicing a "blatant disregard for passenger comfort" in a deliberate, well-calculated effort to discourage patronage and justify the termination of its passenger trains. More specifically, California and Texas government agencies charged that "satisfactory [passenger] service is non-existent" and that the SP had eliminated Pullman coaches, dining cars, and reserved seats in a deliberate attempt to turn away passengers.[21]

Even the exclusive, extra-fare *Golden State* fell on hard times, exemplified in the decline of its dining facilities. The postwar decrease in the number of passengers had a direct effect on the patronage of diners and the cost of maintaining the high standards of these services. For each dollar patrons spent in diners, it was estimated, the railroads incurred expenses of $1.38. As a result, the Rock Island removed table linens and began serving precooked frozen meals. For a while the *Golden State* continued its exemplary service, but, in 1962, the SP made "the most Draconian cuts" when it replaced most diners with "Automat Cars." One railroad historian has declared that this "combination of mechanized service and sterile decor" undoubtedly ruined the enjoyment of any meal.[22]

Frank Kile Turner got caught in the SP's use of Automat Cars in its campaign to eliminate passenger service. In 1966, while on leave from the Marine Corps, Turner made his last trip on the *Golden State* to his hometown with his own family for Christmas. It began with fond memories of past journeys but became a disillusioning experience. The train was late departing and arriving. The Southern Pacific's infamous practice of introducing automated food service spoiled memories of eating exquisitely prepared meals served by gracious, white-coated waiters in tastefully decorated dining cars.[23] To his displeasure, Turner found that this was the case for most of his trip. The message was plain and simple to him—"Next time take a plane or drive." It was no surprise to Turner that the *Golden State* made its last run through Tucumcari less than two years later, in February 1968. Maintaining the railroad passenger service had been a long-term struggle even before the Second World War. In 1938, despite pleas from Tucumcari business leaders, the SP discontinued the *Apache* jointly operated with the Rock Island, even though that run reportedly was showing a reasonable profit.[24] Then, during the war, the railroads made great profits on passenger trains and, mistakenly anticipating the high volume of riders to continue in the postwar period, had spent more than $1 billion on new, luxurious coaches. The boom failed to materialize following the war. Travelers chose cars for short trips and planes for longer journeys. Awakening to the changing world, the railroads set out to remedy their mistaken investments by dumping passenger service altogether. Because of this concerted campaign, one ICC official declared that the passenger train had not died a natural death but, instead, "It was shot in the back."[25]

Rock Island board chairman Jervis Langdon Jr. put a different spin on it to the company's stockholders in 1964. He told them that the railroad would discontinue passenger service reluctantly "but with the firm conviction that the freight service should no longer be asked to absorb the inevitable and growing deficits." As far as public relations were concerned, Langdon said, "inferior passenger service is much worse than no service at all."[26] Besides such considerations, the Rock Island would also justify dropping passenger service by pointing out the major loss of revenue resulting from the removal of Railway Post Office (RPO) cars in 1967 and 1968, a problem shared by other railroads as well. "It was an historic moment—the end of an era," declared the *Tucumcari Daily News*. At one time, in the 1920s, Tucumcari had been the home station of some fifty-five mail clerks, although not all of them lived there, and six trains carrying mail passed through daily. In August 1967, after a total of sixty-four years, an RPO car attached to Rock Island passenger train Number 4 stopped at the local depot on its last run between Los Angeles and Kansas City. The only RPO clerk working out of Tucumcari was assigned temporarily to the local post office before his transfer to a similar permanent position elsewhere. In effect, the Railway Post Office cars were "the last pillar" of support for passenger trains. But mail trains with separate RPO cars carried less and less because trucks and airplanes had taken over increasing amounts of the load. As a result, by 1970 little first-class mail went by rail.[27]

In far-off Washington, DC, when certain passenger runs were axed, the

Interstate Commerce Commission indicated its approval by stating in typical bureaucratic jargon that such trains were not "required by the public convenience and necessity" and that their continuation would "unduly burden interstate commerce." In 1967 this treatment was given to two Rock Island passenger trains, Number 39 and Number 40, running between Kansas City and Tucumcari, but not before the town put up a prolonged fight in protest. The Rock Island rationalized elimination of both runs because they carried mostly mail and express shipments, which had decreased significantly, and the passenger service on both runs had dwindled to only one coach. More than thirty local residents turned up at an ICC hearing held in town in June 1965, and several appeared as witnesses against the cutbacks. After hearings held at Tucumcari as well as Topeka and Pratt, Kansas, the ICC asked the Rock Island to continue the two trains for another year. The railroad complied and then applied again for a discontinuance. Another set of hearings, including three days of testimony at Tucumcari in December 1966, dragged out the protests until the ICC's final decision axing Numbers 39 and 40 in 1967. In addition, the once-popular *Cherokee* passenger and mail run from Tucumcari to Memphis had long since disappeared by 1965; the *Choctaw*, between Amarillo and Memphis, had suffered the same fate; and the *Imperial*, between Tucumcari and Kansas City, was discontinued in 1966. Among others terminated on the T&M route, trains numbered 21 and 22 ceased operations in late 1967. At the same time that the Rock Island whittled away on passenger service to the east, the Southern Pacific waged a similar attack on runs between Tucumcari and Phoenix and Los Angeles—a campaign it also won in 1967.[28]

The details of Tucumcari's loss of the *Golden State*'s premier passenger service, as revealed in ICC hearings conducted in 1967, were even more painful for locals. At 2,762 miles in length, the Golden State Route between Chicago and Los Angeles was the longest continuous rail connection in the United States. Ever since 1902, when the jointly operated endeavor began, Tucumcari had been "a major junction point" where passenger cars, personnel, and locomotives were changed. The two partners, the Rock Island and the Southern Pacific (whose role was inherited by purchasing the El Paso & Southwestern Railroad in 1924), had maintained an "uneasy relationship." For the Rock Island, its share of the Golden State Route was a prized possession, deserving priority consideration. On the other hand, the route had considerably less standing with the SP. In the end, as the ICC hearings revealed, the nature of this uneven partnership brought a conclusion to this Los Angeles–Chicago rail connection.[29] Legendary Route 66, the highway link between the two cities, was memorialized in song, films, television, and popular culture, but the Golden State railroad route, although also providing "kicks" for a multitude of California-bound passengers, received far less attention.

At the ICC session in Tucumcari on the *Golden State*'s fate, twenty-one testified—twenty locals and one from Dalhart, a total of two more than at El Paso—and one of the most enthusiastic crowds of all the hearings turned out.[30] Two general themes emerged in this hearing. First, it was the opinion of those who spoke that the two railroads, and especially the SP, had intentionally sabotaged dining services on *Golden State* trains to rid themselves of such public transportation facilities. Some witnesses also believed that passenger trains would be profitable if the railroads placed more emphasis and spent more money on publicizing their advantages. The ICC concluded, however, that "the record would not support a finding that the carriers attempt to discourage patronage on the trains or that patronage could be increased substantially by promotional means." Second, in one way or another, the testimony contended, in the words of one witness, "that, having encouraged settlement and development of the west for their own purposes, the railroads have a moral obligation to provide [passenger] service." Another local resident stated this opinion succinctly, by saying he found "it hard to believe that the last [passenger] trains are being removed from a town built by and for the railroads."[31]

The year 1968 saw an unmatched number of earthshaking events, including the assassinations of Martin Luther King Jr. and Robert F. Kennedy and the Tet Offensive that brought the end of the Vietnam War. For Tucumcari, on a comparable scale in local history, that fateful year saw an end to the passenger train service the town had enjoyed for sixty-six years, beginning in 1902 soon after its founding. This momentous event abruptly terminated the town's easy access to Los Angeles, Kansas City, and Chicago, and, for the everyday lives of individuals, it changed a personal orientation that brought El Paso, more than three hundred miles away in Texas, "closer" than Santa Fe and Albuquerque, both less than two hundred miles from Tucumcari in the same state.

The nature of the venerable Southern Pacific–Rock Island partnership involved in the Golden State Route determined the fate of passenger service for

Tucumcari. When the ICC permitted the financially challenged Rock Island to discontinue the eastern part of the route, it meant the longstanding enterprise was doomed, and the SP closed the western segment as well. The ICC sanctioned this action in its customary death knell jargon, declaring that the Golden State Route was "not required by the public convenience and necessity" and, therefore, "Investigation discontinued." The *Golden State* passenger train made its last run through Tucumcari on February 20, 1968, and its last stop in Chicago the next day. It was the end of passenger service for Tucumcari. As long feared locally, passenger trains had gone "the way of the passenger pigeon."[32]

On the national scene, Congress created federally owned Amtrak in 1970 to take over the remnants of railroad passenger operations and partially fill the public need for this form of transportation. Tucumcari was not included on an Amtrak route. Behind the industrial rationalizations, official jargon, and statistical technicalities, the fact remained that the disappearance of the traditional passenger train was a grievous loss for the entire nation. For Tucumcari as well as countless other small towns, it resulted in the loss of the community's "absolute center of the universe," the railroad depot.[33]

The caboose, often called the conductor's castle or "crummy" became another casualty of the new era. Officially, this specially equipped railroad car was attached to trains for safety reasons. Because of all the dangers involved in the operation of railroads, the industry as a whole had always been a stickler for strict adherence to safety rules and regulations. As a result, a caboose provided protection for rear brakemen, conductors, and often a flagman when they were not performing their switching and operational duties. Before radio communication, hand and whistle signals were used between the caboose and the engineer. Realistically it was more like a home away from home where the trainmen caught a few winks of sleep, fixed meals on a coal-fired cook stove, and on occasion played dominoes and checkers. The caboose also had office space for the conductor to deal with required paperwork. Protracted negotiations in 1982 and 1985 between the railroads and the unions resulted in the virtual elimination of the caboose. For safety purposes, and reduced operational costs, it was replaced by computerized sensors. Fortunately, the Southern Pacific gave the Tucumcari Historical Museum a vintage caboose, which is among the larger exhibits on the museum grounds.[34]

The Southern Pacific branch line to Dawson, with its train called the Polly,

Railroad caboose, also known as a "crummy." These specialized railroad cars were second homes for conductors where they could relax and do their paper work. Photo by Nancy Stratton Hall.

had survived until the closure of the coal mines there in 1950. At that time the 18 miles of tracks between Dawson and French—where the Polly crossed the Santa Fe Railroad tracks from Raton to Las Vegas—were removed. The SP wanted to end operations on the remaining 114 miles of tracks between Tucumcari and French, beginning with the 45-mile connection between French and Roy.[35] But for the time being, the Polly continued to carry passengers and freight three times a week between Tucumcari and French. With the state Corporation Commission supporting their case, ranchers said they needed the Polly to ship cattle and receive supplies. The Polly had been the exclusive carrier of tank cars for the Carbonic Chemicals Company, located on the Mitchell family ranch near Solano, that pumped wells of carbon dioxide used in making dry ice. Trucks had taken over hauling most of that product. That the remaining tracks were now called the "Roy line" indicated the importance of continued service for that village as well as nearby Mosquero, the struggling county seat of Harding County. An ICC hearing resulted in an order for the SP to continue the Polly's runs. Later, the ICC relented, however, and permitted the railroad to discontinue the unprofitable service as of November 1962.[36]

As soon as the Polly made its last stop at French, a work crew immediately tore up a segment of railroad tracks, foreshadowing the removal of the rest of the line.[37] In effect, this action also symbolized the end of Tucumcari's sixty-year economic partnership with Dawson, which had been especially instrumental in the town's early development and of considerable importance in its continued prosperity. The last run of the Polly featured one of the few mixed passenger and baggage cars left in the country. It was another reminder of changing times in the railroad industry and Tucumcari's past benefits from the Dawson branch line. On October 31, 1962, the Polly ended its long operations.[38]

Between 1960 and 1970 the number of railroad employees nationwide declined by almost 30 percent, from 909,000 to 640,000.[39] Although the loss of jobs at Tucumcari had started in 1964, the years 1967 and 1968 were especially bad for drastic cuts of positions. In 1967 the Southern Pacific had a workforce of slightly more than three hundred at Tucumcari, including thirty-three clerical jobs—with the Rock Island paying for one-half of the clerical salary expense. At the beginning of the year, the SP had warned that, because of streamlining and modernization of its operations, about seventy clerical, mechanical, and yard positions would be eliminated at Tucumcari. Then, in May, the SP announced that fifteen to twenty clerical positions would be abolished immediately, with the option of transfers for those who wanted them. The clerical staff took another hit a few months later when a new computer system in El Paso made such traditional skills nearly obsolete. One of those transferred to El Paso was Democratic state representative Willie Greaser, SP switchman and local railroad union official.[40] And the onslaught had just begun.

About the same time passenger service ended at Tucumcari in 1968 the SP transferred seventy-eight operating crew members—engineers, switchmen, brakemen, conductors, and train maintenance personnel. This left some 185 SP jobs at Tucumcari and about thirty-five retiree families. Most of those transferred were sent to El Paso and others to Tucson and points in California. At the ICC hearing in Tucumcari on the elimination of passenger trains, a railway engineer's wife gave plaintive testimony describing the painful uprooting of such a large number of families and the damage caused to the local economy, particularly the real estate market.[41]

The carnage also claimed the roundhouse and its workforce. Mainly because of diesel dominance that involved locomotives requiring far less and less costly maintenance, as well as different repair facilities, the roundhouse was closed in 1968. The giant turntable and stalls for work on steam engines had become obsolete. A roundhouse foreman recalled that, in 1951, "the diesels were so new that we only had one man who knew anything about them." Now, all of the mechanical adjustments for diesels were done in El Paso. In one devastating blow, Tucumcari lost 105 shopmen's jobs. And in short order the impressive roundhouse was demolished, leaving a conspicuous gap where it had stood for more than half a century. According to a longtime railroader, "the only trace" left to mark the location was a plot of "weedy concrete."[42]

The decade of the 1970s proved to be an especially difficult time for the railroad industry, and for Tucumcari as well. Even though no more passenger trains stopped, freight crews checked in and out of the depot, members of a small clerical staff worked around the clock there, and track and signal maintenance crews operated from the premises. The trainmaster also had an office in the depot. The Rock Island, which, as usual, tottered on the edge of bankruptcy, had not shown a profit since 1967, and had lost more than $100 million since then. It lost $23 million in 1974 alone, and employees were warned of layoffs unless they took voluntary wage cuts. After approval from the Interstate Commerce Commission for a merger with the Union Pacific, the deal stalled, and finally fizzled, over questions about the Rock Island's prospects of eventual profitability. Disintegration of the Rock Island seemed at hand. The railroad's service area and demographics mainly explained its impending demise. Spread out over fourteen states, most of them in the Midwest, the Rock Island depended largely on hauling agricultural commodities and serving a rural population for its freight revenues. The Midwestern rural population, however, was declining and, along with the altered economic realities of the period, including the steadily reduced count of major industries on the Rock Island lines—small in number to begin with—the Rock Island's doom was sealed. In short, as one scholarly economist puts it, "The Rock Island was too long, too lightly trafficked, and too dependent on agricultural origination that was open to competition from ICC-exempt truckers."[43]

Local railroaders and other residents paid especially close attention to the disposition of Rock Island tracks to Kansas City, or what was known as the

"Tucumcari line." The fate of the Rock Island itself was hardly a major concern; the overnight stays of crews operating between Tucumcari and Dalhart, who changed locomotives in the local yards, were about the only reminders of that railroad's presence. What did matter was the Southern Pacific's interest in the Golden State Route from Los Angeles as far as Kansas City, with the crucial connection at Tucumcari, where the SP and the Rock Island met to make a through line. Strangely enough, the Santa Fe Railroad, which already had a Chicago connection through Kansas City, also had designs on this link and opposed the SP bid—mostly for strategic reasons, not altogether for a through traffic link. A delegation of mid-level executives from SP headquarters in San Francisco explained what was at stake. If the Santa Fe won, it would, in all likelihood, abandon at least part of the 673-mile route, thereby bypassing Tucumcari at Vaughn, and, with its existing line via Clovis and Amarillo, have the only through connection between Los Angeles and Kansas City. The effect on railroad employment at Tucumcari, and on SP operations generally, the rail officials said, would be disastrous.[44]

Locals went to work imploring the Interstate Commerce Commission and New Mexico's congressional delegations to give favorable consideration to the SP's cause and the seventy families dependent on the railroad's $1.8 million local payroll, as well as the $50,271.07 in taxes paid annually by the two railroads.[45] As it happened, two SP executives in the thick of the Santa Fe acquisition hailed from Tucumcari and had started their railroader careers as brakemen in the local yards. SP vice president of operations Richard D. Spence revealed in a nationally syndicated newspaper interview that the SP had made an offer to the Rock Island for the Tucumcari-Kansas City link and was waiting for a response. Without predicting the effects on his old hometown, he did say that "dozens of towns and grain elevators in the West" would suffer if the Santa Fe won out. Lawrence F. Furlow Jr., in the contracts department at SP headquarters in San Francisco, was also closely associated with this issue, and remained so until the SP later took over the Rock Island. By that time Spence had moved on to greener pastures.[46]

After the Santa Fe's bid for the Tucumcari Line failed, the Rock Island went into receivership for the third time in 1975. Four years later, the ICC gave temporary authorization to the SP—actually its subsidiary the St. Louis Southwestern Railway, or "Cotton Belt"—to operate over the Rock Island's Tucumcari line between the Pecos River and Kansas City and beyond to St. Louis. On June 10, 1980, the ICC approved the outright sale of the Tucumcari line to the SP-Cotton Belt for $57 million. The Southern Pacific subsidiary had begun operations out of Tucumcari on March 24, 1980.[47] Soon afterward, the SP began extensive restoration and repair work on the tracks between Tucumcari and Topeka, Kansas. As completed, the renewed tracks enabled the SP "to offer competitive rail service to and from Southern California via the Kansas City gateway." As a result, these improvements created more than two hundred temporary construction jobs from Tucumcari east to Topeka. Among the advantages of the SP's acquisition of the new trackage and its subsequent improvements, it became possible to deliver refrigerated West Coast fruit and vegetables to Chicago-area markets by piggyback trains on the third day of shipment.[48]

While SP control of this additional trackage benefitted Tucumcari, the loss of another rail connection had the opposite effect. Streamlining and modernization were the watch words of the 1970s for the railroad industry. In this context reform of the federal regulatory system enforced by the Interstate Commerce Commission seemed inevitable. The main result of this sentiment was deregulation in the Staggers Rail Act of 1980, which had the distinction of including the name of the bill's sponsor, Representative Harley O. Staggers of West Virginia, in the official title of the act. In general, the Staggers Act allowed railroads more freedom to manage their affairs, particularly in setting freight rates charged shippers and in providing or terminating service. As described in a trade publication, the Staggers Act did not free railroads from federal control, but "it left little regulation in place." In fact, the Surface Transportation Board, which replaced the ICC in 1996, was given relatively little of the regulatory power originally wielded by its predecessor.[49]

As a result of the newfound freedom in the Staggers Act, some rail lines that might have facilitated the subsequent increase of freight traffic were hastily ripped up and the rights of way abandoned. The Choctaw Route between Amarillo and Memphis had been an important Rock Island main line for both freight traffic and passenger service. Its extension from Amarillo to Tucumcari, formally the Tucumcari and Memphis Railway, or locally called the T&M, gave the Rock Island transcontinental service through the Southern Pacific. The last train from Amarillo on the T&M tracks arrived at Tucumcari on March 28, 1980, and the tracks collected weeds thereafter awaiting their removal. No longer in use, the T & M rails—233 miles of them as far as Erick, Oklahoma—were torn up and sold for scrap. Elsewhere, other segments of Choctaw tracks were removed and the rights of way abandoned, effectively dismembering the route. Some critics have bemoaned the destruction of the freight shortcut provided by the Choctaw Route between Amarillo and Memphis, which, with the T&M–SP connection at Tucumcari, served transcontinental traffic. On the other hand, another group of rail specialists contends that such action helped promote the industry's long-term goal of the "economies of density." This approach promised increased efficiency and profitability through the elimination of maintenance and operational costs of unnecessary branch lines, allowing the concentration of freight traffic elsewhere. Removal of the T & M tracks from Tucumcari as far as Amarillo could be explained, but not justified by this view, if the tracks between Amarillo and Memphis had remained intact.[50]

In the continual war of nerves inflicted on Tucumcari, as if the discontinuance of passenger service, the wholesale transfers of railroad personnel, and the loss of the roundhouse were not enough, rumors continually circulated that divisional operations would be shifted elsewhere. It all focused on the sixty-mile stub of Rock Island tracks between Tucumcari and Santa Rosa, which had been owned by the Rock Island but controlled by other railroads to reach the Dawson coalfields. With the Dawson mines no longer in operation, and the branch line from Tucumcari removed, the stub could logically be incorporated into the main line and the division point changed to Santa Rosa, the original termination of the Rock Island.[51] The threats of shifting divisional operations to Santa Rosa never materialized but were still numbered among the calamities, real and rumored, that plagued Tucumcari during the 1960s.

The nagging question that mystified Tucumcari and the national railroad industry as well was how the venerable Southern Pacific Railroad, the third-largest US corporation of the 1950s—in league with the likes of Standard Oil, General Motors, and United States Steel—could fall apart in the relatively short span of thirty years or so. Its territory, linked together by 13,000 miles of tracks, stretched from Portland, Oregon, in the north into Mexico in the south, and from Los Angeles to Tucumcari as well as New Orleans. The SP had 60,000 employees, annual operating revenues of $500 million, assets of more than $1.82 billion, and property in California and the West larger than the state of Connecticut. In company terminology this vast western domain was the "Golden

1949 Air View West   Tucumcari, New Mexico

Aerial view of railroad yards looking east with the roundhouse a prominent feature. LeDeane Studio.

Empire." As the problem had always been, however, the SP was a railroad "looking for a destination" because it did not "particularly arrive anywhere." Acquisition of the Rock Island line from Tucumcari to Kansas City and control of the Cotton Belt tracks to St. Louis would only partially alleviate this shortcoming.[52]

As late as the 1970s, a special edition of the popular railroad trade publication, *Trains*, displayed these captions on its cover: "The decade that changed everything" and below, "SP in its prime." In that decade and immediately afterward, however, a shifting national economy and a virtual revolution in the railroad industry, including mergers and bankruptcies of old-line giants, caused unsettling economic conditions. Attempting to adapt and protect its financial stability, the SP had taken the decisive action of diversifying by investment of its profits in high-priced real estate, trucking, telecommunications, mining, energy production, forestry, and pipelines. At the same time, the SP depended too heavily on servicing smokestack industries, such as steel plants and other big manufacturing concerns, many of which closed. By the 1980s its "traditional mother lode" of perishable fruit and vegetables had been lost to trucks and airplanes, and the traffic in lumber and auto parts declined. It relied too long on old-fashioned boxcars, with comparatively higher profits, although it did shift belatedly to flatcars that piggybacked truck trailers but reaped smaller charges.[53] Likewise, the SP was slow in making the transition to intermodal containers. As one critic declares, "It just turned out that intermodal made so much sense that it overcame management ineptitude." On the other hand, the Santa Fe adopted intermodals early on and survived many pitfalls of the day. The decisions made during the relatively long dictatorial reigns of two successive board chairmen, Donald J. Russell and Benjamin F. Biaggini, have also drawn criticism. It was said of Biaggini that he had the "prescience good enough to see 10 years into the future, but not good enough to see 20."[54]

At Tucumcari in the 1970s, Southern Pacific freights still changed crews at the depot, but since the elimination of firemen and most brakemen, as well as cabooses, fewer railroaders checked in there. In 1991 a federal ruling approved only two-member crews of an engineer and a conductor for through freight trains—an action that cost 25,000 jobs nationwide. Previously, five-person crews had been customary, including an engineer, a conductor, two brakemen, and a fireman. And computers in El Paso had completely displaced the clerical staff at Tucumcari. These circumstances reflected one more set of external forces, which Tucumcari neither originated nor controlled, that determined the town's fate.

Proud and aristocratic, the SP was reluctant to accept the necessity of the merger craze. But the Union Pacific dropped a bombshell with the announcement that it had acquired the Western Pacific Railroad, with its operations between Ogden, Utah, and San Francisco. This meant that the UP would no longer exchange freight cars with the SP at Ogden, with the result of a 75 percent loss of business on the SP's Overland Route between Ogden and the SP line in Oregon. With a change of heart on mergers, the SP attempted combined operations with the Santa Fe in the mid-1980s. After delaying for three years, however, the ICC unexpectedly denied the merger on the basis that it was monopolistic, and also probably because of the Santa Fe's arrogance in not wanting to grant any concessions to competing lines. During the prolonged Southern Pacific–Santa Fe joint arrangement, paint jobs on locomotives had included lettering representing both railroads, caused wags to joke later that "SPSF" really stood for "Shouldn't Paint So Fast."[55]

Then next, like "swallowing a whale," the much smaller Denver & Rio Grande Western Railroad "adopted" the Southern Pacific when the D&RGW owner, Colorado billionaire Philip F. Anschutz's Rio Grande Industries, purchased the SP for $1.8 billion in 1988. The two railroads operated jointly as the Southern Pacific, but for most purposes both actually kept and used their traditional names. That was hardly the end of the SP's mergers. In a time replete with such changes, the ICC's successor, the Surface Transportation Board, approved the Union Pacific's acquisition of the Southern Pacific on September 11, 1996. The UP had a voracious appetite for gobbling up other railroads, most recently, the Missouri Pacific, Western Pacific, Chicago and Northwestern, and now, as a package deal, the Southern Pacific along with the Denver & Rio Grande Western. Such conspicuous consumption probably pleased the Santa Fe stockholders but caused near chaos in the new system's operations.

Now it was hardly the minnow swallowing a whale, but more like the indigestion caused by a monster consuming an ox whole. Eager to reap savings from obtaining the SP and the other mergers, the UP cut back on operations at strategic points on the newly acquired lines. Soon there was a rippling effect throughout the UP system that caused bottlenecks for freight traffic much the same as automobiles jammed up on a freeway. In fact, the shock waves spread out to other railroads. As a rail analyst observed, one company's dilemmas "in a network industry like railroading" might quickly become everybody's problems. After a couple of years bogged down in a "service crisis," the UP had recovered enough to launch a major capital upgrading program that included $14 million for "the former SP Tucumcari line." The objective was to improve "time-sensitive traffic" between California and the Middle West. When the UP absorbed its new acquisition, the SP's name and identity were erased and the palatial headquarters at One Market Plaza in the heart of the old San Francisco business district was closed permanently.[56]

The fate of Tucumcari in the resulting Union Pacific chaos became a simple matter of mathematics and geographical location. In the new division designation from El Paso to Dalhart, the distance between El Paso and Tucumcari was 331 miles, with only 93 more miles to Dalhart. Under the Rock Island, separate operating crews had made the relatively short 93-mile run from Dalhart to the division point at Tucumcari, where a Southern Pacific crew took over to Carrizozo (187 miles), and another unit ran to El Paso (144 miles). During the confusion after the Union Pacific absorbed the Southern Pacific, the UP renewed "the railroad presence in Tucumcari," temporarily as it turned out, by bringing back sixty-five operating crew members and their families. Since diesel locomotives could operate farther without stopping than steam locomotives, UP executives reasoned that a Tucumcari-to-El Paso run seemed possible. This distance had one serious drawback, not because the diesels failed to make it, but because federal regulations at that time allowed train crews to work only twelve hours without an eight-hour rest. The cost of repeatedly stopping trains wherever the twelve-hour shift ended and transporting substitute crews to that spot was regarded by the UP as excessive. As a result, the UP decided to cover the distance between El Paso and Dalhart with one crew change at Vaughn (i.e., Dalhart to Vaughn, 195 miles, and Vaughn to El Paso, 229 miles). These mathematical calculations, which satisfied both diesel locomotives and federal regulations, simply left Tucumcari out of consideration as a crew changing point.[57]

The twenty-first century had barely dawned when, in 2001, the last crew change took place at Tucumcari. The UP pulled out the last railroad personnel assigned there—engineers, brakemen, and track crews, along with their families—taking with them a payroll estimated at $4 million. A town official stated the obvious, saying: "It hurt the real estate market. It hurt taxes." In short, the UP's failed Tucumcari-to-El Paso run involving sixty-five operating crew positions, caused a great deal of handwringing over the historic railroad presence in Tucumcari but with few positive results.[58] All too soon the only evidence of the town's past railroad prominence would be fifteen to twenty freight trains speeding through daily, emblazoned with the bright red-white-and-blue Union Pacific shield, as they whipped past the deserted depot and the vacant site of the demolished roundhouse. A UP official blandly warned locals that freight trains would be going "straight through" town at 60 miles an hour with no stops. People at Tucumcari were accustomed to seeing trains stop at the depot and slow down at grade crossings, the railroad representative acknowledged, but from now on they had better get used to faster rail traffic.[59] At the turn of the century not railroads but agriculture—farming and ranching—became the mainstay in the town's struggle to overcome its "way-station" image.

During the three decades following the end of World War II, while Tucumcari wrestled with highway and railroad problems, the town had also paid attention to other transportation events and trends. In 1967 traditional political protocol and the committee assignments of Congressman Thomas G. Morris of Tucumcari had an unusual payoff for the town.[60] The first navy hydrofoil to use water-jet propulsion, a $4 million patrol gunboat prototype developed for experimental purposes, was officially designated the *Tucumcari* (PGH-2). Sometimes called a "flying boat" and classed as the successor of the famous PT boats, the hydrofoil had no propeller but operated on a gasoline-turbine pumping system that sucked water in at back and jetted it out underneath "like a super fire hose" at a rate of one hundred tons a minute. This action caused the vessel to rise five or six feet in the air, and, gliding on three leg-like struts with submerged foils, reach speeds around 50 miles an hour. On July 15, 1967, at Seattle, with a large delegation from Tucumcari looking on, Yetta Kohn Bidegain of Montoya christened the vessel with a bottle of New Mexico water provided by Governor David Cargo.[61]

After the launching ceremony and shake-down test cruises, the crew of thirteen took the seventy-one-foot long, twenty-one-foot-beamed, sixty-ton *Tucumcari* for a tour of combat patrol duty in Vietnam waters. It was armed with twin .50 caliber machine guns on either side, a 40-mm gun on the bow, and an 81-mm mortar at the stern. Then, the Tucumcari was piggybacked aboard its larger support vessel, the USS *Wood County*, for a seven-month deployment in European waters where the craft conducted demonstrations and joint operations before several NATO naval delegations. To match the Soviet Union's latest prototype, a NATO armaments team chose certain features of the *Tucumcari* as requirements for the NATO hydrofoil program.[62]

The vessel had collided with a log in Puget Sound during early tests, which caused serious damage that required major repairs. While cruising off the coast of Puerto Rico in 1972, however, the *Tucumcari* ended active naval service when it ran aground on a reef. In the blasting for removal, it was damaged beyond repair. Miscellaneous memorabilia were at first stored in the local library, then transferred to the Tucumcari Historical Museum, and finally displayed at the convention center.[63]

Over the decades, the train station provided other entertainment to the townspeople as Tucumcari was no stranger to visiting celebrities. During the 1932 presidential election, a crowd estimated at 3,000 greeted Republican incumbent President Herbert Hoover at the local depot as he campaigned the traditional way, standing and waving on the rear platform of his special railroad

USS *Tucumcari*. This US Navy hydrofoil vessel was supposed to serve in the
same role as the famous World War
II PT boat, but it had relatively brief
prominence. Ajax News & Feature
Service / Alamy Stock Photo (Image
ID: PEKP4M).

passenger car. Suggestive of the differences ahead in her husband's New Deal
programs, Eleanor Roosevelt stopped off in an airplane at the local airport long
enough to talk with a small group.[64] In 1940 Hollywood movie star James
Stewart spent twenty-four hours in town when his bright yellow monoplane
made an unscheduled stop at the local airport because of weather conditions.[65]
Later that year a large crowd headed by motel owner and Notre Dame football
player-alum George Lins met a special Fighting Irish streamliner train on the
way for a game in Los Angeles with USC. The high school band was on hand
to play the Notre Dame fight song, and Coach Jimmy Rudd took the Rattler
team aboard the passenger cars to shake hands with the players. By chance the
Hollywood film *Knute Rockne, All-American*, about the famous Notre Dame
player and coach killed in a plane crash in 1931, was being shown at the Princess
Theater. On a couple of occasions, major league baseball teams on passenger
trains stopped over in town and played each other on the local diamond.[66] In
1950, during a fifteen-minute stop of the *Golden State* passenger train, a crowd

of between 1,500 and 2,000 gave "a tumultuous welcome" at the depot to singing cowboy Roy Rogers, his wife Dale Evans, John Wayne, and other Hollywood notables on their way to the premier of the film *Rock Island Trail* in Des
Moines, Iowa. The Quay County Sheriff's Posse made Rogers an honorary
member and gave him a badge. Peter Fonda and Dennis Hopper, along with
sixteen production crew members, stayed overnight in the Circle S Motel while
going to Taos to film scenes of *Easy Rider*. Even an Elvis sighting was reported,
although there was no convincing evidence to confirm the King's actual presence in town.[67] With air travel becoming more popular, however, celebrity-
watching at the train station became much less rewarding.

A longer encounter with celebrities came in the late 1950s with the filming
around Tucumcari of the long-running CBS television Western series *Rawhide*,
starring a budding actor named Clint Eastwood as Rowdy Yates. The highly
popular series, filmed in black-and-white, aired for eight seasons, beginning in
January 1959. It featured a band of cowboys on the fabled Long Drive of the
1860s, taking a herd of cattle from San Antonio, Texas, to the railhead at
Sedalia, Missouri. In a supporting role, bearded Paul Brinegar, who was born
in Tucumcari but left after high school graduation, played cranky drover cook
George Washington Wishbone.[68] Five complete episodes and stock film of
enough for a sixth—all shown the first year of the series in 1959—were shot on
the Spade Ranch north of town. Ranch cowhands sometimes got in the action
as extras, with one playing a cowboy in an episode and an Indian in another.
The cast and crew of sixty-five were in town for six weeks, staying in local
motels and the Conchas Hotel and frequenting Del's Restaurant.[69] Famous for
his jukebox hit "The Purple People-Eater," Sheb Wooley, who played scout Pete
Nolan, visited with an old family friend who had known the Wooleys back in
Erick, Oklahoma. It was rumored that so many smitten local damsels tried to
interrupt the sleep of Clint Eastwood, in his big break as an actor, that he had
to call the police for relief.

During the year 1959, Tucumcari fairly buzzed with Hollywood filming
activity. For several days in February, the thirty-member cast and crew of the
drug-trafficking movie *Switchblade*, starring Robert Hutton, shot scenes in and
around Tucumcari. In addition, the song "Tucumcari" was recorded as a single
by the popular young singer Jimmie Rogers, who in his career had thirteen
number one hits and sold over sixty million records. "Tucumcari" made

Paul Brinegar, born in Tucumcari, portrayed the cook George Washington Wishbone in the CBS TV series *Rawhide* of the 1950s, about a late nineteenth-century cattle long drive. Early episodes of the series were filmed on a ranch near Tucumcari. Courtesy of Darel Greene.

Billboard's Hot 100 list in September, staying there for nine weeks. Rogers did a TV guest appearance on the *Jimmy Durante Show*, and with simulated desert scenery in the background as he walked along on a treadmill, sang his way to "Tucumcari."[70]

In the "Brave New World" that emerged after the Second World War, fascination with the speed of travel by air and the opportunity it offered to visit distant places became a national fixation. Now even small, remote towns expected to have airline service.[71] These postwar expectations by Tucumcari were fulfilled temporarily by Pioneer Airlines of Dallas, Texas. Originally Essar Airways, the carrier changed its name to Pioneer Airlines soon after the war ended. When the federal Civil Aeronautics Board authorized the creation of feeder or local service airlines, Pioneer increased its routes in Texas and expanded into New Mexico. At the peak of operations, Pioneer Airlines served twenty towns and cities in Texas and seven in New Mexico, including Albuquerque, Clovis, Las Cruces, Las Vegas, Roswell, Santa Fe, and Tucumcari.

The inauguration of Pioneer Airlines service at Tucumcari on April 21, 1948, to begin passenger, airmail, express, air freight, and air parcel connections was greeted with the fanfare approaching a Fourth of July celebration. A Boy Scout troop helped direct traffic, and the Sheriff's Posse, dressed in Western attire and mounted on prancing steeds, paraded through the crowd. A typically wicked southwestern sandstorm, with winds reaching 45 miles an hour, blew across the airport tarmac as the *Kit Carson* and *Mirabeau Lamar*, two twin-engine Pioneer airliners, "swooped to a graceful landing" with governors of the two states aboard—Beauford Jester of Texas and Thomas J. Mabry of New Mexico. Following elaborate ceremonies, the two airliners boarded capacity loads of locals for courtesy flights circling the town. Then, the official party accompanied by four local business leaders took off for a repeat inaugural performance in Albuquerque.[72]

A local ground crew of three agents became a fixture at the airport, and war surplus, twin-engine C-47s, rechristened as civilian Douglas DC-3s, started making regular calls. Initially four flights landed and took off daily at Tucumcari. On its eastbound morning and afternoon flights to Dallas, scheduled stops included Clovis and four Texas cities, and two westbound flights out of Tucumcari to Albuquerque included stops at Las Vegas and Santa Fe. In its first year Pioneer agents processed about one thousand passengers, of whom half boarded locally. More than five tons of mail had been loaded and an even greater weight unloaded in that time, or, to put it in numbers, Tucumcari residents had mailed 294,000 letters and received 310,000 on Pioneer flights. In addition, Pioneer handled 2,000 pounds of air express items and 7,500 pounds of air freight shipments. Santa Claus arrived that year aboard a Pioneer flight, and the airline sponsored a performance by a magician, who otherwise served as the airline's district manager. Commenting that Pioneer was providing "excellent service in all phases of air transportation," the *Daily News* editor commented that the airline's performance had been "even better than we had expected."[73]

Local boosters, satisfied that the airport was at last fulfilling long-held expectations for it, claimed that an average of sixty airline passengers a day stopped off there and, in addition, as many as fifty private and charter planes landed there daily. That more aviation gasoline was sold at the airport than anywhere else in New Mexico except Albuquerque only proved its importance. After three years at Tucumcari, however, Pioneer reduced its service by 50 percent, with an airline official saying that the reason was declining local business, adding that "some service is better than none." In fact, reports that the airline might suspend local service altogether had started surfacing in March 1950, and by August 1953 the flight schedule was down to one roundtrip daily. The stay of Pioneer in Tucumcari, which began in 1948, was relatively brief and came to an end in 1953. The airline itself disappeared when it merged with Continental Airlines in 1955.[74] After the departure of Pioneer Airlines, the municipal airport only hosted spasmodic air service in later years.[75] In the early 1970s, Trans Central Airlines, a fledging commuter operation, linked Tucumcari with such larger air terminals as Amarillo, Albuquerque, and El Paso. It provided passenger and air freight service to several small towns and cities in New Mexico and Texas with nine-seat, twin-engine planes. When Interstate 40 opened, catching a flight out of Amarillo or Albuquerque became the most logical option for air travel.[76] Over the years the Federal Aviation Authority made improvements and based a crew of six or more technicians at the municipal airport to operate the air navigation and informational equipment installed there. The FAA also maintained a unit at Mesa Rica near Conchas Dam. Beginning in 1992, the Rotary Club sponsored a popular annual air show at the airport. In a typical show, forty planes would be on display, on the ground and in the sky, including a Japanese Zero and a US twin fuselage P-38, one of the fastest aircraft in World War II. Sure crowd-pleasers would include exhibitions by the US Navy's Leap Frog Parachute Team as well as military formations flown by the 9-jet Canadian Snowbirds and those of the US Army or Navy. Famous figures associated with flight, such as astronaut Frank Borman, attended the event. At the fourteenth show, in 2006, an experienced Oklahoma pilot, also a physician, was killed when he crashed his German-made, single-engine plane in full view of the crowd while making a looping aerial maneuver. The rest of the day's program and festivities planned for the evening were cancelled, and the show was not held on a regular basis afterward.[77]

Transportation interest and excitement around Tucumcari climaxed, or anticlimaxed, with the unsolved mystery of the day—Unidentified Flying Objects (UFOs), sometimes called flying saucers. As early as 1949, multiple sightings of the same object, including reports by a Tucumcari police officer, the Montoya postmaster, and a local newspaper editor, were recorded by an unofficial national UFO register. The image with a vapor trail, described as yellow-amber-orange in color and somewhat smaller than a moon, reportedly moved slowly across the sky, at first wiggling slightly but then making two or three steep dives before leveling off in a blaze of white light and disappearing without making a sound or leaving a vapor trail.[78] In April 1965, several people reported seeing a low-flying object, usually of three or four different colors, flash across the night sky. A railroad switching crew said they saw an orange and blue blaze of light flying toward Clovis. A family on the road north of San Jon had a similar experience, with a three-year-old passenger exclaiming as the object sped by, "Ooh, Grandma's car lighted up!" Military officials at Cannon Air Force Base in Clovis refused to comment on the phenomenon, and a local newspaper columnist dismissed the question as a secret government experiment that nobody needed to know about.[79] Earlier, Roswell had gained lasting fame from a weather balloon that crashed on a nearby ranch. Conspiracy junkies quickly turned the incident into a monstrous government coverup involving an alien spacecraft whose extraterritorial beings were held in secret captivity.[80]

A celestial mystery even closer to home supposedly claimed a major city water storage tank. In mid-December 1951, less than two weeks before Christmas, the big, ground-level tank near the downtown business district collapsed just before dawn, killing four people and injuring three more. A three-million-gallon flood, three blocks wide, and neck-deep in some places, destroyed two businesses, a city warehouse, and fifteen adobe homes. It reached but did not damage the Southern Pacific tracks and other railroad facilities. At first popular speculation favored sabotage, an earthquake, or a mysterious fireball—possibly a meteorite—as the cause. An early-rising resident living across the street reported: "I saw a light streak across the sky and land close to the tank," and continued, "It hit with a roar, and then there was the sound of the tank breaking open." Other witnesses also said they saw a fireball plunge to earth beside the round, steel, 30-foot-high tank just before it exploded. A University of New Mexico scientist observed, however, that a meteor would not bear a flame all the way to earth and that a crater would remain behind where it struck. No crater could be found. A later investigation by professional engineers concluded that the secondhand tank, originally constructed for oil storage, was not suitable to hold water, and also failed because it was improperly welded when re-erected. The city had obtained the tank as surplus material after its use in the construction of Conchas Dam.[81]

On a more worldly level, a decidedly small-scale travel enterprise originated in the town itself. Dominative Roy Smith, the erstwhile hustling, bustling Chamber of Commerce manager, and before that, local postmaster, had always been at the forefront in seizing new transportation opportunities. While Chamber manager, he and his wife Grace, a Civil Service postal clerk, probably became the first locals to make a long-distance commercial airline flight when he attended a national convention in California. Later he donned a driver's cap and introduced the first authentic bus service in Tucumcari. Smith himself often piloted one of the two buses on a scheduled route around town or took groups to distant cities for special events. Smith soon sold his interest in the floundering bus line, and it became another failed transportation enterprise at Tucumcari.[82]

In summary, the transportation history of Tucumcari included passenger train service that had become available in 1902 but ended in 1968. The Southern Pacific absorbed the Rock Island, vacated its own operations at the local terminal, then returned, but only briefly. In measured succession, the Union Pacific took over the SP and pulled out of town, ending the railroad presence. Regular national bus service started in the late 1920s and continued on. Airline and trucking companies came and went. In the end Union Pacific freights whipped through town without stopping and automobile traffic roared around the outskirts on Interstate 40 at 75 miles an hour. It had been quite a ride for a town created on the prairie from scratch by a railroad.

Chapter 8

LIVING WITH THE BYPASS

ity Commissioner King Aitken, waxing philosophical as he peered into the future, quoted Charles Dickens's *A Tale of Two Cities* to express his mood: "It was the best of times, it was the worst of times . . . it was the spring of hope, it was the winter of despair." In 1974 Aitken saw clearly what lay ahead—and what should be done about it. "The completion within the next 10 years of the Highway bypass around the City," Aitken declared, "will necessitate rethinking and relocation of businesses which serve the traveler, and even more importantly, the local customer."[1] A few years later in 1989, the Hollywood film classic *Field of Dreams*, starring Kevin Costner, had the same message, which it contributed to American everyday life in a famous, although mangled, quotation, "If you build it, they will come."[2] In the plot an Iowa farmer hears a voice telling him that if he builds a baseball diamond in his cornfield, the legendary Joseph J. "Shoeless Joe" Jackson will return and play a game there. And that is exactly what happens. The Tucumcari business community might have taken the advice of Commissioner Aitken and this well-known film quotation in adopting a strategy for the Interstate 40 Bypass but it did not.

The original town site company, with the unswerving objective of attaching itself to the transportation center of that time, had obtained land surrounding the railroad depot and established an adjacent business district at the Second and Main Streets intersection. After World War II, a new commercial district appeared along Route 66 in town as many businesses joined the motels, cafes, and service stations there. In effect, the center of business activity shifted from the old downtown to the new transportation magnet. Then came Interstate 40. As one well-traveled California tourist recalls: "One day you took your life in your hands when you tried to cross 66. The day after it was bypassed, you could lie down in the middle of 66 and not be run over."[3] At that time, transplanting businesses from Route 66 to the bypass, traditional stores as well as motels, restaurants, and service stations, might have been the logical option. However, only a scattering of old-line commercial venues appeared there—and most were chain operations, not locally owned. Instead, Tucumcari concentrated on urban renewal and Main Street projects that would entice motorists to pull off the freeway and visit the old business district. In effect, it was an attempt to turn back the clock and restore a moribund business district and an abandoned train depot. What would have happened if the town's attention had been focused on the development of a new business district at the I-40 Bypass is only a matter of speculation, not part of the corporeal record.[4]

A news item in September 2002 states the case simply: "When you mention Tucumcari, N. M. (pop. 5,989) longtime residents say you're likely to hear one of the following: I've driven through there, I've broken down there, or I've spent the night there." Tucumcari boosters liked to say that the population had topped 10,000 or even 12,000 people in the town's heyday. That was never the case. The population reached its peak of 8,419 people in 1950.[5] The boosters now faced the daunting challenge of trying to change Tucumcari's "way-station image" and boost a population that had been "steadily shrinking since the 1950s," and especially so since the 1980s after the Interstate 40 Bypass.

Even before the bypass, but when it was on the way, signs of dissatisfaction with Tucumcari's progress began to surface. About the time of Commissioner Aitken's futuristic advice, the town's mayor was fed up with public apathy, and in his letter of resignation in October 1975 he included an analysis of the town's economic ills:

> We presently have a very flat economy, [with] many people dependent on Retirement income, Social Security, Welfare, and other very limited monies . . . Tucumcari cannot continue to support itself strictly from within and on very expensive taxpayer produced dollars. [We are going] down the "Social Welfare Road" that cannot be reversed.[6]

This description of Tucumcari's income base would remain valid to plague the town for years to come, long after the Interstate 40 Bypass opened.

Only a few years later, City Manager Ray Hohstadt gave an optimistic report on Tucumcari's economic prospects, belittling those folks who had considered things so dismal they thought "the town was going to dry up and blow away." The reason for Hohstadt's belief that the public attitude had changed from negative to positive was obvious. In his view, big national trucking companies, whose semitrucks and trailers frequented I-40, had moved into town to replace the railroads and save the day. Hohstadt might have mentioned that Navajo Truck Lines had maintained a terminal at Tucumcari for several years but reduced its operations to an agency status in 1961.[7] Another early indication of the importance of trucking was the sizable Shipley-Philips Tucumcari Truck Terminal that had been in business since 1958. In fact, the firm opened an expanded million-dollar-plus truck stop in 1975. It occupied more than eighteen acres and was considered "the premier truck stop in New Mexico on the basis of sales volume and facilities." The "Triple T," as it was called, had fueling stations for both gasoline and diesel that served five hundred rigs on some days and reputedly always kept a million gallons of fuel on hand. As early as 1975, the Shipley operation was one of the top twenty privately held companies in the state, having expanded in New Mexico and spread into Arizona. The firm employed sixty-five people locally—and more during the summer rush season—with an annual payroll of $650,000.[8]

Motor freight carriers such as Red Ball had operated out of Tucumcari earlier, but the first of the big trucking companies to stay for several years, Yellow Freight, arrived in town with thirty-three drivers in July 1977. A year-and-a-half later the company had about fifty drivers and expected to continue expanding its operations. Most of the additional drivers had been hired locally. At first the regular Yellow Freight runs out of Tucumcari shuttled freight to Albuquerque, and the drivers returned home the next day with a load, but later an additional leg was added to El Paso. Because of a shortage of suitable housing locally, some transferred drivers made short-term lodging arrangements with the Pow Wow or another motel.[9]

After Yellow Freight, other big trucking firms started establishing terminals or relay stations, usually the latter, on the outskirts near Route 66. Los Angeles–based Transcon Lines, one the ten largest motor freight concerns in the country, was ushered into town with pomp and fanfare not seen since the inauguration of Pioneer Airlines thirty years earlier. The *Quay County Sun* put out a special supplement with ads from local businesses welcoming the trucking firm.[10] Consolidated Freight Lines with 102 drivers and 10 staff members followed

Transcon, as did the Ryder line and the Missouri-Nebraska Express, a long-haul carrier based in St. Joseph, Missouri. Missouri-Nebraska differed from other trucking concerns by using a single 48-foot trailer with two drivers in the cab on runs averaging 1,200 to 1,400 miles. This firm negotiated with the local community vocational college for a truck-driving program to supply its needs.[11]

Once Tucumcari became a popular truck stop, independent truckers who owned their rigs, or hired out to someone who did, began moving their families into town, and an unaffiliated entrepreneur constructed the big Grant Fueling Center. Later, another truck servicing facility, the $2 million Coronado Center, was constructed adjacent to the Grant operation. This installation, intended to appeal to the general public as well as truckers, included more than one hundred dormitory-style motel rooms, a restaurant, convenience store, and a large parking lot for trucks and cars. Increasingly, luxurious truck stops, as differentiated from company terminals and relay stations, continued to be built at Tucumcari, even after a major exodus of trucking companies. In 2007 Love's ushered in a new $4.5 million facility with more amenities than its earlier travel stop, which had opened in 1991. At the same time, Flying J's $6 million establishment seemed to offer all that a trucker or tourist could ever dream of or imagine.[12]

By April 1994, the impact of truck lines on the local economy became readily apparent. Consolidated Freightways and Yellow Freight, along with three independent truck terminals, were listed among the major employers in Quay County.[13] It soon became evident, however, that the trucking companies and their drivers did not fit as well into the local community as the railroads and the railroaders. The railroads, in their heyday, had been the heart and soul of the town, while the trucking presence seemed shadowy and remote—as well as ephemeral, here today, but perhaps gone tomorrow. And to put it plainly, the truck drivers were a strange breed. For one thing, by the 1970s, about one-fourth of the drivers were women, and a husband-wife combination sharing the driving was not uncommon then, and more so now.[14] The truckers were like their railway counterparts in one way, however; both were strong believers in unions. For the drivers, it was the upstart International Brotherhood of Teamsters, which had quickly become powerful after the Second World War under the leadership of brash James R. "Jimmy" Hoffa. It had not helped the truckers' image when Hoffa went to prison essentially for his alleged mob connections.[15]

On the other hand, the longstanding, relatively conservative railway unions and brotherhoods claimed the allegiance of the railroaders. True, the railroaders were identifiable in town because they had good, regular paychecks spent locally, bought not Fords, Chevrolets, or Plymouths but a new Oldsmobile or Buick every three years, and sent their kids to college. Otherwise, they lived pretty much like everyone else. The truck drivers had a different way of life. They always seemed to be gone on a run, and when at home, they were struggling to get caught up on their sleep.

Despite their intense competition, the railroads and trucking companies discovered a common ground of operations when the railroads found it necessary to diversify and try new approaches in transporting cargo. Following World War II, and especially when the four-lane interstates allowed faster traffic, trucks gained a major advantage because of their "speed of service"—that is, quicker delivery time. To remedy this disadvantage, the Southern Pacific and the Rock Island introduced the "Fastest Train to the West," also called the "Gold Streak," a joint express freight service between Chicago and Los Angeles. To facilitate making the run in twenty hours, feverish activity was necessary at scheduled stops—of which Tucumcari was one—in arranging crew changes, switching freight cars, lining up multiple diesel units, shifting freight shipments, and servicing rolling stock. Five diesel units pulled the train, which was limited to sixty freight cars. At about the same time, the more alert railroads turned to piggyback intermodal cargo containers and "auto racks" that could be transported initially on rail flatcars and, when unloaded, hauled the rest of the way by truck. These cooperative measures helped save some railroads from financial ruin. Although Yellow Freight expressed interest in developing intermodal operations at Tucumcari, it went no further than that. Tucumcari did compete for the location of a "mixing center," or drop-off point for the automobiles picked up by trucks pulling auto racks, but the railroad chose Santa Rosa instead.[16]

Above all else, railroad engine crews regarded truck drivers as inferiors, as "truck jockeys," without the comparable skills required to manage a large locomotive.[17] However, at the time the big trucking companies came into Tucumcari, truck drivers had gained the popular image of "Cowboys of the Open Road," a reputation enhanced by the hit song "Convoy," in 1975, and a Hollywood film by the same name in 1978. Another film, *Smoky and the Bandit*

(1977), starring the well-known actor Burt Reynolds, also romanticized the truck driver. In the genre of music involving truckers, the songs "Six Days on the Road (and I'm Gonna Make It Home Tonight)" and "Tucumcari Tonight" were popular fare locally.[18]

But no hint of these romantic aspects surfaced in a public statement made by a local driver's wife. In her trucker husband's view, she said, most people in Tucumcari seemed to believe that the drivers, because of their aggressive union, got "big wages for little actual work." Expressing annoyance at such beliefs, the trucker's wife declared, "Nothing could be further from the truth," and added, "You would be hard pressed to find a more miserable lifestyle than that led by truckers." She then described the company driver's routine in terms suggestive of some similarities with the job of railroader operating crew members:

> The lucky driver has a bid run with a set departure time and regular day off. Extra board drivers don't have even that luxury. The telephone is just as likely to ring at three in the morning as three in the afternoon, giving the driver two hours to report for work. And trucking companies don't care if the weather is fair or foul. If there is a blizzard blowing with gale-force winds and snow eyeball deep to a giraffe, too bad. Freight must move. Moreover, the work of truckers involved certain health problems, such as back, neck, and shoulder injuries, as well as hearing loss and respiratory ailments resulting from the noise and fumes of diesel motors.[19]

The "most dangerous problem of all," however, was getting adequate sleep. At that time an interval of only eight hours was required between runs, which resulted in sleep depredation, and ultimately fatal fatigue at the steering wheel. The average of three trips a week kept the driver away from home ninety to one hundred hours, making a regular home life impossible. This schedule also forfeited any chance of participation in town affairs and sacrificed the pleasures of relaxing holidays, school plays, and little league baseball games. For wives, it was evenings spent nail biting and worrying if the truck had hit black ice or something worse. Especially for wives, it was hard to feel at home in the community when the job might require "you to move to Timbuktu at any time." Yes, the trucker's wife observed remorsefully, "Union truck drivers do make a decent wage. Wouldn't it be wonderful if they also earned a decent living [situation]?"[20]

Not that the townspeople failed to reach out to these strangers in their midst.[21] Sometimes, though, the cordiality seemed forced or fainthearted at best. In November 1994, twenty years after the arrival of the first trucking company, a full-page newspaper ad, sponsored by more than two dozen local merchants, expressed appreciation for the truckers' presence in the city. It proclaimed:

> We Support the Trucking and Railroad Industries in the Tucumcari area Because Trucking and Railroads in Tucumcari Supports Us.

Undoubtedly, to the truckers, the ad was a long-belated thank-you note.

Earlier, the truckers and the trucking companies had called on the town for help in two instances and received either grudging support or outright opposition. First, the independent truckers had a problem of where to park their rigs. According to a city ordinance, they could not park the large trucks in front of their own homes even long enough to change the sheets in the sleeper cabs. The city commission discussed the issue at length, and it got a thorough airing in the local press. The main complaints came from those who said the motors operating the refrigerated trailers, which ran all night, would disturb their sleep and that a truck with trailers could block a neighbor's driveway. In defense of the independents, it was pointed out that they were usually gone for two weeks on runs and only at home for a couple of days at a time. The economic contributions of trucking finally prevailed, to a degree, and the city commission reluctantly changed the ordinance to allow the big trucks, without trailers, to park on residential streets, but with a limit of seventy-two hours.[22]

This halfway concession hardly settled the matter for independents. A disgruntled independent driver wrote the city commission, beginning, "Truckers are real people," and continued that they had families, paid taxes, bought goods, and spent money on services in the community. He said that his national affiliate organization, the Commercial Motor Vehicle Owner/Operators and Drivers, constituted a major part of trucking in Tucumcari, helping to create jobs and stimulate business generally. Then, he laid down a challenge to the commissioners: "The city says 'We support truckers.' . . . You 'support' us but don't want us parking our trailers on any street in Tucumcari. That tells me you do not want us here." If the commission really wanted his kind of trucker to stay, he claimed, it would designate an area for trailer parking. And there the issue rested uneasily.

The most contentious controversy, however, arose over "triples"—that is, permitting a truck, or, in trade jargon, a "tractor," to pull three trailers instead of the limit of two.[23] This issue, which had statewide dimensions, involved primarily the trucking companies. Early on, in 1983, State Representative Clif Moreland of Tucumcari, declaring that the triple trailers would bring at least four more trucking firms and 240 families into Tucumcari, introduced legislation that would extend the length of trucks and trailers on New Mexico interstates from 65 to 105 feet. Moreland attributed the defeat to opposition from the railroads, the state highway and motor transportation departments, and the American Automobile Association (AAA).[24] In February 1988, the new city manager, Hugh Riley, speaking in favor of another pending triple-trailer bill, told a legislative committee that the measure involved "a terribly important issue" for Tucumcari, particularly in keeping trucking jobs. After the bill died in committee again, Riley declared that triple trailers still had a future in Tucumcari and the state.[25]

In this vein, supporters predicted increased economic gains from the longer trailers, including local purchases, additional fees, and service charges. The discussion continued in the press and elsewhere, focusing on whether the economic benefits outweighed the increased road hazards. Although a survey of Tucumcari residents showed that 84 percent of them opposed triples, the city commission, by a 3-to-2 vote, barely endorsed yet another legislative proposal on the issue.[26] The state legislature had apparently listened to the public outcry of the opposition, however, and the result for triple trailers this time was no more favorable than before.

The relatively brief trucking interlude, much shorter in time than the railroad presence, was coming to an end. Transcon was absorbed by another trucking concern and closed its terminal at Tucumcari in April 1990. Consolidated began relocating drivers in late 1993. The others followed suit until the town's first long-distance hauler, Yellow Freight, announced in February 1997 that it would close the local relay point, becoming the last of the big trucking companies in Tucumcari. Acknowledging the exit of the trucking industry, the *Quay County Sun* editor bemoaned the loss of all the trucker families whose departure had come down to "dollars and cents"—to financial decisions made in some distant corporate headquarters. The people of Tucumcari must pull together, the editor advised, to bring in other industry, pointing out, as an example, that Santa Rosa had recently won approval for a new state-authorized, privately operated prison.[27]

Greyhound bus drivers, although usually noticeable at Tucumcari only when picking up and discharging passengers, led a life much like that of truckers—and, to some extent, of railroaders as well. The Greyhound drivers lived by the whims of a dispatcher; often disappointed their children by missing school functions and baseball games; and had an even greater concern for weather conditions because of the tricky nature of icy highways that imperiled the human cargo aboard. Blizzard-like weather, however, often revealed a brotherhood of the thoroughfares. Howard Suttle, who shepherded Greyhound buses for twenty-eight years, beginning in 1951, often drove on Route 66 from Amarillo through Tucumcari to Albuquerque. Suttle later recalled with appreciation the times that truckers stopped and diligently helped shovel a stranded bus out of snowdrifts "so the women and children could get to town."[28] Like truckers, the main problem of Greyhound drivers was catching enough sleep to avoid dozing off behind the wheel. Usually, the big Greyhound buses came and went without any problem except, now and then, kicking off an abusive drunk. In 1949, however, Greyhound drivers and the company itself found themselves in the middle of a prolonged strike for recognition by AFL-affiliated restaurant workers at Tucumcari. The Greyhound company intervened in the labor dispute. To prevent further disruption of its service and avoid additional complaints from passengers, Greyhound threatened to move its bus terminal from the Rondy-voo Cafe to another location unless the restaurant owners settled the strike and signed a union contract. The owners grudgingly complied.[29]

As usual, Tucumcari boosters were desperately seeking available industry to invite into town.[30] In these efforts they cast a broad net trying to haul in new businesses and for a time had success. Launched with a federal grant of $3 million in 1982 and owned by the city, an ethanol plant operated by Oklahoma-based Grain Power Limited and subsequent firms got off to a rocky start. Plagued by problems for several months, Grain Power made its first ethanol shipment of eight thousand gallons in July 1983. Repairs of the plant's vapor system finally allowed release of the consignment to a Farmington refinery, which sold the ethanol to distributors in that area. Prospects of future production for the local market appeared promising since the plant had received two million pounds of milo grain for processing, and, in addition, still had about sixty thousand gallons of ethanol in storage. Blended with unleaded gasoline, the ethanol produced a higher grade of fuel. But the venture had a troubled track record because of equipment failure, shortages of grain for processing, and marketing difficulties. It fell into the hands of a marketing company, closed briefly, then reopened in 1991. Openings, closings, and threatened demolition seemed the destiny of the ethanol plant.[31]

On the national scene involving publicly sponsored projects, the interstate highway system was the biggest single public works undertaking in American history. Yet, interstates like I-40 stirred few, if any, sentimental attachments. As stated succinctly, the new routes were bigger and faster, but because they lacked character, nobody "writes songs about interstates."[32] After Interstate 40 opened all the way, Route 66 did not die but quickly rose to new prominence as a legend. And it reached legendary status in record time. In 1990 novelist and historian Larry McMurtry wrote: "Exit I-40 now and then and look at what can still be seen of recently famous Route 66, which was still a fully viable trail in the days of Keroac and Cassady. It's taken scarcely thirty years for the plains and desert to erase Route 66."[33] Unarguably Route 66 had been "recently famous" as an active highway pulsing with traffic, but instead of being "erased," it became equally renowned as a legend. Route 66 was well on the way to becoming a legend during its lifetime, even before authorization of Interstate 40 in 1956.

How this happened in such a short time is easily explained, starting with vital statistics. Designated as US Highway 66 in 1926, it was called the "Wire Road," because much of the way it ran along the first western telegraph line, and it also was called the "Great Diagonal Way" due to its slanted route through eight states between Chicago and Los Angeles. It started near the intersection of Jackson Boulevard and Lake Shore Drive in Chicago, close to Lake Michigan, and ended at the corner of Santa Monica Boulevard and Ocean Avenue in Santa Monica, in sight of the Pacific Ocean from the Santa Monica Pier.[34] Popularly known as the "Main Street of America," Route 66 was also considered as the "Will Rogers Highway" after the Oklahoma-born newspaper humorist and movie celebrity, although the latter designation did not stick. It was originally 2,448 miles in length, but with subsequent alterations, finally ended up 2,451 miles long. At first

New Mexico contained the longest portion of any state—originally 487 miles stretching from Glenrio to Gallup—but Governor Hannett's cutoff and other adjustments reduced it to 380 miles. Officially, Route 66 lasted from its creation November 26, 1926, to June 26, 1985, when it was decommissioned, or fifty-nine years and seven months. Its doom was sealed, although not immediately delivered, when President Dwight D. Eisenhower signed the bill creating the National Interstate Highway System on June 29, 1956. As of 2001, 350 "driveable miles" of Route 66 remained in New Mexico, of which a mixed graveled and paved 49-mile stretch ran from the Texas line, or Glenrio, through Tucumcari. A second span of 50 miles in length began at the Palomas exit, west of Tucumcari, and continued through Santa Rosa.[35]

To understand the biggest boost Route 66 received for canonization as a legend, it is necessary to go back to the creation of the federal highway system and its numbering. Originally, the cross-country highway from Chicago running through Tucumcari to Los Angeles was designated as US 60. However, the governor of Kentucky reportedly had a special preference for the highway through his state being numbered 60 and won his case. Of the twenty-six unused double-digit numbers left, 66 happened to be one of them, and it was agreed that US 66 should be substituted instead. And what a difference that simple exchange made; undoubtedly "Get your kicks on Route 60" would never have passed muster in a song's lyrics.

Like any popular legend, the mythical Route 66 needed a good theme song as "the anthem of the asphalt."[36] In this regard the highway was dealt an extraordinarily strong hand. In 1946, following the end of the Second World War and his discharge as a captain from the US Marine Corps, Robert "Bobby" Troup and his wife, Cynthia, set out for Hollywood where he hoped to cash in on his talents honed during a stint as the pianist for the Tommy Dorsey Band. The Troups did not travel the whole length of Route 66 on their trip to California, since they started from Harrisburg, Pennsylvania, and reached the popular route after it left Chicago. They drove enough of it, however, for Troup to compose "the lyrical road map" of the well-traveled thoroughfare that included the trademark line, "Get your kicks on Route 66." Those same lyrics zoomed past Tucumcari with, "You'll see Amarillo, Gallup, New Mexico," and on across Arizona to California. The popular recording of Troup's song, by Nat King Cole, hit the market and jukeboxes a week after the Troups arrived in

Hollywood. It became an instant hit. Since the Troups began their trip in Pennsylvania on US Highway 40, he originally thought of writing the song about that road, before his wife pointed out the rhyming advantages of Route 66. It is hard to imagine the lyrics of that hugely popular 1950s song as "Get your kicks" on US 40 or Route 60 instead of the bouncy, rhyming "Get your kicks on Route sixty-six." In other words, the tradeoff, in which Oklahoma gave up the highway number 60 in exchange for 66 saved the day for the iconic song and made it a monumental landmark in American popular culture.[37]

Earlier, before the impact of Troup's song and Nat King Cole's recording, newspaper columnist Ernie Pyle, later the famous war correspondent of World War II, had made a major contribution in familiarizing Americans with Route 66. Between 1935 and 1940, Pyle traversed the route twenty times, while writing a steady stream of human-interest stories in his assignment of reporting on life in America.[38] At the same time, John Steinbeck's Great Depression–era novel *The Grapes of Wrath*, published in 1939, developed a cult following and threw a spotlight on Route 66, especially after it became a Hollywood film. Steinbeck's story cast a pessimistic tone on the journey of Dust Bowl refugees, but it also drew attention to every torturous mile of the route they traveled. Readers of the book and viewers of the film were exposed to the problems caused by the succession of slopes and curves of the terrain as the weary transients passed through Tucumcari, stopping at Santa Rosa in their broken-down, overloaded truck on their way to the Promised Land of California. In fact, as already pointed out, Steinbeck mentioned Tucumcari as part of the trip on the same page that he called Route 66 "the mother road." And he later immortalized Route 66 as the "the road of light" and that "great cross-country highway" of escape and hope, "waving gently up and down on the map" from the Mississippi River to the Pacific Coast. Significantly, by the 1950s, as a reenactment, or "ricochet effect," a steady stream of the migrants who had traveled over Route 66 during the Great Depression and World War II, then had gone back home after the war, were now returning to California on the same highway.[39]

Besides the effects of *The Grapes of Wrath*, both the book and the movie, the highway also received weekly exposure in a popular television series titled *Route 66*, starring Martin Milner and George Maharis, in which two young men drove a Corvette convertible to adventures in various locations. The series ran for four seasons on the CBS TV network, lasting from October 1960 to March

1964. Although *Route 66* helped promote the highway's legendary status, few of the 116 episodes were filmed along the historic route. During the first season (1960–1961), four of the thirty episodes featured New Mexico, but none specifically involved the Tucumcari area.[40]

A latter-day reinforcement, the computer-animated film *Cars*, and its sequel *Cars 2*, had a significant role in the Route 66 legend.[41] Released in 2006 and 2011, the two films feature the voices of well-known entertainers, but all the characters are animated cars and other vehicles. The plot of the original *Cars* involves a rookie, hot-shot race car, Lightening McQueen, as the main character, who is hurrying to the Piston Cup championship at the fictional Los Angeles International Speedway. He is arrested in the town of Radiator Springs, located on old Route 66, and forced to repave a section of road he has torn up. During his unwilling stay, he meets the town's people/cars, comes to respect them for their honesty and simple lifestyle, and falls in love with Sally, a 2002 996-series Porsche 911 Carrera. *Cars* won the Golden Globe Award for Best Animated Feature Film and was nominated for two Academy Awards.

In short, small-town values are glorified in Radiator Springs, which, like Tucumcari, once enjoyed the flourishing tourist trade of Route 66 but has wasted away following the construction of an Interstate 40 Bypass. There is no doubt about Tucumcari's starring role in the film, although Radiator Springs was supposedly a composite of several places along old Route 66. According to Route 66 historian Michael Wallis, the film's advisor and the voice of the Sheriff, who is a 1949 Mercury Club Coupe (police model): "The radiator cap mesa . . . [in *Cars*] is based on Tucumcari Mountain in Tucumcari, N. M. Even the 'RS' painted on the butte mimics the capital 'T' on the side of Tucumcari Mountain."[42]

With this kind of publicity plus a major novel and Hollywood film as well as a jukebox hit song bolstering legendary status, public celebrations could be expected as a natural result. And these civic events now number in the hundreds. To add to the pizzazz, some fifteen Route 66 associations are dedicated to spreading the legend and lore worldwide, including organizations in Canada, the Czech Republic, the Netherlands, Norway, and Japan. In addition, state and city associations have sprung up along the route. In 1999 Congress joined the campaign by providing funds to preserve and restore historic properties on Route 66. In 2003 the National Museum of American History probably

Get your kicks on Route 66 mural. This mural on the side of a building is one of several giving support to the recent slogan that Tucumcari is a "City of Murals." Jay Goebel / Alamy Stock Photo (Image ID: CW91W6).

demonstrated the greatest labor of love by acquiring a 40-by-20-foot concrete section of the highway in Oklahoma. The hunk of concrete was cut into twelve pieces and trucked to Washington, DC, where they were reassembled as an unusual exhibit—a special museum pedestrian walkway. In short, the Route 66 legend has received constant reinforcement and remains alive and well today.[43]

Moreover, in the wake of the Interstate 40 Bypass at Tucumcari, a virtual torrent of celebrations, re-creations, recognitions, and remembrances was loosed up and down the old Route 66, and many of these demonstrations of affection or commercial exploitation passed through or involved Tucumcari. There were magazine and newspaper feature articles, festivals, and celebratory events of all kinds, even a Route 66 Quilt Show. In the midst of all this commemorative activity, Tucumcari claimed the ultimate distinction of being the "Heart of Historic Route 66," a boast that drew loud challenges from other cities, in particular Kingman, Arizona.[44] Early on, in this same vein, a full-blown controversy had exploded between Tucumcari boosters and the Oklahoma Turnpike

Authority, which had erected two large billboards advising tourists to follow a route out of Oklahoma City to California that would take them through Clovis on US Highway 60 instead of via Tucumcari on Route 66. This "battle of the billboards" and blatant "rustling" of the tourist trade subsided when Tucumcari erected four billboards pointing out the shorter distances and better roads in traveling Route 66. Without surrendering, Oklahoma altered the wording on its signage.[45]

City, state, and federal governments also nourished and lavished attention on the Route 66 legend. The Tucumcari Cultural Corridors Committee staged the dedication of the Route 66 Monument, May 17, 1997, in front of the convention center, and threw in a classic car show celebrating the Route 66 heritage. The city commission also contributed to revitalization by voting to change the name of Tucumcari Boulevard to Route 66. In a municipal tribute to the Route 66 legend, the Lodgers Tax Advisory Board renewed its campaign of installing Tucumcari Tonite! signs along major roads leading to the town. Carefully avoiding federally mandated limits on signage along the interstates—with the severity of the restrictions formulated by individual states—the Tucumcari board, starting in 1971, had placed twenty-six of the famous signs by 1988. From Arizona to the west and Oklahoma to the east, eighteen signs dotted I-40, four appeared along US 54, and four more adorned other roads. Each one, headed "Tucumcari Tonite!," told motorists how many miles remained to the city and welcomed them to stop by.[46] Near the First Street exit off I-40, a large, illuminated, two-sided sign added, instead of the mileage left, the greeting, "You're Here," under "Tucumcari Tonite!" For about a year, in 2007 and 2008, the lodgers tax board had dropped the Tonite! signs and substituted instead billboards featuring silhouetted cowboys on horseback and the slogan "Gateway to the West." The board returned to the longtime signage because of its national recognition—now with the boast of "Over 1,200 Motel Rooms."[47]

On the national scene, another billboard battle raged over the restriction of signage along the new interstates. This conflict involved, in the cultural context, aesthetics and natural beauty of the landscape versus commercialism and the opportunity for business advertising. In constitutional terms, as in various cases considered by the Supreme Court, the main issue was government police power versus the First Amendment's guarantee for freedom of expression. The argument for aesthetics gradually won out until the National Interstate Highway

Tucumcari Tonite! sign. These advertising signs were placed along federal highways, mainly Route 66 and later Interstate 40, for more than two hundred miles east and west of town. Jay Goebel / Alamy Stock Photo (Image ID: CWA3F6).

System raised the stakes. From that time on, according to one scholarly assessment, "Commerce won new First Amendment privilege, but beautification was not overwhelmed."[48] On the local level, signage along the interstates was simply a bread-and-butter issue. The expense of advertising with the Tucumcari Tonite! signs and otherwise was substantial, even with state tourism matching funds furnishing up to half of the cost. But it seemed to pay off. "People come into the motel," one owner said, "and tell us they have followed the signs to Tucumcari for many miles." Another motel operator declared of the Tonite! signs, "We're dead without them."[49]

Among other actions taken by state agencies, the Office of Cultural Affairs in Santa Fe placed the Blue Swallow Motel and more than a dozen other Quay County entries on the National Register of Historic Places between 1977 and 2007. Of the fourteen listed, nine had a direct historical connection with Route 66, including two historic districts, at Glenrio and segments of the highway from there to Montoya. Like the Blue Swallow, the Cactus Motor Lodge, built

Final Tucumcari Tonite! sign at Tucumcari—"You're Here." Andre Jenny / Alamy Stock Photo (Image ID: BC25XM).

ten years earlier in 1930, also gained this significant national recognition. Prominently located atop a hillside on the eastern approach to town, the Cactus had been renowned for its adjacent dance hall and creative live music. On the national level, Congress passed the Route 66 Study Act of 1989, which authorized investigation of ways to preserve remaining parts of the highway and memorabilia from that period. Later, congressional legislation created the Route 66 Corridor Preservation Program, administered by the National Park Service, which awarded grants to save and restore historic buildings and landmarks as well as revitalize the old highway. Route 66 has also been designated as a National Scenic Highway.[50]

The Caprock Amphitheatre, located along the Caprock off State Highway 469 about eleven miles south of San Jon, attempted to cash in on the public attention devoted to the Route 66 legend. Modeled after a similar outdoor facility in Palo Duro Canyon near Amarillo, this imposing edifice had a complicated background. An unusual state-owned cultural facility, it was designed by noted Santa Fe architect John McHugh, whose work included the Santa Fe opera house. It was constructed by a Clovis contractor with a mix of private, foundation, and state funds and operated by the nonprofit New Mexico Outdoor Drama Association. Two San Jon women, Betty Philley and Ida Fellers, had been inspired to create a canyon theater after visiting the site. A veritable multitude of enthusiastic backers, mainly from Tucumcari and Clovis, joined the women in bringing the idea to fruition. The theater program at Eastern New Mexico University at Portales pledged to provide casts for the dramatic and musical productions.[51]

After preliminary performances in the summers of 1981 and 1982, and nearly ten years of intense publicity and fundraising efforts, the theater finally opened in the summer of 1985 with a "celebration show," followed two weeks later by "Stage 66's Melodrama," then a concert of fiddle music, and later a dinner show. Among other productions, a musical drama, *The Legend of Billy the Kid*, written by acclaimed playwright of outdoor shows Kermit Hunter, with music by well-known composer Frank Lewin, ran for ten straight seasons. All the opening shows were well attended and subsequent summer performances, often standard melodramas, at first drew sizable crowds. From the beginning, however, the backers thought the theater would attract large numbers of tourists from Interstate 40, and it soon became apparent that this was not the case. Interest in Tucumcari and Clovis waned. At the end the average attendance was only 270 in the 955-seat bleachers. The county had owned the land where the state spent $1.8 million to construct the native-rock facility, including a stage, concessions building, lunch area, and bleachers. But the impressive Caprock Amphitheatre had become a white elephant and the state wanted Quay County to take it. The county commissioners refused. Today, vandalized and weather beaten, the Caprock Amphitheatre remains as a reminder of good intentions worn thin.[52]

An unusually bright spot in the post–Interstate 40 Bypass era was the growth of Mesalands Community College.[53] It was established by state legislation in 1979 as the Tucumcari Area Vocational School (TAVS) to offer vocational programs, and later it was authorized to confer two-year degrees in business administration and computer information systems. The institution steadily expanded the curriculum and administrative structure until it became more like a typical community college, or steppingstone, to a four-year university and was accredited by a national association. As a result of its strategic planning, Mesalands took the bold step of developing programs in paleontology and geology, which led to founding the Mesalands Dinosaur Museum and Natural Science Laboratories. The dinosaur exhibition, located off-campus near old Route 66 in town, is one of the best small museums of its kind in the country. And the way it was established, and is still funded, shows that the town's spirit of civic betterment was still alive. The whole museum enterprise was based on a close-knit partnership between the college and local community members, who contributed significant sums to establish the facility and set up a foundation to support continuing operations. The total of donations and other forms of fundraising amounted to $840,000, an almost unbelievable sum for a depressed town of about six thousand people.[54] The museum, which opened May 6, 2000, and draws about fourteen thousand paid admissions a year, has become "part tourist attraction, part educational facility," filling the bill for boosters as the kind of venue that tempts travelers to exit Interstate 40 and pull into town. As a matter of fact, Quay County contains the most extensive deposits of Triassic period dinosaurs in North America. Moreover, excavations in eastern New Mexico southeast of Raton revealed the Folsom point, dating back ten thousand years, followed by identification of the mammoth-hunting Clovis people, who lived in Blackwater Draw between Clovis and Portales twelve thousand years ago. Besides the overall educational program itself, the most significant contribution of Mesalands College and the museum is the world's largest exhibit of bronze dinosaurs. This unique way of displaying prehistoric animals began with a regular college-credit art course in bronze sculpturing but was given an added dimension by combining scientific paleontology with the artistic aspects. On the assumption that the alloy retains the details and gives better protection to an object, fossils collected in the field and skeletal remains are replicated in bronze with careful attention to anatomical accuracy.[55] Museum visitors can observe faculty and students working on bronze replicas in a special glassed-in section. Although not permitted in most museums, the bronze exhibits can be touched, an important reason the casting process must retain every detail accurately.

An energizing force in the community, the college offers educational opportunities to about eight hundred full-time and part-time students. Reflecting its eastern New Mexico setting, the college has a nationally ranked intercollegiate rodeo team and a research center in wind-energy research. The director of the

Dinosaur Museum. In collaboration with local Mesalands College, the exhibits feature brass skeletal replicas of dinosaurs. Danita Delimont / Alamy Stock Photo (Image ID: CMN6DM).

New Mexico Scenic Byways program became stuck when selecting a "centerpiece" for the 120-mile-long Mesalands Scenic Byway. Then she happened to visit the Mesalands College Museum and saw the bronze dinosaur exhibit. Immediately, as she recalls, "I said, 'This is it.'"[56]

On the other hand, the Tucumcari Historical Museum, founded to pay tribute to the Route 66 legend as well as the railroad presence in Tucumcari, appeals mainly to those interested in Quay County history. As the authorized description claims—and rightly so:

> This museum is different. It is like one giant attic of old stuff. There is stuff piled on top of stuff—under stuff—between stuff—stuffed inside of stuff— and overstuffed stuff. There are two stories of stuff, a basement with stuff, and outbuildings overflowing with stuff. And what constitutes a museum exhibit? Here at Tucumcari Museum, about anything goes. Prized bowling balls, a collection of used cowboy boots, a bucket of particularly colorful

cow-patties, piles of family scrapbooks, bootleg liquor stills, a roulette wheel from one of the old gambling halls, you name it. . . . There is an excellent chance you can dig through stuff and find something that the rest of the world didn't even know existed.

This imaginative listing pretty well describes the range of the museum's holdings in a whimsical way, but the periodic exhibits are of a professional quality. Likewise, the permanent displays outside, spread across a half-city block, include an authentic ranch windmill and a railway caboose, thereby accurately addressing local history and lore. Funded by the city, this facility also helps satisfy the local obsession to attract tourists off the Interstate 40 Bypass.[57]

The guiding spirit in the museum's founding was one of the town's most colorful characters, Elk Drugstore owner Herman Moncus, nicknamed "Corny" for the brand of jokes he told on the local radio station's early morning talk show. Moncus grew up on the family homestead near the Ima community and in outlaw Black Jack Ketchum's canyon hideout, which became known as Moncus Canyon.[58] At age nine his visit to a Santa Fe museum inspired a "life-long desire" to collect "all the history and paraphernalia of the early settler," which he pretty well accomplished. In fact, the Elk Drugstore itself became a sizable museum with his collections "jammed into every nook and cranny" inside and outside a new drugstore building, leaving limited shelf space for the store's wares. Moncus also loaned parts of his hoard to several universities across the country.[59]

In 1958, as his retirement approached, Herman Moncus spearheaded the organization of the Tucumcari Research Institute, which led to the founding of the Tucumcari Historical Museum in the old Central School building. Moncus donated his massive holdings to the new facility, and he was the first full-time curator. Later the museum added the Herman H. Moncus Annex to house a special Route 66 wing.[60]

Besides railroad, dinosaur, and historical museums, Tucumcari has another potential tourist attraction to tempt travelers off Interstate 40 and break the monotony as they whip along at seventy-fiv miles an hour.[61] The small, largely unknown New Mexico Route 66 Museum has exhibits dedicated to the legendary highway. This museum is located immediately behind the sprawling 30,000-square-foot Tucumcari Convention Center with its artistically sculptured

Route 66 Monument in front. A local newspaper predicted that the convention center might have the "strongest impact" on the town's future of any project the city had undertaken recently. The prediction was bolstered by locating a controversial art object in front of the convention hall and adjacent to the old highway.[62]

A tourist attraction itself, the *Route 66 Monument* has been described as "a semi-whimsical tribute to the Mother Road . . . that looks a bit like a Tex-Mex temple made of sandstone tires and serpentine, two-lane road outlines." Artist Tom Coffin has said that the design represents a "Myanesque pyramid." The half-reclining 66s and, at the top, the 1950s Cadillac rear fin are highly polished aluminum to look like chrome, while the three vintage red taillights are cast acrylic that lights up at night. Coffin explained that the composite artistic features represent a car headed West because "cars are what the road is all about." Dedicated in 1997, the city, the state highway agency, and the state arts organization commissioned the *Route 66 Monument* under a program to create public art in nine New Mexico communities.[63]

An emphatic expression of faith in Tucumcari and its future, in the form of a

Route 66 Monument. This artistic tribute to the famed highway beside old Route 66 in Tucumcari represents a luxury automobile headed west. Fred LaBounty / Alamy Stock Photo (Image ID: BK065J).

bank building, came to dominate the downtown business district, beginning in 1974, as completion of the I-40 Bypass loomed ahead.[64] As pointed out earlier in chapter 2, the First National Bank at the southeast corner of the Second and Main intersection became an anchor of the original town site. Henry Burt "H. B." Jones, the bank's longtime president, had been a leading figure in the early business elite that literally put the town on the map. He died in 1941.[65] As an old-style family bank, George Wilbur Jones succeeded his father as president, and when he died in 1987, his son, Henry Barton Jones, became its president. Young Jones had joined the bank in 1967 after finishing college.

Wilbur and Barton Jones had seen no reason the town would not continue to progress, as it had when promoting construction of a $15.5 million federal dam on the Canadian River, followed by a long, successful struggle for a road to that dam. The First National building at the downtown corner of Main and Second was showing its age, however, and no longer provided enough room for expansion. In addition, the urban renewal mall had changed the old town to such an extent that it seemed wise to build a new bank some distance away— about three blocks south, as it turned out. Regardless of where the new location might be, Wilbur and Barton Jones wanted to make a statement that would stimulate the local economy and inspire confidence in the town's future. After all, their bank and the town had prospered together since the family patriarch H. B. Jones moved from Santa Rosa to Tucumcari back in 1910 to join the Goldenberg brothers and the other founding fathers in making something from scratch out of an isolated, struggling railroad community.

The majestic bank the Joneses built on First Street more than made the statement of faith they wanted to convey. Costing about a million dollars (close to $5.5 million today), the structure was situated on a full city block, contained 29,000 square feet of floor space, and required 400,000 toque-colored brick for its walls. Without a Santa Fe look, which the Joneses wanted to avoid, the eclectic architectural style still had a definite southwestern appearance. Four large pillars at the entrance provided the required bank ambiance. Inside, the exposed brick walls surrounded an 8,000-square-foot lobby with custom wood furniture and oak flooring throughout. A drive-in branch on Route 66 at the First Street intersection opened in 1956 and closed when the new bank was built. Altogether, with two remaining branches at Santa Rosa and Las Vegas, the First National now employed 120 people, including the staff for its state-of-the-art computing system. Tucumcari had never seen such splendor in a business build-ing or any other structure.[66] With the bypass still an unknown, the grand new First National Bank represented a sizable financial investment and moral com-mitment in the town's future. In 1997 the Norwest Corporation, part of a large banking chain with headquarters in Minneapolis, purchased the First National Bank of Tucumcari, which, controlled by three generations of the Jones family, had been a mainstay of the local economy for almost a century. H. Barton Jones, board chairman and CEO, said in a public statement, "new realities in banking" required "full-service" components that the local bank could best provide its customers by merging with the larger firm. Otherwise, in the 1990s, major transitions were taking place nationally in the banking industry, result-ing in the consolidation of small and large banks alike. It was hardly a forced sale or one of desperation for First National, which was a viable and profitable business concern at the time of the sale. For the time being, Barton Jones remained as board chairman CEO, as did Craig Cosner, the bank's president. A different administrative structure was installed when the Norwest's corporate parent merged with Wells Fargo several months later, assuming the name of that venerable banking chain as did the Tucumcari bank. Jones retired in 2000, Cosner followed suit in 2006, and the present Wells Fargo branch has become a shadow of the old First National Bank nurtured for a century by H. B. Jones and his descendants.[67]

If any doubt existed that a location on a busy cross-country highway brought more crime and lawlessness, it was dispelled by events on Route 66 even before the heavier traffic on Interstate 40. Tucumcari drew national attention for a series of three baffling murders of young men near town along Route 66. The first victim, a retired navy officer, was discovered stabbed to death beside the highway about five miles east of town in 1946. A hitchhiker was found guilty and sentenced to life in the state prison. A similar murder occurred in 1951 when an unidentified body was reported about a mile from the previous spot. Then, in 1954, an army enlisted man on his way to a new assignment in California was fatally stabbed and beaten in a Tucumcari motel by a hitchhiker when the two became involved in an argument over the Korean conflict. The killer was sen-tenced to life imprisonment. The most difficult to solve of these three "hitch-hiker murders" was the death of the unidentified man found in 1951.[68] In 1939, thirty-three-year-old Claude Moncus, brother of druggist Herman Moncus, became the youngest sheriff in the state and served three staggered four-year terms, a record number in Quay County. Moncus won national recognition for his professional sleuthing by solving the 1951 hitchhiker murder and bringing the killer to justice. His "painstaking and meticulous" detective work started when he dismissed twenty-six other identifications of the victim before fingerprints he sent to the FBI resulted in a positive report. An abandoned car in Amarillo had led Sheriff Moncus on a tedious, time-consuming round of visits to service stations and garages along Route 66 until he came upon a place in Shamrock, Texas, where repair work had been done on the vehicle. Of equal importance, seven people gave detailed descriptions of a second man who had accompanied the car's owner. In a careful search of the car, Moncus found a matchbook from a Sturgeon Bay, Wisconsin, tavern. Combining the firsthand descriptions with the address on the matchbook cover, the sheriff contacted the Wisconsin tavern and got the name of the killer. He had worked there as a bartender. The rest was police routine of circulating information nationwide and an apprehension in California. The accused man, an army deserter, was brought to Tucumcari for trial, sentenced to death in the electric chair, and executed in the state prison at Santa Fe. The case was written up in a national detective magazine, and for years, until his death in 1982 at age seventy-six, Claude Moncus was acclaimed as the small-town sheriff who had solved the "Matchbox Murder."[69]

With Interstate 40 fully operational as a cross-country transportation connection, Tucumcari became exposed to even more complexities of the national crime scene and the work of federal crime prevention agencies. This was the situation when New Mexico state policeman Clifford Hooper, stationed at Tucumcari, stopped a rented minivan on I-40 doing 80 miles per hour in a 75-miles-per-hour zone. He found thirty-one handguns hidden in the vehicle's paneling. The routine stop immediately involved Officer Hooper in the national campaign to halt interstate firearms and drug trafficking. It also quickly led to his association with the Atlanta Police Department as well as several federal law enforcement agencies, including the US Marshals Service, FBI, Drug Enforcement, and Alcohol, Tobacco and Firearms. Hooper was called to testify in New York, where he learned the tangled details of the case.[70] As an indication of the big-time aspects of illegal trafficking on I-40, another state policeman made an arrest at about the same time that netted twenty-five pounds of cocaine valued at $1.1 million. Later, in 2002, state police made a bust involving $59,000 in cash and eighty pounds of cocaine worth about $3 million.[71]

For the Quay County sheriff, the constant hum of traffic on the four lanes of Interstate 40 was occasionally broken by exciting car chases in pursuit of bank robbers or other fleeing felons. More often, however, drug busts became increasingly frequent occurrences. In 1997 Quay County sheriff's deputies made a routine traffic stop on Interstate 40 and arrested two North Carolina men for possession of close to seven pounds of cocaine, and in another stop seized three hundred pounds of marijuana. The sheriff, commenting that this was "right up there" in weight among drug hauls, emphasized that his department was "very adamant about the war on drugs." Later that year the full might of an organized taskforce for the drug war went into action. At five o'clock on an April morning, a small army of more than seventy law enforcement officers from across the region, in addition to state narcotics agents, assembled in the local National Guard Armory, to make a sweep of illegal drug traffickers in Tucumcari itself. The members were easily identified by their bulging bullet-proof vests and weapons displayed conspicuously in plain view. After a briefing by a state narcotics officer, the taskforce converged on the city in the early morning light. A former city manager and twenty-six other Tucumcari residents were arrested mainly on drug-dealing charges involving methamphetamines, cocaine, and marijuana. Large amounts of drugs were seized by undercover agents, and a meth lab was also discovered and destroyed.[72]

The local war on drugs had also involved US customs agents, who took to the air and relentlessly pursued a twin-engine Cessna 206 carrying $375,000 worth of marijuana and two suspected drug dealers—at least one a Tucumcari resident—across Texas, beginning near Alpine and continuing over a good part of New Mexico. Along the way, as the pilot tried cat-and-mouse elusive maneuvers by dipping in and out of the clouds, a New Mexico State Police helicopter joined federal planes in the chase. As a last resort, the pilot landed in a wheat field east of Ragland, pushed out the marijuana, and took off. Finally, the plane ran low on gas and had to land at the Tucumcari airport where both suspects were arrested.[73]

As already indicated, weather always became a consideration in travel on New Mexico roads and highways, including Interstate 40. The worst blizzard recorded in Quay County, in February 1986, piled up snow over two feet deep, and, combined with ice and freezing sub-zero temperatures, stalled semitrucks, buses, vans, and cars on I-40, bringing traffic to a complete standstill. An estimated 3,200 persons crammed every motel and hotel room as well as lobbies, lounges, and restaurants. Another 1,200 found shelter, blankets, and food in the National Guard Armory, school gyms, and churches. The governor, announcing a state of natural disaster, called out the National Guard to rescue stranded travelers and isolated rural families. In some stricken country areas, however, it was impossible to travel even by horseback. City water mains froze and burst, and municipal sanitation trucks were out of commission. Fears of flooding arose when warmer weather thawed the ice and snow, but on the bright side, wheat crops needed the moisture and, according to official reports, the spring grasshopper horde was probably frozen out. The next winter was almost as bad, as eight inches of snow fell in thirty-eight hours, again forcing the closure of area roads and I-40.[74]

Similar weather conditions several years earlier had resulted in one of the saddest tragedies in the annals of local tourist travel. In December 1978, a twenty-one-year-old female navy electronics technician, traveling from San Diego to her home in Kansas for the holidays, got mixed up on highway directions she received at Clovis. Taking a wrong turn at Grady in the nighttime darkness, she wound up at the Quay store and post office where she made the fatal mistake of turning east on a country road instead of continuing twenty miles north to Tucumcari. It was the first big snow of the year. After a few miles the car bogged down, and, apparently while trying to get out chains, the young woman locked the ignition keys inside the trunk. She then started to walk back to the Quay store but froze to death in the sub-zero temperature along the way.[75] A pathetic newspaper photograph showed her last zigzag halting steps etched in the snow before she fell. Ironically, back in the early homesteader days, with settler families living on every 160-acre claim, the doomed woman, guided by a coal-oil lamp's glow from a nearby farmhouse window, could probably have walked to safety. But most of the homesteaders had long since given up and left the area. In its hopeless outcome, this tragic episode seemed to portray the frustrations for Tucumcari in the closing decades of the twentieth century.

Chapter 9

DOWN THE SLIPPERY SLOPE

A s the end of the twentieth century approached, one concerned observer bemoaned the "long, hard road" Tucumcari had been forced to travel in the last few years, adding that the town had changed "from a bustling community to a near village" as people had "swarmed in and then moved out just as fast." Later, at the turn of the century after the I-40 Bypass had almost killed the tourist trade, the trucking companies had departed, and the railroad was leaving town for the second time, a local newspaper editor summed up Tucumcari's misfortunes in the last forty years or so and its prospects ahead, if any. It was hard to assume a positive attitude, he said, "when you drive around town and see empty houses and boarded up store fronts." And it was equally difficult "not to dwell on the negative when one of the town's major economic forces, this time the railroad, is pulling out of town [again], like the trucking industry did not so many years ago." The editor looked hard to see some rays of hope but found few of any promise. In truth, Tucumcari's economy had peaked out in the 1960s and 1970s with the first departure of the railroad and as completion of the I-40 Bypass loomed ahead. Now "hardly an echo" remained of the boom period. Looking ahead, and grasping for some promising signs, the editor took a sudden philosophical approach, declaring that "God helps them who help themselves" and he had a revelation of God's will for Tucumcari.[1]

Quay County's economy now depended mainly on agriculture—ranching and farming—which had never been a predictable source of revenue. Therefore, Route 66, in the transitional stage of turning into a legend, was Tucumcari's most valuable asset. The famous highway had "once brought growth and prosperity to our little corner of the world," the editor said, "and [it is] an asset that keeps the town as alive as it is." A concerted effort to build on the remaining remnant of the tourist trade seemed like the logical conclusion if the town

Main Street West
Tucumcari, New Mexico
August 1959

Tucumcari Main Street, looking west at the Main and Second Streets intersection, the heart of the old business district. LeDeane Studio, Tucumcari.

wanted to survive. But what would get travelers to stop, stay overnight, and spend their money, that was the problem.[2]

In addition, major simultaneous hammer blows, particularly the I-40 Bypass and the railroad pullout, had been delivered by external forces, which Tucumcari had not initiated and possessed little power to control. In the wake of this devastation from the outside, however, the town itself took, or sanctioned, a series of actions that contributed to its decline. In short, a combination of destructive forces, external and internal, resulted in a virtual knockout punch for Tucumcari as a vital commercial center. Of the external forces, sanctioned internally, the most destructive calamity was a federally funded, locally approved, urban renewal project.

Concern about the effects of an interstate bypass, years before it was built, spurred a group of alert civic and business leaders to form a downtown development organization in 1965. This group, fearing that their town would become "just another whistle stop" in the rapidly changing postwar world, decided to make Tucumcari so attractive that tourists could not resist pulling off the freeway and visiting the place. After viewing a film on the renewal of Grand Junction, Colorado, an All-American City, and making an inspection trip there, about sixty persons appeared before the Chamber of Commerce asking it to back a request for the city commission to obtain a similar project for Tucumcari. From the beginning, the local leaders had "in the back of their minds" the idea of saving the original business section around Main and Second Streets by converting it into a modern shopping mall. The trip to Grand Junction, however, apparently resulted in an expanded concept that encompassed much more of the downtown area adjacent to the business district. To accomplish this broader plan, a consulting firm was hired to gather information and present a detailed design of the changes needed to implement the ambitious vision. On November 7, 1968, the city commission approved a resolution recognizing the need for urban renewal and establishing a five-member Urban Development Commission. Throughout these preliminary preparations the town's residents were assured that although a city bond issue might be necessary, every effort would be made to obtain federal funding. The city commission's approval became the first step in the most controversial, and eventually destructive, public undertaking in Tucumcari's history.[3]

With a downtown mall as only one of the objectives, the whole issue of urban renewal received a thorough airing in public meetings, opinion polls, and the press. Federal legislation emphasized the elimination of blighted areas and, for central business districts specifically, that a successful program should "create a climate of change and optimism" to attract commercial and financial firms to invest in the completed renewal district.[4] Following authorization by the city commission in 1968, things moved quickly to produce a "Workable Program" for consideration by the federal Housing and Urban Development Department of a renewal area including the business district and adjacent residential neighborhoods. In fact, the project eventually involved the construction of ninety low-cost housing units as replacements for blighted structures that were demolished. By the time of its completion in late 1973, the Tucumcari urban renewal program had been funded for close to $3 million, and in 1972 alone, had relocated thirty-nine businesses and removed fifty-six families and their residences from the funded area. The responsibility of the town to provide spacious parking lots interspersed in the renewal area fell behind schedule, and with befuddled taxpayers "screaming that the city has gone parking lot crazy," got into more trouble when the designated areas remained mud holes for months because of funding shortages.[5] Otherwise, the wide swaths of vacated spaces where the urban renewal program had swept through like a scythe reminded some locals of the bombed-out cities they had seen in the wartime movie newsreels.

The downtown mall had been the most controversial issue of all. Should it be covered or open became the main question, and the advantages and disadvantages of both arrangements were thoroughly debated, as well as whether there should be any changes at all. In the end the old business district was transformed by shutting down three blocks of Main Street to create the open-air Four Seasons Mall, and by replacing existing buildings behind to the south with three parking lots. Trees and shrubs were planted throughout the mall, canopies placed over the entrances of most businesses, and lights installed for nighttime illumination. Since no automobile traffic was permitted, merchants involved had to redo the backs of their businesses and make them into new entrances that opened onto parking lots. Protracted howls of protest resulted over the costs to the merchants of this reconstruction work.[6] However, the outpouring in a single instance of $3 million for urban revitalization was probably the greatest federal expenditure locally since Conchas Dam and the New Deal work relief programs of the Great Depression.

The rerouting of US Highway 54 with a bypass had long been a problem for the city, and it figured prominently in the urban renewal project. At a cost of $400,000 the state, in cooperation with the city and the local urban renewal agency, worked on constructing a suitable bypass, but apparently conflict over the potential results caused the Highway 54 problem to linger for resolution another day. In fact, it took fifteen years to settle the pesky dilemma by construction of a Highway 54 Bypass that skirted the west side of Tucumcari Lake to connect with the Interstate 40 Bypass at the Mountain Road exit and interchange. The project included a new railroad overpass and exit signs that encouraged tourists to pull off to the old downtown business district.[7]

With the headline "Urban Renewal Overplayed as Bad Guy," a newspaper columnist commented on the raucous name-calling directed at the local project's leadership. He said that the controversial nature of urban renewal itself and the "ever-changing directions" of the federal program had "subjected these loyal citizens to the role of villains." The city Urban Development Commission chair and members had endured blistering attacks for every unfavorable action, real or imagined, they had taken, often as mandated by federal policies. And the commission had frequently been at loggerheads with city officials, particularly as the city tried to protect its political turf against the invasion of a competing body backed by the powerful federal government. At one point the mayor threatened to shut down the whole urban renewal project and disband the local development commission. Most often, though, the local urban renewal agency was accused by individual citizens and city officials alike of a failure to communicate on crucial issues. Some interested locals said that when they asked questions, they always received the same answer: "We are in the planning and survey stages, and do not know just what will be done yet."[8] Undoubtedly service on the Tucumcari Urban Development Commission was a thankless task.

For the dedication and grand opening ceremonies of Tucumcari's impressive Four Seasons Mall on June 1, 1974, the various construction contractors who had profited from building the facility ran a two-page newspaper ad congratulating the downtown merchants on their rejuvenated business locations. Included were photographs depicting broad walkways and architecturally decorative features in front of the businesses. To put it mildly, the downtown mall failed to work the hoped-for miracle of reviving the old business district and the tourist trade.[9] Disappointment with the outcome became apparent a few years after the grand opening when, at the urging of merchants who wanted to free up customer access to their businesses, the city cleared out enough of Main Street to permit one-way traffic through the mall. A year later, in 1983, according to the *Quay County Sun*, the mall had begun to dilapidate: "The canopies had sagged and swayed from the walls causing floods down the front of the buildings. Some of the steel posts for the canopies had begun to crack and the whole area looked sort of depressing and a change was in order." A group of business owners dedicated to redoing the facility and giving it a "Western Look" removed most of the main features of the original design, including the nighttime lighting, but delayed installing the new motif. The city commission considered tearing up the Four Seasons Mall and allowing traffic through Main Street as before but took no further action.[10] Unfavorable judgment of the mall's success was direct and to the point. "When you take a walk along Tucumcari's downtown mall," a local newspaper observed, "one thing is obviously lacking—people." While on a visit to town from Santa Fe, a state official declared: "Tucumcari has the distinction of being one of two communities in the state to try open-air malls. They didn't work, not here or anywhere in the country." As a final verdict, when it came time to extend the urban renewal contract or let it lapse, 76 percent of the property owners involved voted against an extension.[11]

In effect, the failed urban renewal project was paired with the I-40 Bypass since, at the outset, apprehension about the bypass had spurred town boosters to pursue the renewal program. Or one potentially disastrous project of an external origin (the I-40 Bypass) had led straight to another destructive wound, originating externally but sanctioned internally. After the "double whammy" of the I-40 Bypass and the disastrous urban renewal experience, the old downtown district looked more forlorn than ever with the remaining businesses struggling to survive, several landmark buildings destroyed, and the remnants of a decaying outdoor mall left as reminders of good intentions sadly gone wrong.[12]

The prevailing mentality associated with urban renewal had little room for historic preservation or regard for the town's heritage. Instead, the dominant mood favored clearing away the old to make room for the new. In sum, the Tucumcari urban renewal project not only ended as a failure that gutted the original downtown, demolishing several historic downtown business buildings, but it also destroyed some historically important residences beyond Main and Second Streets. The large, vintage home of Royal A. Prentice, which almost certainly qualified for the National Register of Historic Places, fell victim to demolition. Built on South Third Street about 1908, the two-story Prentice residence featured adobe walls eighteen inches thick, a high-pitched roof with three gables, twelve-foot ceilings, and decorative interior woodwork done by craftsmen from St. Louis.[13] Urban renewal claimed this architectural treasure and one-time home of the distinguished pioneer attorney who served with Teddy Roosevelt in the Spanish-American War, recorded the history and archaeology of the surrounding area, and contributed to the acquisition of Conchas Dam.

Demolition also became the fate of the one-story Baca-Goodman House, built at the northwest corner of Third and Aber Streets around 1905 by Benito Baca, a manager of the Gross, Kelly & Company mercantile branch store. The first structure had adobe walls eighteen inches thick. A wood-frame addition about 1920 was made by the next owners, pioneer Jewish grocer Herman Goodman and his wife Beckie (Adler) Goodman. The site itself had been part of the forty acres originating from ex-Union soldier William Kirkpatrick's Civil War land claim, purchased through brokers by Alex Goldenberg to form the Tucumcari town site. Herman Goodman's son, Joseph, who had a major role in local civic, political, and veterans affairs, later made it his family home. The Baca-Goodman House was the first local entry listed on the National Register in 1973. At first civic leaders and city officials, recognizing the pioneer structure's distinctive historical value as part of the community's heritage, were enthusiastic about restoring it. Located inside urban renewal boundaries, however, the historic structure became entangled in bureaucratic red tape. Before its demolition in 1977, the Baca-Goodman House went through a two-year process of delisting from the National Register at a cost of $4,520.27 to the taxpayers. Although distinguished enough to meet the National Register's rigid criteria, the building failed to attract the fancy of the local community and fell under the crunching treads of a bulldozer. Located across the street from the Quay County Courthouse, the historic home succumbed to the urban renewal spirit of improvement by making room for a parking lot. In this same spirit, a local newspaper ran the headline, "Progress Claims Baca-Goodman House."[14]

With the spirit of urban renewal afoot in town, even sacred religious edifices were not safe. Probably the one older building in the entire town with the most architectural distinction was the three-floored, neoclassical red brick First Baptist Church with massive white pillars at the front. Church leaders deemed the building "structurally unsafe and a fire hazard" and unsuitable for further occupation. Citing a study that concluded "remodeling costs would be prohibitive," they rejected suggestions of renovating it, calling in a demolition contractor to level the impressive structure. The ground it had occupied since 1926 was destined to become a parking lot for a modern, stylishly plain vanilla new sanctuary next door. It was simply a matter of out with the old and in with the new. For those who had attended Sunday school in the edifice, it was not that simple. Nor did memories of listening to countless sermons in the spacious sanctuary, with its high vaulted ceiling and heavenly light shining through pale blue windowpanes, help prevent destruction of the majestic old building. But the architecturally classy edifice with cultural significance that would gladden the soul of any historic preservation apostle had to go—and make room for a parking lot.[15]

To add to the destruction of old landmark buildings, the Vorenberg Hotel was also condemned and demolished except for the grisly skeletal remains of its steel-reinforced concrete infrastructure. A former owner recalls that the Vorenberg "had a big railroad business" until the passenger trains were eliminated and the runs for freight crews were changed. By the late 1960s, she said, there was not enough business even "to pay the night clerk's wages," and the doors were closed for good in 1972. In an attempt to save the venerable building, the owner had recommended its listing in the National Register of Historic Places, but the application was turned down in Santa Fe. About this time a town official intoned that he would like to see as much turn-of-the-century architecture as possible spared from urban renewal but added: "You can't change things overnight in government, though. We just try to make sure that buildings they build now conform to city standards."[16]

Town boosters would not give up. Still hoping to turn back the clock and restore Tucumcari as it had been when it was a busy railroad center and tourist mecca, the city next signed on with the New Mexico MainStreet Program, an agency dedicated to the economic revitalization of downtown areas, including adjacent neighborhoods. The state organization, affiliated with the national MainStreet Program, in turn, a subsidiary of the National Trust for Historic Preservation, is a nonprofit, privately funded body. Tucumcari's association with MainStreet has been spasmodic, probably because of the difficulty of obtaining outside funding. The town first became associated with MainStreet in the mid-1980s, just as the urban renewal program faded away, but dropped out for several years and then rejoined in 2006.[17]

The watchword of national MainStreet, "Revitalization of Your Commercial District," had great appeal among Tucumcari boosters. As a result, the local MainStreet envisioned an ambitious program of restoring the old downtown's retail business environment and creating "an arts and theater district centered around the historic train depot" that would attract tourists as well as townspeople. As the *Quay County Sun* stated, however, the community favored restoration of the train station above everything else. MainStreet also developed, with local funding, a Paint the Town program to brighten up four buildings, transforming one into a mid-twentieth century gas station of the Route 66 style, and to sponsor the painting of murals along Route 66 through town. Previously, in 2004, local artists Doug and Sharon Quarles painted a mural celebrating Route 66 on a grocery store wall located along the old road, followed by several other large depictions elsewhere in town. Altogether more than forty murals in

Tucumcari and Quay County, most done by the Quarleses, now make up what the Chamber of Commerce calls the town's "newest landmarks." The payoff for MainStreet's activities, and its proudest achievement, was refurbishing the railroad depot and establishing a museum there.[18]

Built in Spanish Mission Revival architectural style in 1927, the depot had been used jointly by the Southern Pacific and the Rock Island. The new owner, the Union Pacific Railroad, offered the building free to the city but stated that it would not provide any funds for renovation. If the city declined to take the structure, UP officials declared, it would be demolished. After lengthy discussion of the costs required to bring the aging structure up to code, the city commission decided it could not refuse an opportunity to acquire such a historically important property and voted to accept the UP offer.[19] Significantly, in a public meeting later, State Historic Preservation Officer Elmo Baca stressed that the time-worn phrase "community involvement" was essential in any future endeavor involving the depot. In effect, he warned that in the case of a museum, although it was relatively easy to establish one, the hard part came in staffing and operating it afterward. In fact, he stated pointedly that the prospect of a museum might attract a great deal of attention initially but that "they are not revenue producing venues." On the other hand, Baca conceded, there was no official state railroad museum in New Mexico, and a local facility commemorating Tucumcari's railroad history might be a logical goal for the former depot.[20]

From the beginning, the salaried director of Tucumcari's MainStreet emphasized that the depot was the organization's inaugural project to restore the old downtown business district. With $1.4 million in state funds and another $300,000 of federal money, reconstruction was authorized to begin in 2010 of the Tucumcari Railroad Historical Museum, estimated to cost close to $2 million. A broad parklike plaza at the front, also part of the overall design, was added for various kinds of public events and celebrations. On November 4, 2011, the staff kicked off a combination celebration of the New Mexico Centennial Commemoration of statehood and the official opening of the newly remodeled depot museum. The scheduled festivities included, in keeping with the program theme Fired Up!, several specialists in fire displays as well as an official New Mexico Centennial hot air balloon and a vintage Union Pacific steam locomotive, which puffed into the railyards carrying a load of dignitaries. It was an impressive send-off for the new museum and recognition of a job well done on its renovation. The depot had been listed on the National Register of Historic Places in 1990, and, as a capstone, the restoration project received the Architectural Heritage Award from New Mexico MainStreet in 2012.[21]

The annual Rattler Reunion became the biggest tourist attraction of the year for Tucumcari, and, reportedly, "the biggest event of its kind in New Mexico." On the first weekend of August, Tucumcari High School graduates of all classes, not just those of a single class, gather and exchange fond memories at the reunions. Marian Farmer Knapp, THS Class of '45, fostered the successful annual affair, starting in 1971.[22] Until that time, off and on, reunions for a specific class had been staged in a single year. Despite some problems with arrangements, the first annual all-class Rattler Reunion was declared a success, with an attendance of about 350. THS alums had started something big for their old hometown—fifteen years later, in 1986, an attendance of 1,000 was expected.[23]

In the American tradition of "loving a parade," the favorite part of the reunion for locals became the Saturday morning parade in which each class decorated a float, and the members rode on it. These parades became so popular and widely publicized that a New Mexico governor sometimes appeared with state police escorts to lead the floats. In fact, the float assembled by the class of 1978 for the 1998 reunion, a connected and decorated string of vehicles and trailers 265.5 feet long, carrying class members and pulled by a tractor, won international recognition as the longest float in the world from Guinness World Records of London.[24] And so, for the first weekend in August every year, the town was once again the lively tourist Mecca it had been before the Interstate 40 Bypass.

The remnants of rural schoolhouses built, or rebuilt, as WPA public works projects by the New Deal during the Great Depression still stand as reminders of once-proud communities the structures represented.[25] To say that the country folks loved their schools is no exaggeration. As more than buildings for educational purposes, the gymnasiums served as community gathering places on various occasions, from visits by Santa Clause to quilting bees. Of most importance, however, came the high school basketball games, in which a victory by the young players, proudly decked out in school colors, ranked only slightly less important than Kansas City grain and beef prices. Farmers just off their tractors, with calloused hands and leathery, wind-weathered faces—stiffly dressed in starched khaki workpants, white shirt, and coat and tie—never missed any of the games. They knew the rules as well as the scriptures and had no reluctance to disagree with a referee's call and loudly defame the official in such terms as polite society of the day allowed.

For years the plains community of Forrest had a powerhouse high school basketball team, the Pirates, winning the state championship in 1931 and 1933. In the latter year, because of the Great Depression, the Pirates doubted if they could afford the state tournament in Albuquerque until donations of eggs, bacon, home-canned meat and vegetables, and other food made it possible. A caravan of four or five "Model A Fords, and maybe one Chevy" traveled most of the way to Albuquerque on Route 66, passing "more wagons than automobiles" on long stretches that were still rough and unpaved. Forrest defeated Raton 23–18 for the state championship. The Pirates probably would have come out on top the year before, if the whole team had not contracted severe food poisoning and had to sprint off the court frequently, one by one, to relieve themselves. In that championship game against Albuquerque High School, which set a state record for low scores, the final tally was 29–3, with Forrest making only free throws and not a single field goal. From 1928 to 1934 for seven straight years, and for six out of eleven years, 1944 to 1954, the Forrest team continued its winning ways and went to the state basketball tournament until the high school closed in 1957.[26]

Because of their importance across the countryside, weather conditions and the status of rural schools help provide an explanation of the declining population in the satellite settlements surrounding Tucumcari. And one thing was for sure, if these communities were in trouble, Tucumcari merchants felt the pain immediately. Under any circumstances, the population figures for the rural hamlets themselves hardly seem impressive today, but the farm and ranch families in the adjacent areas at the time must also be considered in the total numbers. In the 2010 census, for instance, the population of Quay County stood at 9,041, or less than it had been a century ago. Back in the region's heyday of homesteading, 1900 to 1910, the county's population rapidly increased to 14,912, only to drop by almost one-third, down to 10,444, by 1920. Subsequent droughts, dry spells, and displacements, such as job opportunities elsewhere during World War II, slowed increases until the count, as it inched back up toward the record-setting total of 1910, reached 13,971 in 1950.[27]

The freakish weather of the 1950s delivered a sucker punch to the rural areas of Quay County. In a masterful understatement, one official report stated, "Precipitation in the area is sporadic and variable." The decade of the 1950s was plagued by conditions reminiscent of the Dust Bowl, when the all-time record for the least annual moisture was set at 6.13 inches in 1934. In fact, the *Wall Street Journal* ran an article with statistics claiming that the drought on the southern Great Plains in the 1950s was worse than the 1930s. Annual precipitation from 1902 to 2002 in Quay County averaged 15.91 inches, but for most of the 1950s the individual years measured below that figure. To make the bad weather's influence worse, the driest years were separated periodically to inflict sporadic but cumulative damage, with 1951 receiving about half the usual amount of moisture, or 8.2 inches, and four years later, in 1955, it was only slightly better at 9.66 inches. The total effect of the weather in the rural farming and ranching areas was reflected in the loss of nearly 1,700 people between 1950 and 1960 (13,971 down to 12,279, or a loss of 12 percent). As the full results of drought conditions struck home, even with improved weather in the following decade, the population erosion continued between 1960 and 1970, 12,279 down to 10,903, or more than an 11 percent reduction. In short, then, in the twenty years between 1950 and 1970, Quay County lost well over 25 percent of its rural population. Such a hefty reduction inevitably had an adverse impact on rural school enrollments, and just as certainly the disturbing news caused additional nail-biting in Tucumcari, since the town itself had declined more than 1,200 in population, from 8,419 down to 7,180, in that same twenty-year period.[28]

Behind the statistics was the human distress caused by the weather. The "big drought of the 1950's, . . .[which] was nearly as bad as the dust bowl days of the 1930's," caused more than one farmer to quit and move into town. The 1950s, according to one wheat-farmer wife, were a gut-wrenching ordeal: "The wind blew for days at a time, covering up . . . [fence rows] with dirt and blocking out the sun. Wet blankets were hung over doors and windows to help keep the dirt out." On the other hand, according to another farm wife, the weather was, if nothing else, always unpredictable: "The early 1960's were good years. . . . It rained 6 days and nights without completely stopping." Yet winter cold spells in Quay County could be so severe it seemed a fury had been loosed on the land. Paul Dodge had crusaded in the *Tucumcari Daily News* for good rural roads, and now country folks were using the improved highways to leave the farms and ranches usually for jobs in Tucumcari or another nearby city.[29]

To set the record straight, the so-called dust storms in Quay County were in actuality sandstorms, consisting of reddish sand granules considerably larger than specs of dust. These storms, driven by gale force winds out of the southwest, could penetrate the edges of any window frame and leave a pile of reddish grains inside on the sill. A person could not work outside, or even walk easily, during these sieges. It is difficult to describe the fear and apprehension caused by the sight of one of those rolling, tumbling, encircling dark clouds filling the entire sky to the southwest from the ground up, and raging on like a gigantic billowing tidal wave. On "Black Sunday," April 14, 1935, when the worst sandstorm of the 1930s struck, an eight-year-old boy and his father had been to visit a neighbor and walking back home were caught by swirling darkness in the middle of a partially vacant city block. For the boy, it was the end of the world he had learned about in Sunday school. He could not see his hands in front his face. The lid of a garbage can banged across the prairie nearby, but he could not see it. Finally, the boy grasped his father's hand and the two of them, stumbling along, felt their way home a half-block away.

The drought of the 1950s brought closure to several remaining county schools. In 1951 alone, five smaller Quay County schools were consolidated with others. At Quay the high school had been shuttered in 1941, and the other grades were eliminated in 1955. Porter High School closed after the gym burned down in 1955. Endee was consolidated with San Jon, and the Wheatland schools closed, both in 1956. The next year, the Nara Visa and Forrest High Schools were terminated. In the wheat-growing community of McAlister, the high school had lasted until 1943 when students were bused to Forrest or House. The grade school shut down in 1956. Whether in New Mexico or any other part of the "Waning West," it was true that "there is nothing more painful to a community than seeing its high school boarded up."[30]

Among Quay County's rural communities, only three managed to survive the 1950s and keep their high schools and lower grades intact: San Jon, with the benefits of Route 66 and Interstate 40; House, which gathered students from adjacent closed districts; and Logan. Of the three, Logan not only managed to last but was the only one that thrived, mainly because of recreational tourism resulting from the construction of Ute Creek Dam at the junction of Ute Creek and the Canadian River. Dedicated in 1963, and built entirely with $5 million of state funds, the dam backs up a lake more than fifteen miles long that is a major tourist attraction as well as the source of an ambitious project to supply water for Clovis, Portales, and other Plains communities.[31]

National and state developments helped close rural schools. Improved buses could now travel farther and transport students greater distances to a central location, and county roads had been paved or updated to make the longer trips possible. In addition, New Mexico fell in line with the national postwar fixation on industrial production, in which schools became like factories, with students as units on the assembly line. In this concept the efficiency of large production facilities carried the day, which meant that small industrial plants—and small rural schools—should be eliminated. Moreover, New Mexico was an economically poor state and needed to trim educational budgets where it caused the least pain—that is, in the rural areas with declining populations. In New Mexico and elsewhere during the postwar period, from the 1940s through the 1960s, the number of school consolidations reached record highs. Although student enrollments in the state increased 117 percent during that time, the number of schools declined by 49 percent, from 7,143 to 3,659. In 1951 alone, five Quay County schools were consolidated with others. Average Daily Attendance (ADA) became the determining factor in closing schools, although state legislation made special provisions for the continuation of some "isolated schools."[32]

At Tucumcari, away from distressed rural areas, the locals could relax and forget their troubles in a beautiful swimming pool. Metropolitan Park, also called Five Mile Park, with its trophy swimming pool and adjacent Spanish-Pueblo revival style combination bathhouse and pavilion, surrounded by graveled roads, ponds, and picnic areas, was a real gem that any much larger city would have gladly claimed. In its declining years, however, Tucumcari was unable, or unwilling, to maintain the park and, as a result, abandoned the swimming pool.[33] Even so, the loss of this tourist attraction and local recreation complex occurred despite the prolonged crusade of a small dedicated group to save it, spearheaded by a specially formed civic organization, the Apache Wells Lions Club. Ray Paulson, a retired public-school teacher and coach who backed this movement, managed the pool in the summers until 1977 when the city withdrew its sponsorship.[34]

On the basis that transportation to Metropolitan Park was too costly and its pool increasingly difficult to maintain, the city had crammed a smaller swimming facility into an existing block-square public park in town.[35] Continued efforts for years by the city and various civic organizations to resurrect the Five Mile Park and its pool proved unsuccessful. The park, pool, and bathhouse received every kind of recognition imaginable, including listing on the National Register of Historic Places, but this kind of acclaim failed to attract restoration funds.[36]

This outcome, however, could not erase memories of the park's swimming pool in its heyday when three hundred to four hundred kids and parents splashed in the spacious waters and a larger crowd watched from the pavilion's shaded veranda. Or, during the Second World War, when several recent high school graduates, back home on leave from the armed services, got the idea around midnight of going out to the old swimming hole, building a blazing fire, and climbing over the tall wire fence surrounding the pool for enjoyable skinny dipping in the moonlight. Conditions at the pool had changed considerably by 2005 when Tom L. Lawson returned to town for the Rattler Reunion and the fiftieth anniversary of his high school graduating class. "Driving into Tucumcari," Lawson recalled, "I made a mistake and pulled off the Interstate to go look at the old swimming pool at Five Mile Park—it looked like something on the outskirts of [war-torn] Baghdad." With a "sinking feeling," Lawson quickly turned around and drove away. A few years after Lawson's trip, any hope of resurrecting the park probably ended with a fire that gutted the bathhouse-pavilion, leaving only its exposed adobe walls standing. The city razed the site several weeks later.[37]

Tucumcari Mountain, a 4,976-foot mesa once part of the Llano Estacado, towers almost a thousand feet above the town three miles away.[38] Called the "Lonely Sentinel on the Plains," the stately landmark had served for more than four centuries as a guide to Indian bands and white explorers alike, remaining relatively unchanged by human hands. The inviting springs at the foot below the hamlike collapsed north face probably accommodated Coronado's expedition as well as other travelers, and several generations of Indian bands occupied the site periodically. In 1853 Heinrich B. Mollhausen, a skilled Prussian artist and naturalist, recorded seeing from twenty miles away that "distant mountain rising like a faint blue cloud along the plain." When he got closer, he wrote that "the Cerro de Tucumcari" took on the image of "a gigantic cathedral" standing

majestically above the surrounding level countryside. The railroader and homesteader throngs who arrived in the early 1900s took a different view of the
pristine mountain. Instead of admiring and protecting the distinguished landmark's natural beauty, the newcomers seemingly could not rest until the mountain served some practical profit-making use. The Quay County commissioners
considered but tabled a resolution that would have preserved and protected
Tucumcari Mountain from commercialization.[39]

In this vein a zany idea did come to fruition in the 1950s, when the Chamber
of Commerce sponsored another desperate attempt to stimulate the tourist trade
and cash in on the nearby historic natural wonder. Apparently enamored of the
purely fictional Tocom and Kari legend, these civic boosters set out to erect the
replica of an Indian village on Tucumcari Mountain. For the village itself, the
chamber envisioned several sixteen-foot-tall teepees of raw cowhide stretched over
slanted poles. A high school art class agreed to paint authentic symbols on the
teepees. It was rumored that the area was salted with imitation arrowheads and
trinkets. Although Comanches had most recently dominated the surrounding
territory, the project was advertised as an Apache Indian village.[40]

An elaborate ceremony celebrating Tucumcari Mountain Day and launching
the Indian village included appropriate hoop-de-la for the momentous occasion,
including a free barbecue, motorcycle mountain-climbing demonstrations up
the nearby slopes, and several other special attractions. For the occasion, the
village of teepees was named "Tucum-Taka-Luk." To add "a natural look" to the
twenty-five teepees erected by the Chamber of Commerce, two native families,
not Apaches or Comanches but from the Santo Domingo Pueblo, circulated
among the guests. They sold their artworks at the replica of a hogan. The Tucumcari Mountain Project was inaugurated with the firm belief that it would start
"a new era for our local tourist industry." Most of "the more than 1,500 persons"
attending the opening celebration, however, were from the surrounding area—as
would be the case for later events. The Chamber of Commerce had managed to
get a rough, narrow road, painfully visible against a backdrop of the Plains
beyond, gouged into the mountain's northeast flank. But the cluster of peaked
teepees was barely visible to motorists approaching town from the east. The
project drew widespread local support for a couple of years, and then lost steam
when it failed to boost the tourist trade appreciably.[41] Four bedraggled teepees,
their rawhide coverings hanging loosely from pole frameworks and flapping in

the wind, did last long enough to be depicted overlooking Tucumcari on a classic panoramic postcard.

In the unrelenting quest to make Tucumcari Mountain useful, local boosters got the support of US Representative Thomas G. Morris of Tucumcari, who enlisted the National Park Service in the cause. The federal agency made a study of the mountain with the possibility that it might be eligible, as proposed locally, for designation as a national park or national monument and thereby a tourist attraction. The Park Service rejected the proposal.[42] As late as the 1970s, another short-lived proposal envisioned hollowing out the mountain's interior for an underground shopping mall and using the dirt and rock to fill up Tucumcari Lake, "thus reclaiming that land for useful purpose." With an eye on the tourist trade, an editor observed, "Think of the interest a hollow mountain would generate for the area."[43]

The mesa's significant elevation and isolated location in the Canadian corridor had led Indian bands to use it for sending messages with smoke and flashing mirrors, and army troops out of Fort Bascom also utilized it for similar purposes. In the 1930s, when air traffic started getting congested, the federal government placed a powerful directional beacon on Tucumcari Mountain. At night the beacon's long, yellow beam swept in a solid arc from horizon to horizon, stirring young boys to imagine that, somehow, they might climb aboard the bright, glowing image and ride it all the way across the heavens.[44] Later, additional towers to relay radio, telephone, television, and other electronic signals were erected on the small second story, or biscuit. Meanwhile, upperclassmen at the local high school had started the annual initiation ritual of having freshman males do the heavy work of carrying buckets of whitewash up the slopes to paint a large letter *T* formed with rocks high on the mountainside facing the town. A recent touch involved the local Rotary Club's outlining of the *T* on the first plateau with solar-powered lights to illuminate it at night. The great mountain, filling up the sky to the south, served as a constant reminder that it had no practical purpose.[45]

In the first years of the town's settlement most townspeople only seemed interested in what the word *Tucumcari* meant ("to lie in wait for someone or something to approach"), not in any real or imagined lore concerning the mountain itself. That all changed in 1907 when a Methodist minister, immersed daily in the lyrical episodes and Good-vs.-Evil lessons of the Scriptures—and probably still captivated by his college course in Shakespeare—concocted a pure and undefiled morality tale strikingly similar to Romeo and Juliet's tragic romance. Over time the original tale evolved into what can be considered a semiofficial version.

THE LEGEND OF TUCUMCARI MOUNTAIN

Wautonomah, an Apache chief, knew that he would die soon, and he was troubled about who his successor would be. The two best warriors were Tonopah and Tocom, who were deadly enemies and rivals for the hand of Kari, the daughter of Wautonomah. Kari loved Tocom and despised Tonopah. Wautonomah summoned Tonopah and Tocom and told them, "I must die soon and one of you will succeed me as chief. Tonight, you must take your knives and meet in a duel to determine the question between yourselves, and the one who survives shall be chief and have my daughter Kari for his wife."

The two rivals met that night on a secluded slope of the mountain and fell upon each other in a fight to the death. Unknown to them, Kari had learned of the duel and now hid nearby. Just when Tocom had disarmed his enemy and seemed about to win, the treacherous Tonopah broke all the rules and drew out another knife he had secretly hidden away and plunged it into Tocom's heart. Kari immediately rushed from her hiding place and struck her own knife into the heart of Tonopah. Then, in grief, she went to the side of her dead lover, picked up his knife, and stabbed herself with it.

When Wautonomah happened upon the death scene, he was stricken with remorse for arranging the duel, and seizing the knife in Kari's bosom, he plunged it into his own chest. In his last, gasping breath, he cried out, "Tocom-Kari, Tocom-Kari!" In time, the old chief's last words came together as "Tucumcari" and furnished a name for the mountain as well as the town that arose three miles away.[46]

The legend has attracted widespread attention. As pointed out previously, it is true that the Apaches at one time occupied much of eastern New Mexico—that is, until the Comanches drove them out and took over. The legend would be slightly more accurate to make it a Comanche tale. Although the mountain is privately owned property, the county road on the east flank, now running all the way up on top of the biscuit, is used as a hiking path, and by technicians in four-wheel-drive vehicles going to service the towers on the mountain.

The Hollywood film *The Last Picture Show* (1971), based on Larry McMurtry's novel of the same title, joined the fate of a star-crossed Texas town and its equally distressed people with that of the local movie theater, which was about to close. The austere black-and-white production conveyed the desired effect of doom.[47] Ten years after the movie's release, as the Interstate 40 Bypass neared completion and Tucumcari's downtown urban renewal project unraveled, the Princess Theater told a similar tale of woe. Once the community's prized movie house, in near ruins it remained standing. The first of three fires had ravaged the downtown building in 1943, during the Second World War, and two more had swept through it later.[48] Although declared structurally sound, it had been boarded up since the last blaze in 1962. Left in this dilapidated condition, it stood isolated and unclaimed amid urban renewal's flashy Four Seasons Mall. The only occupants for twenty years had been a flock of pigeons who made their home on the premises. At one time Arch Hurley and his son Milas had owned two downtown theaters, the Princess and the Odeon as well as a drive-in movie venue on Route 66. The Odeon had become part of the Commonwealth Theatres chain of Kansas City, but it later returned to local ownership. The mortgage holder gave the Princess to the local schools for an auditorium; however, the renovation price tag of $500,000 to make the conversion into a six hundred-seat hall required approval of a special tax levy. Perhaps forgetting all the times they had lost their troubles and worries watching Hollywood fantasies in the darkened interior, the voters turned down the levy.[49]

And so, the grand old Princess Theater, in the heart of the fancy Four Seasons Mall and the successor MainStreet Program, continued to collect mold and pigeon droppings. For those with eyes and ears to pay heed, however, the aged theater held an archive of memories: Humphrey Bogart in *Casablanca*, muttering those immortal words, "Of all the gin joints in all the towns in all the world, she walks into mine"; the seductive Mae West, she of the remarkably ample bosom who aroused strange, new feelings in young boys, as she repeated the trademark invitation in all her film roles, "Come up and see me some time!"; and Buck Jones, a genuine old-time cowboy, not a bespangled phony who sang and played a guitar, but the real thing, who kissed no women, only his beloved horse Silver, and fought the bad guys singlehanded the entire movie despite a mortal wound and a blood stain, or maybe catsup, blotted across his chest. Those memories and many, many more were stored away in the old Princess Theater.

With the town down for the count as the twenty-first century approached,

Princess Theater. Located on Main Street adjacent to renovated urban renewal-sites, the abandoned Princess, once the community's prized movie house, has suffered a series of disastrous fires. Photo by Nancy Stratton Hall.

Odeon Theater, representative of a moderate art deco style, is recognized as an example of an old-time movie house. It is still in operation. Jay Goebel / Alamy Stock Photo (Image ID: CW91RY).

there seemed few indignities left for it to endure. Wrong! For several reasons many towns and cities fought against the retail giant Walmart coming into their communities. Not Tucumcari, where Quay County officials actively courted Walmart to come in and perhaps buck up the lagging retail sector, or at least provide additional employment. In a rare action for Walmart, it refused the welcome mat offered by the county. A Walmart executive said that he had visited Tucumcari several times and concluded that the town lacked sufficient population to support one of his firm's stores. Usually, the mega-giant retailer looked for a place with at least 10,000 to 12,000 people, whereas the town had an estimated population of 5,989 in 2004, and the county only slightly more than 10,000 people. A city official emphasized the traffic flow on Interstate 40 and the number of tourists passing through the town itself, but received little encouragement that Walmart's decision would change anytime soon.[50]

Gambling in New Mexico is regulated by two state agencies. The Racing Commission issues licenses to operate horseracing tracks and monitors the Pari-mutuel betting horseracing industry, while the Gaming Control Board gives licenses for gambling at these sites and oversees their gaming operations. The number of licenses is strictly limited for such venues, called "racinos."[51] In 2008, following lengthy deliberation, the announcement was made that the number of racino licenses already issued would be increased from five to six after consideration of the proposals from interested communities. Representatives from Tucumcari, Quay County, Logan, and San Jon quickly formed the Quay County Gaming Authority and hired Logan attorney Stanley Frost, former district judge, as its executive director. Charged with drawing up the county's bid for the coveted sixth license, Frost and the board of directors organized Coronado Partners LLC to run the proposed Coronado Park Racetrack and Casino at Tucumcari. Don Chalmers, millionaire Albuquerque auto dealer, became the principal investor in the enterprise.

It was big-time speculation involving a potential multimillion-dollar payoff. The estimated cost ranged between $55 and $60 million, with an annual payroll of $8.9 million for three hundred new jobs, and an annual economic impact of $114.7 million. A later study predicted that first-year gross receipts would be $79 million, increasing to $89 million by the fifth year, and directly and indirectly a racino would create 1,264 local jobs the first year and 1,458 jobs by the fifth year. Besides the racetrack, the casino would feature six hundred slot machines.

Raton emerged as Tucumcari's main opponent in the statewide competition for the sixth license. That Raton had a failed racetrack in its La Mesa Park, which closed in 1992, seemed no disadvantage. Also, in southern New Mexico, Hobbs was already operating the fifth licensed racino, and the racing industry, for seasonal scheduling purposes, indicated that it wanted the new facility located farther north than Tucumcari.[52]

Despite this kind of troubling opposition, Tucumcari bared its soul to obtain the sixth license. At last, there was the possibility of an attraction that would cause drivers to pull off the I-40 freeway and visit the town. Tucumcari's ace in the hole, financial backer Don Chalmers emphasized, was its proximity to Amarillo, Texas, located in a state that prohibited casino-style gambling. In fact, authoritative predictions indicated, he said, that 66 percent of a local casino's revenue would come from Texas. As a result, he continued, gambling revenue at Tucumcari would be "money coming from another state into our state," and not "just trading dollars within a community" as would be the case with Raton. For this reason alone, but also because the Raton proposal's backers were Canadians, Chalmers concluded that the economic benefit would be "several times greater" at Tucumcari than at Raton. Or, as Stanley Frost, county gambling authority director put it, the racino was Tucumcari's one big opportunity to get new jobs and economic opportunity. "We won't have another chance like this," Frost said, continuing, "Tucumcari is losing its population base and is dying on the vine." A local newspaper editor saw the big picture of decisive historical turning points:

> Tucumcari was built for train travelers more than 100 years ago. Its heyday was spent catering to visitors along the Mother Road—Route 66—in the 1950s and '60s. But now, with the racino plan, there's a chance to create the next round of glorious days with more potential for tourism than ever before. Coronado Park Racetrack Casino is what we need to put Tucumcari back on the map. It all made good sense, but would it be enough to deliver the highly prized sixth license?[53]

Tucumcari went the distance in preparations when the State Racing Commission came to hold the third of its hearings on granting the sixth license. Businesses and city work crews hung banners and placed posters all over town showing local support for the racino. Even a prominent minister said he backed the proposal because of its employment opportunities. Flyers were circulated inviting everyone in the county to show up in the convention center's parking lot just before the hearing for "the biggest Tailgate Party" ever. Some 1,200 attended the hearing inside and another 200 stood outside noisily showing their support of the county's proposal. The local gambling authority and its financial backers presented their case effectively, and the demonstrations of public support were convincing. But the New Mexico Racing Commission granted the sixth license to Raton. It had been a long, hard four-year ordeal for the entire community, ending in gut-wrenching disappointment. And the racing commission's decision hardly ended the affair, since Raton failed to build the racino, extended court action followed, and the possibility remained that the sixth license was still available. Tucumcari was left in limbo with a gambling authority in place and the racino's site strategically located on a pie-shaped plot in town between the I-40 Bypass and historic Route 66—just waiting if fate should ever beckon favorably. Meanwhile, the county gaming authority merged with the Tucumcari Economic Development Corporation, which joined city and county officials in a renewed fight to capture the elusive sixth license.[54]

As emphasized previously, Tucumcari was caught in a tug-of-war between external and internal destructive forces. The town did not stand alone in this struggle. In fact, countless other places felt the effects of the shifting winds of industrial development in the years after World War II. Urban centers in the state, like Albuquerque and Las Cruces, and those more distant, like Phoenix and Denver, boomed with economic and population growth. One revealing comparison involved Las Vegas, Nevada, and Tucumcari. Las Vegas was already an established settlement, but both took off as towns in the early 1900s with the arrival of railroads almost simultaneously in each place. In the 1940 census, they were still roughly similar in size, with Tucumcari just over 6,000 population and Las Vegas over 8,000. Today, there is no comparison—Las Vegas has well over two million people in its metropolitan area, while Tucumcari numbered 5,363 in 2010 and will probably have fewer than 5,000 in the next census.[55]

What happened to Dawson, a specialized mining center, provided an extreme example of the powerful external forces at work in industrialized America after the Second World War. Once the largest coal producer in New Mexico, Dawson was a company town of nine thousand population and ten mines, coal sorting and cleaning facilities, tall, belching smokestacks of 124 coking ovens, and other machinery and rail lines. Although built on the scale of an eastern industrial complex, its remote, isolated location in northeastern New Mexico suggested an obvious contrast with those broad, intensely developed areas. As detailed earlier, the copper giant Phelps Dodge Corporation, which purchased the mines in 1906, created a model company town with all the urban amenities for the variety of workers who hailed from Europe, Asia, and other parts of the world. These improvements included a high school with forty teachers.[56]

Despite strict safety measures, two deadly mine explosions literally rocked the town and the surrounding area. The first disaster in 1913 killed 2 rescue members and all but 23 of the 286 workers underground, and the second, in 1923, accounted for 123 deaths. Otherwise, Dawson prospered for forty years but changes in the outside industrial world eventually brought its downfall. Natural gas and electricity for cooking and heating, as well as oil furnaces, were cleaner and more efficient for the costs. And the same forces that damaged Tucumcari—the replacement of coal-burning steam locomotives with diesel engines and reorganizations in the corporate world—also helped spell the end for Dawson. Phelps Dodge shut down the last mine in 1950, razed the town, and with a few exceptions sold everything, lock, stock, and barrel, to a Phoenix salvage concern. Only a few houses remained for use by a ranch.[57] Like the loss of trade from the dwindling Plains communities, the disappearance of Dawson coal rail shipments through Tucumcari and the wholesale and retail business coming over the 132 miles of connecting tracks, as well as the diminished railroad employment, hit the town hard.

Other towns in the West experienced chaotic conditions, as mining of various kinds and oil and gas production as well as agricultural and railroad activity went through boom-and-bust cycles. In Robert Pirsig's book, *Zen and the Art of Motorcycle Maintenance*, the author halts his travels and tries to relax in a park, and then looks around at his surroundings:

It isn't restful. A change has taken place and I don't know quite what it is. . . . There is a pallor of dust in the air. Empty lots here and there between the buildings have weeds growing in them. The sheet metal equipment sheds and water tower are like those of previous towns but more spread out. Everything is more run-down and mechanical-looking, and sort of randomly located. Gradually I see what it is. Nobody is concerned anymore about tidily conserving space. The land isn't valuable anymore. We are in a Western town.[58]

The scene laid out before Pirsig is the "Waning West," a region that the rest of the country knows little about. It is a West that has consistently lost population in every census for decades, where the tombstones in the cemetery outnumber the residents in town, where the rough set of ruts along every section line once led to 160-acre homesteads but are now blocked by the locked gates of big ranches, and where For Sale signs are everywhere but there are no buyers. Many western towns and counties have fewer people now than they did a hundred years ago.

One sure sign of a declining community appeared when daily newspapers became weeklies or ceased to exist. At Tucumcari evidence of the town's distress was obvious when Paul Dodge's prized publication, the *Tucumcari Daily News*, suffered its death throes in the late 1970s. The paper began in 1905 on a weekly basis, as the *Tucumcari News*, merged with the *Tucumcari Times*, and became the *Tucumcari Daily News* in 1933. It reverted to a biweekly starting June 3, 1972, resuming its earlier title, the *Tucumcari News* until May 23, 1977, then merged with a Santa Rosa journal to form the *Tucumcari News-Digest*, and finally ceased publication December 23, 1977. At the time of the biweekly reduction, a front-page announcement explained that the publisher felt an "obligation and responsibility" to provide "the best paper Tucumcari can afford." Then, explaining that there was no other choice, the notice pointed out that costs of publication had increased significantly, while the town's population had decreased, which had cut into circulation income. Although circulation brought in only 20 percent of the total revenue, the decrease in population during the past six or seven years had been accompanied by the loss of no less than a dozen sizable business advertisement accounts when those firms shut down. As a result, the *Daily News* had to "tighten its belt or go with the rest of them."[59]

Despite the financial troubles that led to its closure, this venerable news organ had inaugurated a new era of mass communication with Dodge's proprietorship in 1923 and, before his death in 1937, the introduction of a daily edition in 1933. Every Quay County homesteader community worth its salt had a newspaper at one time or another, as evidenced by the files of some twenty county papers, including several in Tucumcari, preserved in digital collections. But Paul Dodge had introduced modern journalism in that part of eastern New Mexico. Meanwhile, before the demise of the *Daily News*, three enterprising local women—Laura Latham McKenzie, Susan L. Gellinger, and Sandra Tompkins—believed the town needed another news venue and began publication of the *Quay County Sun*. After some faltering steps, they got the new paper up and running before it was sold to a Portales publisher.[60] It should be noted also that for years the *Daily News* had as its chief local competitor the weekly or biweekly *Tucumcari American*, which also issued a daily edition briefly.

Among other signs of distress was the decreasing number of cars, or at least the number of car dealerships. In the immediate post–Second World War period close to a dozen dealerships handled most models and makes Detroit produced. Customers could choose among Ford, General Motors, or Chrysler models, or turn to other American makes such as Studebaker, Nash, Hudson, and Willys-Knight. Newcomers such as the Kaiser-Frazier also had models available. By 1983 only two dealerships remained in business—Ford and General Motors. Retired NFL Chicago Bears football linebacker Brian Urlacher, who grew up in Lovington and played at the University of New Mexico, acquired the General Motors dealership in Tucumcari as one of his holdings. When this venue closed in 2013, it was the last local franchise dealership.[61]

Indications of the town's slide down the slippery slope continued to mount. In the spring of 1965, Tucumcari High School announced the largest graduating class in its history—168 seniors. Despite the emerging railroad pullout and an incipient Interstate 40 Bypass, Tucumcari was at its peak, flying high. Twenty-five years later, near the turn of the century, the number had dropped to 70 graduates, or a calamitous decrease of close to 60 percent.[62] Since then, for budgetary reasons, the local school system has gone on a four-day week, and the spring 2016 high school senior class numbered about 60 graduates. During that time the school board laid off teachers and dealt with steadily falling enrollments. What happened to Tucumcari from its peak years until a half-century later is clearly reflected in these statistics.

The wise men of the community, mainly a steady succession of newspaper editors, analyzed, debated, discussed, and refuted what was wrong with the town and how it could be fixed without coming to any consensus. Meanwhile, a series of incidents and controversies occurred that were representative of

Tucumcari's free-fall decline. With the expectation of better service and lower rates, the pundits approved of the Southwestern Public Service's (SPS) arrival to take the place of the defunct municipal power plant, but they howled in protest when SPS merged with a larger firm and closed its office in town. "It seems as though the big company," one editor concluded, "feels the little town of Tucumcari isn't worth dealing with." Another incident occurred when a state police lieutenant, disciplined for mishandling a drug case, was demoted and transferred from Albuquerque to Tucumcari. An Albuquerque newspaper, in discussing the case, insinuated that the officer's transfer to such a "boon dock" assignment was more than adequate punishment for his offense. Up in arms over this insult, the city commission instructed the city manager to tell state police authorities in no uncertain terms that Tucumcari was neither a boondock town nor a penal colony, which he did. The reply from the state police chief was full of apologies and explanations, and there the matter rested.[63]

The pinch of the I-40 Bypass on existing motels was clearly revealed in December 1990, when the owner of a Main Street lodging approached the city commission with an unusual request. As a member of the local economic development council, he submitted a petition to the commission asking for a five-year moratorium on the construction of additional motels anywhere inside the city. He said that three major chains had plans to build locally, and if they did so, the results would be disastrous because, the owner declared, "The tourist pie is finite." More motel rooms would only mean smaller pieces or none for those already in the business. The commission took no action on the petition, and such action, if taken, would likely have been an illegal restraint of trade. But the number of abandoned motels along Route 66 Boulevard today clearly shows that the size of the pie was indeed finite.[64]

With the end of the twentieth century approaching, other troubling issues indicated Tucumcari's decline. A Census Bureau report in 1994 revealed that Quay County was losing population at a higher rate than any other county in the state—a 3.4 percent decrease to 10,457. Especially alarming was the sharp decrease in the number of young people, who, a county official speculated, took temporary employment elsewhere or went off to college and, because of the lack of good jobs locally, never returned. It seemed the discouraging indicators of decline would never end: that Tucumcari ranked third in the state for violent crimes; that the county had an unusually large number of welfare recipients;

that not only did the town's population continue to drop, but it showed no signs of changing; that small, locally owned businesses were disappearing and not being replaced. And so on. An editor of the *Quay County Sun* reiterated the common theme uttered repeatedly in the last few years: "Tucumcari is going through some tough times right now. And townspeople seem to be grim-faced and worried. Tucumcari is not dead yet. Not by a long way." Another editor of the *Sun*—the only newspaper left now, and barely kept alive by paid obituaries and the required legal notices—had the right idea. He emphasized his main point by saying, "It's time for Tucumcari residents to quit dwelling in the recent, and not so recent, past and look forward to a better tomorrow." It was possible, he conceded, to "learn some positive lessons from the past," and reminded his readers that "Tucumcari was once a thriving city, not, as some now perceive it, a city that is drying up and blowing away."[65]

When it had been a prosperous railroad and tourist center, Tucumcari was respected and admired on every hand. It had won the distinction of New Mexico's Blue Ribbon City in 1970 for its livability and efforts in promoting tourist and industrial development.[66] In the heyday of Paul Dodge as editor of the *Tucumcari Daily News*, the main enemies, or competitors, were substantial places like Amarillo and Clovis, but now the main foe was upstart, smallish Santa Rosa. Once the town started sliding down the slippery slope of decline, it seemed that everybody wanted to take a crack at Tucumcari. In 1994 the East Coast elitist *Wall Street Journal* joined the pack by dispatching into the hinterlands a traveling correspondent who eventually stumbled upon Tucumcari and Santa Rosa. Like the neighborhood bully egging on two younger kids to fight, the transient journalist reported from Tucumcari that Santa Rosa wanted "a piece of Tucumcari's cheesy prosperity as a traveler's rest." The front-page article quoted one Santa Rosa motel manager as saying, "Tucumcari advertises over 2,000 rooms, and probably 1,800 of them wouldn't be usable for anybody with any class." Another motel operator added the cryptic quote, "Their city is dying real rapid." The Tucumcari mayor regarded the strange utterances coming out of Santa Rosa as fighting words, but chose, nevertheless, to take the high road. He replied to the insults by emphasizing, in near poetic terms, his city's renowned, artful neon signage. "If you come in at night," he said, "it looks like a piece of black velvet with diamonds thrown out across it." Lillian Redman, crusty as ever in her last years holding sway at the Blue Swallow Motel, reverted to her early days as a Harvey Girl dealing with a bilious customer, and commented tartly, "They're just a very small town." The big city reporter had the last word, pronouncing his judgment on both towns by emphasizing their convenient locations for tourists in need of lodging between Albuquerque and Amarillo: "In reality, neither place has much going for it except geography and beds."[67]

Tucumcari may have survived this round, but Santa Rosa got the upper hand in the rivalry when it obtained a privately operated state prison, and Tucumcari, despite its best efforts in Santa Fe to secure a similar facility, failed to do so. Also, in another loss for Tucumcari the Union Pacific chose Santa Rosa for the location of its "mixing center," or drop-off point for carloads of automobiles brought by freight trains to be picked up and hauled elsewhere by trucks.[68]

Back in August 1979, even though more disappointments lay ahead at that time, it seemed like the last straw when Alex Sands had announced that the Sands-Dorsey Drugstore would close after sixty-five years at the southwest corner of Main and Second Streets.[69] Sands, grandson and namesake of famed lawman Alex Street and son of a firm's founder, Leon Sands, stated the reason precisely for the decision to close after such a long history as an anchor of the local business community, "We're just not making any money." Robert Wicks, the store's longtime pharmacist, now retired, spoke for many in the community when he commented: "It's sad. A lot of people grew up with Sands—it's a landmark." He was exactly right. Sands-Dorsey's fountain area had been a community social center for young and old alike, where dating couples came for a soda or milkshake, businessmen met over coffee and made deals, and older, retired seniors sought out friends for company. Professional boxing matches had once been held upstairs before the introduction of offices there, while the basement below had regularly hosted high-stakes poker games. More recently, a back room humorously called the "City Hall Annex," was the scene of a regular morning coffee klatch where a mix of the town's old-timers and current business leaders met to exchange gossip, tell jokes and stories, and discuss politics and business affairs. In addition, besides prescriptions, the store also sold a wide variety of goods from bottled liquor to firearms.[70]

In 2007 a disastrous fire left the Sands-Dorsey building in ruins. After years of wrangling over who had the responsibility of cleaning up the mess, the city finally obtained funding to do the job that would meet environmental requirements. With the last remains of Sands-Dorsey gone at the corner of Second and

Sands-Dorsey Drugstore was a community gathering place for people of all ages and sold everything from prescriptions to bottled liquor. After closing, it was hit by fire, and the debris was hauled away. Photo by Nancy Stratton Hall.

Main, it seemed that Tucumcari was giving up. The Vorenberg Hotel across the intersection at the northeast corner had experienced a similar fate. As for the rest of the surviving original business district, the local police blotter recorded, early in the evening of August 9, 2008, an anonymous phone call that two small children were playing in the middle of Main Street.[71]

Chapter 10

SOME WENT RUNNING

rances McDaniel Prentice was the wife of Southern Pacific telegrapher Sylvester Prentice, son of longtime Tucumcari lawyer Royal A. Prentice, who was the patriarch of a large local clan of generational offspring. All of which is a way of saying that Frances Prentice spoke from seasoned as well as shared firsthand knowledge when she remembered Tucumcari as an important regional railroad center and the junction point of the Southern Pacific and two Rock Island lines, as well as the Dawson branch. Because of all the operational and administrative functions occurring at several levels, she pointed out, Tucumcari "offered a unique opportunity" for beginning employees to learn the most important aspects of railroading and go on to high-level positions in the industry as several had done.[1]

As proof of this assertion, numerous executives had started working in the industry at Tucumcari or had significant experience there, and later became officers of major national and regional lines, industry associations, and similar bodies involving most parts of the United States. In fact, so many had done so that the town could rightfully boast of a national impact on the railroad map. In a humorous example of the town's outreach, so many Southern Pacific executives at SP headquarters at one time or another hailed from Tucumcari that the staff referred to the "Tucumcari Crowd."

In a related circumstance, when the railroads were hiring freely after World War II, it seemed that the main influence in who got the best jobs was whether your father or some other close relative was, or had been, a railroader. As a result, most of those included in Frances Prentice's observation about Tucumcari as a springboard for future rail executives were second-generation railroaders—that is, they were following in the footsteps of their father or a close relative.[2] Of those in the second generation who got their start in railroading at Tucumcari, Richard

La Cita Restaurant with an interesting entrance is representative of the many Mexican food eateries along old Route 66. Courtesy of Carol M. Highsmith.

D. Spence rose to the greatest heights in the industry. After World War II naval combat service in the Pacific, Spence began in the Tucumcari railyards as an apprentice brakeman in 1946, and twenty-three years later, at age forty-four, became the youngest vice president the Southern Pacific had ever appointed. At age fifty he was president of Conrail, the biggest railroad conglomerate in the United States.[3]

Every member of Spence's immediate family except his mother was employed at one time or another by a railroad, starting with his locomotive engineer father, two older brothers, a brother-in-law, and a sister, who held a clerical position at the division headquarters. When Spence was born at home on the kitchen table, attended by railroad physician Dr. Joseph M. Doughty and a midwife, family legend said that he had flopped off the counter where he was placed after his birth. Siblings teased him the rest of his life, claiming that he had hit the floor on his head and was never "quite right" afterward. Another interpretation might be, however, that Dick Spence came into the world thrashing about with ambition and determination to make a name for himself in the life ahead. While growing up in Tucumcari, he seemed intent on fulfilling the second version by taking every part-time job and seizing every opportunity that presented itself in the smallish railroad town and tourist mecca. In high school he starred in both football and basketball, excelled scholastically, had leading roles in class plays, and won election as student body president. Like mythical heroes Superman and Batman, Spence also saved the day for the high school band at football games. As the band's only reliable trombone player, he would quickly change from his gridiron togs into a band uniform for the halftime musical performance at midfield, and afterward swiftly switch clothing again to play in the second half. Dick Spence volunteered for the US Navy and left school in the middle of the spring semester of his senior year.

Spence's various part-time jobs had been necessary because of finances at home. Earlier, his father, locomotive engineer Andrew Doke Spence, had owned or leased the OK garage and gas station on the side, an activity strictly forbidden by the railroad at that time, and he was fired. Doke Spence left town in search of railroad employment elsewhere, and as Dick Spence wrote later, "My father disappeared forever."[4] Her husband's absence in the depths of the Great Depression of the 1930s "quickly became a disaster" for Myrtle Spence, left to fend for herself and feed a family. And so Richard D. Spence, who developed supreme self-confidence and became president of the railroad conglomerate Conrail, did not grow up "with a silver spoon in his mouth" but, instead, had once lived with the daily family dilemma of wondering where the next meal was coming from.

Perhaps because he was the youngest member of the family, with a doting mother and considerably older siblings, Dick Spence had the talent of becoming a prodigy—of being recognized for his potential and rewarded for his accomplishments. Such personal qualities plus an undergraduate degree from UCLA, a specialized program in transportation management at Stanford, and another advanced program for senior executives at MIT undoubtedly aided Spence in his rise to the top in the railroad industry. He graduated that same year, 1943. During World War II in Tucumcari, it was usual to approve graduation for those who volunteered for the armed forces (which was almost always the navy) in the final semester of their senior year. This was the case for many. You could only volunteer at seventeen—or be drafted, almost certainly for the army infantry, at eighteen, if you stayed for commencement. Those were the facts of life at that time.

After graduation from UCLA and working summers for the SP as a brakeman out of Tucumcari, Spence returned to California with the intention of entering Loyola University Law School. Before enrolling, however, he was offered a job as a terminal trainmaster at Lordsburg with a salary of $550 per month. He accepted immediately. From the Lordsburg assignment Spence rose steadily through the Southern Pacific ranks. In 1962 Richard D. Spence, delivered as a baby by a railroad physician on the kitchen table in Tucumcari, New Mexico, received word of his advancement to One Market Plaza, SP headquarters in San Francisco, as assistant general manager.[5] He was on his way up the SP managerial ladder. One extraordinary achievement had probably drawn the attention of the SP brass more than any other. In the winter of 1953–1954, while on a temporary assignment in the mountains between Roseville, California, and Sparks, Nevada, Spence had arrived just in time to witness a monster snowstorm. Following the telephoned instructions of SP President Donald J. Russell, he forged through a blinding blizzard to rescue track workers and lead them to safety. Then, for two days, he tended the passengers trapped in a mountain pass aboard the premier SP train City of San Francisco. From then on, Russell undoubtedly remembered him for a difficult job done successfully.

Spence soon settled into his new job at SP headquarters. He traveled over the SP system evaluating terminals, branch lines, equipment, rail yards, shop repair and replacement operations, and other company facilities. Advanced to assistant vice president–system operations in 1967, he was appointed vice president–operations in 1969, at age forty-four, the youngest VP–Ops the SP ever had. As he gained experience and regular promotions, Spence testified at congressional hearings in Washington on railroad matters and learned the fundamentals of national politics. He also met and struck up friendships with senior officers of other railroads, particularly eastern lines, and officials of national industrial associations.[6]

In his memoirs Spence is evasive about his part in the Southern Pacific Railroad's pullout from Tucumcari. While cruising among the historic Greek islands of the Aegean Sea during an extended family vacation, he received a message of an impending trainmen's strike at Tucson. "We (Southern Pacific) had earlier closed Tucumcari, New Mexico as a terminal," he later wrote, adding, "We had moved people, such as my brother-in-law, Dean Shockley, a yardmaster, to Tucson as part of the closure." To Spence's relief, the trainmen's strike ended by the time he reached Istanbul. This convoluted reference to the SP pullout from Tucumcari, interspersed in his recollection about a strike at Tucson, is the only time that Spence wrote in his memoirs about the SP's exit from his hometown. In a 2002 telephone conversation with the author, he commented that he had a hand in implementing the shutdown but added no details.[7] Under the prevailing circumstances, it is doubtful that Richard D. Spence or anyone else could have prevented the closure. Ironically, in January 1968, at the same time the SP was in the process of drastically reducing its local activities and transferring employees, the Tucumcari/Quay County Chamber of Commerce held a banquet honoring a group of former residents who had become well known in their chosen fields. Two executives from Southern Pacific headquarters in San Francisco, Richard D. Spence, assistant vice president of system operations, and Lawrence F. Furlow Jr., assistant vice president in the contracts department, were among the honored guests.[8]

Spence had gone to St. Louis to finalize SP's purchase of the Alton and Southern Railway and was conferring with company lawyers in his hotel room when he received a message from Tucumcari that his mother had been attacked and robbed in her home and was hospitalized in critical condition.[9] He dropped the legal papers he was reading, chartered a plane, and flew to Tucumcari without delay shortly before Myrtle Spence died from her wounds. Spence brought in two SP detectives to assist city and county lawmen in the investigation and offered a $5,000 reward for apprehension of the murderer. Following a tip, the city police arrested a seventeen-year-old Hispanic boy, whom Myrtle Spence had befriended and paid to do chores. The young defendant was given a life sentence in the state prison, but was later injured in a prison riot, released, and reportedly returned to Tucumcari.[10]

It was certainly no surprise in railroad circles when, in the early 1970s, seven northeastern and midwestern lines went into bankruptcy and the federal government created Amtrak to continue passenger service. In addition, at that time the US Railway Association was formed and funded to develop a plan that would save what was left of the stricken companies. The surprise came when President Gerald Ford named a Los Angeles insurance executive, not a railroad official, as president of USRA. When appointed, Edward G. Jordan compared the new rail combination to the struggling US Postal Service and alluded to his lack of railroad experience, saying that he was "'a little known president' of 'an unknown company.'"[11] Several months after his original appointment, the USRA board named Jordan chairman and chief executive officer of Consolidated Rail Corporation, or Conrail, the agency authorized to take over and revive the bankrupt railroads.[12] Conrail was scheduled to become wholly independent on April 1, 1976, Conveyance Day or Activation Day, when USRA would set the new corporation free to either sink or swim. Meanwhile Jordan and his team, many of whom, like their chief, had no hands-on experience with railroads, set out to establish headquarters in Philadelphia and hire staff personnel. Eventually the professional staff numbered 170.[13]

In mid-1975 a representative of the USRA board offered Richard D. Spence the position of Conrail president, or chief operating officer.[14] Before making a decision, Spence conferred with formidable SP president Benjamin Franklin Biaggini. Described by a railroad periodical as "emperor of the Southern Pacific," Biaggini had served as president of the SP since 1964. Donald J. Russell retired and vacated the chairmanship of the board of directors in 1972, and Biaggini was expected to move up, leaving the presidency open for some younger SP executive. Usually, the current vice president of operations became the "crown prince" in such circumstances. Would Biaggini tell current VP–Ops Richard D. Spence, implicitly at least, that he should stick around to become the next SP president? Or would the older man tell him, "Take the Conrail job!" meaning that Spence was out of the running for SP president. Shortly afterward, Biagggini was quoted in the press as calling Spence "the best operating man in the industry." But, in effect, Spence got the message from Biaggini in their meeting that he was not in the running for the presidency. As Spence recorded it in his memoirs, "Mr. Biaggini congratulated me and seemed sorry that I was leaving, but he also understood what a tantalizing opportunity I had ahead of me."

Spence's goodbye to former chairman Russell was brief, and the reply probably what he had expected to hear from Biagggini. Russell exclaimed, "You could have been President!" Spence stated publicly that he left the SP because of the challenge offered by the Conrail presidency. After taking the job, he told the new workforce, "I honestly believe that Conrail is our best chance to save America's private sector rail industry from the threat of financial collapse and nationalization." According to insiders, Spence became disillusioned that he would not be SP president "and wanted to run his own railroad."[15] When Biaggini moved up to chairman a year later, his hand-picked successor, Denman McNear, who had been Biaggini's assistant for more than three years, was named president. McNear had taken a crucial step in his railroading career when he became trainmaster at Tucumcari.[16]

For Richard D. Spence the presidency of Conrail involved the seemingly impossible task of taking over six different bankrupt railroads in seventeen states of the Northeast and Midwest—the Penn Central, Central Railroad of New Jersey, Erie Lackawanna, Lehigh and Hudson River, Lehigh Valley, and Reading—and blending them together into one efficiently operating rail line called Conrail.[17] Different modes of operation and management among the six railroads were only the beginning. Negotiating new USRA-mandated contracts with all the labor unions and brotherhoods took an inordinate amount of time and patience. Replacing thousands of miles of deteriorated tracks and obtaining at least three hundred new locomotives were horrendous tasks. In fact, "the most immediate problem" was motive power, mainly locomotives, many of which, Spence determined, were "virtually falling apart."[18] And on and on. On top of all these challenges, it was necessary to constantly assure Congress and the USRA of satisfactory progress toward Conveyance Day, or Activation Day, on April 1, 1976, when Conail would become an independent operation.

Spence's biggest problem, however, was his boss, Conrail's chairman and CEO Edward G. Jordan. Or, as Spence put it, there was a "great distance" between him and the chairman. They had different styles of management and different approaches on almost everything else. More specifically, Spence regarded Jordan as a poor "problem solver," and the kind of corporate executive who relied on an "imperial presence" arising from his lofty position. In labor relations, while Spence worked patiently to establish a common ground between labor and management, Jordan favored a get-tough policy that implied that the union leaders "would eventually just let Conrail have its own way." On the other hand, Spence adhered to the concept he had known at the Southern Pacific that emphasized a family relationship within a tightly knit "traditional authoritative, hierarchical management structure."[19] Published accounts described Jordan's management style as "autocratic," which often resulted in a "personality mismatch." Spence's principal shortcoming, it was said, arose from his long career in operations. He was such "an avid railroader, so imbued with the art of running trains that he sometimes forgets the need of profitability."[20] Whatever the case, bad chemistry existed between Conrail's top two executives.

After a relatively smooth Conveyance Day and more than two years as chief operating officer, or "the outside man," to Ed Jordan's role as chief executive officer, or "the inside man," it became obvious, according to Spence, "that Ed Jordan and I would never make a team." Quite simply, Spence declared, "Among other things, we neither admired nor liked each other." At first, rumors circulated that Ed Jordan would resign or be fired as chairman, but instead, when the board of directors convened in a special meeting at the Philadelphia headquarters on June 26, 1978, Jordan asked for Spence's removal and got his wish.

No reason for Spence's departure was given in a brief announcement saying only that he was "leaving his position as president and chief operating officer immediately." *Railway Age* asked, "Was he pushed or did he jump?" Questioned about whether Spence had been asked to leave, a Conrail spokesman pointed out that the board's statement said nothing about a resignation. Initially, Conrail had performed better than expected economically, but later, the *New York Times* reported, it was "suffering severe financial problems." Reliable reports indicated that some USRA board members were dissatisfied with Spence's efforts to reduce expenses and not reluctant to see him go. There were rumors that the board was also upset by reports that a thousand employees on the payroll could not be identified. Likewise, there was criticism that freight cars scheduled or urgently needed in certain locations had not shown up on time. In fact, Spence's management of operations had "drawn sharp criticism" in Congress and a $2.3 million fine by the Interstate Commerce Commission. When one board member expressed his support, however, Spence recalled, "I told him honestly that I could not work with Mr. Jordan." In fact, Conrail's politicized structure and failure to meet unreasonable expectations required a scapegoat, and either Spence or Jordan had to go. It was an easy choice. Spence as "Mr. Outside" in charge of operations, where steel wheels hit steel rails—or failed to do so—seemed the obvious culprit. On the other hand, Jordan as "Mr. Inside," shielded by his higher position in Philadelphia headquarters, seemed above the chaos.[21]

Richard D. Spence left the plush Conrail quarters in Philadelphia after two years and eight months with a guaranteed salary of $135,000 for two more years. He could have taken it easy for several months or even a year, but he wasted no time licking his wounds. Instead, he soon accepted an offer to become president of the Louisville & Nashville Railroad, commonly known as the L&N. Under Spence's leadership L&N "staged a stunning financial comeback in just two years," reversing a $31.2 million loss in 1978, the year he became its president, to a $28.8 million profit in 1979.[22] He was recognized in Congress for his "record of outstanding performance as a railroad man" in rescuing L&N, and he was designated in an industry publication as one of the nation's most admired railroad executives. In 1979 his total compensation rose from $158,000 to $241,000 a year (about $840,000 today).[23] After the disappointments at Southern Pacific and Conrail, Richard D. Spence had now reached the peak of his railroad career.[24]

As a result of the railroad merger craze, Spence later served as executive vice president of operations for Family Lines and the Seaboard System from 1980 to 1984, and then retired to become a railroad consultant until 1990.[25] In retirement he enjoyed a Florida home with his socially prominent second wife as well as another residence in Scotland close to a golf course. He made a profitable investment in an English firm that produced "nappies" or disposable diapers.[26] Richard D. Spence had almost forty-five years in railroading, mostly on an upward executive trajectory. In a newspaper obituary of Spence's death in Florida, on his ninetieth birthday, April 7, 2015, proper attention was devoted to his illustrious railroad career and his personal attributes as well as "his great jitterbug dance moves."[27]

Although not all of them were at Southern Pacific headquarters at the same time, the easily identifiable members of the Tucumcari Crowd included Dick Spence, Larry Furlow, Roy Penix, and Charles Babers. Harold F., "H. F." or "Fulkie," Fulkerson from Tucumcari was the district superintendent at nearby Watsonville.[28] Following in his father's footsteps, Roy Penix had taken a job with the SP in signal maintenance at Deming, dropping out of high school at Tucumcari and stretching his age a bit to do so. It was 1942, at the beginning of the Second World War, and the railroad desperately needed workers. Later, when a question arose about his age—which was seventeen by now—Penix joined the navy and thus kept his SP seniority intact. In time, after the war, Roy Penix moved up to become an assistant signal engineer at the company headquarters.[29] Lawrence F. "Larry" Furlow Jr. was assistant vice president in the SP contracts office.[30] Both he and Spence came from railroad families, grew up together in Tucumcari, and, as members of the high school graduating class of 1943, joined the navy at about the same time. After his navy discharge Furlow first worked in a clerical position at the division offices but, like Spence, soon signed on as a brakeman. Close behind Spence, he became assistant trainmaster at Lordsburg, and, on his high school classmate's trail, they both eventually landed at SP headquarters and formed the nucleus of the Tucumcari Crowd.

Roy Penix often conducted business with other members of the Tucumcari Crowd. He soon learned that Spence had the hands-on reputation of covering a great many miles on "walking trips" through SP terminals and rail yards, and not sitting in his office waiting for the phone to ring. In contracts, as mentioned previously, Larry Furlow had a major role in the SP's lengthy on-again, off-again negotiations to acquire the bankrupt Rock Island. Roy Penix sometimes consulted with Furlow on interpretations or changes the railroad unions wanted to make in their contracts. The Tucumcari Crowd also included, as a later addition, General Manager Charles T. Babers, who was Penix's boss on the organizational chart. When the two conferred on business matters in the general manager's office, Penix found Babers to be a cordial and effective executive. Without a college degree or even a high school diploma, Roy Penix had forty years of solid practical experience in the SP signal system when he took early retirement in 1983.

Unpretentious and unimpressed with formalities, Charles T. Babers was a second-generation railroader who got his start at Tucumcari and jumped through the hoops all the way to SP headquarters in San Francisco.[31] Babers, while a switchman in the local yards, might well have risen to similar heights on the other side of the industrial scene. Because of his hearty, forceful personality and organizational skills, he was becoming a prominent figure in local railroad union circles, and the Brotherhood of Railroad Trainmen wanted him to become a full-time field representative. At about the same time, however, he caught the eye of Rio Grande Division superintendent W. R. Adair, who, accompanied by several other SP officials, came from El Paso to give the main talk and hand out awards at a highly successful safety meeting. In charge of the Family Night affair attended by four hundred people, Babers put on a show that would have pleased a professional party organizer. Some four dozen talented young people from the community presented vocal, instrumental, and choral group music, starting with a bottle, fife, and jug chorus. There was an Elvis

Presley impersonation in pantomime, door prizes, inviting refreshments, and dancing to the music of an orchestra. Babers also introduced the uniformed Pacific Diesels Little League baseball team, of which he was the manager. Several longtime railroaders commented that this was the best safety meeting they had ever attended.[32]

At the end of the meeting, Superintendent Adair's secretary called Babers aside and invited him to El Paso to chair the Rio Grande Division safety meeting, which he attended but did not preside. He did, however, have an opportunity at that affair to meet and mingle with several company officials from SP headquarters, including J. W. Corbett, who had been trainmaster at Tucumcari and was now SP vice president of operations. Later, when W. R. Adair retired as division superintendent, the employees chipped in a dollar apiece to buy him a car, and Babers was chosen to make the presentation at a fancy banquet in an El Paso hotel. He must have done an outstanding job because afterward he was offered an appointment as assistant trainmaster at Carrizozo. A routine local safety awards meeting provided Charles Babers with the opportunity to join management levels of the Southern Pacific Railroad.

Babers had become a second-generation railroader following a family tragedy. When he was nine years old, his father, Josh Babers, a section foreman near Tucumcari, had gone on a quail hunting trip along the Dawson branch when he was severely wounded in an accidental shotgun blast. The others in the hunting party loaded the wounded man on a motorized handcar, hustled him to Tucumcari, and put him aboard a baggage car for El Paso. The Babers family followed close behind on the Golden State passenger train. Josh Babers reached El Paso alive but died in the hospital, leaving a wife and three young sons. Clyde Wells, who had been a member of the hunting party, married the widow and helped raise the three boys. The couple also added a daughter, Lucretia, and another son, Marvin, who, as we shall see, also had a notable career in the railroad industry. Employment opportunities were scarce during the Great Depression, but Clyde Wells had found a job on the clerical staff in the division offices.

Charles Babers drew more important posts in the SP system. To prepare him for the challenging responsibilities ahead, the railroad enrolled him in Harvard University's famed General Management Program. By the time he finished the rigorous Harvard program, Babers felt he was ready for whatever advancement the SP might offer him.

After the usual assignments for budding SP executives, Babers was appointed assistant general manager at the San Francisco headquarters and then general manager. For a year Babers headed the labor relations department before returning to his former duties. In an impromptu interview after retirement, Babers recalled the stress of his executive duties:

> There wasn't any time off, there wasn't any leisure time and phones were ringing all hours of the day and night no matter where you were. Vacations or wherever, why, you were getting phone calls, you were having to make decisions, [and] there would be some labor problem, [and] you'd have to go back [home] and sit down with those guys and argue it out. . . . I never was where a strike was called when I was around and could get to them before they did it.

After heart bypass surgery, Babers never returned to his office. "I figured, what the heck," he reasoned for not going back and retiring instead, "I've gotten myself in this condition by working 24 hours a day, seven days a week, 365 days a year."[33]

Like Spence, Babers as general manager got to hire his own combination chef-bartender on the private railroad car assigned to him for his frequent trips over the SP system. Probably the highlight of his entire SP career came in 1980 when the City of Tucumcari celebrated Charles Babers Day and presented him with the key to the city. The ceremony was also occasioned by the ribbon-cutting celebration for the SP's acquisition of the Rock's Tucumcari Line to Kansas City. To add luster to the occasion, SP General Manager Charles T. Babers, who got his start as a switchman in the local yards, had arrived with his personal chef in a luxurious private railroad car, which was switched to a sidetrack in full view of the old downtown. At the formal ribbon-cutting program in a packed city hall, Babers was the featured speaker. Before his remarks, in which he stressed the necessity of concerted communal action to keep SP operations in town, a Tucumcari High School Class of 1949 graduate sang all verses of the THS team's Rattler fight song.[34] For Charlie Babers, this special occasion in his old hometown, accompanied by his personal chef and in his private railroad car, was the payoff for all of those midnight phone calls, headaches arguing with union officials, and interrupted family vacations.

Frank Kile Turner followed a different route to the executive level of railroad management. As previously indicated in chapter 6, he grew up in a local railroad family but used Tucumcari indirectly as a springboard for a career in the industry. His father, Frank N. Turner, began a long association with railroading as a "call boy" (usually a young person who called crews for their next run) for the El Paso & Southwestern Railroad, retired as a Southern Pacific conductor, and at his death in 1994 at age ninety-two, was the last living employee of the old EP&SW.[35] In short, an impressive parental example, plus growing up in a railroad town, undoubtedly instilled railroad blood in young Frank Turner. Whatever the case, after attending New Mexico Military Institute at Roswell and East Texas State University (now Texas A&M University at Commerce) where he graduated in 1961, he served eight years as a Marine Corps officer, including thirteen months in Vietnam.

In 1969 Turner was honorably discharged from the Marine Corps as a captain and began a thirty-seven-year railroad career. He started as a management trainee with the Norfolk and Western Railroad and continued with that line in operations positions, including superintendent and general manager, until its merger with the Southern Railroad. In 1988 he became vice president of operations, and a year later president and CEO, for the Midsouth Railroad, which was later sold to the Kansas City Southern. Next, Turner changed from regional railroads to the CSX system where he held the position of vice president of field operations and intermodal. He returned to smaller lines when, in 1998, he was chosen as president of the American Shortline and Regional Railroad Association, a trade organization representing four hundred small and regional railroads with Congress and government agencies, headquartered in Washington. When he retired in 2002, Congress recognized him for his "visionary leadership in the railroad industry." As a personal example, Frank Kyle Turner's career with several different companies showed, in graphic detail, the frenzied railroad merger craze in the last three decades of the twentieth century.[36]

Dick Spence's competitor for the SP presidency, who won out, had unorthodox credentials for the job. Denman K. McNear grew up in Petaluma, California, not in eastern New Mexico; his family was in the feed and grain business, not railroading; nor did he get his start in the trade at Tucumcari. McNear's Tucumcari rail assignment, nevertheless, helped determine his future with the Southern Pacific Railroad. A graduate of MIT in civil engineering, McNear was fresh out of college when, in 1948, he took an engineering job in construction with the SP's Sacramento Division. During the next seven years at Sacramento, he headed a surveying party for a challenging major construction project, the Roseville Hump Rail Yard, and afterward became general track maintenance foreman. Then he advanced to SP headquarters where he served for a year as the system's construction engineer. All of his SP service so far had been in engineering, not operations, the usual path to the company's top executive positions. One day the general manager called McNear into his office with the surprising news that he would be transferred to an obscure place McNear had barely heard of called Tucumcari, not in engineering, but in a completely different capacity, as trainmaster, an operations position.

McNear was astounded. After locating Tucumcari on a map, he started wondering about the reason for his apparent exile to such a remote spot and thinking about what his new duties might entail. As McNear later recalled, "Operations at Tucumcari was really the first step in my career to CEO [of the SP system]." In fact, he eventually became SP chairman, president, and CEO simultaneously. Undoubtedly a crucial move in Denman McNear's distinguished railroad career came when he was "exiled" to Tucumcari, where he gained essential operational experience monitoring rail traffic between there and Dalhart and Carrizozo, 1955 to 1957. The unusual action of transferring him from one department to another indicated that he seemed to have potential for the company's executive ranks. According to a widely circulated rumor, when a young employee showed promise, he was often sent as a trainmaster to Tucumcari with its complicated divisional connections to prove himself. He had also apparently gained an advantage in the running for SP president by serving as Ben Biaggini's assistant and as an SP vice president after stints in operations at Tucumcari and elsewhere. McNear had pleasant memories of his two years in Tucumcari: of "Two Gun Harry" Garrison meeting passengers at the trains and enticing them to his sandwich joint; of living, as a bachelor, in a company house formerly occupied by a family of ten; of the help he received in learning to perform his duties as trainmaster; and of the local merchants' custom of always, without fail, saying after you paid a tab, "Hurry back."[37]

Third-generation railroad executives comprise another category of those who, in one way or another, used Tucumcari as a springboard to start their careers in the industry. Charles Edward Babers, son of Charles Thomas Babers, fits in this classification. His career in railroading not only ran in a straight line from his grandfather, Josh Babers, the section foreman whose death resulted from a hunting accident, to his father, the SP general manager. Also, he was recruited by the same SP official who hired his father.[38] Although he had the brains and work ethic for success, his family status and some fatherly advice along the way may well have smoothed his advancement through the ranks. Babers also provides an example, as a child in a railroad family and in his own career, of the constant movement from one assignment to the next involved in the ascendancy of aspiring young rail executives. For most of his life, from his birth at Tucumcari in 1951, while his father worked in the local yards as a switchman, to his own retirement sixty years later in 2011, he was constantly changing schools and adjusting to a different neighborhood. Then, in his own career, he was regularly fitting in at his next job location and worrying about his own family's wellbeing. By the time his daughter was in the sixth grade, it was the sixth school she had attended. His son had been enrolled in three high schools by the time he graduated. Babers has said that except for concerns about his family the frequent moving was never an issue for him personally because he liked meeting different people and finding out about new places. But the demands of the railroader life on wives and mothers of growing families can well be imagined. With their husbands away much of the time, childcare and family affairs were left in their hands, as well as the main responsibilities of frequent packing and unpacking in the case of sudden announcements of transfers to new locations.

When Babers was six years old, his father became assistant trainmaster at Carrizozo and the family started shifting around the Southern Pacific system as the elder Babers moved up in SP management. In a remarkable coincidence, when his father was an assistant superintendent of the SP Los Angeles Division in 1969, he worked with another assistant superintendent, Arnold G. Bays, who had hired him as a switchman at Tucumcari almost twenty years earlier. It was hardly a random selection, then, when this same SP official who had hired his father called young Babers and asked if he would like to work for the SP as a brakeman. Young Babers had signed on briefly as a switchman with the Santa Fe Railroad after his high school graduation and was now a college freshman. Bays said that the SP always needed help during Christmas holidays, and he could hire Babers as an experienced employee because of his work for the Santa Fe.

That was how Charles E. Babers began his SP career as a third-generation railroader—the same way his second-generation father had done before him—by working during the holidays and summers for two years before becoming a full-time brakeman and being promoted to conductor in 1972. He then "did a lot of booming around," spending three to eight months at various locations between Yuma, Arizona, and Watsonville, California, and up the SP San Joaquin Division to Fresno. In 1976 he accepted a management position as assistant trainmaster at Bakersfield, California. In the next thirteen years, he moved ten times in executive assignments at locations from Southern California to Texas and Kansas, including a couple of stops at SP headquarters in San Francisco. Not surprisingly, his transitory lifestyle delayed marriage until he was twenty-seven years old and fell in love with a railroad secretary's daughter at Yuma. He had known her earlier as a childhood friend when his father was assigned to the Yuma division headquarters. Thereafter, as the SP passed into other hands, Babers worked in the new headquarters at Denver, and after its sale to the Union Pacific in 1996, for seven years at the Edward H. Harriman Center in Omaha as the director of positions. In 2004 he applied for a position in the Pacific Northwest in the intermodal department and retired there in 2011. Babers's Oregon retirement home was his thirty-seventh residence, and the one he liked best. Sizing up his railroading career, Charles E. Babers wrote, "The best years of my career were during the timeframe of the 60's–70's and 80's before regulations and technology changed much of what had made railroading the thing of legend."

Marvin Lee Wells was a fourth-generation railroader, who got his inspiration for railroading, although not his actual start in the trade, at Tucumcari.[39] His paternal great-grandfather was a bridge and building supervisor for a Tennessee railroad, and his grandfather, the original Marvin Lee Wells, was an SP road-master at various locations in the Tucson and Rio Grande divisions, including at Tucumcari. From this point on, the railroad connections become more complicated. Wells was the uncle of Charles E. Babers and the half-brother of Charles T. Babers, whose widowed mother had married Clyde Wells of the SP division headquarters clerical staff. Born in 1947, Marvin was the son of Clyde Wells and Lucretia Babers Wells. In short, young Wells had strong railroad bloodlines, which were strengthened by growing up in the busy railroad center of Tucumcari. Wells recalled that as a kid in Tucumcari the elite Little League team was the Southern Pacific Diesels. Coached by railroaders, the Diesels wore uniforms like their idols, the New York Yankees. "Every kid wanted to play for the Diesels," Wells remembered. Although not drafted by the Diesels at age seven, he had a satisfactory Little League career playing for the Kiwanis team against them.

After high school graduation in 1965, Marvin Wells got the tough summer job at Yuma, Arizona, of icing down freight cars of the Southern Pacific's subsidiary, the Pacific Fruit Express, for the fast shipment of Southern California and Arizona fruit and vegetables to East Coast markets. Then, in the familiar pattern followed by Dick Spence, the Baberses, Lawrence Furlow, and other Tucumcari college students, Wells hired out as a brakeman at Yuma to work holidays and summers until he graduated from Eastern New Mexico University at Portales at mid-year 1965–1966. With his diploma in hand, Wells was hired as an SP assistant trainmaster in the San Francisco Bay area, working mainly at San Jose and Oakland, and then was selected for the SP Management Development Program. Among the executive positions he held were superintendent of the Tucson division and general manager of the southwest region, which included Tucumcari. Wells continued with the Union Pacific after it took over the Southern Pacific and was director of transportation services when he resigned to become general manager of the Port Terminal Railroad Association in Houston in 2001.

At Houston Marvin Wells took on a far more complicated job than any assignment he had held with the Southern Pacific or Union Pacific. The Port Terminal Association was a collaborative venture of three different, competing major railroads—the Union Pacific Railroad, BNSF Railway, and Kansas City Southern Railway—which meant there were three masters to serve. Then, straddling the Houston ship canal, the PTRA was dedicated to provide railroads entering the city with equal access to the Port of Houston and the industrial concerns located along the waterway, which on occasion might get "sticky." Also, the fairly large executive team of twenty-five members and the hundreds of employees sometimes presented management problems. In addition, the PTRA served 150 industries and 225 local clients and handled about 500,000 railroad cars annually. At the same time the PTRA served firms involved in a wide range of products, such as chemicals, grains, foods, autos, and others. When Marvin Wells retired and moved to Florida in January 2012, Houston area rail groups recognized his managerial skills in running the complex Port Terminal Railroad Association and asked him to share his views as an invited speaker.[40]

With the influence of Dick Spence's career in operations that encompassed the West, East, and South; Frank Kyle Turner's tenure with regional lines in the Southeast, Middle West, and nationally; and the careers of Roy Penix, Lawrence Furlow, and the Baberses and Wellses (fathers and sons), the railroad impact of Tucumcari pretty well reached all across America. And the careers of Frank Kile Turner and Marvin Wells had notable significance because they applied their earlier experience to the administration of national or regional railroad trade associations. Others, although not hailing from Tucumcari, had gained valuable experience in local assignments. Denman K. McNear got his first taste of railroad operations at Tucumcari and rose to become SP board chairman, president, and CEO simultaneously. Likewise, James W. Corbett had been trainmaster at Tucumcari in 1948, retiring as SP vice president–system operations in 1960; and Ralph V. Currier, trainmaster, 1956–1959, became SP manager of transportation rules and training at San Francisco headquarters. These examples help suggest Tucumcari's effect on individual lives and the town's widespread influence in the railroad industry as well.[41]

And for those who stayed behind in Tucumcari, the railroad offered significant social mobility. Conductors, engineers, and trainmasters might have left a failed homestead to find a job on the railroad in some capacity and worked their way up in the local rail hierarchy. In the small western town where income counted for more than cultural refinement, the erstwhile country boys who climbed the local railway ladder to good, steady salaries found themselves boosted several notches in respectability and prestige in local society. As mentioned earlier, the railroaders were easily distinguishable because they were the ones who bought a new Oldsmobile or Buick every three years, not a Ford or Chevy, and sent their sons to college and enrolled their daughters in a teacher's training school.

Tucumcari and Quay County had experienced three different major waves of incoming population. The Jewish Founding Fathers and their associates of various faiths who joined them, although indispensable in the town's creation, were relatively few in numbers. Much more numerous, the second wave consisted of railroaders and those attached to them, who came with the town's establishment as a regional rail center in the early twentieth century. Accompanying the railroaders, hordes of homesteaders poured in at about the same time to get free land. A third mixed group was drawn in later by the development of the Route 66 tourist trade, the construction of Conchas Dam, and the subsequent general growth of the town. A subgroup might also be noted, that is, the boomerang homesteader offspring, who, having passed through the town on their way to the country when they arrived, fled the rural areas and returned to the county seat seeking jobs on the railroad or, in the case of daughters, to get a railroader husband. Of the three main groups, the railroaders ranked the highest in the eyes of locals because of their substantial incomes and the use they made of their money and, also, of great importance, because of their association with a major national industry. This connection with the outside world of corporate business and finance remained hard to overlook when it was exhibited daily for all to see in the feverish activity of huge locomotives pulling passenger and freight trains past the depot, the rail yards, and the roundhouse on a massive network of steel rails that stretched over the horizon.

A fourth major group accumulated gradually, from the beginning and over the years. This was the Hispanic people, who at first drifted into town from the early sheep ranches and the villages along the Canadian River and its tributaries, and later from more distant places. Few in the first three groups, overwhelmingly Anglos, reckoned that Hispanics had any identifiable position in local society. As a result, the Hispanics were relegated to the north side of the railroad tracks and to the custodial jobs of carmen, which involved cleaning and servicing railroad passenger trains. Most other railroad jobs, especially in the elite operations crews, were off limits for them. As the railroads and railroaders pulled out, and many other Anglos left for greener pastures with the collapse of the tourist trade and the town's decline, the Hispanics stayed put. By the turn of the twenty-first century they had become the majority in the local population, and they inherited the remnants of the town.

Chapter 11

THE OTHER SIDE

Conclusion

The lives of Henry Max Goldenberg and Benjamin Munoz, half-brothers who had the same Jewish mother, exemplified the complicated ethnic web of Tucumcari and Quay County. The elder of the two, Henry Goldenberg, had the same surname name as the mercantile Goldenbergs, although not part of that pioneer family. His El Paso Jewish mother had married a Jewish husband, Jacob Nathan Goldenberg, who died, leaving her to fend for herself. She remarried, this time to a Hispanic husband, Leon Munoz, who got a railroad job in Tucumcari and moved the family there in 1909. Henry Goldenberg, born of two Jewish parents but raised by Hispanic stepfather Leon Munoz on the north side of the tracks, identified culturally with his neighbors. He attended mass regularly at Saint Anne's Catholic Church, became an altar boy, and took two Hispanic wives.

Goldenberg later recalled, "I grew up on the north side of town—that is where it is rough and tough and ornery." Henry Goldenberg learned these facts of life the hard way. His stepfather, Leon Munoz, abandoned the family, forcing seventeen-year-old Henry to drop out of high school and find work that would support his mother and three younger siblings.[1] In time, as a member of the city governing body twice, he became a spokesman for the Hispanic community. Goldenberg developed talents that served him well in obtaining employment with the Southern Pacific Railroad for twenty-nine years, winning elections, and acquiring one home on Third Street—well south of the tracks—and later another, larger residence on Fifth Street farther south. His Jewish roots, however, always remained submerged in the Hispanic culture north of the railroad. His job with the SP as a supervisor of custodial workers who did chores reserved for Hispanics was hard, dirty work. As his son remembered, "My mother seemed to always have the washing machine going." Often mistakenly considered a relative of the financially well-off pioneer Goldenbergs, he once commented, "People tell me that I must have a lot of money—but [I tell them] they got the wrong guy." Then, revealing his long cultural identification with the local Hispanic community, Henry Max Goldenberg usually added, "I have made about 40,000 or 50,000 adobes, though."[2]

Younger brother Ben Munoz grew up in the same northside home as Henry Goldenberg, mainly under the care of their Jewish mother, and with only a relatively brief, shadowy influence of his father Leon Munoz. After graduation from Tucumcari High School, where he excelled in Spanish classes and his other studies, Ben Munoz put his language skills to work serving Hispanic depositors as a teller at First National Bank. In keeping with his position in the community's main financial institution, he joined the Rotary Club as well as the prestigious First Baptist Church. As a member of the church choir, he met and fell head-over-heels in love with its pianist, Dorothy Doughty. She was the attractive only daughter, with two doting brothers, of the town's most prominent physician and deacon in the First Baptist Church, Dr. James M. Doughty, who, as stated previously, had arrived as a railroad doctor. From that point on, the life of Ben Munoz would become drastically different from that of his half-brother Henry Goldenberg and a world apart from his origins on the north side of the railroad tracks.

Following a couple of years at Hardin-Simmons, a leading Texas Baptist college, Dorothy Doughty taught school briefly. Meanwhile, Ben Munoz, bolstered by his expertise in Spanish, had become a mainstay at the First National Bank, especially by dealing in Spanish with Hispanic customers. He would later increase his prestige when selected for the extra assignment of city treasurer.[3] The romance of Dorothy Doughty and Ben Munoz led to their marriage and to a new role for him in one of Tucumcari's leading families. Reportedly, after Dorothy Munoz died as the result of complications from childbirth, no other funeral in Tucumcari had witnessed as much shared grief or as many banks of flowers as her funeral rites in the First Baptist Church sanctuary. Afterward, Ben Munoz and the surviving male child became regular members of the Doughty household. It was said that Dr. James Mitchell Doughty never got over being unable to save his beloved daughter's life. He soon retired, his finances suffered, and the family had to move from a much larger home in an upscale neighborhood into a small, markedly modest house across town. His daughter died in 1936, and he followed in 1941 at age sixty-three. Following Dr. Doughty's death, Ben Munoz became the main breadwinner of the family. As befitting a rising star at the First National Bank, he joined local civic and business organizations and became choir director of the First Baptist Church and a vice president of the bank. He later remarried, this time to the daughter of a prominent Anglo Democratic Party leader, and fathered another child.[4] He and his half-brother Henry Goldenberg spoke occasionally, when they happened to meet, but otherwise led different lives in the same town. Ben Munoz crossed the chasm of the railroad tracks to live comfortably on the Anglo southside. Henry Max Goldenberg also moved to the southside with his second Hispanic wife, but, according to his son, he "was born a German Jew but had a Mexican stepfather, so he felt culturally Mexican."[5] One of the brothers is buried in the Protestant part of the Tucumcari cemetery and the other in the Catholic section.

A disillusioned newspaper publisher, when leaving town, plaintively asked why "the colorful religious and historic culture" of the Hispanic people was hidden and ignored in Tucumcari and Quay County.[6] This was a reasonable question since Hispanic hunters, traders, and shepherds—the *ciboleros, comancheros,* and *pastores*—had traveled across every square mile of the county and left their marks behind where railroads and highways would soon appear. Following Tucumcari's founding in 1901, the incoming throngs of homesteaders forced the Hispanic sheep ranchers to leave the Plaza Larga Creek district between Tucumcari Mountain and Mesa Redonda and seek grazing lands farther west.[7]

Fabriola Cabeza de Baca was the daughter of a prominent Hispanic rancher who at one time grazed fifteen thousand head of sheep, tended by twelve to fifteen herders and their vigilant dogs, along Plaza Larga Creek near Tucumcari Mountain. She astutely observed that most Hispanic settlers and traders may have "vanished" from the countryside, but "the names of hills, rivers, arroyos, canyons, and defunct plazas linger as monuments to a people who pioneered into the land of the buffalo and the Comanche." She continued in the same vein, "These names have undergone many changes, but are still known and repeated." Then she added a virtual indictment, "Very likely many of those who pronounce them daily [now] are unaware that they are of Spanish origin." A myriad of place names—from the large Texas Panhandle city of Amarillo to the Plaza Larga, Ruveulta, and Pajarito Creeks, as well as Puerto, Rana, Tuscocoilio

Canyons—substantiate her claim.[8] In fact, as more examples, south of town beyond Tucumcari Mountain and Saddleback (officially labeled "Bulldog") mesa stands a third butte, Mesa Redonda (often mistakenly mixed gender "Mesa Redondo"). On beyond lies El Llano Estacado's lofty rim-rock originally named La Ceja (the Eyebrow) by Hispanic traders but now called the Caprock. As for the vast Llano Estacado (Staked Plain, singular not plural) itself, the designation arose not from Spanish conquistadors pounding down stakes to measures distances, but from later Hispanic traders on the treeless Plains using stakes to tether their horses. In addition, the corruption of *zanjon* (deep gully) into San Jon identifies a creek and the nearby village. Likewise, the once-flourishing homesteader village of Nara Visa originated from an arroyo-hewn creek named for one Narvaez, a Hispanic sheepherder of the 1880s. The prime example, of course, is the Canadian River, labeled "Rio Colorado" (Red River) by early New Mexicans, and *Goo-al-pah* by the Indians. Its current designation likely came not from the presence of Canadian fur traders but from the descriptive words *canada* or *canadon*, Spanish terms applied to the upstream deep canyons by Hispanic observers.[9]

It was often said for years that Tucumcari had no race problem, which was largely true. Until the late 1930s, with the construction of Conchas Dam and the stimulus of other New Deal work-relief projects, only a handful of permanent black residents lived there. But the town did have an ethnic and cultural divide as pronounced as a separation of racial groups. That part of eastern New Mexico next to the Texas Panhandle was often called "Little Texas" and "Lapland"—where Texas lapped over into the neighboring state. The New Deal–era Quay County Courthouse in Tucumcari, which bears almost no influence of New Mexico's Indian-Spanish-Mexican heritage common in a great number of the state's public structures, tells the whole story in architectural terms. A specialized study of New Mexico courthouses has this description: "The building is virtually indistinguishable from many of the courthouses in the neighboring panhandle of Texas."[10] The same characterization might be applied to certain transplanted Texas cultural traits.

Without a sizable black population in their midst, many Tucumcari Anglo residents regarded Hispanics on the north side of the tracks with a similar racial disdain. At the 1998 Rattler Reunion, one Hispanic woman recalled the social structure at the local high school thirty years earlier in the 1960s, saying, "There

Quay County Courthouse. The structure's typical New Deal architectural style, with little hint of New Mexico's Hispanic heritage, identified the area as "Lapland" (where Texas laps over) with a border-state cultural bias. Jay Goebel / Alamy Stock Photo (Image ID: CW91X8).

was a real feeling in those days of separate lives for Hispanics and whites, nothing like today." That she used the term *whites* instead of *Anglos* spoke volumes, placing Tucumcari's social structure squarely in the national racial conflicts of the post–World War II period, when the separate-but-equal judicial doctrine was under attack and overturned by the Supreme Court.[11]

During the Democratic Party dominance of Tucumcari and Quay County, particularly about the time of the Second World War, the Hispanic north side of the railroad tracks was always a safe borough. Jovial, round-bellied Blas Jimenez, who usually chomped on a big cigar and wore a Western-style hat, was the precinct chairman and known as "Mayor of the Northside." For thirty years, beginning in 1946, Jimenez owned and operated the El Rancho Bar, which doubled as precinct headquarters. To give him added prestige, as well as more actual clout, he was sworn in as a special deputy sheriff. With a prominent role in politics, he served as a spokesman for Hispanics, helped them with their

problems, and delivered the vote. Blas Jimenez also was president of the Spanish-American Club that met in the El Rancho Bar, renamed "Jimenez Hall,"
when the group gathered.[12]

Another guiding spirit north of the tracks, although not in a political sense,
was Father Robert Hammond, the parish priest at Saint Anne's Catholic
Church from 1934 to 1952. Hammond was born in Syria, educated and ordained
for the priesthood in Jerusalem, and obtained a PhD degree in Rome. He came
to New Mexico in 1930. Distinguished by close-cropped hair and sharp facial
features, he drove a big black car, smoked long cigars, and managed his flock
with an iron hand, including the education of its youngest congregants. Until
well after the Second World War, when it closed at the end of the spring term
in May 1968, Saint Anne's parochial school maintained classes through the
eighth grade with Dominican nuns as the teachers.[13]

The transition from parochial school to the public high school could be
traumatic for Hispanic youngsters. Large parts of the student body, it sometimes seemed, were made up of "Stomps," Anglo boys who came to school
wearing cowboy boots and big Western hats, and "Chukes," imitators of the
dress and style of southwestern Mexican American street gangs. The Stomps
and Chukes often got into heated arguments and fights. At a Rattler Reunion,
Joanne Valverde recalled a big showdown fight in 1968 between Hispanic and
Anglo boys that resulted from "a long period of bad feelings between the two
[bunches]." Even though the Anglo and Hispanic girls "always seemed to get
along," Valverde remembered, the two groups never mixed or mingled at school
or after classes.[14] Father Hammond saw to it that the Hispanics stayed in the
parochial school through the eighth grade and made it to the ninth grade in the
public high school. From then on, it was difficult for him to keep up with them,
and particularly the boys dropped out in large numbers in a year or two.

After serving almost twenty years at St. Anne's, Father Hammond was transferred to Raton. Later, in Pennsylvania, Hammond devoted his retirement to
the scholarly study of medieval philosophy, having already published two volumes on the subject, and he was finishing a third. According to local legend,
when asked where he wanted to go after death, heaven or Tucumcari, he hesi-
tated a long moment. In 1968 he returned to his beloved Tucumcari and assisted
in the parish until his death at age eighty-five in 1980. He was buried in the local
cemetery's separate Catholic section among the graves of those he had served in

the longest tenure of a priest at Saint Anne's parish. Father Robert Hammond left close to a half-million dollars in his estate for college scholarships to go to Saint Anne parishioners who graduated from Tucumcari High School and met specified scholarly qualifications.[15]

Life north of the railroad tracks for Hispanic kids was no picnic, even under the stern guidance of Father Hammond, but they had one distinct advantage over Anglo juveniles. The Hispanic kids had command of Spanish, a strictly foreign language to the Anglos. In the occasional hostile confrontations by members of the two groups, the northside forces understood perfectly the insults shouted at them in the vilest English profanity, while the Anglo troops had little understanding of the extreme contempt aimed their direction in the Spanish word for male goat combined with various vulgar terms. That was the Hispanic kids' secret defense in any situation; they could always withdraw and speak Spanish among themselves, automatically excluding Anglos and pushing them to the fringes. The armed confrontations began with the usual exchange of blistering insults shouted across the no man's land provided by the railroad tracks, followed by hurled caliche clods. When the piles of clods were exhausted, the battle groups gradually melted away. The Hispanic boys returned to their bleak homes with faded, peeling paint, on windswept, unpaved streets adjacent to the railroad tracks The Anglo kids stopped off for a soda at the Sands-Dorsey Drugstore on Main Street on the way to their neatly painted or stuccoed homes along paved, tree-lined streets several blocks south of the tracks. There were two different, well-defined worlds. For the Hispanic kids, one of them recalled, "Church life was not only our spiritual life and school, but also our social life. Maybe that was also true for the . . . [Anglo] kids. We didn't know too many of them."[16]

Sometimes the ethnic division in Tucumcari took a strange twist. Although the great majority of Saint Anne parishioners were Hispanics, several prominent Anglos also adhered to the Catholic faith. Among them was long-time Tucumcari lawyer Royal A. Prentice, who had served as a sergeant with Theodore Roosevelt's Rough Riders in the Spanish-American War, and afterward for eighteen months in the Philippines with the regular army. The Rough Rider ranks contained numerous recruits from New Mexico. When Roosevelt became president, he took care of his former troops by backing many of them for federal appointments.[17] Prentice's knowledge of shorthand had led to a temporary

Royal A. Prentice served with Theodore Roosevelt's Rough Riders in the Spanish-American War, and afterward as a civic and business leader in Tucumcari. Courtesy of Royal A. Prentice II.

assignment at Rough Rider headquarters and daily association with the commander. Thus, the president himself undoubtedly had a hand in the appointment of Prentice as register of the federal land office in Tucumcari during the heyday of homesteading in 1908. Prentice later established a law practice, specializing in land titles. An accomplished photographer and archaeologist, he wrote several historical accounts of early local history, including a detailed, scholarly series of newspaper articles on the Coronado Expedition of the 1540s. The Museum of New Mexico in Santa Fe holds a collection of his photographs, artifacts he found, and other research material measuring 7.5 linear feet in length.[18]

As pointed out previously, Prentice built a landmark adobe home on Third Street for his large family, and he became the patriarch of a sizable extended clan, all of whom were members of Saint Anne's. For granddaughter Christine Prentice Hays, attending parochial school gave her "the opportunity to experience a culture different from my own since 'Anglos' were the minority and

Hispanics were the majority." In this role reversal, comparable to that of Hispanics in local society, she learned to adjust but found it hard "to be accepted and to be a part of a group with strong ties to a heritage and tradition different from your own." This childhood exposure served Christine Prentice Hays well, however, when she later moved to Miami, Florida, with its large Hispanic population, and she found no difficulty adjusting to the local culture. It was like "coming home," she said.[19]

The conscience of pre–Second World War Tucumcari, Paul Dodge of the *Tucumcari Daily News*, pretty much followed the language usage and prejudices of the day, for example, referring to "Slant Eyed Mongrels" on reporting an incident in China. In one notable instance, however, Dodge spoke out clearly for racial equality, contrary to public opinion locally. Access to a public education was probably the main issue in the small black community at Tucumcari. The local school board and school administrators for years reflected the town's southern or border-state discriminatory viewpoint by barring black children from the existing public schools, but they offered no separate schooling for them. Even though state law mandated black children could attend public schools unless provided for otherwise, school officials consistently ruled out alternative arrangements on the basis of budgetary limitations. Dodge rose to his editorial best in criticizing this argument, writing that when it came to public schooling, black children were equal to anyone else and had the same rights as white children. His plea fell on deaf ears. It was not until the fall of 1941 that a "negro school" with eight students and a "colored teacher" opened on the north side of the railroad tracks. By 1944 the school board had hired a college graduate with two years of teaching experience as the sole teacher in the north side school. After World War II, the city leased land to the school board and helped acquire a war surplus structure for a black school.[20] In time, with the momentous Supreme Court decision in *Brown v. Board of Education* of 1954 that struck down the "separate but equal" doctrine, African American students were regularly admitted to the Tucumcari public schools.

Popular recognition of an ethnic heritage occurred as the number of Hispanics in the local population became great enough to sway election returns. The evidence of such influence appeared when Hispanics took over two all-important posts—both previously reserved for Anglos only—the administration of justice and control of police power. In 1954 Jacob V. "Jake" Gallegos, who had previously served as city attorney and assistant district attorney, was appointed district judge, and soon thereafter he won the first of three elections for six-year terms before voluntarily retiring. Since Gallegos came from an old-line Hispanic family in New Mexico and married Mary Letcher, the granddaughter of prominent Jewish merchant Adolph Letcher, his political success was not altogether surprising.

Law enforcement probably had the greatest importance in the everyday lives of Hispanics. As the number of Hispanics increased, they occupied important positions in policing agencies. Paul Velasco and Ted Garcia served by appointment as police chief. John Barreras topped the Democratic primary by eighteen votes in a field of seven candidates for county sheriff and won in the general election. Hispanics also claimed other positions previously reserved for Anglos. Oscar Hernandez was elected president of the Chamber of Commerce, and Joe Leon Carlos Moya won a seat on the three-member board of county commissioners. Ralph Moya served as mayor and Raphael Martinez as municipal judge. By 1992 there was a Hispanic city manager as well as another city police chief.[21]

Shared problems, or the sharing by one ethnic group of the other's special problems, could breach the railroad tracks as a barrier and join Anglos and Hispanics together in a worthy cause. Such had been the case in 1937 when "one of the greatest mass tragedies in the history of New Mexico" and the largest outbreak of botulism in the state's public health annals struck in Tucumcari's Hispanic community. At a large reunion of an extended Hispanic family, the members of three generations had enjoyed sizable helpings of traditional food featuring green chili peppers, home-canned in glass jars, which contained the toxin causing botulism. Altogether nine people who ate the chili peppers died and eleven more were sickened but lived. Those who survived probably owed their lives to the brand new public health laboratory at the University of New Mexico in Albuquerque, which quickly identified the specific type of botulism toxin involved and quickly telegraphed the information to Dr. James M. Doughty in Tucumcari so he could administer the correct antitoxin.[22]

The best human-interest story, however, unfolded on the local level. The *Daily News* first informed the community that botulism was a dread disease, "as rare as it is deadly—one that saps life's air from the lungs of nearly all its victims." Then, proclaiming that "Tucumcari has always done its part—and always will," the newspaper set up the Botulism Victims Relief Fund. "Some of these unfortunate victims," the front-page notice explained, "are unable to bear the financial burden of proper care and treatment . . . [,] yet it is not fair that the hospital and undertaker should be shouldered with all the load." As a result, in support of the affected families, the special fund gave hundreds of locals an opportunity to contribute to a worthy cause and show the bereaved families that the town was on their side "in this hour of darkness." Jacob V. Gallegos, then city attorney, served as treasurer of the successful fund drive.[23]

One of the most significant indications of the increasing numbers and growing influence of Hispanics came in the high school athletic teams, particularly football. In the late 1960s, the names of Hispanic players became more common on Rattler gridiron rosters, which had seldom been the case previously. And significantly the first names usually were no longer traditionally Hispanic, such as Juan, Eloy, or Manuel, but now more likely were the same as Anglo teenagers, such as Art, Chris, or Pat. Moreover, by the 1990s Hispanic names tended to dominate the rosters. In the same vein, for Anglos returning to their hometown after several years' absence, it was remarkable to hear Hispanic mothers, while in the grocery store line, scold a wandering small child in English instead of Spanish. Most significant of all, in 2000, the public-school superintendent was Felix Jimenez; the high school principal, Adrian Cordova; the athletic director, Tom Trujillo; and the school board president, Eddie Encinas. By the 1970s black football players also became more obvious in team photographs and their names appeared more frequently in newspaper accounts.[24]

Federal census statistics in 1982 revealed that New Mexico had the highest percentage of Hispanics of any state—36.6 percent.[25] Recognition by Hispanics at Tucumcari of this distinction for the state, as well as their awareness of the civil rights movement nationally, became apparent in a series of events exhibiting a growing communal spirit and an inclination to take direct action. Hispanics formed the Concerned Citizens for Stable City Government organization and, referring to themselves in racial terminology of the civil rights movement as a "minority," challenged the Anglo city commission on some of its actions. An estimated 150 to 200 Hispanic residents gathered in front of the public school administrative offices to protest the hiring of an Anglo superintendent instead of a Hispanic, whom the protesters believed was more qualified. Hispanic businessmen, declaring that a "barrier of communication" existed between them and the Tucumcari/Quay County Chamber of Commerce, announced their intention of forming their own separate chamber to meet their special needs. By the 2000 census, Hispanics had become a majority in Tucumcari—51.39 percent in a total population of 5,991—and from that point on, they had a voice in civic and political affairs and held most of the elective and appointive positions of importance.[26]

Soon after the founding of Tucumcari, when Tom Hodges arrived at the Puerto community southeast of Tucumcari during the early days of homesteading, he may have been the only African American in Quay County.[27] Actually Hodges, born in 1870 at the height of post–Civil War Reconstruction in western Tennessee, was brought to New Mexico by Silas Wilson Hodges, who homesteaded on the east side of Puerto Creek near the Norton community. At the death of Silas Hodges, his cousin and fellow homesteader across Puerto Creek, John Milton Hodges, took Tom Hodges under his wing. Tom Hodges had been brought to Quay County under quasi-indentured-servitude conditions, and he worked in this arrangement for room and board plus a small stipend the rest of his life. For him, Southern social customs prevailed in that remote part of territorial New Mexico. He slept in a separate outlying building, ate at a nearby kitchen cabinet instead of the family table, and did not join in family social gatherings and conversations. Once, on a rare trip to the county seat for a day, he was invited to lunch in a married Hodges daughter's home. When it came time for the meal, she said, "Tom, since only you and I are here, I have fixed a place for you at the table with me." To which he replied, "No mam, I'll just eat over here on the cabinet." And so, the two of them ate at their separate places in the small kitchen, chatting about the crops and weather. The daughter's husband, deciding that Tom Hodges would like to mix and mingle with those of his own race, took him across the railroad tracks to the northside's Rocket Inn, where African Americans gathered to eat and drink. After only a few minutes, he wanted to leave. When asked why so soon, he replied, "Those are strange people!"

In one notable episode, the Puerto community forgot racial barriers and included a black man as one of their own. Tom Hodges had established a homestead claim, and when a neighboring rancher threatened to take it away from him, community leaders told the rancher in terms unheard thereabouts since open range days, that they would not permit it. In another instance Tom Hodges himself joined the "white man's world." At his death in 1952, at age eighty-two, he was buried in the little Puerto cemetery among the numerous graves of the Hodges clan with whom he had lived, but separately, most of his life.[28] This was the last resting place for a man who had lived all those years on Puerto Creek, never traveling more than twenty-eight miles to the county seat.

On occasion African Americans faced a Jim Crow system of separatism in Tucumcari that united Anglos and Hispanics on the same side. In 1931 county sheriff's officers caught a group of African Americans playing poker, apparently a forbidden group entertainment for blacks, arrested the whole lot, and ordered them to get out of town. Jack Stanton, janitor at the Piggly Wiggly grocery store, was one of those exiled, as was his fourteen-year-old son Quinn. One night shortly after the poker incident Quinn Stanton encountered a Hispanic deputy sheriff, an argument developed, and the deputy shot the young African American in the leg as he ran from the scene. The Hispanic deputy said that the black lad cussed him.[29] Physicians who attended the boy determined that the wound was so serious that the leg had to be amputated, but they could not get him admitted to the Tucumcari hospital because of his race. Subsequently, young Quinn Stanton died in an Amarillo hospital as the result of infection in the leg wound. The boy's mother said that he would be buried in Amarillo because she feared trouble if the body was returned to Tucumcari for interment. The county sheriff, the boy's mother reported, told her to bury her son in Amarillo and give the bills to the sheriff's office.[30] Further details about this troubling racial incident, it seems, were apparently buried in an Amarillo grave.

Another incident of violence and bloodshed, this time involving Anglo and Hispanic antagonists, started with an argument at a dance, followed by a fight in which the Anglo was stabbed. After recuperation, the Anglo met the Hispanic on a Main Street sidewalk on a busy Saturday afternoon and shot him in the left breast at close range. A large blood stain remained visible in the concrete to mark the spot for several weeks. After deliberation overnight, a jury acquitted the Anglo, who had pleaded self-defense.[31]

Other crimes of violence occasionally roiled the precarious ethnic and racial situation at Tucumcari.[32] In 1951 the "horror-of-horrors" in crime for a southern or border state—the rape of a white woman by a black man—caused a furor at Tucumcari. Sheriff Claude Moncus observed that it was the first time in Quay County that such a mixed-race crime had been committed. At the time an African American from Kansas was tried and sentenced to twenty-five to thirty years in prison, but not before causing an uproar of racial animosity in the community.[33]

The most noteworthy racial crime of violence began when state police officer Sherman L. Toler Jr., twenty-seven years old, made a routine traffic stop about ten miles east of Tucumcari on Interstate 40 and issued a speeding citation to the black driver of a black Cadillac with California license tags. A passing truck driver reported to police that he had seen "a police officer fighting with a black man," and that the African American had taken the officer's gun during the scuffle and shot him with it. In fact, an autopsy of the policeman's body revealed that he had been shot five times, four times in the upper body and once in the left hand, and that he had been struck in the head with a blunt object at least twice. Officer Toler left a wife and three children. The suspected shooter and a female companion were arrested two miles from the murder scene at a roadside convenience store. In a state farther south than New Mexico, this kind of crime would have called for a lynching, but fortunately the accused black man, who reportedly had a long criminal record, lived to face capital felony murder charges in court.[34]

District Judge Stanley Frost, declaring that he found too much "public excitement in Quay County" to seat a fair and impartial jury, granted a change of venue to Fort Sumner and DeBaca County. This was the same judicial district and, therefore, Frost would still be the presiding judge at the trial, but with a DeBaca County jury. Public defender Benjamin Gonzales, who represented the defendant, questioned the change of venue but conceded that since this was "probably the premier capital case in the state right now," it would be hard to find an impartial jury anywhere in New Mexico. The trial at Fort Sumner, in which the defendant's attorneys claimed that he had only acted out of fear for his life when Officer Toler pointed a drawn gun at him, ended with a conviction of second-degree murder. Judge Frost subsequently handed down a seventeen-year prison term.[35] Locals were left to wonder if the black killer of a white state policeman beside a nearby freeway would have received the death penalty if the trial had been held in Tucumcari.

If the rural people of Quay County cheered and virtually worshipped their high school basketball teams, which was true, these sentiments were only a little less pronounced at the county seat—for football. In the eyes of teenage players, their coaches, epitomized by the legendary Jim Rudd, were godlike figures, who could stand on Tucumcari Mountain and hurl lightning bolts at opposing teams, destroying their will to win.[36] Basketball and football games were community social events as well as expressions of community loyalty, which compelled the attendance of young and old alike, whether or not they knew the difference between a ten-yard penalty and a sentence of life imprisonment for murder.

Tucumcari enjoyed its share of accomplished athletes. Basketball was a crowd pleaser, especially when Tucumcari won the state championship at home in its new gym in 1950.[37] But whatever the case, football was the name of the game—the high school sport that drew the most local attention and sent players to the college level. Two families, each with three athletic sons, provided prime examples of local athletic prowess. On one hand, in the late 1940s and into the 1950s, there were the three Babers brothers—Charles, Donald, and James—with Don, once called a "sports immortal," appearing most often in the newspaper sports sections.[38] Later, in the 1970s and 1980s, the three David brothers—Mick, Stan, and Rod—took Tucumcari High School sports, it was said, to an unmatched level in football, basketball, and track.[39] Of the three David brothers, the youngest, Rod, seemed to have the most athletic ability. He started in football as a freshman, as a sophomore led the Rattlers to the state finals in basketball and set the record in scoring, and as a junior took his team to a state title in track. Some sports experts predicted that he would be an Olympic contender in the decathlon. To one Albuquerque sports columnist, Rod David "wasn't just a star; he was a whole solar system, perhaps the best all-around athlete to come out of New Mexico," and "a nice, modest kid" with the body of "a Greek god" because of which gave him the nickname of "Rock." He seemed to have everything, including a football scholarship at Texas Tech. However, in a shocking tragedy that devastated the town as nothing else had ever done before, he took his own life. It was his senior year and a pleasant April day, when he broke up with his girlfriend in the morning, drove home from school that afternoon, loaded a 20-gauge shotgun, and standing outside in the driveway, put the gun against his chest and pulled the trigger. A city employee reading water meters found the body in a pool of blood.[40]

An estimated 2,500 people, most of them weeping or, in disbelief, too stunned to cry, attended the memorial service in the Rattler Gym where Rod and his brothers had played and won so many basketball games. His gold-colored casket with copper trim stood under the south goal. After the funeral service, people did not hurry away but lingered in small groups as if to console one another. A fund was established for a memorial display case in the high school to house Rod's trophies and other sports memorabilia. Someone placed a light on his cemetery tombstone. For years his classmates and other townspeople, who made regular pilgrimages to his grave, were left to wonder what had made him do it. Perhaps the "athletic system" that accepted nothing but winning had taken his life. Or the expectations of a goal-oriented father and his own standards were so high that even he could not meet them, and he had snapped. Regardless, as the Albuquerque sports columnist concluded, "a golden god was gone," and the fragile community had suffered an irreparable loss as it was already sliding down a slippery slope.[41]

With the community's excitement about high school sports, it was not surprising that another traumatic happening, and one that served as a disillusioning climax to the disappointments of the late twentieth century, involved a football game. In 2000, after several drought years of mediocre-to-miserable football results, Tucumcari fans enjoyed a 12–0 win season, including playoff games, and looked forward to capping the year with a perfect finish by the Rattlers winning the state championship.[42] As befitting the times, the Rattlers were nicknamed—in military style—the "Elite Strike Force Team." During the season, even the "Church Lady" had devoted one of her weekly religious newspaper columns to a discussion of that week's Rattler victory over Lordsburg, commenting: "Life is very much like the game of football. We face an enemy that is going to hit us hard and try to make us give up the fight."[43]

The number of fans driving the 225 miles over snow-covered roads to Eunice for the state championship game was unbelievable, and, according to a newspaper report, they were about to see "probably the best AA football game in the history of the sport." That Tucumcari had already defeated Eunice during the regular season, 31–21, had, according to the *Albuquerque Journal*, "whipped hometown fans into a frenzy." This time, however, the Eunice Cardinals fought the Rattlers to a 7–6 Tucumcari lead with 48 seconds to go. The Cardinals had a first down on the two-yard line and tried three times to push the ball over but were stopped by the Rattler defense. With only inches to go, and the last six seconds ticking off the clock, Eunice got off one last play. A video later showed the play stopped short of the goal line and no time left on the clock. Thinking they had won, the Tucumcari coaches, bench players, and fans swarmed onto the field claiming a victory. But an official, who either threw a late flag or one unnoticed previously, ruled that the Rattler defense had lined up offside, that three-tenths of a second remained on the clock, and that the penalty gave Eunice one more play. With zeros flashing on the scoreboard the Cardinals kicked an eighteen-yard field goal to win 9–7. The figurative weeping, wailing, and gnashing of teeth for weeks in Tucumcari can well be imagined. Numerous protests of the "late phantom penalty call" and an appeal to the state athletic association were useless.[44] It was another painful disappointment among others of recent years. The ill feelings ran so deep that local school officials thought it wise to cancel the next home basketball game with Eunice.

Already on the ropes and hanging on for dear life, Tucumcari suffered the ultimate indignity—belittlement in a popular novel. In Larry McMurtry's *Some Can Whistle* (1989), one of the characters has disappeared to some unknown remote location—as stated in the novel, probably a place "as far afield as Tucumcari." McMurtry's fictional depiction, as applied to Tucumcari at the turn of the twenty-first century, realistically involved a scholarly controversy among historians between the Triumphalists and Revisionists. Mostly an argument among college professors, it ended with the Revisionists winning and the emergence of the New Western History. In short, the Triumphalists believed that the conquest of the West promised both financial and spiritual rewards and had a happy ending. On the other hand, the Revisionists contended that winning the West had resulted in no victory at all but destruction of the environment as well as spiritual disillusionment.[45]

In the early 1900s, eastern New Mexico remained largely unoccupied in an American West that supposedly had been filled up by the 1890s. The problem was that the people who moved into the open lands of Quay County and planted crops and helped build a railroad and tourist town, firmly believed in the Triumphalist concept—that their endeavors would produce endless bountiful harvests from the soil and perpetual freedom from the boom-and-bust pitfalls of corporate America in the East. Droves of disillusioned homesteaders, realizing the folly of their faith in the stingy soil, started leaving early and kept on leaving as subsequent droughts and hard times convinced them there was no happy ending. Some realists, such as the Goldenbergs, lived the dream and cashed out in time; other early entrepreneurs moved on west to California or stayed just long enough during the plush days to die in place before the rasping horns of diesel locomotives and the strangling highway bypass caught up with them. But the surrounding rural areas were left as abandoned as if evacuated by military decree and the town a mere shell of its once-prosperous, vital state. True, Howard Kohn skillfully assembled the T-4 ranch of more than 100,000 acres, but each of the dozens of failed homesteads that made up a substantial portion of the T-4 represented a disappointed settler family who disproved the Triumphalist theory. And what can be said about the three hundred or four hundred railroaders who had worked for the Southern Pacific at its peak of local operations, many of whom were transferred elsewhere? Their children and grandchildren grew up in El Paso, Phoenix, or some place in California where their fathers or grandfathers had ended up after diesel locomotives and the railroad merger craze doomed Tucumcari as a division point.

One high school graduate of 1955, returning for his fiftieth class reunion at the annual Rattler Reunion, made the point in a plaintive recollection:

> My Tucumcari is gone, the one I knew from childhood to graduation. As a child, the universe did not extend beyond Tucumcari. Tucumcari was my universe. Now, all of the places where I played as a youngster are gone. Southern Pacific is no more. Many landmarks that I remember, including our THS [Tucumcari High School building], and our football field, are gone.[46]

Tucumcari lasted sixty-five years as a viable railroad town, from 1901 to the 1960s, and a little less time, 1926 to 1981, as a prosperous tourist mecca. That was a long time in the saga of the American West. At least Tucumcari's fate was not as bad as what happened to the coal mining town of Dawson, which once was larger than Tucumcari. The Phelps Dodge Corporation, it will be recalled, created a company town with a population of nine thousand with all the amenities of city life.[47] But a sharp decline in the use of coal made its mines obsolete. The entire town of Dawson was razed and carted off as salvage—simply wiped off the map. Tucumcari survived.

NOTES

Introduction

1. *Tucumcari Pathfinder*, April 26, 1902. Parts of this chapter were previously published as D. Stratton, "The Jewish Founding Fathers of Tucumcari," 25–62.

2. Schwantes, *The Pacific Northwest*, 199. See also for succinct statements on the effects of transportation development in the West, Etulain and Malone, *The American West*, 4, 36–45, 232–38.

3. Theroux, *The Great Railway Bazaar*, 1; Catton, *Waiting for the Morning Train*, 253; Kawabata, *Snow Country*, 15, 74; Platonov, "Among Animals and Plants," 123.

4. The South Canadian River, which is called the Canadian River in this study, runs through New Mexico and the Canadian corridor, while the North Canadian originates in Colorado before joining the southern branch in eastern Oklahoma.

5. The amounts local boosters donated are based on random reports circulating in town at that time. For a specific example, see *Tucumcari Daily News* (hereafter *TDN*), August 7, 1934, when $600 was collected "out of the pockets of the people here in Tucumcari" to send a delegation led by Hurley to Washington for lobbying. See also, *TDN*, March 31, 1937, for another solicitation of these funds. Hurley estimated that he had spent $10,000 of his own money for such purposes. *TDN*, February 4, 1941.

6. *TDN*, April 10, 11, 1934. The Pirates won, 12–7.

7. The detailed information on Hurley's arrival, the accompanying ceremony, and his speech came from *TDN*, July 30, 31, August 1, 2, 1934.

8. For a succinct discussion of the importance of railroads in twentieth-century America, see Wilner, "Railroads in the 20th Century."

9. Faulkner, *Light in August*, 162.

10. The survival of small railroad stations has been a continuing struggle. For examples, see Johnston, "Small Town Stations in Flux," 20.

11. Steinbeck, *The Grapes of Wrath*, 103.

12. E-mail, Phares Huggins, Sasebo, Japan, to the author, September 12, 2000, copy in possession of the author.

13. A local newspaper mentioned that Abner Weaver of Weaver Brothers & Elviry was staying a few days at the Blue Swallow. *TDN*, July 11, 1941.

14. An oft-told apocryphal tale about the glimmering summer heat waves, which frequently appeared in various forms, involved two hitch hikers on Route 66. One of the pair suddenly sat down beside the road and started taking off his shoes. When asked by his companion about this strange behavior, he replied that he had to take off his shoes to wade through the large puddle of water on the road ahead. The illusion of a puddle had been created by heat waves dancing on the black-topped highway.

15. Producer Sterling Siliphant's popular *Route 66* television series, which ran on CBS for four seasons (1966–1969), featured two handsome young men who roamed the West in a white Corvette car. The writing and recording of the hit song, "Get Your Kicks on Route 66," is discussed later in chapter 8.

16. Gwynne, *Empire of the Summer Moon*, 199–20, 222–23. Haley points out that Quanah Parker and the Quahadas were familiar with Tucumcari Mountain. See Haley, *Charles Goodnight*, 308.

Chapter 1

1. Whipple, "Report of Exploration for a Railway Route," pt. 1: 3–36, 39, 132, pt. 2: 76–77.

2. Max Goldenberg gave his recollections of these early events in a speech reported verbatim in *Tucumcari News and Times*, May 27, 1911, hereafter cited as *TN*.

3. Moncus and Knapp, eds., *Quay County, 1903–1985*, 15–18. Smith and Street were probably named as figurehead top executives of the town site company to avoid concerns about anti-Semitism. In one notable source, however, several scholars agree on the relative absence of that bias in the American West. See Rischin and Livingston, eds. *Jews of the American West*.

4. The Tucumcari Townsite and Investment Company was officially organized November 22, 1901, and the articles of incorporation were notarized in Clayton November 23, 1901, and certified and filed in the territorial secretary's office in Santa Fe on November 30, 1901. See Moncus and Knapp, *Quay County*, 16. Another valuable source of information on Tucumcari and Quay County is Whittington, *In the Shadow of the Mountain*.

5. Keleher, *The Fabulous Frontier*, 293–94; Myrick, *New Mexico's Railroads*, 91–92.

6. Noel M. Loomis and Abraham P. Nasatir, *Pedro Vial and the Roads to Santa Fe* (Norman, OK: University of Oklahoma Press, 1967), 403–4. Julyan, *Place Names of New Mexico*, 362, cites a 1777 burial document mentioning an Indian battle at "*Cuchuncari*," which may be an earlier recorded reference to Tucumcari Mountain.

7. *Pathfinder*, April 26, May 3 and 24, July 19 and 26, August 16 and 30, 1902; Hinshaw, *Tucumcari*, 38, 44; P. Stratton, *The Territorial Press of New Mexico, 1834–1912*, 294. Reference is made to rail operations between "Liberty Junction" and Santa Rosa in Memorandum of Agreement Covering divisions between the Dawson Railway and the Rock Island System, 1901, Box LTA-52, FF 7, Southern Pacific Railroad Collection, Special Collections, University of Texas at El Paso Library, hereafter cited as SP Collection UTEP.

8. Tucumcari was officially recorded as a "village" in March 1902, a "town" August 16, 1906, and "The City of Tucumcari" August 5, 1908. It became the county seat of Quay County, formed by the territorial legislature February 28, 1903. For the town itself, see Minutes of the Quay County Board of County Commissioners, August 16, 1906 (Tabulation of votes in election for incorporation of Tucumcari as a town—65 in favor, 45 against); Board of Trustees, Town of Tucumcari, Application to change the Incorporated Town of Tucumcari, New Mexico to a city, July 30, 1908; Territory of New Mexico, Executive Proclamation, Approval of the Application to Change the Incorporated Town of Tucumcari to a city, August 5, 1908, signed George Curry, Governor. City Manager J. A. Fleming to Alberta Miller, New Mexico secretary of state, July 9, 1964, stated that Tucumcari had been "incorporated as a Village in the year 1902, but [we] have no Article[s] of Incorporation." Hinshaw, *Tucumcari*, 52, states that Tucumcari was incorporated as a village in March 1902 under the Territorial Village Act. The date of the town designation is based on the county commissioners' confirmation of the votes cast in a special election held August 11, 1906. See Office of the New Mexico Secretary of State, Santa Fe. A map recording the earliest property ownership is in the Quay County Clerk's Office; see also Dedication on [*sic*] Plat of Tucumcari, NM, January 20, 1902, Tucumcari City Clerk's Office.

9. For examples of the legend, see Moncus and Knapp, *Quay County*, 14–18; Hinshaw, *Tucumcari*, 1–23.

10. The Jewish residents of Las Vegas formed a religious organization, the Congregation Montefiore, in 1884 and constructed a temple in 1888. Tobias, *A History of Jews in New Mexico*, 111–12. For more details on early Jewish residents in Tucumcari and New Mexico, see D. Stratton, "Jewish Founding Fathers," 35–62; Niederman, "A Better Life: Jewish Pioneers Add to State's Cultural Richness," 60–62; Levinson, "American Jews in the West," 286–88; Rischin and Livingston, *Jews of the American West*, 20.

11. "Way Back Then," *TDN*, June 2, 1952; Manuscript of interview with Henrietta Wertheim Goldenberg (wife of Alex Goldenberg), Los Angeles, CA, October 30, 1958, Jacob Rader Marcus Center of the American Jewish Archives, Jewish Institute of Religion, Hebrew Union College, Cincinnati Branch, Cincinnati, OH, hereafter cited as AJA; and Arthur W. Goldenberg (a feature article on his father), *TDN*, June 22, 1967. See also Twitchell, *The Leading Facts of New Mexican History*, 3:490–92. Alex Goldenberg became a US citizen at Las Cruces, NM, April 27, 1888. Typewritten affidavit headed "United States of America" (filed as part of Goldenberg land claim), US Land Office, Clayton, NM, Entry No. 4264, December 23, 1902, Land Entry Records, General Land Office, Department of the Interior, RG 49, National Archives and Records Administration (NARA), Washington, DC. Henrietta Wertheim Goldenberg died in 1963 at age ninety-six in Newport, RI; her funeral and burial were in Tucumcari. *TDN*, March 12, 1963, and obituary of Emma Wertheim Goldenberg, wife of Max B. Goldenberg; *TDN*, June 2, 1957.

12. Tobias and Payne, *Jewish Pioneers of New Mexico: The Ilfeld and Nordhaus Families*, 1–12. This booklet is in a series in which all the entries have the same main title, *Jewish Pioneers of New Mexico*; the first reference gives the full title, but hereafter only the subtitle.

13. US Land Office, Clayton, NM, Entry 2824, April 4, 1901 (Wertheim), Entry No. 2887, May 18, 1901 (Alex Goldenberg), Entry No. 2888, May 18, 1901 (Smith), Land Entry Records, General Land Office, Department of the Interior, RG 49, NARA, Rocky Mountain Region, Denver, CO. According to the Quay County Clerk's files in Tucumcari, the three homesteads were patented and eligible for entry in county records in the category as follows: Wertheim entry patented December 27, 1906, recorded June 26, 1907, Misc. Book I, p. 92; Alex Goldenberg entry patented March 11, 1905, recorded April 24, 1905, WD Book I, pp. 329–30; Smith entry patented April 17, 1905, recorded July 27, 1906, WD Book I, pp. 595–98, and July 8, 1908, Patent Book I, p. 16. After Smith died in May 1902, the heirs, on March 13, 1906, sold their patented interest in the forty acres to James A. "Alex" Street and, as a silent partner with a one-half interest, Alex Goldenberg.

14. US Land Office, Clayton, NM, Entry No. 4264, December 23, 1902, Land Entry Records, General Land Office, Department of the Interior, RG 49, NARA, Washington, DC. This extensive file of documentation includes items dated from 1877 to 1910. The Riley tract was patented March 17, 1903. As stated in the narrative, and verified here, Goldenberg filed the essential paperwork for this particular tract at the Clayton land office on November 23, 1901.

15. US Land Office, Clayton, NM, Lieu Land Selection No. 4804, November 25, 1901, LEF, RG 49, NARA. Such trades in paper certificates that represented tangible property were perfectly legal and common practice at the time.

16. Keleher, *The Fabulous Frontier*, 240–51; Clark, *Then Came the Railroads*, 235–36; Myrick, *New Mexico's Railroads*, 84–85. For the historical background of Dawson, see Keleher, *Fabulous Frontier*, 250–54, 265–68, and, by the same author, *Maxwell Land Grant*, chap. 16; Pearson, *The Maxwell Land* Grant, chap. 8, and 215–16.

17. Unless cited otherwise, the information in this section on the construction of the Rock Island line to the Pecos River was taken from Myrick, *New Mexico's Railroads*, 141–47, and two contemporaneous articles in *Railway Age*: "The Rock Island's New Line to El Paso" (November 8, 1901): 526–28, and "Rock Island Bridge over the Canadian River in New Mexico" (December 8, 1901): 658–60. For the Rock Island's construction progress, see the following 1901 issues of *Railway Age*: June 7 (p. 612), June 14 (p. 658), June 28 (p. 710), August 9 (p. 116), September 20 (p. 294), November 8 (p. 548). For construction of Charles B. Eddy's part of the line between Carrizozo and the Pecos River, see Myrick, *New Mexico's Railroads*, 85–86.

18. *El Paso Herald*, February 1, 1902; Myrick, *New Mexico's Railroads*, 71–92; Keleher, *Fabulous Frontier*, 240–58, 259–81.

19. Schwantes and Ronda, *The West the Railroads Made*, 39–42; *Railway Age* (February 7, 1902): p. 181; *Railway Age* (February 21, 1902): 234; Myrick, *New Mexico's Railroads*, 85–91.

20. Schneider, *Rock Island Requiem*, 39.

21. *Railway Age* (March 7, 1902): 294; *Railway Age* (May 9, 1902): 758; *Pathfinder*, August 16, 1902.

22. Myrick, *New Mexico Railroads*, 91–92; *Denver Daily News*, February 8, 1902,

quoted in *Pathfinder*, May 9 and 24, 1902; Walker, *SPV's Comprehensive Railroad Atlas of North America*, 30, 42; *Pathfinder*, August 9, 1902.

23. *Pathfinder*, August 9, 1902.

24. *Montoya Republican*, October 18, 1907; June 5, 1908; and December 24, 1909; *TDN*, July 14, 1940; and August 15, 1953. An article in the *Pathfinder*, April 26, 1902, stated that Liberty was now abandoned and that the businesses there had moved their goods to Tucumcari and were constructing new buildings. See also, *TN*, Special Agricultural Edition, June 14, 1923.

25. Parish, *Charles Ilfeld Company*, 208–9.

26. Alex Goldenberg to W. A. Hawkins, general attorney, El Paso & Southwestern Railroad, August 26, 1903, and Hawkins to E. C. Lindlay, general attorney, Rock Island Railway, August 21, 1907, Box LCR-11, FF 9, SP Collection, UTEP; *TDN*, November 2 and 6, 1933. An extensive file on legal disputes between the Goldenbergs and the railroads, from May 14, 1912, to February 10, 1915, is in Box L-6, FF 9 and 10, SP Collection UTEP.

27. *Pathfinder*, May 10 and 17, 1902; *Albuquerque Citizen*, May 13 and 16, 1902; *El Paso Herald*, May 12, 1902; *Albuquerque Journal*, June 21, 1904; *Prescott (AZ) Weekly Journal-Miner*, June 29, 190.

28. A detailed account of Smith's shooting death was reported in the *Pathfinder*, May 17, 1902, and an eyewitness reminiscence by early settler and later sheriff Fred White is in *TDN*, Special Edition, January 29, 1945. The best firsthand account, however, is *Albuquerque Citizen*, May 16, 1902, with background articles May 12, 13, and 14, 1902.

29. *Albuquerque Citizen*, May 14, 28, and 30, 1902; *Tucson Arizona Daily Star*, May 17, 1902; *Prescott (AZ) Weekly Journal-Miner*, June 29, 1904; *Quay County Democrat*, June 18, 1904; *Albuquerque Journal*, June 21, 1904; *Alamogordo News*, September 16, 1905; *El Paso Herald*, September 22, 1905.

30. *Little Rock (AR) Democrat*, August 6, 1904; *El Paso Herald*, February 20, 1902; *Phoenix Republic*, March 17, 1902; *Tucson Daily Star*, June 5, 1905; recollections of Herman Moncus, *TN*, December 30, 1975. The different versions of the bloody cowboy-rail worker episode are summarized in Hinshaw, *Tucumcari*, 49–50.

31. Keleher, *Fabulous Frontier*, 253, 267–70; Myrick, *New Mexico's Railroads*, 100–101.

32. *Pathfinder*, August 2 and 9, 1902. This issue also included this prediction from the *Santa Fe New Mexican*: "Tucumcari is to have railroad shops, round-houses, electric light and power works and other improvements."

33. Keleher, *Fabulous Frontier*, 253–56.

34. Smith, *Coal Town*, chap. 2; Covert, *Dawson the Town that Was*; typewritten manuscript, Esther Rogers Gafford, "Dawson," n.d., Phillip and Yetta Bidegain Collection, Tucumcari. Gafford, who lived in Dawson for several years, recalled the difficulty, because of language differences, of sharing grief with families of mine disaster victims in a diverse population "made up largely of Greeks, Slavs, Italians, French, Welch, Scotch, Mexicans, a few Germans, and Chinese."

35. Schwantes, *Vision and Enterprise*, 139–44. See also, Smith, *Coal Town*, chap. 5.

36. *Albuquerque Journal*, November 8, 1905; *El Paso Herald*, July 24, 1905.

37. *Actual Settler*, June 24, 1905; *TN*, July 6 and 13, August 24, 1907.

38. *Albuquerque Journal*, November 8, 1905; *El Paso Herald*, July 24, 1905.

39. Ward, "On Time: Railroads and the Tempo of American Life," 89; Bartky, "The Invention of Railroad Time," 13–22. On the temperature, see "Way Back Then," *TDN*, January 10, 1952, which reprinted a newspaper account of 1912.

40. Myrick, *New Mexico's Railroads*, 147–48.

41. *TN*, September 14, 1907; and Hinshaw, *Tucumcari*, 76–91, which has an extensive list of homesteader communities. See, for selected examples, feature stories on several early communities in *Review*, magazine of *TDN*, for Bard, October 29, and, for Nara Visa, December 31, 1965. For the most complete list with the most detailed information, however, see Moncus and Knapp, *Quay County*, 85–169.

42. *TN*, May 27, 1915; *TDN*, July 23, 1937.

43. *QC Sun*, March 5, 1983.

44. *TN*, May 10, 1902; Recollections of Roy H. Smith, *TDN*, February 13, 1940.

45. The information on William Morland Lancaster is from *Review*, magazine section of *TDN*, March 18, 1965, and "Genealogy Report: Descendants of John Atkinson, Sr.," Genealogy.com, 2004, https://www.familytreedna.com/public/y-dna-haplotree/A.

46. *Actual Settler*, January 14, 1905.

47. Moncus and Knapp, *Quay County*, 677. The Quay County statistics on rainfall and population decline are taken from *Historical Homesteads and Ranches in New Mexico: A Historic Context*, Historic Preservation Division, New Mexico Office of Cultural Affairs, Santa Fe, March 2008, 19.

48. On the Kohns' move to Montoya, see *Pathfinder*, July 26, 1902. The actual purchase date was May 2, 1902. Originally called Rountree, for the first postmaster, it became Montoya in 1902, shortly after the Rock Island track-laying crew's arrival. Julyan, *Place Names of New Mexico*, 233; Sharon Fried, *Heart & Soil*, 42–48.

49. *TN*, August 1, 1908; *Tucumcari Sun*, February 4, 1916; Montoya *Republican*, April 3, 1908; *TN*, August 1, 1908. The information about the two Kohn brothers, George and Charles, and brother-in-law Albert Calisch was gathered mainly from scattered news items and ads in the *Montoya Republican* and its successor, the *Montoya Democrat*, between October 18, 1907, and June 8, 1917. A biographical sketch of Calisch is in Twitchell, *Leading Facts of New Mexican History*, 3:502–3.

50. *Golden State Route*, 6; *Pathfinder*, July 26, 1902. *Montoya Republican*, August 7, 1908; May 28, 1909; November 22, 1912; April 13 and December 5, 1913; May 8 and August 14, 1914; April 26, 1915; March 3, 1916; *Montoya Democrat*, June 1, 1917; *Tucumcari Sun*, September 14, 1917. The first issue of the newspaper under its new title, *Montoya Democrat*, appeared January 31, 1916. Hinshaw, *Tucumcari*, 70–71, discusses the shift to a Democratic majority in Quay County.

51. Solomon H. Kohn, president, Chrome Steel Works, Brooklyn, NY, to Howard L. Kohn, February 4, 1891, December 11, 1902, May 18, 1903, Bidegain Collection. Solomon Kohn accumulated more wealth when he sold Chrome Steel to Crucible Steel, a part of Andrew Carnegie's industrial empire that became the foundation of United States Steel

in 1901, the world's first billion-dollar corporation. See Sharon Fried, *Heart & Soil*, 22. The Kohns were fortunate to have such a wealthy relative since Jews often had difficulty obtaining loans from regular banks, especially those in the East. On the growth of Montoya, see *Montoya Republican*, November 8 and December 6, 1907.

52.   *Montoya Republican*, January 28 and February 4, 1916; *Montoya Democrat*, April 27, 1917; *Tucumcari Sun*, February 4, 1916, and April 27, 1917. Hannah Goldenberg's obituary is in *TDN*, November 2, 1965.

53.   For Kohn's mercantile interests at this time, see *Montoya Republican*, April 21, 1916.

54.   Handwritten, Clara B. McGowan (age fifteen), "My Autobiography," n.d., and typewritten copy, Pearl Baker McGowan Cude, "My Life Story," September 1955, both in Bidegain Collection. Sharon Fried, *Heart & Soil*, 132–33, has the exact dates of these events.

55.   *TDN*, November 2, 1933; *Tucumcari Sun*, November 12, 1915.

56.   At the time of his death, Kohn reportedly had ongoing Partido contracts, in various stages of fulfillment, for 3,000 head of cattle, spread out over several eastern New Mexico counties. For an example of his partido contracts, see Stratton, "Jewish Founding Fathers," n64, 60–61. See also, on the Partido system, Baxter, *Las Carneradas*, 28–37, 48–49, 94–101.

57.   *QC Sun*, April 6, 2016. Jane O'Cain, abstract of interview with Yetta Kohn Bidegain, May 13, 1996, Oral History Program; *QC Sun*, February 19, 1997; copy, Form WR-16, A Report on Examination of Range Land, US Department of Agriculture, Agricultural Adjustment Administration, Western Division, May 8, 1937, in Bidegain Collection. Clara Kohn may have been the first woman in Quay County to use a hyphenated name, Kohn-Williams, in her brief marriage to T-4 ranch foreman J. H. "Skeet" or "Skeeter Bill" Williams Jr., which began in 1934. It was Williams who, during the Dust Bowl drought of the 1930s, managed the rail shipment of the T-4 herd, numbering 2,729 head, to Chihuahua, Mexico, where the cattle grazed from 1934 to 1937. See Sharon Fried, *Heart & Soil*, 67–69.

58.   Presently the T-4 Ranch consists of more than 186,000 acres, plus leases on an additional 15,000 acres of state land, or about 315 square miles, in Quay, Guadalupe, and San Miguel Counties. With a grazing program set at 40 acres "per cow unit," the ranch comfortably supports 2,500 cattle. Members of the extended Bidegain family also engage in farming and the breeding of quarter horses. By 1997 the Bidegains were the fifth-largest landowners in New Mexico, and by 2010 the forty-seventh largest in the United States. On the present holdings, see Memorandum, "T-4 Cattle Company Ltd.," n.d., Bidegain Collection; and Sharon Fried, *Heart & Soil*, 67–93, 192. See also, *Crossroads*, "Who Owns New Mexico, the State's 40 Largest Private Landowners"; Estes, "The Land Report," 48; Williams, *The Big Ranch Country*, chap. 15.

59.   Marcus, *To Count a People*, 137–38.

60.   *TN*, November 18, 1926.

61.   *TN*, January 5 and July 5, 1928; *TDN*, April 30, 1941. The Randle Hotel closed for

renovation in June 1948 and reopened two months later, renamed the Conchas Hotel. In 1960 the structure underwent extensive remodeling that produced seventy-three rooms, two apartments, a coffee shop, an enlarged lobby, and a lounge. On April 25, 1970, the Conchas Hotel burned to the ground. At that time, permanent renters, mostly railroaders and clerks on Railway Post Office cars, occupied only fifteen rooms. *QC Sun*, April 29, 1995.

Chapter 2

1. *TDN*, August 24 and 26, 1937.

2. *Las Vegas* (NM) *Daily Optic*, August 23, 1937; *Kansas City Star*, August 25, 1937.

3. Whitehead, *The FBI Story*, 113–18; *Clovis* (NM) *News-Journal*, May 3, 1937.

4. *TDN*, August 9, 1941; *Phoenix Arizona Republic*, August 24, 1937.

5. *Kansas City Star*, August 25, 1937.

6. *TDN*, August 24, 1937; Hornung, *Fullerton's Rangers*, 161–69; Doherty, *Just the Facts*, 186–88; Nash, *Citizen Hoover*, 23; *Phoenix Republic*, August 24, 1937; Grann, *Killers of the Flower Moon*, 115–16, 134, 164, 169, 178, 193, 216, 310, 314; Modell, *Ruth Benedict*, 180–82; Franz Boas, Hamburg, Germany, to Ruth Fulton Benedict, August 1, 1931, in Mead, *An Anthropologist at Work*, 408–9.

7. *Phoenix Republic*, August 24, 1937.

8. *TDN*, August 24 and 25, 1937.

9. Unless specified otherwise, the general information on the national scene is taken, without citation, from Colin J. Davis, *Power at Odds: The 1922 National Railroad Shopmen's Strike*. On the possible effects of the shopmen's strike, see also Bryant Jr., "Development of North American Railroads," 16. For a general description of organized labor in the West, see Etulain and Malone, *American West*, 80–83.

10. During the manpower shortage of the First World War, a few thousand women were hired in the shops by the country's railroads, including the Southern Pacific, but the female workforce had been obliterated by the time of the shopmen's strike. Davis, *Power at Odds*, 41–43.

11. For examples of the Brown system as applied by the SP, see Southern Pacific Company (Pacific Lines), *Schedule of Pay and Regulations*, May 1, 1928. For a succinct explanation of Brownie demerits, see Fall Brook Railway Company, "General Superintendent G. R. Brown's 'System of Discipline,'" https://www.fallbrookeailway.com/g_r_brown.html. See also, King as told to Mahaffey, *Main Line: Fifty Years*, which states that the number of Brownies for dismissal from the SP was ninety. In an example of the Brownie system as used by the SP, in the case of a locomotive inspector at the Tucumcari roundhouse in 1929, the entry read: "For your failure to note and report front end of left main rod hot and bushing out on Rock Island engine 4046 on arrival Tucumcari on train No. 3, June 3rd, resulting in 15-minute delay to train No. 2 out of Tucumcari, I am assessing your personal record with a reprimand. In view of the fact that defect in this particular case was difficult of detection, we are showing leniency by only assessing your

record with a reprimand." Typewritten copy, dated July 22, 1929, in possession of the present author. How the shopmen's strike affected another community, Aurora, Illinois, is the subject of Flynn, "The Railroad Shopmen's Strike of 1922 on the Industry, Company, and Community Levels."

12.   At Tucumcari at least 122 EP&SW shopmen walked out; at Amarillo, Texas, 110 miles away, the number was about 500 for the various rail lines there, including an unknown number of Rock Island operating crew members who made runs to Tucumcari on the T&M line. Since the EP&SW ran the shops at Tucumcari, all the shopmen there were presumably employed by that company. *Amarillo Daily News*, July 1, 1922.

13.   General Memorandum, A. E. Sweet to "All Employes of the Mechanical Department, Who Voluntarily Left the Service at 10:00 A. M., July 1st," dated July 5, 1922. The Rock Island issued a similar decree for Amarillo, quoted verbatim in *Amarillo Daily News*, July 7, 1922.

14.   Files of Tucumcari newspapers for dates of the strike have mysteriously disappeared from public depositories. The information here is from State of New Mexico, Quay County, affidavit of Eugene Gordon, master mechanic of the El Paso & Southwestern System, transcribed at Tucumcari, NM, July 19, 1922 (similar documents hereafter cited as affidavit, name, place transcribed, date; EP&SW titles are usually omitted); H. B. Harding, land and tax agent, to Hawkins, July 15, 1922; affidavits, P. G. Burnham, special agent, Tucumcari, M. O. Scobee, employee, El Paso, TX, C. D. Beeth, superintendent at Tucumcari—all July 19, 1922. These items, as well as most other documents and correspondence used in this chapter, came from Box L-23, Southern Pacific Railroad Collection, University of Texas at El Paso Library, El Paso, TX. Hereafter the box designation will be omitted for such material.

15.   Joint affidavit, G. V. Davis and S. M. Monroe, El Paso, July 19, 1922. Among several firsthand accounts of the depot incident involving the two young icers, these are the most informative: McElroy to Hawkins, July 20, 1922, Howard Avant, Tucumcari police officer, to L. U. Morris, EP&SW general superintendent, El Paso; and affidavits, C. D. Beeth, Tucumcari, P. G. Burnham, Tucumcari, and M. O. Scobee, El Paso, all three July 19, 1922.

16.   Affidavit, Ernest Simpson, Quay County sheriff, Tucumcari, August 1, 1922, and on events at Montoya, affidavits of Dan Alderette and Sam Adger, El Paso, July 19, 1922.

17.   The information on the Fall-Hawkins relationship and the Hawkins Act is taken from Keleher, *Fabulous Frontier*, chap. 12; and Stratton, *Tempest over Teapot Dome*, 68–72. Hawkins's superior at Phelps Dodge in New York City gave full approval as "necessary and judicious" for both his strategy and tactics in dealing with the shopmen's strike at Tucumcari. Hawkins to William Church Osborn, EP&SW general counsel and member of Phelps Dodge board of directors, July 25, 1922; Osborn to Hawkins, July 31, 1922.

18.   Hawkins to William Church Osborn, July 25, 1922; Fall to Hawkins, July 20, 1922, and enclosed copy of Fall to Daugherty, July 20, 1922. Harry H. McElroy was sent to Tucumcari by his boss, W. A. Hawkins, as an undercover observer of the strike, and he frequently reported what was happening. See McElroy to Hawkins, July 20 and 24, 1922, and McElroy to Eugene Gordon, EP&SW master mechanic at Tucumcari, August 4, 1922.

19.   Hawkins to William Church Osborn, July 25, 1922; exchanges of coded telegrams between Hawkins and W. F. Dickinson, Rock Island general solicitor, Chicago, July 7–11, 1922; three letters on the same date, Dickinson to Hawkins, July 11, 1922, and another letter, July 18, 1922; coded telegram, Hawkins to J. F. Hogan, EP&SW general agent in Chicago, July 10, 1922; two letters, Hawkins to Dickinson, July 15 and 25, 1922; three legal documents headed: District Court of the United States, District of New Mexico, El Paso and Southwestern Company vs. International Association of Machinists, et al., No. 899 Equity: "Bill for Injunction," July 20, 1922;the restraining order, July 22, 1922; and a copy, "In Chancery," the subpoena form, n.d.

20.   General information about the sudden appearance of deputy marshals comes from W. F. Dickinson to Hawkins et al., July 17, 1922; Hawkins to A. E. Sweet, August 21 and 23, September 15, 1922; Sweet to Hawkins, October 13, 15, and 20, 1922, and Sweet to A. L. Hawley, EP&SW general auditor, August 3, 1922; F. L. Hunter, EP&SW purchasing agent, to Hawkins, October 24, 1922; Hawkins to Hunter, October 30, 1922. Most of the arms and ammunition were returned to the railroad for sale as surplus, but one Colt revolver was reported as stolen and two cartridge belts as well as three hundred cartridges came up missing.

21.   McElroy to Hawkins, July 24, 1922; coded telegram, Hawkins to McElroy, July 25, 1922; Hawkins to William Church Osborn, July 25, 1922. Without the political clout he enjoyed in New Mexico, Hawkins had less luck getting the cooperation of federal and state authorities in Texas. The US marshal in San Antonio agreed to assign only five deputy marshals to the major rail hub at El Paso where four railroads and 3,800 strikers were involved. The El Paso County sheriff and his deputies as well as the city police, however, essentially sided with the railroads in the strike. Telegram, A. E. Sweet and Hawkins to D. A. Walker, US marshal, San Antonio, July 19, 1922; telegram, Walker to Sweet, July 20, 1922; R. M. Henry, EP&SW chief special agent, to Seth B. Orndorff, El Paso County sheriff, August 12, 1922; El Paso Herald, June 30 and July 4, 1922.

22.   Temporary Injunction, El Paso and Southwestern Company vs. International Association of Machinists, et al., No. 899 Equity, District Court of the United States for the District of New Mexico, August 3, 1922; Albuquerque Morning Journal, July 26, 1922; Hawkins to Dickinson, July 25, 1922; E. R. Wright, Santa Fe attorney representing EP&SW, to Hawkins, August 3, 1922, and telegram, Wright to McElroy, August 1, 1922. A temporary restraining order is usually issued when immediate action is necessary, while a temporary, or preliminary, injunction is given only after the defendants have had a chance to reply. A permanent injunction is issued following an actual trial.

23.   Davis, Power at Odds, 126–36; Giglio, H. M. Daugherty and the Politics of Expediency, 146–52; Daugherty with Dixon, The Inside Story of the Harding Tragedy, chaps. 11 and 12; Dean, Warren G. Harding, 114–21. Davis's book is the standard account of the shopmen's strike; the best short version is Murray, The Harding Era, chap 8 (quote on Wilkerson injunction, 255).

24.   Stratton, Tempest over Teapot Dome, 209–10.

25.   E. R. Wright, Santa Fe, to Hawkins, October 16, 1922, and two letters Hawkins to Wright, October 20, 1922, and January 17, 1923.

26. El Paso & Southwestern Company, *Ninth Annual Report*, 7; Hawkins to Wright, January 17, 1923; Murray, *Harding Era*, 264. Lists of strikers' names with those of return-ing workers marked with a red *X*, attached to T. Paxton, EP&SW superintendent of motive power, to Hawkins, January 13, 1923. Rodden, *The Fighting Machinists*, 73, is the source for the lack of a raise until 1941.

27. Davis, *Power at Odds*, 36–39, 164–65; Wilner, "Railroads in the 20th Century"; Bryant, "Development of North American Railroads," 16; *TDN*, August 31, 1949.

28. *Pathfinder*, June 16, 1902.

29. *TN*, April 12 and May 3, 1917.

30. *Tucumcari American*, April 27, 1917; *Tucumcari Sun*, April 29, 1917; *TN*, May 3, 1917; Canning, *The Most American Thing in America*, 155–59, 176–79, 188, 199–204.

31. *Tucumcari Sun*, October 5, 1917.

32. *TDN*, October 9, 1934; and April 8, 1936; *TN*, January 17, October 10, and December 26, 1918; and May 19 and 26, August 4, 1921.

33. *Tucumcari Sun*, August 31, 1917; *TDN*, June 13 and 20, 1918; *TDN*, October 9, 1934, April 8, 1936.

34. *TN*, April 27, 1917.

35. *TN*, July 4, 1918.

36. *TN*, May 2 and October 10, 1918.

37. Myrick, *New Mexico's Railroads*, back cover.

38. Schwantes, *Vision and Enterprise*, chap. 7.

39. See map, "Southern Pacific Traffic Density, 1995," Saunders Jr., *Main Lines*, 273. Railroad scholar Philip F. Beach pointed out the difference in profits between the two main routes. Philip F. Beach, Eatonville, Washington, telephone interview by the author, October 3, 2002, transcript in possession of the author.

40. *TN*, January 7, 1911; November 4, 1915; *Tucumcari American*, December 11, 1919; *Quay County*, 273; *TDN*, October 2, 1941, May 13, 1952. E-mail, Robert M. Doughty II, Alamogordo, New Mexico, October 28, 2020, to the author, copy in possession of the author, provides information on what brought his grandfather, Dr. James M. Doughty, to Tucumcari.

41. Orsi, *Sunset Limited*, 27–29; Aldrich, *Death Rode the Rails*, 168–69; *TDN*, Septem-ber 10, 1937; Wilner, "Railroads in the 20th Century."

42. Lewis, *Chasing the Cure in New Mexico*, 4, 18–19; Gilbert, "The Cry Was: Go West, Young Man, and Stay Healthy," 138–49.

43. Lewis, *Chasing the Cure in New Mexico*, 61, 70, 206.

44. Ibid., 1–2.

45. *TN*, December 4, 1919.

46. Jack R. Hanna, Albuquerque, New Mexico, son of Hugh and Mabel Hanna, inter-view by the author, October 4, 2015, video recording in possession of the author; "Hugh Hanna," typewritten genealogical chart of Hanna family, courtesy of Jack R. Hanna.

47. One reason New Mexico did not attract homesteaders earlier was because most of it seemed "to be a permanent grazing region." Dale, *Range Cattle Industry*, 121.

48. Sanchez, Spude, and Gomez, *New Mexico*, 188.

49. For the dangers of grade crossings, see Aldrich, *Death Rode the Rails*, 124–29, 213–15; Middleton et al., eds., "Grade-Crossing Safety," *Encyclopedia of North American Railroads*, 495–99; *Trains*, February 2008, 20–21; *TN*, August 31, 1907; *Tucumcari Sun*, July 28, 1916.

50. *TDN*, February 4, 1937.

51. *TN*, November 28 and December 5, 1908; March 25, 1911; August 12, September 8 and 23, and October 7, 14, and 28, 1915.

52. Etulain and Malone, *American West*, 61; *TN*, June 14 and 17, 1910; *Albuquerque Morning Journal*, June 17, 1910; Moncus and Knapp, *Quay County*, 638.

53. *TDN*, February 18, 1933. For other examples of Miss Ulmer's Hudson news columns with arguments for prohibition, see *TDN*, January 2 and September 8, 1933. See *TN*, April 28, 1921; and March 24, 1932, for automobile and bootlegging locally, and March 24, 1932, for the appearance of "Big Time Racketeers" in cars.

54. Amarillo was in the Central Time Zone, but apparently an adjustment was made to accommodate the flight to Albuquerque, which was on Mountain time.

55. Transcontinental & Western Air became Trans World Airlines in the early 1950s. Unless cited otherwise, the account of the T&WA plane crash in this section is a composite of information taken from typewritten copy, Transcontinental & Western Air, Western Region Aircraft Accident Board, Findings on Accident #104, Kansas City, MO, September 7, 1933; interoffice correspondence, dated September 2–3, related to this crash; typewritten copy, Precinct No. 3, Quay County, New Mexico, "Coroner's Inquest," Quay, NM, August 30, 1933: Trans World Airlines (TWA) Records, Collection No. K0453, the State Historical Society of Missouri, Research Center, Kansas City, MO. For additional information, see *TDN*, August 29, 30, 31, and September 1, 1933; *Albuquerque Journal*, August 30, 1933.

56. Jewell D. Stratton was not related to the author.

57. Moncus and Knapp, *Quay County*, 568.

58. T&WA Aircraft Accident Board Findings, Accident #104, August 29, 1933, TWA Collection.

59. Unless cited otherwise, the account in this section on the Golden State train wreck is mainly a composite of information taken from *TDN*, August 29, 30, 31, and September 1, 5, and 7, 1933; and four Associated Press articles, August 29 and 30, 1933, online.

60. *El Paso Herald-Post*, August 30, 1933. Letter to the editor, *TDN*, September 7, 1933, recounts a rumor circulating earlier that there was erosion at the bridge.

61. *Albuquerque Journal*, August 31 and October 11, 1933; *TDN*, August 31 and September 7, 1933; *Clovis News-Journal*, November 3, 1933; *El Paso Herald-Post*, November 4, 1933; *El Paso Times*, November 5, 1933.

62. *TN*, January 7, 1914; January 31 and May 2, 1929; US Census Reports, Cities, Population by Decades, New Mexico, 1930, https://en.wikipedia.org/wiki/Tucuncari_New_Mexico.

63. *TN*, September 26, 1929.

Chapter 3

1. *TN*, September 20 and October 4, 1923; February 18, 1926.

2. *TN*, October 4, 1923; February 18, 1926.

3. *TDN*, April 1, 1935; June 9, 1937.

4. Watts, *The People's Tycoon*, 1–10, 343–47, 533–36; Etulain and Malone, *American West*, 40–41, 235–37; Schwantes, *Going Places*, 120, 125; Sutton, "Way Back When," 135–48; Patton, *Open Road*, 60.

5. Donovan, *Wheels for a Nation*, 150.

6. Cray, *Chrome Colossus*, 204–5. Automotive historian James Flink uses the term *automobility* in describing the mass interest in cars before most people could afford to buy them and later when widespread ownership had created an *automobile culture*. See Flink, *The Car Culture*, 29, chap. 6; and by the same author, *America Adopts the Automobile, 1895–1910*, 73; and, for the cultural influence of Western women, Etulain and Malone, *The American West*, 156–63.

7. An excellent source for both technical details and general information about road building to the 1920s is MacDonald, "The History and Development of Road Building in the United States.

8. Schwantes, *Going Places*, chap. 4; MacDonald, "History of Road Building in the US," 35–53; Etulain and Malone, *The American West*, 40–41. For the effects on Quay County of the 1916 act and subsequent legislation to 1921, see *TN*, April 15, 1921.

9. Hokanson, "To Cross America, Early Tourists Took a Long Detour," 58, 61.

10. Moncus, "Taking a Ride with Some Old Directions"; McAlavy and Kilmer, *High Plains History of East-Central New Mexico*, 125–26. *QC Sun*, August 5, 1995, has a feature article on Stand Rock, or Monument Rock. Etulain and Malone, *The American West*, 61; *TN*, June 14 and 17, 1910; *Albuquerque Morning Journal*, June 17, 1910; Moncus and Knapp, *Quay County*, 638. As early as 1901, automobile clubs in the East were cooperating in a movement to place signs and guideposts marking the main routes between major cities. Flink, *America Adopts the Automobile*, 209–10.

11. Kelly, *Father of Route 66*, chaps. 8 and 9. Early on, in 1928, Route 66 gained nationwide publicity in an event that was like a "traveling circus" involving a footrace of about two hundred contestants running along the highway from Los Angeles to a point in Oklahoma. Only ninety-three runners were left at the end when the first one to cross the finish line collected the $25,000 prize. Sonderman, *Images of America*, 7.

12. *TDN*, September 28, 1973, contains an official brief history of highways in New Mexico. See also, *TDN*, October 22, 1964, for a semiofficial account of Route 66's cactus computers.

13. *TN*, September 28, 1973, contains an official brief history of highways in New Mexico. See also, *TDN*, October 22, 1964, for a semiofficial account of Route 66's historical background.

14. *TN*, August 27, June 18, and September 10, 1915; April 20, 1916; June 15, 1920; *American Legal News* 32 (February 1921): 19.

15.   *TN*, June 4,1914; Goddard, *Getting There*, chap. 3.

16.   McAlavy and Kilmer, *High Plains History of East-Central New Mexico*, 126; Flink, *America Adopts the Automobile*, 203–10.

17.   *TN*, March 4, 1920; April 15 and August 4, 1921.

18.   *TN*, March 25 and July 22, 1920. San Jon, east of Tucumcari on the Ozark Trail route, had an Ozark Hotel. *TN*, April 8, 1920.

19.   *TN*, March 12, 1915.

20.   *TN*, May 28 and July 30, 1914; June 1, 1916.

21.   *TN*, December 7 and 14, 1916.

22.   *TN*, February 18, 1914; November 25, 1915; July 28, 1921.

23.   *QC Sun*, Progress Edition, August 28, 1977, A-10; Harding County Biographies: Pool and Hawkins Family, 2–3; *TDN*, October 26, 1970, has a firsthand account of building the Logan highway bridge.

24.   *TN*, March 18, 1920.

25.   For an example of early complaints about US 54's deplorable condition, see *TDN*, February 27, 1935.

26.   In 1932, Paul Dodge reported that his examination of the main roads leading out of Tucumcari had found all of them in terrible condition, blaming the county Democratic machine, whose members, he said, were more interested in getting state jobs than the plight of local roads. *TN*, -March 10, 1932.

27.   Stone, "Fields of Hope," 72–74. Clovis made a more questionable bargain by trading its support to Portales in exchange for backing its bid to obtain an armory where popular wrestling matches of that day could be held.

28.   *QC Sun*, April 2 and November 19, 1915; *TN*, August 12, 1920.

29.   *TDN*, November 12, 1934. Dodge's South Road was designated State Road 18 and later was changed to SR 209. *QC Sun*, June 20, 1988.

30.   *TDN*, May 5, 1932; and April 21, 1936. In April 1935, a US Highway 54 association was formed in Tucumcari with O. S. Greaser as president. Dodge described US 54 as a "rolly coaster." *TDN*, April 26, 1935.

31.   *TDN*, April 29 and May 27, 1936.

32.   *TDN*, June 28, 1921; *TDN*, May 26 and August 26, 1936.

33.   *TDN*, January 16 and 23, 1934.

34.   *TDN*, June 20, 1934.

35.   *TDN*, January 16 and September 25, 1934; April 28, July 10, and August 26, 1936; August 6 and September 21, 1937.

36.   *TDN*, November 28, 1934; June 1, 1936; January 26, February 8 and 9, and March 31, 1937. At the time of Cutting's death, Dodge indicated that he had supported the senator in two elections, presumably also in 1928. *TDN*, May 7, 1935. For Cutting's 1934 election and death in 1935, see Lowitt, *Bronson M. Cutting*, chaps. 23 and 25; and Keleher, *Memoirs*, chap. 11.

37.   *TDN*, August 15 and 19, 1934; July 13, 1936.

38.   *TDN*, March 15, 1937.

39. *TDN*, July 9, 1936; March 15, 1937.

40. *TDN*, July 8 and 9, and March 29, 1935; March 3, 1936.

41. *TDN*, June 18, 1934; April 21, 1936.

42. *TDN*, June 18, 1934; April 21, 1936.

Chapter 4

1. Ellis, *The Bell Ranch as I Knew It*, 154. There are two branches of the Canadian River, north and south, before they join in eastern Oklahoma. The branch in New Mexico is the South Canadian, but in this study will be called the Canadian River.

2. *TN*, September 20 and October 4, 1923; February 18, 1926; Rogers, *Tucumcari Project*, 6–8; Moncus and Knapp, *Quay County*, 499; *TDN*, September 30, 1935; June 24, 1941.

3. *TDN*, Special Edition, October 5, 1937; *TDN*, April 24, 1947, and obituary, September 7, 1956.

4. *TDN*, July 8, 1935. Paul Dodge devoted one of his "Man About Town" columns to an impromptu historical background of Conchas Dam, based on conversations with local business leaders. See, also, a long newspaper account, for which Hurley was interviewed, Elmer T. Peterson, "Hurley's Dream Resulted in Conchas Dam," *Oklahoma City Daily Oklahoman*, January 26, 1941, reprinted in *TDN*, February 4, 1941. In a letter to Governor R. C. Dillion of New Mexico, May 28, 1928, Hurley reported on his activities promoting construction of Conchas Dam, reprinted in *Santa Fe New Mexican*, June 14, 1928. For Royal A. Prentice's early interest in a Canadian River dam and his invitation to General Goethals for an inspection tour, see Moncus and Knapp, *Quay County*, 499; *TDN*, April 24, 1947; September 7, 1956.

5. *TDN*, August 7, 1934; and March 31, 1937; Special Edition, June 24, 1941; *Daily Oklahoman*, January 26, 1941.

6. David Phillips, "Arch Hurley Conservancy District," 9.

7. Ibid., 1; Welsh, *A Mission in the Desert*, 18–21; Clark, *Water in New Mexico*, 227–32, 259–62.

8. *TDN*, September 23, 1941.

9. *TN*, February 18, September 28, October 3, and November 7, 1932; *TDN*, January 1, 1935.

10. *TDN*, November 14 and December 18 and 27, 1934; January 1 and 15, 1935.

11. *Clovis News-Journal*, October 24, 1933; *TDN*, May 7, 1934.

12. *TDN*, May 7, 1934.

13. *TDN*, November 16, 1934; February 5, April 2, and May 15, 1935.

14. *TDN*, October 22 and December 11, 1934; April 5, 1935.

15. *TDN*, April 29 and August 6, 1935.

16. *TDN*, October 21 and November 15, 1935.

17. Melzer, *Coming of Age in the Great Depression*, 10–16, 22–28, 112, 132–34, 177, 228. The broad federal mandate assigned to the CCC as it applied to Metropolitan Park is outlined in Clark, *Water in New Mexico*, 244–45.

18. *TDN*, August 26, 1935; April 26 and July 22, 1936.

19. *TDN*, November 14, 1935; March 18, 1936; Melzer, *Coming of Age in the Great Depression*, 71. The source of the flagstone was undoubtedly Mesa Redonda, not Tucumcari Mountain, as the CCC enrollee recalled.

20. *TDN*, November 14 and 15, 1935; April 21, 1936. As an example of how the CCC enrollees mixed in locally, their softball team usually demolished opponents in the city league. *TDN*, March 18, 1937.

21. *TDN*, August 27, 1935.

22. *TDN*, Special Edition, October 5, 1937, contains a list of local and county WPA projects until that time. A later partial list is in *TDN*, January 29, 1940. Private contractors scornfully claimed that WPA (Works Progress Administration) stood for "We Piddle Around." They claimed that the local undertaker was summoned to collect the body of a WPA worker but failed because he couldn't tell which one was dead.

23. The essential information on Hannett's shortcut is from Hannett, *Sagebrush Lawyer*, 127–28, 163–64, and the appendix, 277–89, which contains highway engineer E. B. Bail's account of the difficulties in carrying out Governor Hannett's orders to construct the shortcut. See, also, Mann, "Irate Governor Paves the Way," 61; Sanchez et al., *New Mexico*, 209–10.

24. *Amarillo Globe-Times*, April 7, 1970; *Clovis News-Journal*, April 7, 1970; Hilleson, "Roadside Attractions Give Character to 66 Towns," 50–52.

25. Steinbeck, *The Grapes of Wrath*, 103, 171; Sanchez et al., *New Mexico*, 244.

26. *TDN*, August 6, 14, 23, September 17, 18, October 13, November 9, 12, and December 13, 1934; February 14, 1941; Remley, *Bell Ranch*, 263–70. It should be noted that the Agricultural Adjustment Act included crop reduction as one of its aims and that not only cattle but also hogs and sheep were part of the government's buying and killing program. In fact, references in the press to "plowing under little pigs" caused a public uproar. Hurt, *Problems of Plenty*, 67–69.

27. *TDN*, August 16, 1934.

28. *TDN*, August 6, 1934; January 23, 1941.

29. Welsh, "Mission in the Desert," 21–23; Shelburg, "Conchas Dam," 2–3.

30. Welsh, "Mission in the Desert," 22.

31. Remley, *Bell Ranch*, chap. 6. On Mitchell's Tequesquite Valley ranch, see *TDN*, June 31, 1971.

32. *TDN*, April 11, October 19, and November 7, 1938; Mitchell quoted in *Amarillo Daily News*, June 27, 1941.

33. Remley, *Bell Ranch*, 294–96.

34. Ibid., 95.

35. Associated Press feature article, *TDN*, May 31, 1937.

36. Welsh, "Mission in the Desert," 24; Remley, *Bell Ranch*, 295.

37. *TDN*, Special Edition, June 24, 1941. In January 1942, the CE headquarters was moved and the name changed to the Albuquerque District. *TDN*, January 16, 1953.

38. Welsh, "Mission in the Desert," 26, n40, n.p.; Rogers, *Tucumcari Project*, 10;

Associated Press feature article, *TDN*, May 31, 1937; Mulhouse, *Abandoned New Mexico*, 82–83.

39.   *TDN*, November 14, 1935.

40.   *TDN*, Special Edition, June 24, 1941; Welsh, "Mission in the Desert," 25–26. As depicted in Hinckley and James, *Ghost Towns of Route 66*, 100–103, Newkirk is today, like many other early twentieth-century settlements, a ghost town. Besides some lodging available at Newkirk, the Corps of Engineers built dormitories for individual workers, and frame quadraplexes and rows of sandstone and adobe houses for families on the Conchas town site. In addition, schools, an infirmary, a mess hall, movie theater, billiard parlor, nine-hole golf course, tennis courts, a hunting lodge with swimming pool, and other facilities were built. Many workers, and would-be workers, lived in makeshift structures in fringe communities, such as Gate City, Mesa Rica, and Hooverville. Welsh, "Mission in the Desert," 26, 29–30, and n40 & 41.

41.   Sanchez et al., *New Mexico*, 243–44; Welsh, "Mission in the Desert," 27; Hans Kramer, Captain, District Engineer, US Army Corps of Engineers Office, Conchas Dam, NM, to Samuel H. Stratton, National Reemployment Service, Tucumcari, NM, December 18, 1936, in the possession of the author. In this letter Kramer restated the CE's earlier commitment regarding the hiring of WPA workers.

42.   Kirksey, Lauriault, and Cooksey, *Weather Observations at the Agricultural Science Center*, 1. Although Conchas Dam was in the eastern part of San Miguel County, weather patterns were similar to those in adjoining Quay County.

43.   *TDN*, May 2 and 5, September 22, and October 30 and 31, 1941; November 7 and 17, 1975; "The Arch Hurley Irrigation District," and "History and Status of the Tucumcari Project"—both Arch Hurley Conservancy District.

44.   Rogers, *Tucumcari Project*, 8–9; Clark, *Water in New Mexico*, 385–86; "Arch Hurley Irrigation District"; Hinshaw, "A Gift of Water," is an excellent detailed account of the Arch Hurley Conservancy District until 1965.

45.   Rogers, *Tucumcari Project*, 24. The conservancy district claims that the Tucumcari Project "has about 41,000 acres of irrigable land," or an original 42,214 irrigable acres, subsequently adjusted to 41,397 acres, with 32,000 acres "actually irrigated each year . . . on a 25 year average." "Arch Hurley Irrigation District" and "Project History of the Arch Hurley Conservancy District."

46.   *QC Sun*, April 22, 2014; Phillips, "Arch Hurley Conservancy District," 19.

47.   Rogers, *Tucumcari Project*, 8–9; Clark, *Water in New Mexico*, 385–86; Hinshaw, "A Gift of Water."

48.   Clark, *Water in New Mexico*, 325–27, gives a detailed presentation of the legal complexities of water rights involved in this case, while Welsh, *A Mission in the Desert*, 35–36, gives a streamlined version.

49.   "History of the Coronado Celebrations," in George P. Hammond, *Coronado's Seven Cities*, 77–82; WPA Writers' Program of New Mexico, ed., *New Mexico*, xxiv–xxxvi.

50.   *TDN*, Special Edition on the Coronado Cuarto Centennial, July 29, 1940. See also editorial, October 18, 1940.

51.   See *TDN*, Special Edition, June 24, 1940, which covers the planning for both the opening of Conchas Lake and the Highway 66 Association convention, and *TDN*, June 30 and July 1 and 2, 1940, for reports on the events. The series of articles starts March 4, 1940, with several historical installments by Royal A. Prentice titled, "Coronado East of the Pecos," and runs continually thereafter until the Entrada.

52.   In 1952, in a ceremony at the Texas–New Mexico state line, the National Highway 66 Association formally dedicated Route 66 as the "Will Rogers Highway," but the designation did not stick and, in time, was largely ignored. *TDN*, May 12, June 9, 24, and 27, 1952.

53.   *TDN*, June 7, 1941.

54.   *TDN*, October 5, 1936; May 10, 1937.

55.   Pauline Sartain, interview by Mary Grooms, *Tucumcari News*, July 25, 1975.

56.   *TDN*, January 25, June 3, 11, and 14, and July 6, 1937.

Chapter 5

1.   Details of the *Arizona*'s sinking in this section are from Lord, *Day of Infamy*, 53. 68, 71, 88, 94–97; Jasper et al., *The USS Arizona*; Stillwell, ed., *Air Raid: Pearl Harbor!*

2.   Lord, *Day of Infamy*, 95; Mitsuo Fuchida, "I Led the Air Attack on Pearl Harbor," 13.

3.   Jasper et al., *USS Arizona*, chaps. 6 and 7.

4.   Masterson, "Arizona Survivor," 171–75; Jasper et al., *USS Arizona*, 13; Moncus and Knapp, *Quay County*, 427. The grave of Clifford Griffin from Cherokee, Oklahoma, who later lived in Tucumcari, is also in the local cemetery. He was a Pearl Harbor survivor but not as an Arizona crew member. *QC Sun*, December 18, 2019.

5.   *TDN*, December 23, 1941; July 8, 1942.

6.   On the above-ground fuel oil tanks at Pearl Harbor, see Irwin, *Silent Strategists*, 60–61, 192, 199; D. Stratton, *Tempest over Teapot Dome*, 240–44, 345; M. Davis, *Dark Side of Fortune*, 135–37, 146–49, 286–88.

7.   Lord, *Day of Infamy*, 135.

8.   *TDN*, February 26, 1940.

9.   Fred S. Witty Jr., Johnson City, Tennessee, telephone interview by the author, December 8, 2015, transcript in possession of the author.

10.   *TDN*, March 4 and 6, 1940.

11.   *TDN*, May 10, 1940.

12.   *TDN*, May 31, 1940. Blind-Tigers were places that sold liquor illegally.

13.   Hallam, ed., *Chronicles of the Crusades*, 242–45; Dickson, "Children's Crusade."

14.   *TDN*, June 4, 1940.

15.   Ibid.

16.   Bailey, *A Diplomatic History of the American People*, 717–18.

17.   *TDN*, June 17, 1940. See also, August 20, 1940, which portrays Sarah D. Ulmer's character and fortitude in killing a huge rattlesnake on her "Thousand Acres Ranch" near Hudson.

18.   McMurtry, "The West Without Chili," 38, 40–41.

19. *TDN*, October 21, 1938; September 27, 1941.

20. *TDN*, April 12, 1940; July 1, August 12 and 13, September 1, October 28, and December 22, 1941.

21. *TDN*, April 28, 1938; October 22 and December 17 and 18, 1941.

22. *TDN*, October 10, 1940; January 3 and 15, 1941.

23. Joy Louise Barrick Batson, 50th Reunion, Class of 45.

24. Personal correspondence of Joy Louise Barrick, August 23, 1942–November 20, 1944, in possession of the author. This correspondence is the source of her quotes and the references to her in this section and is not cited separately.

25. The categories of gasoline rationing cards: A, 3–4 gallons per week for the average passenger car driver; B and C, supplemental rations for essential passenger car drivers tailored to individual needs; TT, for commercial transportation, such as trucks and buses; E and R, for farmers and others engaged in essential work. Office of War Information, Report on Civilian Gasoline Supply, online.

26. Sopronyi, "Watching the Radio," 44–49.

27. Tuttle Jr., *"Daddy's Gone to War,"* 154–61.

28. Arany et al., *The Reel List*, 19, 74, 279.

29. *TDN*, December 16, 1941.

30. *TDN*, February 17, 1940; Sanchez et al., *New Mexico*, 261, 271.

31. *TDN*, July 21, 1942. At that time an article in a West Texas newspaper, based on information from a Tucumcari resident, claimed that it was "the hardest hit of all towns in the Southwest" by wartime conditions, and both businesses and people were leaving in droves. The *Daily News*, on July 25, 1942, responded that implying Tucumcari was virtually a ghost town was simply an outrageous lie.

32. *TDN*, July 11, August 1 and 5, October 1, 1941; February 26 and June 12, 1942.

33. *TDN*, April 28, July 21, and August 4, 1942.

34. The official designation of the pre-glider pilot unit was 9th Glider Training Detachment, Elementary/Advanced Training School, 36th Flying Training Wing, Western Flying Training Command, US Army Air Corps. Spencer, *Combat Glider*; contract Flying School Airfields, Database summary, February 4, 2005.

35. An alternate rumor-mill explanation of the air base quest, which is hardly creditable, claimed that opposition from church leaders, based on predictions of a military installation's degrading influence on town morals, discouraged federal officials from locating such a base at Tucumcari.

36. Daylon Chafin, Ardmore, OK, to the author, n d. [December 1945], in possession of the present author. *Amarillo Daily News*, December 28, 1945.

37. *Actual Settler*, July 19, 1905.

38. Fred L. Bailey, recording secretary, BRC Fa. 527, to editor, September 24, 1941, in *TDN*, September 24, 1941.

39. *TDN*, October 28, 1938; *Albuquerque Journal*, October 4, 1942.

40. *TDN*, October 9, 1934; April 8, 1936.

41. *TDN*, February 2 and March 29, 1940.

42. *TDN*, March 23 and 31, April 2, 4, and 8, 1942. Of the three mayoral tickets in the field, the Non-Partisan Ticket headed by R. L. Payne—also a railroader, as were two of the other four candidates on this slate—played only a minor role in the campaign.

43. *TDN*, March 30, 1942.

44. *TDN*, April 3, 1942.

45. *TDN*, March 29, 1944; August 28, 1947.

46. *TDN*, March 30 and April 1, 1944.

47. *TDN*, March 28, 1944.

48. *TDN*, March 29, 30, and 31, April 1 and 3, 1944. Besides his accomplishments while mayor, Priddy could claim the distinction of hosting for dinner in his home boyhood friend and Hollywood celebrity Gene Autry, then starring in matinee Westerns as the "Singing Cowboy" with his equally famed mount, "Champion the Wonder Horse." Autry and Champion were in the area on a public appearance tour.

49. *TDN*, April 3, 1944.

50. *TDN*, April 3, April 7, and November 21, 1944; January 10, February 15, and March 6, 1945.

51. *TDN*, March 28, 1944.

52. Middleton et al., *Encyclopedia of North American Railroads*, 604–8; Keleher, *Fabulous Frontier*, 268–70; *TDN*, March 29, 1944; August 28, 1947.

53. Huddleston, *Uncle Sam's Locomotives*, 95–99; Hofsommer, *The Southern Pacific*, 196–98.

54. Moncus, "Train Ride . . . [Is] Trip Down Memory Lane," *QC Sun*, November 9, 2011.

55. Hofsommer, *The Southern Pacific*, 200–202.

56. Edna Jacquelyn Stiles Kirkis, Tucson, Arizona, telephone interview by the author, July 20, 2004, transcript in possession of the author. For James Harland Stiles's career painting and designing signage, see Kirkus, *The Man Who Put Lights Along Route 66*.

57. Newell, "Railroaders in Olive Drab," 7–13.

58. *TDN*, July 16 and 22, 1947; August 5, 1954.

59. Newell, "Railroaders in Olive Drab," 7–13; Official Army Register for 1960, vol. 1, p. 990, https://www.archives.gov/research/military; and ibid., Regular Army Retired List, January 1, 1963, vol. 1, p. 738, https://www.archives.gov/research/military; Moncus and Knapp, *Quay County*, 540. Harold H. Sharpe came from a railroader family. His father, James H. Sharpe, retired as a locomotive engineer from the Southern Pacific in 1953, having started railroading with the El Paso & Southwestern Railroad in 1907. *TDN*, December 11, 1968.

60. *TDN*, July 21, 1944; January 2 and 29, March 5, and November 3 and 15, 1945.

61. *TDN*, January 10, 1941, January 26, July 26, August 6, 9, 14, 31, September 7, October 25, 1945.

Chapter 6

1. *TDN*, June 13, 19, 28, July 7, 11, 15, 1955.

2.   Robert J. Samuelson, *Washington Post*, reprinted in *Spokane* (WA) *Spokesman-Review*, July 12, 2016.

3.   "American Automobile Industry in the 1950s," *Wikipedia*.

4.   Cray, *Chrome Colossus*, 236.

5.   Schwieterman, *When the Railroad Leaves Town*, xvii; Bachman, "The Open Road," 43.

6.   Jakle, Schulle, et al., *The Motel in America*, 18, chap. 18.

7.   The information in this section on Kemmons Wilson is from his autobiography, with Robert Kerr, *Half Luck and Half Brains*, chaps. 6–8, 20; Jakle et al., *The Motel in America*, chap. 9; Halberstam, *The Fifties*, 173–79. The owners of the Tucumcari franchise, Allen Green & Associates, announced the firm's intention to construct Mirage City, a $2.5 million amusement park near its Holiday Inn that would supposedly rival Disneyland and Six Flags Over Texas. Preliminary planning progressed until the proposal apparently ran afoul of the Interstate 40 Bypass design for a traffic interchange and off ramp. *TDN*, October 12, 19, 20, November 16, and December 8 and 9, 1964.

8.   The first Holiday Inn in Memphis, Tennessee, was styled "Holiday Inn—HOTEL—COURTS," but the chain's signage was later changed to "Holiday Inn—Motel," and finally, as Wilson's lodgings spread and became well known, to "Holiday Inn." Mahar, *American Signs*, 134.

9.   *TDN*, June 12 and November 13, 1964; *QC Sun*, February 12, 2003; May 5, 2007; Jakle et al. *The Motel in America*, 270, 282.

10.   For the motel's evolutionary history in the United States, see Jakle et al., *The Motel in America*, 18–22, chaps. 2–3; *Albuquerque Morning Journal*, August 19, 1922; L. H. Robbins, "America Hobnobs at the Tourist Camp," 9, 19.

11.   E-mail, Gil Hinshaw, Hobbs, New Mexico, to the author, September 22, 2002.

12.   Moncus and Knapp, *Quay County*, 414–15; *TDN*, March 3, 1936; December 12, 1952; May 12, 1961; *QC Sun*, Progress Edition, August 28, 1977, B-7, C-2, C-10.

13.   *TDN*, Gateway Edition, June 20, 1961; June 3, 1963; March 4, 1995; *QC Sun*, January 30, 1993; September 7, 2005; Moncus and Knapp, *Quay County*, 414–15.

14.   Ad in *QC Sun*, Sunscape supplement, September 4, 1993; *QC Sun*, Progress Edition, August 28, 1977.

15.   Thornton, "Bettie Ditto," 24; *TDN*, March 19, April 10 and 15, 1936; August 14 and 16 and December 9, 1964; April 26, 1965; *QC Sun*, September 18, 1993; November 19, 1997; March 7, 29, and 31, 1999; March 2, 6, 2002; September 7, 2005; January 9 and 12, 2008.

16.   E-mail, Phares P. Huggins, son of W. A. Huggins, Sasebo, Japan, to the author, September 12, 2000; *TDN*, April 18, 1942. W. A. Huggins stated his skills in a 1936 newspaper ad: "I Do All Kinds of Plaster, Stucco, Brick Work, Bathroom Tiling and Cement Work." *TDN*, May 6, 1936. In recent years much restoration work has been done by owners Dale and Hilda Bakke, such as updating electrical equipment and neon signage and placing 1939 Bell rotary-dial phones in the rooms. More recently owners Kevin and Nancy Mueller, along with son Cameron and his wife Jessica, have continued to restore the Blue Swallow. "Blue Swallow Motel, History," Blue Swallow website. Previous owner

Dale Bakke, a licensed master electrician familiar with construction, also did extensive repairs. The Bakkes owned the Blue Swallow from 1998 to 2005. Niederman, "Hometown Spotlight," 14; Arkin, "Neon Lights up Route 66," 2; National Register of Historic Places Registration Form, Blue Swallow Motel, National Park Service, US Department of the Interior, Washington, DC, August 1993. The Muellers sold the Blue Swallow to Bob and Dawn Federico of Crystal Lake, Illinois, in July 2020. *QC Sun*, July 16, 2020.

17. In 2005 the Blue Swallow was advertised for sale at $165,000. *QC Sun*, September 24, 2005. In 2018 it was listed for $1.2 million. *QC Sun*, September 5, 2018.

18. Telephone interview by the author with Phares P. Huggins, Portland, Oregon, December 19, 2001; *TDN*, September 14, 1953. See also, National Register Form, Blue Swallow Motel, August 1993. Some of the information in this document is incorrect.

19. *TDN*, June 28, 1954.

20. *TDN*, June 28, 1954; June 12, 1961; Warranty Deed Book, Block 31, Aber Addition, Quay County Tax Assessor's Office, and Real Estate Mortgage Records and Warranty Deeds, 1939–1998, Quay County Clerk's Office, both Tucumcari.

21. *TDN*, June 12, 1961; Moncus and Knapp, *Quay County*, 406–8, 511; Wallis, "Route 66: Cruising down America's Mother Road," 25–27, and by the same author, "Mother Road Journey," 42–43.

22. On Harvey Girls, Harvey Houses, and the El Tovar Hotel, see Stephen Fried, *Appetite for America*, chap. 12; 204–11, 244–45; *QC Sun*, April 18, 1998; Henderson, "Meals by Fred Harvey," 60–61; Poling-Kempes, *The Harvey Girls*, 81. On reliable reports that Lillian Redman had been a Harvey Girl, see Wallis, "Mother Road Journey," 42–43; *QC Sun*, March 5, 1997. Sonderman, *Route 66*, 91, states that Lillian Redman was a Harvey Girl at Kingman and Winslow, Arizona, and ran her own restaurant at Gallup before she returned to Tucumcari in the late 1940s.

23. Moncus and Knapp, *Quay County*, 407; *QC Sun*, April 13 and May 18, 1998. For an example of British tourists drawn to the Blue Swallow soon after the Second World War, see *TDN*, August 23, 1947. The Blue Swallow sign, with the upper part painted a pale blue and the lower section a darker hue, has been recognized for the artistic use of colors to emphasize "thematic content," much like a comparative advantage of color over black-and-white television. Mahar, *American Signs*, 90–91.

24. *Smithsonian*, March 1986, 126.

25. *QC Sun*, January 7, April 18, and May 13, 1998. For the ownership of the Blue Swallow after Lillian Redman, see Wallis, "Mother Road Journey," 42–43; *QC Sun*, November 12, 1997; September 16, 1998; February 18, 2006.

26. Quoted in Wallis, "Route 66," 27. For other examples of the attention given to the Blue Swallow and Lillian Redman in connection with Route 66, see Howarth, "The Okies," 339; Worobiec and Worobiec, *Icons of the Highway*. Lillian Redman sold the Blue Swallow to Gene and Shirley Shelton, who came from Virginia looking to purchase some historic commercial property in the Southwest. *QC Sun*, November 12, 1997. Of the subsequent owners of the Blue Swallow, Dale and Hilda Bakke were vigilant to keep original features, such as the tiles in the showers, in the extensive restoration and repairs they did.

27. Niederman, "Hometown Spotlight," 14; Arkin, "Neon Lights up Route 66," 2. In the early 2000s, the New Mexico Route 66 Association spearheaded federally funded neon restoration along old Route 66, in cooperation with the National Park Service and its Route 66 Corridor Preservation program. The neon eligible for restoration along Route 66 had to predate 1970 and could not be part of a commercial sign, a requirement that left out most of the vintage neon in the state. "Neon Restoration Continues," *Route 66 New Mexico* (Spring 2005): 9. In another program recognizing historic signs, the State Register of Cultural Properties listed five in Tucumcari located at the former Lasso Motel, the Blue Swallow Motel, the La Cita Restaurant, the Paradise Motel, and the abandoned Ranch House Cafe. *QC Sun*, May 1, 2002.

28. *TDN*, December 21 and 22, 1945; August 2, 1954. Later interest in the improvement and routing of US 54 focused on making it four lanes, obtaining a bypass around the old business district, and where to connect it with US 66 or Interstate 40.

29. *TDN*, December 22, 1945; May 20, 1968.

30. *TDN*, August 12, 1943.

31. *TDN*, October 5, 1946; June 17 and July 10 and 22, 1947, covers most aspects of the Bell Ranch sale. See Remley, *Bell Ranch*, 294–303, for the mid-twentieth-century forces at work that influenced the Red River Valley Company's decision to sell the Bell Ranch. Albert K. Mitchell also acted as the agent in the sale of his family's ranch holdings in northeastern New Mexico.

32. *TDN*, May 1, 2, and 21, 1946; April 30 and May 3 and 7, 1947; November 24, 1951.

33. *TDN*, May 16, 1950.

34. *TDN*, August 28, 1944; May 2, 7, and 14, and July 2, 1947; May 16, 1950; August 10 and 17, 1951.

35. *TDN*, May 3 and 4, 1947.

36. See *TDN*, September 29, 1951; July 5, 1952; February 25 and March 10 and 31, 1953; May 17 and July 21, 1957, for examples of the installment-plan paving of SR 104.

37. *TDN*, July 12, 1956; November 24, 1969; *Tucumcari News*, April 30–May 2, 1972; *QC Sun*, May 24, 1981.

38. For pictorial examples of bloodshed on Route 66 in Carthage, Missouri, see photographs by William Carl Taylor in *Route 66: A Trail of Tears*.

39. *TDN*, August 29, 1949. For discussion of New Mexico's drunken driving problem, see Richardson, *Between Worlds*, 323–25.

40. *TDN*, June 13 and 21, July 3 and 28, and December 22 and 29, 1961. For other examples of highway construction graft and corruption, see *TDN*, December 22, 1966; and November 2, 1967, in which state highway commissioners, the chief highway engineer, and a legislator were indicted for misappropriation of state funds. A major aspect of the 1960s spoils system in New Mexico—the allocation of state jobs and appointments—is described in Brennan, "Spoils System Still Flourishes in New Mexico."

41. *TDN*, March 2 and April 4, 1951; *TN*, May 1 and June 20, 1974; *QC Sun*, May 13 and 24, and July 15, 1981.

42.   *TDN*, September 10, 1952; April 8, 1953. Flagrant traffic violations still resulted in a ticket; firms participating in Operation Coffee were reimbursed from a general fund.

43.   Sutton, "Way Back When," 135–36; *TDN*, August 30, 1955, and May 16, 1966.

44.   *Review*, magazine of *TDN*, December 31, 1964; *TDN*, August 3, 1966; April 10, 1970; March 23, 1971; and December 16, 1981.

45.   *Amarillo Globe-Times*, April 7, 1970; Mann, "Irate Governor," 61.

46.   MacKaye, "The Townless Highway," 92–95. See also a companion article by MacKaye and Mumford, "Townless Highways for the Motorist," 347–56, which suggests that the proposed type of highway be called a "freeway." Both articles were part of a scholarly, idealistic urban planning movement, in vogue among intellectuals at that time, with Robert Moses, who fathered the New York parkway and expressway systems, as the titular leader.

47.   Greany, comp., "Principal Facts Concerning the First Transcontinental Army Motor Transport Expedition, Washington to San Francisco."

48.   Eisenhower, "Report on Trans-Continental Trip"; Ambrose, *Eisenhower*, 2:250–53, 301, 326, 391–92, 527–28, 547–48; Pach Jr., and Richardson, *The Presidency of Dwight D. Eisenhower*, 106, 123–24.

49.   Lewis, *Divided Highways*, 50–55, 90, 97–123, 139; "Transcript of National Interstate and Defense Highway Act (1956)," http://www.ourdocumrnts.gov/doc.php?doc=88; Weingroff, "Federal-Aid Highway Act of 1956, 1–12.

50.   Lewis, *Divided Highways*, 136–38.

51.   "The U.S. Highway System," 92, 99, 106, 109, 111.

52.   *TDN*, October 9 and November 2, 1944; December 3, 1945; Thomas J. Mabry to Thomas H. MacDonald, commissioner, Public Roads Administration, Washington, DC, March 30, 1948, in *TDN*, April 1, 1948. In 1946 a large newspaper ad, signed by "U.S. 66 Highway Democrats" and headed, "Wake Up! Don't Be a Sucker," claimed that a deal cooked up in Washington had the objective of routing a "Super four-lane highway" from Amarillo through Clovis to Clines Corner and on to Albuquerque, leaving out Tucumcari completely. *TDN*, November 4, 1946.

53.   *TDN*, March 22, 1949.

54.   *TDN*, July 6, September 4, and November 15 and 22, 1949. Later, under the mantra of smoothing the flow of traffic through town, the city placed two traffic lights on Route 66. *TDN*, September 11, 1952.

55.   *TDN*, August 4, 15, 16, and 18, 1952.

56.   Lewis, *Divided Highways*, 138.

57.   Cameron, "How the Interstate Changed the Face of the Nation," 60, 125; Lewis, *Divided Highways*, 153, illustration between 210–11.

58.   *TDN*, March 8 and July 15, 1960.

59.   The essential facts on the anti-bypass movement and the law are in "The By-Pass Story," news bulletin of the New Mexico Communities By-Pass Association, published as a supplement of *TDN*, September 17, 1963. See also, Lewis, *Divided Highways*, 153; *TDN*,

February 13 and 25, March 22, July 21 and 31, and December 13, 26, and 30, 1963; September 25, 1964; February 24, 1966.

60.   *TDN*, "By-Pass Story," September 17, 1963; *TDN*, April 23 and December 13, 1963.

61.   *TDN*, December 30, 1963.

62.   Significantly, 1964 was also the year that the railroad started pulling out of Tucumcari.

63.   *TDN*, September 2, 4, 23, and 24, October 6, and December 14, 1963; December 3, 1965; October 16, 1970; *QC Sun*, February 23, 1978.

64.   *TDN*, April 3, 1967.

65.   Moncus and Knapp, *Quay County*, 536–37; Kenneth Schlientz was the son of Southern Pacific car inspector Samuel L. Schlientz, who came to Tucumcari in 1927. *Tucumcari News*, November 14, 1975.

66.   *TDN*, March 12 and June 8, 1967.

67.   See *TDN*, September 10, 1971, for an example in a newspaper photograph of Mayor Schlientz's political style in action when accepting the Blue Ribbon City award for Tucumcari.

68.   In 1978 Quay County gained more political clout at the state capital when red-haired, sweeping mustachioed Lawrence (now styled "Larry") Ingram of Tucumcari became state Democratic Party chairman. *TDN*, April 30, 1978.

69.   *QC Sun*, December 29, 1981, has a convenient summary of the implementation, and lack thereof, of the 1964 agreement. See also, *TDN*, October 14, 1970; January 20, 1972. Senator Montoya's visit to Tucumcari is covered in *TDN*, October 22, 1976. Montoya failed to mention that the fifth exit off I-40, intended for access to the city airport, was located almost five miles east of town.

70.   Lewis, *Divided Highways*, 143–45.

71.   *TDN*, November 17 and December 15, 1976; Roberts, "Ode to a Freeway," 21; *TDN*, January 1, 1964; November 24, 1969.

72.   *QC Sun*, February 23, 1978; May 3 and 31, June 21 and 28, and December 24, 1981; *TDN*, August 8, 1949; December 3, 1965; February 20 and 21, and January 21, 1966; November 24, 25, and 28, 1969; March 9 and 27, 1967; March 24 and October 9, 1970.

73.   Cameron, "How the Interstate Changed the Nation," 78–81, 124–25; Snyder, "President Dwight Eisenhower and America's Interstate Highway System"; Cox and Love, "40 Years of the U.S. Interstate Highway System"; Etulain and Malone, *The American West*, 233–38.

Chapter 7

1.   *TDN*, November 21, 1949.

2.   Moncus and Knapp, *Quay County*, 497–98. Sylvester Prentice's work as a railroad telegrapher was representative of "the day when railroading and 'code' were inseparable in the safe operation of trains." For instance, telegraphy enabled a dispatcher to contact

a trainmaster, who gave a written order to an engineer and conductor for their next run, and to send messages for safety measures. "Fantrip: Dots and dashes forever?" *Trains* (May 2006): 76. The railroads and the Western Union Telegraph Company developed simultaneously, and each had a major role in uniting the nation following the Civil War and in permitting the disparate sections to communicate easily with each other thereafter. Fraily, "Ultimate Technology," 48–49.

3.   *QC Sun*, November 30, 1978; Chicago, Rock Island and Pacific Railroad Company, *Annual Report*, 1965, 4–5, https://www.ebay.com/itm/373333149405.

4.   Goddard, *Getting There*, chap. 3; pamphlet, speech by Harry H. McElroy, "New Mexico and Her Railroads," Kiwanis Club, Tucumcari, NM, September 21, 1926, reprinted by *Tucumcari American*, September 25, 1926, 4–5; *Hartford* (CT) *Courant*, November 11, 1977. The problem of competition with trucks is explained in detail in *Southern Pacific Bulletin*, March–April 1988, 36, ASU Libraries. It should be noted that the SP had significant holdings in trucking subsidiaries. See, for example, Southern Pacific Company, *Annual Report*, 1964, 8. In May 1949, for the first time, airline passenger mileage was greater than Pullman sleeping car passage mileage. Kube and Keefe, "70 Greatest Railroad Engineering Feats: 1940–1955," *Trains* (November 2010): 66–73.

5.   "Trains of the 1950s: Railroading's Decade of Change," *Classic Trains*, Special Edition No. 12, 2013, in which the entire edition is devoted to articles on that decade.

6.   Four articles in three special editions of *Classic Trains*, designated by edition numbers: Grant, "Beset by Competition, Rising Costs, and Regulation, American Railroads in the 1960s Responded with Mergers . . . and a Retreat from the Passenger Business," 10–12, hereafter cited as Grant, "Railroads Beset by Problem"; Pinkepanik, "How the Diesel Changed Railroading," 8–19; McDonnell, "Timeline to Victory," 36–43; Dill, "Southern Pacific's Painted Ladies," 86–91. A veteran railroad reporter summarized the steam-to-diesel revolution as well as other changes in the industry, in a masterful one-page article: Phillips, "Every 20 years, Railroading Reinvents Itself," 10.

7.   Davis, *Dark Side of Fortune*, 29–33; Botz, *Edward L. Doheny*, 11–15; Myrick, *New Mexico's Railroads*, 67–69; "Cheap Oil," *Railway Age*, November 15, 1901, 555. Edward L. Doheny was better known for his part in the Teapot Dome naval oil scandal of the 1920s.

8.   Stindt, "The Last Days of Southern Pacific Steam," 101–13.

9.   *TDN*, April 6, 1953.

10.   "Diesel Victory: Railroading's Epic Switch from Steam," *Classic Trains*, Special Edition No. 4, 2006. This entire edition contains articles on the switch to diesels.

11.   Unless cited otherwise, the detailed information in this section on railroads in Tucumcari was based on a typewritten manuscript by Frank Kile Turner, "Train Time in Tucumcari," n.d., copy in possession of the present author. Turner, a retired railroad executive with the rare combination of scholarly skills and firsthand knowledge of railroads, did research for this manuscript in old timetables, family records, and railroad literature. As apparent in this account, he grew up in Tucumcari in its heyday as a rail center. His father, Frank N. Turner, began as a "call boy" (usually a young man who called operations crews for their next run) for the El Paso & Southwestern and retired as an SP conductor.

12.   *TDN*, December 16, 1963; Schwantes and Ronda, *The West the Railroads Made*, 151–54; Morgan, "We'll Adjust, But It Won't Be Easy,"112. Several classic New Mexico depots are depicted in the photographs of Fenton Richards, "Vanishing Depots," 51–59.

13.   The original title was the Golden State Limited, but the "Limited" was dropped March 18, 1947. Loper, "Steel Rails to the Sunbelt," 28. *TDN*, September 28, 1953, has revised schedules for the Imperial and the Cherokee.

14.   For example, in 1929 the passenger train Californian left Chicago for the West Coast at 10:15 a.m., Sunday; arrived in Tucumcari, Monday at 8:10 p.m. (Central Time); and departed at 7:35 p.m. (Mountain Time) for a stopover of twenty-five minutes. On a similar run the Apache passenger train was delayed only fifteen minutes at Tucumcari, while westbound passengers on the T&M line from Memphis, making a connection locally, might have to wait thirty minutes to do so. The prestigious Golden State Limited halted only ten minutes. *Rock Island Time Tables*, Chicago, Rock Island and Pacific Railroad, Chicago, IL, May 1929, in possession of the author.

15.   *TDN*, November 25, 1958.

16.   Hilleson, "Roadside Attractions," 50. The local Chamber of Commerce compiled a list of some fourteen songs, including "Two Gun Harry from Tucumcari," with Tucumcari in the title. Tucumcari/Quay County Chamber of Commerce, "Songs of Tucumcari," 2009–2010, https://www.lyrics.com/lyrics/Tucumcari.

17.   *TDN*, October 14, 1989.

18.   In December 1960, local boosters launched Operation Tucumcari, which, in attempt to entice them to stopover in town, served hot coffee to the flood of Minnesota motorists on Route 66 going to, and returning from, the Rose Bowl in Pasadena, California, where the University of Minnesota Golden Gophers lost, 17–7, to the University of Washington Huskies. *TDN*, December 8, 1960.

19.   Goldenberg, "My Hometown." The Pullman sleeping cars ran "seamlessly, but separately" in agreements with a multitude of railroads that contracted with them to operate individually joined to regular passenger trains. By 1937 the Pullman Company had about eight thousand sleeping cars available for service on various rail lines. Fraily, "Ultimate Passenger Train," 46–48.

20.   Morgan, "Go West, Middle-Aged Man, Go West," 93.

21.   Loper, "Steel Rails to the Sunbelt," 26; Grant, "Beset by Competition," 12; *TDN*, April 22, 1966; Southern Pacific Company, *Annual Report*, 1967, 3. The date of the source cited here, and hereafter, is the date of publication, not the year covered in the report, which would be the preceding year.

22.   Zaga, "The Best on Wheels," 70–71.

23.   Dan Phillips, "The Road to Rescue," 23.

24.   One newspaper editor calculated that discontinuing the Apache would result in the loss to Tucumcari of one-third of its passenger, mail, and express services, and the layoff of three operating crews. *TDN*, December 29, 1937.

25.   Machalaba, "Railroading's Biggest Blunders," 54; Phillips, "Road to Rescue," 23–25.

26. "Getting the Mail Back on Track," *Trains* (March 2015): 6; Grant, "Beset by Competition," 11–12; *TDN*, March 31, August 22, October 2, and December 11, 1967; Rock Island Railroad, 1964, *Annual Report*, 5.

27. Nelson, "Rise and Decline of the Rock Island Passenger Train in the 20th Century," 740, 743, 755; *TDN*, August 22, 1967. Klink Garrett as told to Toby Smith, *Ten Turtles to Tucumcari: A Personal History of the Railway Express Agency*, tells the history of the REA through an agency official's career from 1934 to 1973; *Tucumcari News*, May 13 and June 15, 1920.

28. US Interstate Commerce Commission of the United States (Finance Reports), vol. 328, 648–63; *TDN*, April 26, June 22, September 17, October 4 and 15, November 5 and 8, 1965; February 1, September 30, November 13 and 17, December 8 and 9, 1966; August 21 and 22, 1967; Nelson, "Rise and Decline of the Rock Island Passenger Service," 729–64; Schneider, *Rock Island Requiem*, chap. 3.

29. Loper, "Steel Rails to the Sunbelt," 22, 28, 31.

30. *TDN*, December 11, 1967, reported only twenty witnesses at Tucumcari.

31. US Interstate Commerce Commission, *Decisions of the Interstate Commerce Commission of the United States)*, vol. 331, 768–83, appendix D, 783–97; P. Nelson, "Rise and Decline of the Rock Island Passenger Train"; *TDN*, April 26, 1965.

32. US Interstate Commerce Commission, *Decisions*, vol. 331, 768; Loper, "Steel Rails to the Sunbelt," 22, 26, 31; *TDN*, February 20, 1968; June 6, 1972. Earlier, in November 1965, the SP stated that it was losing $810,000 a year on the passenger runs between Phoenix and Tucumcari. *TDN*, November 4. 1965.

33. Wilner, "Railroads in the 20th Century"; *QC Sun*, January 1, 1983.

34. Jackson, "Cabooses May Be Rolling Toward the End of the Line," 100–110.

35. *TDN*, May 5, 10, and 11, 1955.

36. Ibid., April 18, 1955; May 3 and August 29, 1961; February 23, March 5, May 29, and November 7, 1962.

37. *Albuquerque Journal*, November 9, 1962. Front-page articles in the *TDN*, May 3, 1961, and March 26, 1962, discuss the importance of the "Roy Branch" and, in the latter issue, the ICC hearings held in town on the line's impending closure.

38. *TDN*, September 18, 19, and 24 and November 7, 1962.

39. Grant, "Beset by Competition," 12.

40. *TDN*, May 18 and November 10, 1967. On Greaser's candidacy for state representative, see *TDN*, February 29, 1952.

41. US Interstate Commerce Commission, *Decisions*, vol. 331, 794.

42. On the roundhouse location and elimination, see Bill Reynolds in Steve Winston, "Tucumcari Born with a Railroad Boom," *Albuquerque Journal*, March 11, 1979.

43. Schneider, *Rock Island Requiem*, 297–301. For the steady decline of the Rock Island, see three articles in *Trains*: Hilton, "'Infra-canin-ophilia," 66; Ingles, "Rock Island Lines, 1964," 46–47, with a detailed map; and Machalaba, "Railroading's Biggest Blunders," 52–53. *Trains* devoted its March 1983 issue to articles on the Rock Island's demise, with the caption on the cover, "SIC TRANSIT GLORIA."

44. *Railway Age*, January 31, 1977, 8; *Tucumcari News*, April 15 and 24, 1975. An editorial in the *TDN*, June 8, 1966, claimed that if the Santa Fe acquired the Rock Island trackage, Tucumcari would become little more than a mail-train stop.

45. *Tucumcari News*, April 10 and 14, and July 1, 1975; January 18, 1977.

46. Ibid., April 17 and May 1, 1975.

47. *QC Sun*, March 16, 1980. The Ithinkican Railroad, a strange independent line, largely dreamed up by an Amarillo promoter, also offered service from Tucumcari to Kansas points. *QC Sun*, March 18, 1980.

48. *Railway Age*, April 24, 1978; July 10 and, 27, 1981; *New York Times*, December 4, 1979, and *Washington Post*, June 11, 1980, both online; Southern Pacific Company, *Annual Report*, 1982, 2–3; *QC Sun*, January 21, March 4, and June 3, 1981 See also, the statement of SP President D. K. McNear, which outlines the involvement of the SP and the Cotton Belt with the Tucumcari Line until the sale, in US Congress, Senate, Rock Island Transition Act, Hearing before the Subcommittee on Surface Transportation of the Committee on Commerce, Science, and Transportation, S 2246, S2253, SJ Res. 139, 96th Cong., February 20, 1980, 125–27. The question of why the subsidiary Cotton Belt instead of its parent, the SP, became the buyer of the Rock Island involved issues characteristic of the railroad industry. For instance, the Cotton Belt was already a member of the administrative body facilitating use of the St. Louis terminal, the Terminal Railroad Association of St, Louis, and the SP was not. Gaining membership in this association, jointly owned by some of its competitors, might have been difficult for the SP. Morgan, "The Rock Reborn," 49–50.

49. A series of articles in *Trains* covers the Staggers Act and deregulation: Gallinger, "Railroads Face Possibility of Tighter Regulation," 10–12; Giblin, "The Road to Deregulation," 58–65; Blaszak, "Ultimate Change," 24–33; Sweeney, "Explaining the Surface Transformation Board," 7.

50. *TDN*, February 8, 1967; *QC Sun*, March 25, 1981; Machalaba, "Railroading's Biggest Blunders," 57; Caves, Christensen, and Swanson, "The Staggers Act, 30 Years Later," 28–31; Myrick, *New Mexico's Railroads*, 147–49. Harwell, "The Rock Island Is A-OK," 30–35, discusses the removal of Choctaw Route tracks and what happened to the line's remnants.

51. *TDN*, December 30 and 31, 1964; January 6, 7, and 14, May 18, June 2, September 8 and 17, 1965; December 30, 1966.

52. Wilson and Taylor, *Southern Pacific*, 206–7.

53. Middleton, "Piggyback Champion," 76–81.

54. The importance of the intermodal is discussed in Kaufman, "What Intermodal Needs Next"; and two articles in *Trains*, September 2013: Smith-Peterson, "The Spigot," pt. 2, pp. 33–40, 54; and Machalaba, "Railroading's Biggest Blunders," 54–55. The SP ran an ad campaign in major periodicals and newspapers extolling its diversified investments. *QC Sun*, June 13, 1983. In another major plan for survival, Biaggini tried unsuccessfully to find a suitable railroad merger partner. See "75 People You Should Know," 58.

55. The essential information in this section is from Walsh, "Why the Southern Pacific Failed"

56. Of the extensive coverage of the SP collapse and associated events, these are a few samples: Kaufmann, "Capital Investment," 1–5; and the following in *Trains*: Frailey, "Let Us Now Praise Union Pacific," 15; Frailey, "Union Pacific on the Mend," 9, 11–12; Murray, "Looking for a Silver Bullet," pt. 1, 32; Grant Niemann, "The Lord of the Night," pt. 1, 42–47; Machalaba, "Railroading's Biggest Blunders," 55.

57. In *QC Sun*, January 24, February 7, and June 17, 1998; the mathematics and logic of the UP position regarding Tucumcari are spelled out.

58. *New Mexico Business Weekly*, September 20, 2002, https://www.yelp.com/business/new-mexico-business-weekly-albuquerque. See *QC Sun*, March 25 and April 29, 1998, for examples of handwringing.

59. *QC Sun*, August 24, 1979.

60. *TDN*, October 30, 1967; December 31, 1970; April 28 and September 17, 1971; March 20, 1977; *QC Sun*, November 9, 1991; November 17, 2001; Boeing Marine Systems, "The First Family of Hydrofoils."

61. *TDN*, May 16, 1968; *TDN*, February 22 and 23, 1978; *QC Sun*, November 13 and December 25 and 29, 1977; November 9 and 17, 2001.

62. *TDN*, September 28 and November 14, 1970.

63. *TDN*, January 25 and 26, 1940; *Review*, magazine section of *TDN*, October 22, 1972.

64. *TDN*, September 28 and November 14, 1932.

65. *TDN*, April 26, 1950; June 17, 1968.

66. *TDN*, April 10 and 11, 1934; December 4 and 5, 1940; July 25, 1941.

67. *TDN*, April 26, 1950; June 17, 1968.

68. *TDN*, April 21, 1985. Tucumcari "reclaimed" Brinegar as one of its own, tracking his later acting career and awards. Although born in Tucumcari, Brinegar, whose court reporter father often moved the family to a new job opportunity, said that he considered all of New Mexico as "my home town."

69. *TDN*, September 18 and December 31, 1959. Tucumcari has recently capitalized on the filming of *Rawhide* in the area by staging a two-day event called Rawhide Days, in which children of some of the stars attend and perform. *QC Sun*, March 23 and April 6, 2016.

70. *TDN*, February 12 and September 13, 1959. Probably because of its rhyming possibilities, Tucumcari has been used in both the titles and lyrics of several songs. In 2010 the Tucumcari/Quay County Chamber of Commerce compiled a list of fourteen songs for a Rhino Records CD, *Songs of Tucumcari*. Drabanski, "Songs of Tucumcari," 15–16.

71. Bilstein, "The Airplane and the American Experience," 115–17.

72. *TDN*, July 31, 1949, summarizes the early years of Pioneer Airlines. Previously, in 1946 the Tucumcari Air Service, affiliated with the Toth Aircraft and Accessories Company of Kansas City, leased the airport facilities and scheduled air freight service, which apparently lasted only a short time. *TDN*, June 15, 1946. In 1944 Essair Airways, later Pioneer Airlines in 1946, was the first airline in the United States to fly CAB-authorized short-haul feeder or local service air connections.

73. *TDN*, April 18, 25, 29, and 30, August 25, and October 26, 1948; May 1 and November 17, 1949.

74. *TDN*, March 23, April 19, and November 16, 1949; March 7, 1950; May 3 and November 16, 1951; August 1, November 17, and December 5 and 14, 1953.

75. *Review*, magazine of *TDN*, June 3, 1966.

76. *TDN*, April 11, 1969; August 28 and September 2, 1970.

77. An article and full-page ad describe the Rotary Air Show in *QC Sun*, September 15, 2006, and the air show fatality is reported in *Albuquerque Journal*, October 4, 2006.

78. National Investigations Committee on Aerial Phenomena, Case Directory, Category 1, Distant Sightings, AFOSI Case 42, Tucumcari, NM, March 27, 1949, online.

79. *TDN*, August 3 and 4, 1965. In 1979, Governor Bruce King told Pentagon officials, who wanted to base rotating MX missiles in eastern New Mexico, it would be best "to base the MX in Nevada or Utah." King, *Cowboy in the Roundhouse*, 237–38. The local Chamber of Commerce also voted to oppose "wholly, totally, and unequivocally" placement in the area of another Cold War defense project, in this case, MX Missile System sites. *QC Sun*, January 21, 1981.

80. Roush, "In Alien Territory," 52–56, 58.

81. *TDN*, December 13, 1951; *Louisville* [KY] *Courier Journal*, December 14, 1951; Barnhart et al., "Tucumcari Tank Failure," 435–41.

82. *TDN*, August 21, 1949; December 1, 1965.

Chapter 8

1. *TDN*, March 29, 1974, Annual Progress Edition, "Know Your City" section.

2. The quote in the film is actually, "If you build it, he will come," referring to legendary baseball great "Shoeless Joe" Jackson. For a candid review of the film, see Easton, "Diamonds Are Forever."

3. Jim Conkle, quoted in Hingley, "The Spirit of Historic Highway Becomes an Americana Destination," 8, 10, 12.

4. Early on, the I-40 Bypass did not have a magnet-like attraction, like a bank or supermarket, that would draw in other businesses. Opened later, in 2007, the Flying J Travel Plaza had a few of those magnetic qualities. This facility, built on fourteen acres with parking for 136 semi-tractor-trailers, had a special appeal for truckers, offering them the amenities of showers, restaurant food, and the like. *QC Sun*, November 7, 2007.

5. *New Mexico Business Weekly*, September 23, 2002, online edition.

6. *Tucumcari News*, October 9, 1975. Mayor Saltz had complained earlier. Ibid., April 26, 1974; *Tucumcari News Digest*, September 23, 1977; *QC Sun*, September 11, 2004.

7. *TDN*, August 30, 1961; *Tucumcari News*, May 7, 1975; *QC Sun*, July 9, 1980.

8. *TDN*, December 19, 1967; *TDN*, April 13, 1976; *QC Sun*, Progress Edition, August 28, 1977, A-9, C-9, D-8; November 12, 1978; May 3, 1995.

9. *QC Sun*, December 19, 1967; June 29, July 13, and August 28, Progress Edition, A-9; October 23, 1977; December 21, 1978; July 9, 1980.

10. *QC Sun*, June 8 and 22, and July 2, 1980; July 14, 1982.

11. *QC Sun*, December 1 and 11, 1982; February 19 and March 19, 1983; April 9, 1988; July 2 and 9, 1980. Mesalands Community College continued to train truck drivers, even after most of the big trucking companies left town. *QC Sun*, June 18, 2005.

12. *QC Sun*, January 9, 1987; July 25, 2007.

13. *QC Sun*, April 30, 1994.

14. *RoadKing*. "More and More Couples are Trucking Together—and Loving It."

15. On Hoffa and the Teamsters, see Sloane, *Hoffa*, 32–34, 36–37, chap. 12.

16. Giblin, "Trains vs. Trucks," 37–41; *QC Sun*, December 21, 1978; March 11, 1995.

17. "There's a Difference Between Engineers and Truck Drivers," 20–21, uses the term *truck jockey*. Ranger once worked as a locomotive fireman. Information on the "Gold Steak" is in *TDN*, May 24, 1961. The animosity between truck drivers and railroaders existed even though the railroads and the trucking industry faced some of the same competitors—nonunion trucking, airlines, and barge traffic.

18. Sloane, *Hoffa*, 291. For some of the real-life adventures of a trucker, see Murphy, *The Long Haul*.

19. Tarter, "Truck Drivers, Families [*sic*] Lives Aren't Easy." As an example of the hazards truckers faced close to home, a near record snowfall in 1983 caused several local drivers to become involved in accidents. *QC Sun*, February 2, 1983.

20. Tarter, "Truck Drivers."

21. *QC Sun*, March 30, 1994, Special Edition, section B.

22. The independent truckers' parking problem is covered in *QC Sun*, January 11 and February 8, 1989; August 6, 1994.

23. "A Guide to Truckers Slang."

24. *QC Sun*, February 19 and March 5, 1983.

25. *QC Sun*, February 10 and 20, 1988.

26. *QC Sun*, January 28 and February 1, 1989.

27. *QC Sun*, April 25 and October 17, 1990; November 6, 1993; July 22, 1995; February 15, 1997.

28. A dedicated Continental Trailways driver was acclaimed a hero and spent four days in the Tucumcari hospital as a result of his experience with winter weather. After his bus got stuck in a snowdrift on Route 66 east of the Texas state line, the driver walked thirteen miles to Glenrio through freezing weather and snow often waist deep to bring help to fourteen passengers and a young baby. *TDN*, February 6 and 20, 1956.

29. *TDN*, November 16 and 17, December 22, 1949; Suttle, *Greyhound Tales from Route 66*, iii–v, vii–x, 33–52. For Greyhound's history and its own labor relations, including several strikes, see Schisgall, *The Greyhound Story*, especially 57, 60, 69, and chap. 33.

30. See *TDN*, December 1, 1951, for the second in a series of three articles analyzing the steps necessary to achieve industrial development.

31. *QC Sun*, May 3, 1981; September 9, 1989; April 10, May 18, and December 28, 1991. An item in the *New Mexico Business Weekly*, September 20, 2002, stated that the ethanol plant had been vacant for eleven years. More recently, in 2016, scientist and

inventor Bob Hockaday and his company, Energy Related Devices, bought the defunct plant. Hockaday had "strategic plans to outfit it as a biorefinery, a business that would create not just jobs, but an ecosystem within the community." Bulletin, New Mexico State University, Las Cruces, News Center, Las Cruces July 1, 2016, online; *QC Sun*, April 8, 2014.

32. Fritz LaRue, Letter to the Editor, 7.

33. McMurtry, "How the West Was Won or Lost," 32.

34. In Chicago, the starting point was shifted from time to time with changing traffic patterns, and, on the Pacific end, an alternate termination would be a junction with old US Highway 101. Originally, before its fame, the highway ended in downtown Los Angeles, but an extension to Santa Monica was made in 1936.

35. Pitel, "New Mexico's Route 66 Corridor"; Pew Jr., "Goodbye to Main Street 66," 47–51; Patton, *Open Road*, chap. 16.

36. This term is used by Pitel, "New Mexico's Route 66 Corridor."

37. The information in this section on the creation of Route 66 and the song about the famous highway came from Kelly, *Father of Route 66*, chap. 9; and Wallis, *Route 66: The Mother Road*, 6–10, passim. Wallis's spirited account contains sidebars, 9–15, of Bobby Troup's firsthand story about how he composed the song "Route 66," and about Nat King Cole's rendition of it.

38. Edwards, "The Object at Hand," 32, 34. An abbreviated version of the Michael Wallis book is "Route 66: Cruising Down America' s Mother Road," 24–31.

39. Steinbeck, *The Grapes of Wrath*, 103, 171; Associated Press article, *TDN*, February 15, 1951. In a characterization of the town's sad plight after it went into sharp decline, one outside journalist wrote of the main family in the *Grapes of Wrath*, "Tucumcari . . . is the last place the Joads would know, and it's about the last place where some folks would still recognize the Joads." Pew Jr., "Tucumcari Tonight!," 33.

40. Rosin, *Route 66*, 94–95, 108–11, 247.

41. The essential information on the film comes from *Cars* (2006), *Family Entertainment Guide*, https://www.com/family-entertainment-guide; McDonald, "The Real Route 66 Inspirations Behind Disney's Cars Land."

42. Quoted in McDonald, "The Real Route 66 Inspirations."

43. "Route 66 Museum Likely will be in Tucumcari Convention Center"; *Albuquerque Journal*, January 26, 1947; May 24, 1948; December 13, 1952; Edwards, "Antique Road Show," 34. Patton, *Open Road*, pt. 4, chaps. 16–19, "Gone to Look for America," has an excellent detailed description of the Route 66 legend and its creation. Founded in 1928, Ralph Richardson's general store at Montoya, which housed the local post office, featured old-fashioned manually operated gas pumps in front, was the social center and "everything else to ranchers and train crews from miles around," and remained a remnant of old Route 66 rural culture until the late 1990s. Pew Jr., "Route 66: Ghost Road of the Okies," 29.

44. *Albuquerque Journal*, December 2, 2004, Business Section, p. 7; Hingley, "The Spirit of Historic Highway," 8, 10, 12.

45. *TDN*, June 17 and 23, July 6, 7, 9 and 23, August 9, 1965.

46. Supposedly the original Tonite! signs boasted 2,000 motel rooms, but the number was reduced to 1,200 or 1,500, which were more realistic estimates. A 1993 publication to promote tourism contained a list of thirty-two motels in Tucumcari. This may not have been a complete listing. If every motel listed had 40 rooms—which is unlikely—the total would be more than 1,200 rooms. However, some of the newer chain motels, such as the Holiday Inn, did have 60 to 100 rooms, which makes the boast of 1,200 total more likely. *Sunscape*, Visitor's Guide to Tucumcari & Quay County, *QC Sun*, Spring/Summer 1993.

47. In 1956, to attract tourists, the Chamber of Commerce launched an ambitious program to place "300 or more" large signs advertising the town and individual merchants for "300, 400 and 500 miles" distance along all major roads. The signs were in an "Indian motif," with the message that a "Heap Fine City" was ahead so many miles, and "with the name 'Tucumcari' hyphenated for easier pronunciation." *TDN*, February 14, 1956. For other local actions regarding signage, see *QC Sun*, May 13 and 17, September 27, and December 13, 1981; August 6, 1988; June 25, 2008; *TDN*, May 27, 1966; October 4, 1971; *Albuquerque Journal*, June 15, 2008. In 1971, with completion of Interstate 40 in New Mexico in prospect and under the threat of losing federal funds, the state highway agency started restricting signs and billboards by requiring a permit and a location at least 660 feet away from the roadway. *TDN*, June 2, 1971. The signage issue continued to be a problem for several years. See *TDN*, June 21, 1974; June 30 and November 30, 1977; *QC Sun*, January 2, 1977; November 16, 1978; February 13, 1999; *New Mexico*, January 2018, 69. Sonderman, *Route 66*.

48. Jackle and Sculle, *Signs in America's Auto Age*, xxi–xxxiii, 156–66.

49. *QC Sun*, August 6, 1988; June 25, 2008. Other mottos were tried, but Tucumcari Tonite! in some combination of wording, or alone, managed to survive. *QC Sun*, April 7, 2004. For thorough coverage of notable signs on Route 66, including Tucumcari and New Mexico, see

50. *QC Sun*, September 25, 1993; August 12, 1995; May 10, 1997; August 20, 1999. See *QC Sun*, November 3, 1999, for information on the Cactus Motor Lodge.

51. The principal information for the Caprock Amphitheatre is from Don McAlvy, "New Mexico's Caprock Amphitheatre," in Moncus and Knapp, *Quay County*, 725; *Amarillo Globe-News*, June 17, 1997; *QC Sun*, Progress Edition, August 28, 1977, B-6; March 25, 1981; January 8, 1986.

52. *Amarillo Globe-News*, June 17, 1997. In the same general area just south of San Jon, a private company developed a wind farm that was scheduled to have up to 100 giant electricity-producing windmill turbines. There are other wind farms near House and Fort Sumner. *QC Sun*, May 15, 2004; *Santa Fe New Mexican*, January 31, 2009.

53. Unless cited otherwise, the information on Mesalands Community College and the Mesalands Dinosaur Museum and Natural Science Laboratories is from "Mesalands Community College," and "Mesalands Community College," *Wikipedia*.

54. For examples of the Dinosaur Museum's fundraising efforts, including the large number of donors by name and other early activities to launch the project, see *QC Sun*, April 14, 1999; March 10–12, May 3–5 and 6–9, 2000.

55. Nelson, "Molten Beauty," 40–47. In Mesalands' annual Big Pour event, which attracts a multitude of outside participants, molten iron ore is transformed into objects for artistic uses. K. Nelson, "Molten Beauty," 40–47.

56. Evans, "Scenic Byway Adventures," 28–29; *QC Sun*, May 18, 2004.

57. Tucumcari Historical Museum, https://www.yelp.com/biz/tucumcari-historical-museum-tucumcari.

58. The essential biographical information on Herman Moncus is from *Albuquerque Journal*, September 19, 1999; Moncus and Knapp, *Quay County*, 451–53; Lynn Moncus, "Comments from the Canyons," *QC Sun*, January 4, 1981, and *QC Sun*, obituary, January 4, 1981; *Clovis* (NM) *News Journal*, June 24, 2014.

59. *TDN*, February 19, 1968.

60. *TDN*, May 20, 1965; February 26, May 29, and June 3, 1968; *QC Sun*, January 4, 1981. *TDN*, December 30, 1975, has a long biographical article on Herman Moncus, which was reprinted from the *Southwest Heritage Quarterly*, Fall 1975 issue. Not only did the last passenger train come through Tucumcari in February 1968, but a similar historical event occurred later that year when the Elk drugstore, a venerable community social center, closed in August. *QC Sun*, July 8, 1994; August 5, 1998.

61. *Route 66 Guide*, 2005, Freedom Newspapers of New Mexico, Clovis, has descriptive articles on the Tucumcari Historical Museum and Mesalands College's Dinosaur Museum.

62. *QC Sun*, January 5 and July 16, 1994; op cit., special trade supplement, section A, March 26, 1994.

63. "Route 66 Monument," online *Guide to Offbeat Tourist Attractions*, http://www.roadsideamerica.com/tips/14802; Garcia, "Route 66 Museum Likely in Convention Center," *QC Sun*, August 23, 2012.

64. The essential information on First National Bank and its new building came from telephone interviews, H. Barton Jones, Belton, Texas, with the author, September 21 and October 24, 2016, transcripts in possession of the author.

65. *TDN*, February 7, 1940; March 19 and 31, 1941.

66. *QC Sun*, April 20, 1994. An architectural drawing of the new First National Bank, displayed across the front page above the masthead of the *Tucumcari News*, August 30, 1974, showed a panoramic view of the new building.

67. *QC Sun*, January 22, 1997; February 20, 2008. See also, Moncus and Knapp, *Quay County*, 740.

68. Murphy, "Tucumcari's History as Scene of Hitchhiker Slayings Recalled."

69. *TDN*, November 3, 6, 7, 8, 9, and 28, 1951; Murphy, "Tucumcari's History"; *Gallup* (NM) *Independent*, March 19, 1952; *Santa Fe New Mexican*, September 26, 1954; *Review*, magazine of *TDN*, December 1, 1965; *Albuquerque Journal*, June 12, 1982; *QC Sun*, December 24, 1978; April 26, 1997; July 1, 2014.

70. *QC Sun*, March 27, 2002. Hooper seemed to have a special talent for finding hidden drugs. Stopping a van for a lane violation, he discovered eighty pounds of cocaine worth more than $3 million in a separate compartment of the gas tank.

71. *QC Sun*, January 16 and March 27, 2002.

72. *QC Sun*, January 8, and April 9 and 19, 1997. In 1993 local police conducted an undercover operation lasting four months that led to the arrest of fourteen town residents, while a similar undercover program snared nineteen suspects in Roosevelt and Curry Counties. *QC Sun*, October 2, 1993. Earlier, in 1970, a drug raid had netted eighteen local youths, many of them teenagers; in 1971, six men were indicted; and, in 1974, a raid in Portales and Roosevelt County resulted in fifty arrests. *TDN*, December 7, 1970; January 13, 1971; *Tucumcari News*, August 27, 1974.

73. *QC Sun*, December 20, 1986.

74. *QC Sun*, February 12, 1986; December 16, 1987.

75. *QC Sun*, December 19, 1978.

Chapter 9

1. *QC Sun*, October 17, 1998.

2. Ibid.

3. *TDN*, December 29, 1965; *Tucumcari News*, July 25, 1973.

4. *Tucumcari News*, March 30, 1972; July 24 and September 3, 1973.

5. *Tucumcari News*, November 19, 1973, summarizes the achievements of the urban renewal project. See also, July 27, 1973, on relocations, August 24 and 31, 1973, on parking lots, and July 23, 1973, on a workable plan.

6. *Tucumcari News*, November 19, 1973; *TDN*, March 30, 1972.

7. *Tucumcari News*, November 19, 1973; *QC Sun*, June 24, 1982; November 5 and 30, 1988.

8. *QC Sun*, July 27, August 3, September 3, and November 12, 1973.

9. A concerted effort to develop a new business district along the I-40 Bypass might have been a wiser strategy, but apparently no grants, subsidies, or other funding was as readily available for such projects as urban renewal for established downtowns.

10. *QC Sun*, June 24 and December 1, 1982; September 17, 1983.

11. *QC Sun*, September 24, 1985; January 27, 1990.

12. *Tucumcari News*, July 23, August 24 and 31, November 19, 1973; *New Mexico*, February 2003, 36, tells the story step-by-step of the urban renewal project

13. Moncus and Knapp, *Quay County*, 498.

14. Baca-Goodman House, National Register of Historic Places, online; Benito Baca obituary, *TN*, July 5, 1928; September 10, 1973; Moncus and Knapp, *Quay County*, 499; *QC Sun*, January 26, 1977; August 30, 2006; August 17, 2016.

15. *TDN*, February 15, 1963; November 1, 1968.

16. *QC Sun*, November 30, 1978; July 1, 1979.

17. Tucumcari rejoined the MainStreet program officially in December 2006. *QC Sun*, December 7, 2006.

18. *In the New Mexico Tradition: The Impacts of MainStreet, 1985–2013*, 23–24; *QC Sun*, September 24, 1985; June 13, 1987; October 1, 1988; April 30, 2005; June 6, 2012; *Visitor*

Guide: Tucumcari/Quay County, New Mexico; W. Thompson, "Murals Celebrate Tucumcari," 6.

19.   *QC Sun*, August 7 and 24, 2002. Several other New Mexico towns were remodeling railroad depots or had the chance to acquire one. Thompson, "Return to Glory."

20.   *QC Sun*, April 15–17, August 19–22, 2000.

21.   Tennant, "Tucumcari Depot"; *QC Sun*, September 28, November 2 and 9, 2011; June 6, 2012.

22.   Typewritten, Marian Farmer Knapp, "First Annual Rattler Reunion Highlights," 1971, in possession of the author. In this newsletter, Knapp lists many of those in attendance and mentions some of the practices that became annual events, such as an "All Class-Former Resident Reunion," in the first week of August, which the thirtieth anniversary class would be in charge; special recognition would be given to other decimal classes, and the reunion would be an annual affair. Tucumcari High School graduated its first class of eight seniors in 1913—six young women and two men. Bob Nelson, "Turn Back, oh Time in thy Flight," *Review*, magazine of *TDN*, April 1, 1966.

23.   *TDN*, June 2, 1957; August 4, 6, and 9, 1971; *QC Sun*, July 30, 1986; August 1, 1990; Moncus and Knapp, *Quay County*, 396–97.

24.   *QC Sun*, June 28–30, 2000. A later world record for the longest parade float, set in China, February 6, 2012, represented a marching dragon of paper and bamboo held together with wooden planks, and measured 2,596.8 feet long. Gallery: Weird Guinness World Records, pt. 1, File No. AY 107165358, https://www.guinnessworldrecords.com/world-records/longest-parade-float. See also, *Tucumcari News*, July 8, 1974; *QC Sun*, July 30, 1986.

25.   Unless cited otherwise, general information on the various Quay County rural schools is taken from the entries on these communities in Moncus and Knapp, *Quay County*. Also, see especially for early evidence of the importance of their schools in Quay County's rural communities and individual coverage of each place, *TDN*, Special Edition, September 30, 1935. Another indication of the declining rural population was the closure of rural post offices. See, for example, the demise of post offices at Ima, Jordan, and Montoya. *TDN*, May 3 and July 27, 1955; *QC Sun*, June 1, 1980.

26.   Moffett, "Oran Caton," 70–72; B. Nelson, "End of an Era—Forrest School Closes"; *QC Sun*, November 7 and 10, 2007; Moncus and Knapp, *Quay County*, 238–40. Such low scores as those included here were not uncommon at that time. For one reason, the rule requiring both teams to return to center court for a jump ball after each basket tended to slow down the game, and, also, there was no three-point shot nor a shot clock limiting how long a team could keep the ball before shooting at a basket. In the 1930s there were no classifications, or divisions, in New Mexico based on a school's size, and tiny Forrest could be matched against Albuquerque's only high school of that day.

27.   Forestall, comp. and ed., *Population of Counties by Decennial Census, 1900 to 1990*. Local reports on the weather and its influence on the declining population, including drought conditions in most of the state, are found in *TDN*, May 27, 1956; May 24, 27, and 30, and June 13, 1960. In addition, in 1960, the water delivered to farmers from Conchas

Dam was the smallest amount until that time. *TDN*, October 28, 1960. Moreover, irrigation water had been delivered only periodically during most of the 1950s. *TDN*, August 28, 1953; May 19 and 20, 1955.

28. The Quay County weather statistics are taken from Kirksey, Lauriault, and Cooksey, *Weather Observations*. *TDN*, December 31, 1953, has weather as the main highlight of 1953, and numerous issues of the newspaper from 1950 to 1960 tend to confirm this assessment for the decade of the 1950s. Secretary Benson visited Tucumcari in April 1955. *TDN*, April 25 and May 5, 1955. Although drought conditions prevailed in the 1960s and 1970s, the five-year period beginning in 1984 recorded five straight years of above-normal moisture, the longest such span in Quay County. *QC Sun*, January 11, 1989. The *Wall Street Journal* article, May 5, 1955, included a statement by H. W. Ingram, president of the Citizens Bank in Tucumcari, that deposits were $100,000 less in 1955 than the year before.

29. Moncus and Knapp, *Quay County*, 376, 424, 456, 531; *Tucumcari News*, May 3, 1932; *TDN*, April 21, 1936.

30. *TDN*, August 25, 1955; May 15, 1956; May 1 and 2, July 16, 1957; May 20, 1960; January 22, 30, 1968. On the Nara Visa school, see Cammack, "Nara Visa, the Town that Refused to Die," and also on Nara Visa as well as other schools, *TDN*, May 27, 1966; McAlavy and Kilmer, *High Plains History of East-Central New Mexico*, 101–6. For the love affair with schools across the West, the source is Wyckoff, "Life on the Margin: The Evolution of the Waning West," 35.

31. *TDN*, May 9 and 13, 1963; March 7, 1967. On the authorization of and the benefits for Logan from Ute Creek Lake, see *TDN*, March 10, 1959; *QC Sun*, Progress Edition, August 28, 1977; June 17 and September 13, 1981.

32. "A History: The Growth of School Size in New Mexico," 8; *TDN*, July 16, 1957.

33. General information on Metropolitan Park is found in *QC Sun*, October 22, 1978; and US Department of the Interior, National Park Service.

34. *Tucumcari News*, July 6, 8, and 21, 1976; *QC Sun*, April 23 and October 22, 1978.

35. *QC Sun*, October 1, 1976; June 1 and September 11, 1978.

36. For examples of efforts to resurrect Five Mile Park, see *QC Sun*, February 16, 1983; January 10, 1998; February 12, 2000; January 18, 2006; December 20, 2017.

37. Tom L. Lawson, "Rattler Retrospective," *Rattler Reunion Newsletter*, Tucumcari High School, Tucumcari, NM, 2006, 36; *Route 66 News*, June 13, 2010; *QC Sun*, January 4, 1997; January 7, 1998; Metropolitan Park, National Register of Historic Places, 1995.

38. Geological and chronological statistics on Tucumcari Mountain are taken from Trauger and Bushman, *Geology and Ground Water in the Vicinity of Tucumcari*.

39. Mollhausen, *Diary of a Journey from the Mississippi to the Coasts of the Pacific*, 1:269; *QC Sun*, April 13, 1978.

40. *TDN*, May 22, 1956; February 27, March 12 and 31, April 10 and 24, May 14 and 23, and June 27, 1957; February 28, 1958.

41. *TDN*, May 21, 22, 26, and 28, June 26, 1957; April 25, June 3 and 5, 1958; and January 9, 1959.

42. *TDN*, December 21, 1964; January 20 and April 5, 1965.

43. *Tucumcari News*, March 26, 1976.

44. *TDN*, January 20, 1959; October 2, 1964.

45. *TDN*, November 24 and December 17, 1971. For the various projects proposed for Tucumcari Mountain, see *TDN*, April 9, 1951. See also, "A Hike Up Tucumcari Mountain," for pictures of the roadway up the mountain. And for possible origins of the idea for the Indian village, see K. Phillips, "Tucumcari, N. M.—The Photographer." In 1978 the Quay County Commission considered but tabled a resolution that would have preserved and protected the mountain from commercialization. *QC Sun*, April 13, 1978.

46. *QC Sun*, November 30, 1978; July 1, 1979.

47. See, for instance, Moser, "Saboteur in Texas," 26–28, on McMurtry's connection with rural Texas towns and his literary accomplishments.

48. *TDN*, May 18, 1943; February 29, 1944.

49. *QC Sun*, May 9, 1979; April 24, 1981; December 1, 1984; October 26, 1991; and special Quay County visitors' edition, October 29, 1994. In 1989 the Odeon Theater was listed as part of the Commonwealth Theatres chain of Kansas City, which operated 250 screens—both indoor and outdoor—in an eleven-state area, but later returned to local ownership. An experienced state-contracted cultural historian declared that the Odeon "retains a strong feeling of a pre–World War II motion picture theater," and its modest representation of the art deco style of architecture was the best of any extant theater left in the state. Ramon Martinez, who began working part-time in the Odeon as a teenager, bought the theater and kept it in operation. *Tucumcari News*, June 29, 1989; *QC Sun*, July 29, 2006. See especially, Isenberg, *We'll Always Have Casablanca*.

50. *QC Sun*, May 1, 2004.

51. *QC Sun*, April 21 and October 2, 2004. A summary of Tucumcari's quest for the sixth license is in Brunt, "3 Groups Vying for State's Last Race Track License." The final contenders were Tucumcari, Raton, and the Downs at Santa Fe, a closed racetrack backed by the Pojoaque Pueblo and Canadian investors.

52. *QC Sun*, August 13, 2008; October 21, 2015.

53. Brunt, "3 Groups Vying for Last License"; *QC Sun*, August 3 and 27, 2008.

54. *QC Sun*, July 13 and August 13 and 27, 2008; October 21, 2015.

55. Rothman, *Neon Metropolis*, xx; Moehring and Green, *Las Vegas: A Centennial*, chap. 2, 84–92, 106–08, 132–37; *QC Sun*, April 3, 2003.

56. Schwantes, *Vision and Empire*, 229–30. In fact, not only at Dawson but the coal industry elsewhere in New Mexico suffered "virtual extinction." Keleher, *Memoirs*, 222–24. For general information on Dawson, see Covert, *Dawson, the Town That Was*; and, in Bidegain Collection, typewritten, Mrs. Jess Gafford (Esther R. Rogers Gafford), "Dawson," n.d. Both works are firsthand accounts by people who lived in Dawson during its heyday.

57. *TDN*, April 12, 1950.

58. Pirsig, *Zen and the Art of Motorcycle Maintenance*, 61.

59. *TDN*, June 30, 1972; *Albuquerque Journal*, July 1, 1972; November 23, 1975. Earl Guthmann published the *Roy Record* in neighboring Harding County for more than

thirty-five years until the county's population dropped from about 10,000 to 1,700 in 1958. Harding County became the only one in the state without a doctor, dentist, lawyer, hospital, newspaper, or bus service. Interview with Guthmann, *TDN*, July 13, 1961.

60.   *QC Sun*, November 4, 2000, contains a history of local newspapers, especially of the *Sun*. See also, *Tucumcari News*, May 19, 1977.

61.   *QC Sun*, March 9, 1983; April 4, 2013.

62.   Office of the Principal, Tucumcari High School, Tucumcari, NM, 2018; *QC Sun*, November 17, 1990.

63.   *QC Sun*, March 16, 1980; February 8, 1997.

64.   *QC Sun*, December 15, 1990.

65.   US Bureau of the Census, Quay County, NM, 1994, online; *QC Sun*, January 15 and 25, 1986.

66.   *TDN*, September 25 and 29, 1970.

67.   *Wall Street Journal*, Eastern Edition, December 22, 1994, A1 & A5. See also, *QC Sun*, December 28, 1994, for a rejoinder to the *WSJ* article. Civic-minded groups recently launched a campaign to preserve and restore the town's remaining neon signs, prized with an alarming number hauled off by outside collectors, with the objective of establishing a local "neon park." Biggers, "Destinations: Tucumcari," *New Mexico*, September–October 2021, 28–36.

68.   *QC Sun*, March 11 and 25, October 7, and December 6, 1995.

69.   *QC Sun*, August 5, 1979. Sands-Dorsey was the drugstore's formal name, but usually it was just called "Sands." Leon Sands and Herman Dorsey purchased the drugstore together, and later Sands became the sole owner. *TDN*, August 19, 1958.

70.   *QC Sun*, June 9 and 13, 2007.

71.   *QC Sun*, June 9 and 13, 2007; August 9, 2008.

Chapter 10

1.   Moncus and Knapp, *Quay County*, 497–500.

2.   James Lerke, Tucumcari, NM, interview by the author, October 10, 2001, transcript in possession of the author.

3.   *TDN*, October 2, 1969, apparently relying on an SP news release, states that Spence was the youngest vice president. The main source of information on Richard D. Spence's railroad career was the handwritten, 170-page memoir he wrote especially for this book. Copy of the transcript in possession of the present author. No further footnotes will be used in this section for this source, although additional information will be cited. Unless cited otherwise, the newspaper articles in this chapter are clippings attached to Spence's handwritten memoir for this book. The *D* in Spence's name stood for Dee, from his mother's brother, Dee Roach.

4.   *Tucumcari News*, March 6, 1924, reported that engineer A. D. Spence had accidently driven a railroad spike through his left hand while trying to dislodge the spike from a coal stoker.

5. *Sacramento Bee*, November 28, 1962; Circular No. 2, Office of Vice President–System Operations, Southern Pacific Company, San Francisco, CA, May 19, 1967, copy in possession of author; R. G. Ottman, "Keep 'Em Rolling on Time," *Southern Pacific Bulletin*, January 1971, 2–4, Department of Archives and Special Collections, Arizona State University Libraries, Tempe.

6. *Sacramento Bee*, September 23, 1969; *TDN*, May 30, 1967; October 2, 1969. The *Tucumcari Daily News* took special pains to point out that, at age thirty-three, Spence had been the youngest SP division superintendent when he took that position at Sacramento, and forty-four when he was appointed a full-fledged vice president.

7. *TDN*, February 5, 1965; Richard D. Spence, Ponte Vedra, Florida, telephone interview by the author, February 5, 2002, transcript held by author. In 1975, while vice president of operations, Spence was also involved in the SP acquisition of the so-called Tucumcari line, the 637-mile Rock Island mainline from Tucumcari to Kansas. *New York Times*, May 1, 1975.

8. *TDN*, January 17, 1968.

9. *TDN*, July 15, 1971. A summary and the details in Myrtle Spence's murder and the trial of her assailant are in *TDN*, December 13 and 30, 1971.

10. *TDN*, July 16 and 19, August 13, 16, and 31, and December 30, 1971; *Tucumcari News*, October 8, 1974; November 29, 1975. The Myrtle Spence murder trial was briefly interrupted by the assassination of District Attorney Victor C. Breen. Seeking revenge for his brother's previous conviction, the sniper, recently released from the state mental hospital, killed Breen instantly with a rifle shot fired from two hundred or three hundred feet away. *TDN*, December 1, 2, 3, and 6, 1971.

11. *Railway Age*, June 30, 1975.

12. *New York Times*, December 29, 2001.

13. "Activation Teamwork," *Conrail*, company publication, April–May 1976.

14. *New York Times*, September 27, 1975. Spence's salary at SP had been $100,000 a year, whereas in the new position it was $135,000 a year; Jordan's was $202,000 annually. *Wall Street Journal*, March 4, 1976. A local newspaper proudly ran the banner front-page headline, "Former Tucumcari Newsboy Heads Rail Corporation," *Tucumcari News*, April 1, 1976.

15. *New York Times*, March 28, 1976; R. D. Spence, "A Message from the President," *Conrail*, company publication, April–May 1976. In his remarks Spence also said, "My own experience in this industry goes back to 1946 when I first went to work for the Southern Pacific, as a brakeman, out of my hometown of Tucumcari, New Mexico."

16. In 1967 an announcement that McNear had been promoted to "vice president of the company," also stated, "McNear, who has been assistant to the president of the transportation firm since late 1963, will take over his new Executive Department position April 1." *TDN*, March 23, 1967. For McNear as trainmaster at Tucumcari, see *TDN*, May 5, 1955.

17. A seventh ailing company, the Ann Arbor Railroad, originally designated to become part of Conrail, was sold to the state of Michigan.

18.   Machalaba, "Railroading's Biggest Blunders," 48. See *Railway Age*, October 31, 1977, for one of these problems and Spence's solution, and *Railway Age*, March 28, 1977, for the problem of motive power. The Penn Central, the largest of the six, still suffered from its forced combination with the New York Central in 1968 and bankruptcy in 1970.

19.   *New York Times*, March 28, 1976.

20.   Rush Loving Jr., "Conrail Is Still Seeking the Route to Profitability," 120–24. For the woes of railroad management, see "Commentary: Inside the Mind of Michael Ward," 14–15.

21.   *Wall Street Journal*, September 13, 1976; December 13, 1977; June 27, 1978; *Railway Age*, March 28, 1977, 17–19; July 10, 1978, 8; September 25, 1978, 11; *New York Times*, June 25, 1978; *Washington Post*, June 27, 1978; *Business Week*, July 10, 1978, 25; *Philadelphia Daily News*, June 27, 1978. US Representative Frederick B. Rooney Jr., of Pennsylvania, a member of the Conrail board, stated that Spence's dismissal was "not merely finding a scapegoat" for the railroad's poor performance and unfavorable publicity. This source also reported that Spence had resigned under pressure from Congress, the ICC, the Justice Department, and USRA. Quoted in *Journal of Commerce*, June 27, 1978, 2, 3, 29.

22.   Saunders, *Main Lines*, 150; Moeller, "New L&N Chief Is Mapping out the Route to Recovery," *Louisville Courier-Journal*, November 5, 1978.

23.   *Nashville Banner*, December 31, 1980; *Family Lines*, company publication, September–October 1979.

24.   After Conrail recorded two successive profitable quarters in 1980—an accomplishment some credited largely to Spence—Edward J. Jordan resigned as chairman to pursue other employment. A seven-months' search for Spence's replacement, in which several seasoned rail executives refused an offer, ended with the hiring of an automobile company vice president with no railroading experience. Middleton et al., *Encyclopedia of North American Railroads*, 343–45, 631–33, 956–57; Burns, *Railroad Mergers*, 66–69, 88–93, 126–27. In 1987 the sale of the federal government's 85 percent share of Conrail for $1.65 billion to private investors—and eventually to CSX—remained the biggest divestiture of federally owned property until the sale of the government's 78 percent share of the Elk Hills Naval Petroleum Reserve in California to the Occidental Petroleum Corporation for $3.65 billion in 1998. Three articles in *Trains*: Loving, "The Prize," 30–39; Murray, "Looking for a Silver Bullet," 26–39; and Frailey, "Conrail Lives!" 18–31. See also Stratton, *Tempest over Teapot Dome*, 347.

25.   *Nashville Banner*, December 31, 1980; *Family Lines*, company publication, September–October 1979.

26.   Dick Spence to classmates of 1943, in *Letters from Classmates of 50 Years Ago*.

27.   *Jacksonville Beach* (FL) *Times-Unio.* 2015, http://www.legacy.com/obituariestimesunion.

28.   Harold F. Fulkerson was an employee and officer of the Southern Pacific for thirty-nine years, retiring in 1980. He died November 1, 1995. *QC Sun*, November 4, 1995. See also, Moncus and Knapp, *Quay County*, 306–7, 571.

29.   Typewritten copies, Houston L. Penix, "Texas to New Mexico in a Covered

Wagon, 1907," n.d.; Roy Penix, "My Story," n.d., and Roy Penix, Lindon, UT, telephone interviews, March 24 and April 6, 2002, all three transcripts in possession of the author; Roy Penix to the author, April 1, 2002; *QC Sun*, January 7, 1981. The autobiographical accounts, interview, and correspondence cited here provide the information on Roy Penix's SP career.

30. The essential information on Lawrence F. Furlow Jr. is taken from *San Jose* (CA) *Mercury News/San Mateo County Times*, May 27, 2012, http://www.mercuynews+news+obituaries. Lawrence F. Furlow Jr., to Clifton L. Moreland, July 13, 1993, in *Letters from Classmates of 50 Years Ago*; Turnbeaugh, *Tucumcari High School Rattler Football Greats*, 219; Ottman, "Keep 'Em Rolling on Time," 2. Furlow's father, L. F. Furlow Sr., worked for the Santa Fe, El Paso & Southwestern, and Southern Pacific railroads before he retired at Tucumcari as SP chief car inspector in 1955. *TDN*, September 21, 1960.

31. Unless indicated otherwise, the information on Charles T. Babers is from a letter to the author, April 28, 2002, and from a telephone interview with Babers, Tucson, Arizona, by the author, July 8, 2002, transcript in possession of the author.

32. *TDN*, March 17, 1957, has the details of the program Babers arranged for the SP safety awards dinner.

33. Babers interview, July 8, 2002.

34. *QC Sun*, February 27 and March 24, 1980.

35. See Moncus and Knapp, *Quay County*, 594, for biographical information on Frank N. Turner. For Frank Kile Turner, see chapter 6 of this account; Frank K. Turner, "My Bio," Rattler Reunion newsletter, Tucumcari High School, Tucumcari, NM, 2007, and "Frank Turner," Texas A&M University at Commerce, Alumni Board, n. d., https://www.classmates.com.

36. In retirement, Turner is still closely associated with the railroad industry in several ways. He has been a partner in a small east Texas short line; president and CEO of the Cumbres and Toltec Scenic Railroad, headquartered at Chama, New Mexico; and board member of a tourist line, the Black Hills Central Railroad in South Dakota. As indicated earlier in chapter 6, Turner developed a strong youthful attachment to the Tucumcari depot and is presently board chairman of the restored depot's Tucumcari Railroad Museum. In the same household, Turner's wife, Roselie, is distinguished in her own right, having published six books.

37. The information on McNear came from Denman K. McNear, Kentfield, California, telephone interview by the author, October 10, 2005; McNear to the author, November 4, 2005, with personal vita enclosed—all in possession of author. Although the Petaluma branch of McNear's family had been in the feed and grain business for one hundred years in California, his maternal grandfather spent his career with the New York Central Railroad in the East. Gold, "Denman McNear '48." In 1955 new trainmaster D. K. McNear was "rapidly getting acquainted" at Tucumcari. *Southern Pacific Bulletin*, June 1955, 36, ASU Libraries.

38. The information in this section on Charles E. Babers came mainly from a letter,

Babers to the author, August 11, 2016; Babers, Newberg, Oregon, telephone interview by the author, August 29, 2016, notes in possession of the author. *QC Sun*, March 9, 1988, has the announcement of Charles E. Babers's appointment as the assistant superintendent of a Southern Pacific subsidiary, the St. Louis Southwestern (Cotton Belt) Railway at Kansas City.

39. Biographical information came mostly from Marvin L. Wells, Palm Coast, Florida, telephone interview by the author, July 15, 2016, notes in possession of the author; e-mail, Wells to the author, October 17, 2016.

40. Port Terminal Railroad Association, *Port Terminal Railroad Infrastructure*, Houston, TX, n.d., http://www.houstontx.gov/events; US Gulf International Commerce Club, "Announces April Speaker—Marvin Wells," Houston, TX, April 7, 2010, http://www. houstontx.gov/events.

41. On McNear, Corbett, and Currier at Tucumcari and afterward, see Southern Pacific Company, *Annual Report*, 1960, 10, ASU Libraries; *TDN* March 10, 1944; July 19, 1948; July 18, 1956; June 23, 1960; and January 25, 1967.

Chapter 11

1. *QC Sun*, November 30, 1978; January 27, 1980; Henry C. Goldenberg, *A Tribute to My Father*, 12, 29, 38.

2. *TDN*, March 1, 1940; August 25, 1948; *QC Sun*, November 21, 1974; February 24, 1982; November 30, 1978; January 27, 1980. See also, Henry C. Goldenberg, *A Tribute to My Father*.

3. *TDN*, April 21, 1936.

4. *QC Sun*, March 18, 1991.

5. *QC Sun*, November 30, 1978; January 27, 1980. Quotation is from Henry C. Goldenberg, *A Tribute to My Father*, 7.

6. *QC Sun*, December 30, 2000; *Actual Settler*, January 7, 1905.

7. *TDN*, October 17, 1962, has the recollections of Arthur E. Curren, former publisher of the *Tucumcari Times*, who arrived in 1901 when his father established the first newspaper, the *Pathfinder*. This newspaper faithfully recorded the delivery by pastores of large wool clips. See *Pathfinder*, 1902, ff.

8. Cabeza de Baca, *We Fed Them Cactus*, xxiii, 66–79. The contributions and accomplishments of Fabiola Cabeza de Baca, "writer, home economist, and historian . . . [who practiced] the arts of remembering, storing, moving, preparing, persuading, and extending" the early Hispanic culture of New Mexico, and who lived to be ninety-seven, are discussed in Scharff, *Twenty-Thousand Roads*, chap. 5.

9. Cabeza de Baca, *We Fed Them Cactus*, xxiii, 66–67, 138–39; Morris, *Llano Estacado*, 254–56; Flores, *Caprock Canyonlands*, chap. 7. See places listed alphabetically in Julyan, *Place Names of New Mexico*. On Nara Visa and its name, see Kathy Cammack, "Nara Visa, the Town that Refused to Die," and by the same author, "Ranches Grow Larger, but Children Fewer."

10. Whisenhunt, *New Mexico Courthouses*, 30.

11. *QC Sun*, August 5, 1968.

12. Moncus and Knapp, *Quay County*, 377; *TDN*, January 15, 1942.

13. Moncus and Knapp, *Quay County*, 666, 700; *TDN*, August 18, 1969; *Tucumcari News*, November 5, 1976; Henry C. Goldenberg, "My Hometown."

14. Henry C. Goldenberg, "My Hometown"; *QC Sun*, August 5, 1968.

15. *TDN*, June 24, 1952; *QC Sun*, April 11, 1982; Henry C. Goldenberg, "My Hometown." Tucumcari also had a bilingual Southern Baptist Church, Igesia Bautisa Rayo de Luz (The Beam of Light Baptist Church). See *QC Sun*, March 21, 1992. The Mount Calvary Baptist Church served African American parishioners. The Northside Baptist Church also had a black congregation, but its pastor arranged a merger with the Mount Calvary Church. Moncus and Knapp, *Quay County*, 516, 707.

16. The *Tucumcari Daily News* had carrier routes all over town, most with thirty or forty paying subscribers. North of the railroad tracks was different—there were only seven or eight paying subscribers in that entire section of town. The lone carrier was instructed, however, to fold forty or fifty papers, leave a copy with every paying subscriber, and toss the rest indiscriminately into other yards. How long this circulation system lasted is unknown. The ending quote is from Henry C. Goldenberg, "My Hometown."

17. President Theodore Roosevelt's record of backing federal appointments for former Rough Riders—more than forty received plum positions—tends to substantiate the family's claim that the White House had a hand in Royal Prentice's land-office assignment. Gardner, *Rough Riders*, 21–24, 52, 64–65, 71–72, 266–68.

18. *TDN*, May 1, 1949; Moncus and Knapp, *Quay County*, 497–500; Henry C. Goldenberg, *A Tribute to My Father*; Royal A. Prentice Photograph Collection, 1893–1958, New Mexico History Museum, Palace of the Governors, Santa Fe, NM. The entry for this collection contains a biographical sketch on Prentice. In addition, the Fray Angelico Chavez History Library, Palace of the Governors, Santa Fe, NM, has the Royal A. Prentice Papers.

19. Moncus and Knapp, *Quay County*, 342, 499.

20. *TDN*, August 29 and September 23, 1941; August 24, 1944; July 18, 1947.

21. *TDN*, March 27, 1956; January 16, 1961; *QC Sun*, January 1, 1983; July 11, 1992.

22. Greenfield, *A History of Public Health in New Mexico*, 147.

23. *TDN*, November 19, 1937.

24. On increasing numbers of Hispanic football players, see Turnbeaugh, *Tucumcari High School Rattler Football Greats*, 136–42, 179–91. On the number of black players, Turnbeaugh, 148–62, especially photograph 294, and, for example of blacks in newspapers, Cornell Evans and Sammy Kent, *Tucumcari News*, December 13 and 31, 1976; September 19, 1977; *QC Sun*, January 2, 1977.

25. *QC Sun*, July 28 and November 10, 1982. Texas had the second-highest percentage of Hispanics in its population with 21 percent, while California had 19.2 percent.

26. *QC Sun*, September 7, 1988; April 24, 1991; February 5–7, 2000. By 2015–2016, the Hispanic count had increased to 3,078, or more than 57 percent of Tucumcari's 5,363 total population. US Census Bureau, Current Hispanic or Latino Population, Tucumcari,

New Mexico, 2016, 2015 with Demographics and Stats by Age and Gender, http://www.
census.gov.suburbanstats.org/race/New-Mexico.

27.   The 1910 census reported one black individual and a black family, besides Tom
Hodges, in Quay County, including Tucumcari. By 1940 the count had increased to 102
individuals, almost all of them living in Tucumcari, http://www.census,gov.censusrecords.
com.

28.   In Moncus and Knapp, *Quay County*, 350–52, members of the Hodges family
comment on Tom Hodges's life among them.

29.   *Tucumcari News*, November 12, 1931, has a lengthy account of the clash between
the deputy sheriff and Quinn Stanton.

30.   *Tucumcari News*, November 12, 1931.

31.   *TDN*, November 11, 1940; April 8 and 9, 1941.

32.   *TDN*, January 9 and 10, 1941.

33.   *TDN*, May 7 and 17, 1951.

34.   *QC Sun*, March 8 and 29, 1986.

35.   *QC Sun*, August 27, November 12, and December 10, 1986. Under any circumstances state patrol officers faced constant danger. In his first twenty-five years with the
patrol, Jerry Brunk, stationed at Tucumcari for many years, had been hit by vehicles five
times at highway incidents. *TDN*, September 5, 1962.

36.   On Rudd's sterling qualities and coaching career, see Moncus and Knapp, *Quay
County*, 529–30; *Review*, magazine of *TDN*, October 15, 1965; *QC Sun*, October 25 and
November 1, 1981.

37.   Local sports fans still marveled a half-century later at the state basketball championship won by Coach Rudd's team in 1950. *QC Sun*, February 9–11, 2000.

38.   Moncus and Knapp, *Quay County*, 187; Turnbeaugh, *Rattler Football Greats*, 63, 69,
79–80, 202–4, 264–71; *TDN*, November 25, 1948; August 16, October 31, and November
7 and 28, 1951; February 22, 1968. Don Babers rose to prominence in the US Army's Ordnance Corps, heading several projects that developed tanks and other heavy weaponry. For
information on Lieutenant General Donald M. Babers, see US Army, Ordnance Corps Hall
of Fame Inductees, 1987, http://www.goordinance.army.military/hof/halloffameinductees;
Moncus and Knapp, *Quay County*, 187; *QC Sun*, September 25, 1982, Close to home among
high-ranking military officers, Richard R. "Si" Reid attained the rank of major general
in the National Guard of New Mexico. It seems appropriate to also include Carl E. Berg
among Tucumcari's success stories, as the only person of record who has become a billionaire ($1.1 billion in 2013) through real estate investments in Silicon Valley and various ven-
ture capitalism enterprises. Moncus and Knapp, *Quay County*, 199–200; *Wikipedia*.

39.   Unidentified newspaper account, March 7, 2000, quoted in Turnbeaugh, *Rattler
Football Greats*, 215; Toby Smith, "Recollections of a Golden God."

40.   Smith, "Recollections of a Golden God." Several years later Rod's father wrote
and published a book that gave a great deal of information about his son's life but no satisfactory explanation for his death. See Ward S. David, *Ask Not for Victory*. The title came
from a prayer found in one of Rod's scrapbooks.

41.   *QC Sun*, April 11 and 14, 1984; November 22, 1995; Smith, "Recollections of a Golden God"; Logan, "Mourning Tucumcari Remembers Rod David With Hymns, Prayers"; Laise, "Rod David: Life, Death and the System."

42.   The Rattlers had two perfect consecutive 10–0 football seasons in 1948 and 1949, and, in 1979, they won twelve games, including playoffs, and lost none. By a vote of the state's sportswriters, the Rattlers were named "mythical" state champs in 1948, before the official title was established by a playoff game. The Rattlers were Class A state champions in football in 1959. In later years, their fortunes were much worse. In 1987, when the Tucumcari team won three games and lost eight, it did finally end a twenty-one-game losing streak. *Albuquerque Journal*, October 20, 2000; Turnbeaugh, *Rattler Football Greats*, 67, 69, 75, 79, 159, 173; *TDN*, November 25 and December 1, 1949; November 27, 1959; *QC Sun*, November 29, 2000.

43.   *QC Sun*, November 15, 2000.

44.   *QC Sun*, November 21 and December 30, 2000; *Albuquerque Journal*, October 20 and November 19, 2000; March 14 and 15, 2001; *Santa Fe New Mexican*, November 19, 2000.

45.   McMurtry, *Some Can Whistle*, 75. McMurtry summarized succinctly the scholarly controversy between the Triumphalists and the Revisionists, and the emergence of the New Western History in "How the West Was Won or Lost," 32–38.

46.   Arce, "Reunion Retrospective," 22–23.

47.   Etulain and Malone, *The American West*, 244–46. Phelps Dodge later closed several of its other mining-related properties.

BIBLIOGRAPHY

Aldrich, Mark. *Death Rode the Rails: American Railroad Accidents and Safety, 1828–1965.* Baltimore: Johns Hopkins University Press, 2006.

Ambrose, Stephen E. *Eisenhower, Volume II: The President.* New York: Simon and Schuster, 1984.

Arany, Lynne, et al. *The Reel List: A Categorical Companion to Over 2,000 Memorable Films.* New York: Delta, 1995.

Arce, Ray. "Reunion Retrospective." *Rattler Reunion Newsletter,* Tucumcari High School, Tucumcari, NM, 2006, 22–23.

Arch Hurley Conservancy District. "History and Status of the Tucumcari Project." Tucumcari, NM, n.d.

———. "The Arch Hurley Irrigation District." Tucumcari, NM, n.d.

Arkin, David. "Neon Lights up Route 66." *Route 66 Guide,* June 2004, 2.

Bachman, Ben. "The Open Road." *Trains* (January 2009): 43.

Bailey, Fred L. BRC Fa. 527, to Editor. *Tucumcari Daily News,* September 24, 1941.

Bailey, Thomas A. *A Diplomatic History of the American People.* 10th ed. Englewood Cliffs, NJ: Prentice-Hall, 1980.

Barnhart, Charles E., et al. "Tucumcari Tank Failure: New Mexico Society of Professional Engineers." *Journal American Water Works Association* 44, no. 5 (May 1952): 435–41.

Barradas, Samuel. "A Guide to Truckers Slang." *Truckers Report.* https://www.thetruckersreport.com/library/a-guide-to-truckers-slang/.

Barrett, William P., Juliet Casey, Daniel J. Chacon, Nick Kryloff, Dan McKay, Susan Montoya, and Martin Salazar. "Who Owns New Mexico: The 40 Largest Private Landowners." *Crosswinds.* June 1997. http://www.williampbarrett.com/CrossLand/.

Bartky, Ian R. "The Invention of Railroad Time." *Railway History* 148 (Spring 1983):13–22.

Baxter, John O. *Las Carneradas: Sheep Trade in New Mexico, 1700–1860.* Albuquerque: University of New Mexico Press, 1987.

Biggers, Ashley M. "Destinations: Tucumcari." *New Mexico* (September–October 2021): 24–36.

Bilstein, Roger. "The Airplane and the American Experience." In *The Airplane in American Culture,* edited by Dominick A. Pisano, 115–17. Ann Arbor: University of Michigan Press, 2013.

Blakeslee, Donald J. "Which Barrancas? Narrowing the Possibilities." In *The Coronado Expedition to Tierra Nueva: The 1540–1542 Route Across the Southwest*, edited by Richard Flint and Shirley Cushing Flint, 252–66. Niwot: University Press of Colorado, 1997.

Blakeslee, Donald J., Richard Flint, and Jack T. Hughes. "Una Blanca Grande: Recent Archaeological Evidence and a Discussion of Its Place in the Coronado Route." In *The Coronado Expedition to Tierra Nueva: The 1540–1542 Route Across the Southwest*, edited by Richard Flint and Shirley Cushing Flint, 309–20. Niwot: University Press of Colorado, 1997.

Blaszak, Michael W. "Ultimate Change: Free to Compete." *Trains* (October 2010): 24–33.

Boeing Marine Systems. "The First Family of Hydrofoils." n.d.

Bolton, Herbert E. *Coronado: Knight of Pueblos and Plains*. New York: Whittlesey House; Albuquerque: University of New Mexico Press, 1949.

Brennan, Francis X. "Spoils System Still Flourishes in New Mexico." *Tucumcari Daily News*, August 6, 1963.

Brunt, Charles D. "3 Groups Vying for State's Last Race Track License." *Albuquerque Sunday Journal*, August 3, 2008.

Bryant Jr., Keith L. "Development of North American Railroads." In *Encyclopedia of North American Railroads*, edited by William D. Middleton, et al., 11–17. Bloomington: Indiana University Press, 2007.

Burns, James B. *Railroad Mergers and the Language of Unification*. Westport, CT: Quorum Books, 1998.

Cabeza de Baca, Fabiola. *We Fed Them Cactus*. 2nd ed. Albuquerque: University of New Mexico Press, 1994.

Cameron, Juan. "How the Interstate Changed the Face of the Nation." *Fortune* (July 1971): 60, 125.

Cammack, Kathy. "Nara Visa, the Town that Refused to Die." *Tucumcari Daily News Review*, April 1, 1966.

———. "Ranches Grow Larger, but Children Fewer." *Tucumcari Daily News Review*, May 27, 1966.

Canning, Charlotte M. *The Most American Thing in America: Circuit Chautauqua as Performance*. Iowa City: University of Iowa Press, 2005.

Catton, Bruce. *Waiting for the Morning Train: An American Boyhood*. Detroit: Wayne State University Press, 1987.

Caves, Douglas W., Laurits R. Christensen, and Joseph A. Swanson. "The Staggers Act, 30 Years Later." *Regulation* (Winter 2010–2011): 28–31.

Chicago, Rock Island, and Pacific Railroad Company. *1964 Annual Report*. 1965, 4–5.

Clark, Ira G. *Then Came the Railroads: The Century of Steam to Diesel in the Southwest*. Norman: University of Oklahoma Press, 1958.

———. *Water in New Mexico: A History of Its Management and Use*. Albuquerque: University of New Mexico Press, 1987.

Covert, Fredericoi Caraglio. *Dawson, the Town That Was: A Family Story*. Albuquerque: Far West & Associates, 1984.

Cox, Wendell, and Jean Love. "40 Years of the US Interstate Highway System: An Analysis—The Best Investment a Nation Ever Made." *Highway & Motorway Fact Book*, June 1996.

Cray, Ed. *Chrome Colossus: General Motors and Its Times*. New York: McGraw-Hill, 1980.

Cude, Pearl Baker McGowan. "My Life Story." September 1955, Phillip B. and Yetta Kohn Bidegain Collection, Tucumcari, NM.

Dale, Edward Everette. *The Range Cattle Industry*. Norman: University of Oklahoma Press, 1930.

Daugherty, Harry M., with Thomas Dixon. *The Inside Story of the Harding Tragedy*. New York: Churchill Co., 1932.

David, Ward S. *Ask Not for Victory*. San Diego, CA: Torch, 1992.

Davis, Colin J. *Power at Odds: The 1922 National Railroad Shopmen's Strike*. Urbana: University of Illinois Press, 1997.

Davis, Margaret Leslie. *Dark Side of Fortune: Triumph and Scandal in the Life of Oil Tycoon Edward L. Doheny*. Berkeley: University of California Press, 1998.

Dean, John W. *Warren G. Harding*. American Presidents Series. New York: Times Books, Henry Holt, 2004.

Dickson, Gary. "Children's Crusade." *Encyclopedia Britannica*, March 18, 2018. https://www.britannica.com/event/Childrens-Crusade.

Dill, Tom. "Southern Pacific's Painted Ladies." Special edition, *Steam Glory 2. Classic Trains* no. 5 (2007): 86–91.

Doherty, Jim. *Just the Facts: True Tales of Cops and Criminals*. Batesville, AR: Prose, n.d.

Donovan, Frank. *Wheels for a Nation*. New York: Thomas Y. Crowell, 1965.

Drabanski, Emily. "Songs of Tucumcari." *New Mexico* (November 2010): 15–16.

Easton, Nina J. "Diamonds Are Forever: Director Fields the Lost Hopes of Adolescence." *Los Angeles Times*, April 21, 1989.

Edwards, Owen. "The Object at Hand: Antique Road Show." *Smithsonian* (November 2003): 32, 34.

Eisenhower, Lt. Col. D. D. "Report on Trans-Continental Trip." November 3, 1919, NAID #1055071, Dwight D. Eisenhower Library, Museum and Boyhood Home, Abilene, KS.

Ellis, George F. *The Bell Ranch as I Knew It*. Kansas City, MO: Lowell Press, 1973.

El Paso & Southwestern Company. *Ninth Annual Report, 1922*. General Collections, St. Louis Mercantile Library, St. Louis, MO.

Estes, Casey. "The Land Report." *Magazine of the American Landowner* (Fall 2010): 18.

Etulain, Richard W., and Michael P. Malone. *The American West: A Modern History, 1900 to the Present*. 2nd ed. Lincoln: University of Nebraska Press, 2007.

Evans, Laurie. "Scenic Byway Adventures: Mesalands Scenic Byway." *New Mexico* (June 2004): 28–29.

Fall Brook Railway Company. "Superintendent G. R. Brown's 'System of Discipline.'" https://www.fallbrookrailway.com/g_r_brown.html.

Family Entertainment Guide. "Cars (2006)." https://www.imdb/family-entertainment-guide.

Faulkner, William. *Light in August.* New York: Vintage Books, 1972.

Fehrenbach, T. R. *Comanches: The Destruction of a People.* New York: Da Capo, 1994.

Flink, James J. *America Adopts the Automobile, 1895–1910.* Cambridge, MA: MIT Press, 1974.

———. *The Car Culture.* Cambridge, MA: MIT Press, 1976.

Flores, Dan. *Caprock Canyon Lands: Journeys into the Heart of the Southern Plains.* Austin: University of Texas Press, 1990.

Flynn, James R. "The Railroad Shopmen's Strike of 1922 on the Industry, Company, and Community Levels." PhD diss., Northern Illinois University, DeKalb, 1993.

Forestall, Richard L., ed. *Population of Counties by Decennial Census, 1900 to 1990, New Mexico, Population Division.* US Bureau of the Census, Washington, DC, 1995.

Form WR-16, A Report on Examination of Range Land, US Department of Agriculture, Agricultural Adjustment Administration, Western Division, May 8, 1937. Phillip B. and Yetta Kohn Bidegain Collection, Tucumcari, NM.

Fortune. "The US Highway System." (June 1941): 92–99, 106, 109, 111.

Frailey, Fred W. "Conrail Lives!" *Trains* (October 2012): 18–31.

———. "Let Us Now Praise Union Pacific." *Trains* (June 2002); 15.

———. "Ultimate Passenger Train: Audacious Luxury." *Trains* (November 2010): 46–48.

———. "Ultimate Technology: The Continental Nervous System." *Trains* (November 2010): 48–49.

———. "Union Pacific on the Mend." *Trains* (July 2005): 9, 11–12.

Fried, Sharon. *Heart & Soil.* Santa Fe, NM: Ranch & Family, 2010.

Fried, Stephen. *Appetite for America: Fred Harvey and the Business of Civilizing the Wild West—One Meal at a Time.* New York: Bantam, 2010.

Gafford, Esther Rogers. "Dawson." n.d. Typewritten manuscript. Phillip B. and Yetta Kohn Bidegain Collection, Tucumcari, NM.

Gallinger, Jason. "Railroads Face Possibility of Tighter Regulation." *Trains* (June 2006): 10–12.

Gardner, Mark Lee. *Rough Riders: Theodore Roosevelt, His Cowboy Regiment, and the Immortal Charge Up San Juan Hill.* New York: William Morrow, 2016.

Garrett, Klink, as told to Toby Smith. *Ten Turtles to Tucumcari: A Personal History of the Railway Express Agency.* Albuquerque: University of New Mexico Press, 2003.

Genealogy.com. "Genealogy Report: Descendants of John Atkinson, Sr." 2004, https://www.geni/com/people/john-atkinson.

Giblin, Jim. "The Road to Deregulation." *Trains* (September 2008): 58–65.

———. "Trains vs. Trucks." *Trains* (March 2007): 37–41.

Giglio, James N. *H. M. Daugherty and the Politics of Expediency.* Kent, OH: Kent State University Press, 1978.

Gilbert, Bil [*sic*]. "The Cry Was: Go West, Young Man, and Stay Healthy." *Smithsonian* (March 1983): 138–49.

Goddard, Stephen B. *Getting There: The Epic Struggle Between Road and Rail in the American Century.* Chicago: University of Chicago Press, 1996.

Gold, Liz. "Denman McNear '48: Railroad Executive Stays True to Fraternity." *MIT Technology Review* (June 21, 2011). https://www.technologyreview. com/2011/06/21/258840/denman-mcnear-48/.

Goldenberg, Arthur W. Interview. *Tucumcari Daily News*, June 22, 1967.

Goldenberg, Henrietta Wertheim. Interview, October 30, 1958. Jacob Rader Marcus Center of the American Jewish Archives, Jewish Institute of Religion, Hebrew Union College, Cincinnati Branch, Cincinnati, OH.

Goldenberg, Henry C. "My Hometown." *QC Sun*, August 5, 1968.

———. *A Tribute to My Father, Henry M. Goldenberg.* Santa Clara, CA: privately printed, n.d.

Goodman, Jack. *While You Were Gone: A Report on Wartime Life in the United States.* New York: Morrow, 1946.

Grann, David. *Killers of the Flower Moon: The Osage Murders and the Birth of the FBI.* New York: Doubleday, 2019.

Grant, H. Roger. "Beset by Competition, Rising Costs, and Regulation, American Railroads in the 1960s Responded with Mergers . . . and a Retreat from the Passenger Business." Special edition, *Trains of the 1960s: Challenging Times for America's Railroads. Classic Trains* no. 3 (2004): 10–12.

Grant Niemann, Linda. "The Lord of the Night." Pt. 1. *Trains* (September 2006): 42–47.

Greany, William C., comp. "Principal Facts Concerning the First Transcontinental Army Motor Transport Expedition, Washington to San Francisco." July 7 to September 6, 1919, NAID 33#12005074, Dwight D. Eisenhower Library, Museum, and Boyhood Home, Abilene, KS.

Greenfield, Myrtle. *A History of Public Health in New Mexico.* Albuquerque: University of New Mexico Press, 1962.

Gwynne, S. C. *Empire of the Summer Moon: Quanah Parker and the Rise and Fall of the Comanches, the Most Powerful Indian Tribe in American History.* New York: Scribner, 2010.

Hagan, William T. *Quanah Parker, Comanche Chief.* Norman: University of Oklahoma Press, 1993.

———. *United States–Comanche Relations: The Reservation Years.* New Haven: Yale University Press, 1976.

Halberstam, David. *The Fifties.* New York: Fawcett Books, 1993.

Haley, J. Evetts. *Charles Goodnight: Cowman & Plainsman.* New ed. Norman: University of Oklahoma Press, 1949.

Hallam, Elizabeth, ed. *Chronicles of the Crusades: Nine Crusades and Two Hundred Years of Bitter Conflict for the Holy Land Brought to Life Through the Words of Those Who Were Actually There.* New York: Weidenfeld & Nicolson, 1989.

Hamalainen, Pekka. *The Comanche Empire.* New Haven, CT: Yale University Press, 2008.

Hammond, George P. *Coronado's Seven Cities.* Albuquerque: US Coronado Exposition Commission, 1940.

Hannett, Arthur Thomas. *Sagebrush Lawyer.* New York: Pageant, 1964.

Harding County Biographies: Pool and Hawkins Family, Harding County, NM., NMGenWeb, https://www.tributes.NMGenWeb.

Harwell, Jeffrey A. "The Rock Island Is A-OK." *Trains* (June 2012): 30–35.

Henderson, James David. *"Meals by Fred Harvey": A Phenomenon of the American West.* Fort Worth: TCU Press, 1969.

"A Hike Up Tucumcari Mountain." *Route 66 News.* September 29, 2008. https://www.route66news.com/2008/09/29/a-hike-up-tucumcari-mountain.

Hilleson, K. "Roadside Attractions Give Character to 66 Towns." *New Mexico* (February 1989): 50–52.

Hilton, George W. "Infra-canin-ophilia." *Trains* (March 1983): 66.

Hinckley, Jim, and Kerrick James. *Ghost Towns of Route 66.* Minneapolis: Voyageur, 2011.

Hingley, Audrey T. "The Spirit of Historic Highway Becomes an Americana Destination." *American Profile* (May 13–19, 2012): 8, 10, 12.

Hinshaw, Gil. "A Gift of Water: Legacy for Quay County." *Review,* magazine of *Tucumcari Daily News,* October 1, 1965.

——. *Tucumcari: Gateway to the West.* n.p.: iUniverse, 2010.

Historical Homesteads and Ranches in New Mexico: A Historic Context. Historic Preservation Division, New Mexico Office of Cultural Affairs, Santa Fe, March 2008.

"A History: The Growth of School Size in New Mexico." *Think New Mexico* (Fall 2008): 8. https://www.thinknewmexico.org/wp-content/uploads/pdfs/SmallSchools.pdf.

Hodge, Frederick W., ed. *Handbook of American Indians North of Mexico,* vol. 1, A to G. Washington, DC: Smithsonian Institution, Bureau of American Ethnology, Bulletin 30, 1910.

Hofsommer, Don L. *The Southern Pacific, 1901–1985.* College Station: Texas A&M University Press, 1986.

Hokanson, Drake. "To Cross America, Early Tourists Took a Long Detour." *Smithsonian* (August 1985): 58, 61.

Hornung, Chuck. *Fullerton's Rangers: A History of the New Mexico Territorial Police.* Jefferson NC: McFarland, 2005.

Howarth, William. "The Okies: Beyond the Dust Bowl." *National Geographic* (September 1984): 339.

Huddleston, Eugene L. *Uncle Sam's Locomotives: The USRA and the Nation's Railroads.* Bloomington: Indiana University Press, 2002.

Hurt, R. Douglas. *Problems of Plenty: The American Farmer in the Twentieth Century.* Chicago: Ivan R. Dee, 2002.

Ingles, J. David. "Rock Island Lines, 1964." *Trains* (October 2005): 46–47.

In the New Mexico Tradition: The Impacts of MainStreet, 1985–2013. New Mexico MainStreet, New Mexico Economic Development Department, Santa Fe, NM, February 2014, 23–24. https://www.placeeconomics.com/wp-content/uploads/2016/08/new-mexico-eia-report_placeeconomics.pdf.

Irwin, Manley R. *Silent Strategists: Harding, Denby, and the US Navy's Trans-Pacific*

Offensive, World War II. Rev. ed. Lanham, MD: University Press of America, 2013.

Isenberg, Noah. *We'll Always Have Casablanca: The Life, Legend, and Afterlife of Hollywood's Most Beloved Movie*. New York: W. W. Norton, 2017.

Jackson, Donald Dale. "Cabooses May Be Rolling Toward the End of the Line." *Smithsonian* (February 1986): 100–110.

Jacob Rader Marcus Center of the American Jewish Archives, Jewish Institute of Religion, Hebrew Union College, Cincinnati Branch, Cincinnati, OH.

Jakle, John A., and Keith A. Schulle. *The Motel in America*. The Road and American Culture Series. Baltimore: Johns Hopkins University Press, 1996.

———. *Signs in America's Auto Age: Signatures of Landscape and Place*. Iowa City: University of Iowa Press, 2004.

Jasper, Joy Waldron, James P. Delgado, and Jim Adams. *The USS Arizona: The Ship, the Men, the Pearl Harbor Attack, and the Symbol that Aroused America*. New York: Truman Talley Books/St. Martin's, 2001.

Johnston, Bob. "Small Town Stations in Flux." *Trains* (July 2016): 19–21.

Julyan, Robert. *Place Names of New Mexico*. Albuquerque: University of New Mexico Press, 1998.

Kaufman, Lawrence H. "Capital Investment: UP's Catch-Up Strategy." *Railway Age* (November 1999): 1–5.

———. "What Intermodal Needs Next." *Railway Age* (April 2000): 25–27.

Kawabata, Yasunari. *Snow Country*. Translated by Edward G. Seidensticker. New York: Berkley Medallion Books, 1960.

Keleher, William A. *The Fabulous Frontier: Twelve New Mexico Items*. Rev. ed. Albuquerque: University of New Mexico Press, 1962.

———. *Maxwell Land Grant: A New Mexico Item*. Rev. ed. Albuquerque: University of New Mexico Press, 1983.

Kelly, Susan Croce. *Father of Route 66: The Story of Cy Avery*. Norman: University of Oklahoma Press, 1988.

King, Beatrice A. "The Talk of the Town." *New Yorker* (April 9, 2018): 17–18.

King, Bruce, as told to Charles Poling. *Cowboy in the Roundhouse: A Political Life*. Santa Fe, NM: Sunstone, 1998.

King, Ernest L., as told to Robert E. Mahaffey. *Main Line: Fifty Years of Railroading with the Southern Pacific*. Garden City, NY: Doubleday, 1948.

Kirksey, Rex E., Leonard M. Lauriault, and Patricia Cooksey. *Weather Observations at the Agricultural Science Center at Tucumcari, 1905–2002*. Agricultural Experiment Station, Report 751, New Mexico State University, Las Cruces, July 2003.

Kirkus, Edna Jacquelyn Stiles. *The Man Who Put Lights Along Route 66: Memories of James Harland Stiles*. Tucson, AZ: Wheatmark, 2010.

Kohn, Solomon H. Letters to Howard L. Kohn, February 4, 1891, December 11, 1902, May 18, 1903. Phillip B. and Yetta Kohn Bidegain Collection, Tucumcari, NM.

Kube, Kathi, and Kevin P. Keefe. "70 Greatest Railroad Engineering Feats." *Trains* (November 2010): 59.

La Botz, Dan. *Edward L. Doheny: Petroleum, Power, and Politics in the United States and Mexico*. New York: Praeger, 1991.

Laise, Jim. "Rod David: Life, Death and the System." *Fort Worth Star-Telegram*, May 15, 1984.

LaRue, Fritz. Letter to the Editor. *New Yorker* (October 12, 1998): 7.

Lawson, Tom L. "Rattler Retrospective." Tucumcari High School. Tucumcari, NM, 2006, 36.

Levinson, Robert E. "American Jews in the West." *Western Historical Quarterly* 5 (July 1974): 286–88.

Lewis, Nancy Owen. *Chasing the Cure in New Mexico: Tuberculosis and the Quest for Health*. Santa Fe: Museum of New Mexico Press, 2016.

Lewis, Tom. *Divided Highways: Building the Interstate Highways, Transforming American Life*. New York: Penguin Putnam, 1999.

Logan, Paul. "Mourning Tucumcari Remembers Rod David with Hymns, Prayers." *Albuquerque Journal*, April 12, 1984.

Loomis, Noel M., and Abraham P. Nasatir. *Pedro Vial and the Roads to Santa Fe*. Norman: University of Oklahoma Press, 1967.

Loper, James L. "Steel Rails to the Sunbelt: The Golden State and Sunset Routes." *Passenger Train Journal* (July 1991): 28.

Lord, Walter. *Day of Infamy*. New York: Bantam, 1958.

Loving Jr., Rush. "Conrail Is Still Seeking the Route to Profitability." *Fortune* (March 13, 1978): 120–24.

———. "The Prize." *Trains* (July 2006): 30–39.

Lowitt, Richard. *Bronson M. Cutting, Progressive Politician*. Albuquerque: University of New Mexico Press, 1992.

Mabry, Thomas J. to Thomas H. MacDonald, commissioner, Public Roads Administration, Washington, DC. March 30, 1948, in *Tucumcari Daily News* (April 1, 1948).

MacDonald, Thomas H. "The History and Development of Road Building in the United States." Annual Convention of the American Society of Civil Engineers, Philadelphia, October 6, 1926, National Transportation Library, US Department of Transportation, Washington, DC.

Machalaba, Dan. "Railroading's Biggest Blunders." *Trains* (September 2015): 54.

MacKaye, Benton. "The Townless Highway." *New Republic* (March 12, 1930): 92–95.

MacKaye, Benton, and Lewis Mumford. "Townless Highways for the Motorist: A Proposal for the Automobile Age." *Harper's Magazine* (August 1931): 347–56.

The Magazine of the American Landowner. "The Land Report." (Fall 2010): 48.

Mahar, Lisa. *American Signs: Form and Meaning on Route 66*. New York: Monacelli, 2002.

Mann, Sue Bohannan. "Irate Governor Paves the Way." *New Mexico* (February 1989): 61.

Marcus, Joseph Rader. *To Count a People: American Jewish Population Data, 1585–1984*. Lanham, MD: University Press of America, 1990.

McAlvy, Don. "New Mexico's Caprock Amphitheatre." In Moncus and Knapp, *Quay County*, 725.

McAlavy, Don, and Harold Kilmer. *High Plains History of East-Central New Mexico*. Clovis, NM: High Plains Historical Press, 1980.

McDonald, Brady. "The Real Route 66 Inspirations Behind Disney's Cars Land." *Los Angeles Times*, January 5, 2013.

McDonnell, Greg. "Timeline to Victory: Six Decades of Landmark Events in the Battle of Steam vs. Diesel." Special edition *Diesel Victory: Railroading's Epic Switch from Steam. Classic Trains* Special Edition no. 4, (2006): 36–43.

McElroy, Harry H. "New Mexico and Her Railroads." Pamphlet and speech at Kiwanis Club, Tucumcari, NM, September 21, 1926, reprinted by *Tucumcari American*, September 25, 1926, 4–5.

McGowan, Clara B. "My Autobiography." n. d. Phillip B. and Yetta Kohn Bidegain Collection, Tucumcari, NM.

McMurtry, Larry. "How the West Was Won or Lost." *New Republic* (October 22, 1990): 32–38.

——. *Some Can Whistle*. New York: Pocket Books 1989.

——. "The West Without Chili." *New York Review of Books* (October 22, 1998): 38, 40–41.

Mead, Margaret, ed. *An Anthropologist at Work: Writings of Ruth Benedict*. Boston: Houghton Mifflin, 1959.

Melzer, Richard. *Coming of Age in the Great Depression: The Civilian Conservation Corps Experience in New Mexico, 1933–1942*. Las Cruces, NM: Yucca Tree, 2000.

Memorandum. "T-4 Cattle Company Ltd." Phillip B. and Yetta Kohn Bidegain Collection, Tucumcari, NM.

Memorandum of Agreement Covering Divisions Between the Dawson Railway and the Rock Island System, 1901. Box LTA-52, FF 7, Southern Pacific Railroad Collection, Special Collections, University of Texas at El Paso Library.

Middleton, William D., et al., eds. "Grade-Crossing Safety." *The Encyclopedia of North American Railroads*. Bloomington: Indiana University Press, 2007.

Middleton, William G. "Piggyback Champion." Special edition *Trains of the 1950s. Classic Trains* no. 12 (2013): 76–81; reprinted from *Trains*, September 1956.

Modell, Judith Schachter. *Ruth Benedict: Patterns of a Life*. Philadelphia: University of Pennsylvania Press, 1983.

Moehring, Eugene P., and Michael S. Green. *Las Vegas: A Centennial History*. Reno: University of Nevada Press, 2005.

Moeller, Philip. "New L&N Chief Is Mapping Out the Route to Recovery." *Louisville Courier-Journal*, November 5, 1978.

Moffett, Ben. "Oran Caton: Sports Eased Hardscrabble Life for Albuquerque Educator." *New Mexico* (November 2007): 70–72.

Mollhausen, Balduin. *Diary of a Journey from the Mississippi to the Coasts of the Pacific with a United States Government Expedition*. 2 vols. Translated by Mrs. Percy Sinnett. London: Longman, Brown, Green, Longmans & Roberts, 1858.

Moncus, Lynn. "Taking a Ride with Some Old Directions." *QC Sun*, May 31, 2003.

———, "Train ride . . . [Is] Trip Down Memory Lane." *QC Sun*, November 9, 2011.

Moncus, Mary Lynn, and Marian D. Knapp, eds. *Quay County, 1903–1985*. Lubbock, TX: Craftsman, 1985.

Morgan, David P. "Go West, Middle-Aged Man, Go West." Special edition *Trains of the 1960s: Challenging Times for America's Railroads. Classic Trains* no. 3, (2004): 93.

———, "The Rock Reborn." *Trains* (March 1983): 49–50.

———, "We'll Adjust, But It Won't Be Easy." Special Edition, *Trains of the 1960s: Challenging Times for America's Railroads. Classic Trains* no. 3 (2004): 112.

Morris, John Miller. *El Llano Estacado: Exploration and Imagination on the High Plains of Texas and New Mexico, 1536–1860*. Austin: Texas State Historical Association, 1997.

Moser, Benjamin. "Saboteur in Texas." *New York Review of Books* (May 27, 2004): 26–28.

Mulhouse, John M. *Abandoned New Mexico*. Charleston, SC Arcadia, 2020.

Murphy, Finn. *The Long Haul: Tales of Life on the Open Road*. New York: W. W. Norton, 2017.

Murphy, Vera. "Tucumcari's History as Scene of Hitchhiker Slayings Recalled." *Albuquerque Journal*, January 17, 1954.

Murray, Robert K. *The Harding Era: Warren G. Harding and His Administration*. Minneapolis: University of Minnesota Press, 1969.

Murray, Tom. "Looking for a Silver Bullet: The East After Conrail. Part 1." *Trains* (September 2005): 26–39.

Myrick, David F. *New Mexico's Railroads: A Historical Survey*. Rev. ed. Albuquerque: University of New Mexico Press, 1990.

Nash, Jay Robert. *Citizen Hoover: A Critical Study of the Life and Times of J. Edgar Hoover and His FBI*. Chicago: Nelson-Hall, 1972.

Nathan, Fred, and Kristina Gray Fisher. "A History: The Growth of School Size in New Mexico." In *Small Schools: Tackling the Dropout Crisis While Saving Taxpayer Dollars*, 8. Santa Fe: Think New Mexico, 2008.

National Investigations Committee on Aerial Phenomena. Case Directory, Category 1, Distant Sightings, AFOSI Case 42, Tucumcari, NM, March 27, 1949, https://www.thinkaboutitdocs.com/49-march/ufo-alien.

Neeley, Bill. *The Last Comanche Chief: The Life and Times of Quanah Parker*. New York: Wiley, 1995.

Nelson, Bob. "End of an Era—Forrest School Closes." *Tucumcari Daily News Review*, May 27, 1966.

Nelson, Kate. "Molten Beauty." *New Mexico* (March 2018): 40–47.

Nelson, Paul C. "Rise and Decline of the Rock Island Passenger Train in the 20th Century." *Annals of Iowa* 41 (Fall 1971): 740, 743, 755.

"Neon Restoration Continues." *Route 66 New Mexico* (Spring 2005): 9.

Newell, Clayton R. "Railroaders in Olive Drab: The Military Railway Service in World War II." *Army History* (Fall 2013): 7–13.

New Mexico Communities By-Pass Association. "The By-Pass Story." *Tucumcari Daily News* supplement, September 17, 1963.

Niederman, Sharon. "A Better Life: Jewish Pioneers Add to State's Cultural Richness." *New Mexico* (October 2000): 60–62.

———. "Hometown Spotlight: Tucumcari Gets Its Kicks." *American Profile* (October 23, 2004): 14.

Noyes, Stanley. *Los Comanches: The Horse People*. Albuquerque: University of New Mexico Press, 1993.

O'Cain, Jane. Abstract of interview with Yetta Kohn Bidegain, May 13, 1996. Oral History Program, New Mexico Farm & Ranch Heritage Museum, Las Cruces, NM.

Office of War Information. Report on the Civilian Gasoline Supply, October 13, 1943. Great Plains During World War II. Center for Digital Research in the Humanities, University of Nebraska–Lincoln, 2008.https://plainshumanities.unl.edu/homefront/rationing.htm?section=homefront.

Orsi, Richard J. *Sunset Limited: The Southern Pacific Railroad and the Development of the American West, 1850–1930*. Berkeley: University of California Press, 2005.

Ottman, R. G. "Keep 'em Rolling on Time." *Southern Pacific Bulletin* (January 1971): 2–4.

Pach Jr., Chester J., and Elmo Richardson. *The Presidency of Dwight D. Eisenhower*. Rev. ed. American Presidency Series. Lawrence: University Press of Kansas, 1991.

Pacific Lines. *Schedule of Pay and Regulations for Trainmen*. May 1, 1928.

Parrish, William J. *The Charles Ilfeld Company: A Study of the Rise and Decline of Mercantile Capitalism in New Mexico*. Cambridge, MA: Harvard University Press, 1961.

Patton, Phil. *Open Road: A Celebration of the American Highway*. New York: Simon & Schuster, 1986.

Pearson, Jim Berry. *The Maxwell Land Grant*. Norman: University of Oklahoma Press, 1961.

Pew Jr., Thomas W. "Goodbye to Main Street 66." *American West* (September–October 1984): 47–51.

———. "Route 66: Ghost Road of the Okies." *American Heritage* (August 1977): 29.

———. "Tucumcari Tonight!" *American West: The Magazine of Western History* (January–February 1980): 33.

Phillips, Dan. "The Road to Rescue." *Classic Trains* (July 22, 2011): 23.

Phillips, David A. "The Arch Hurley Conservancy District: A Study in Persistence." Arch Hurley Conservancy District, Tucumcari, NM, 2002. Unpublished report by SWCA Environmental Consultants, Albuquerque, NM.

Phillips, Don. "Every 20 Years, Railroading Reinvents Itself." *Trains* (May 2003): 10.

Phillips, Kenneth. "Tucumcari, N. M.—The Photographer." *Four Corners—A Literary Excursion Across America*. n.d. https://www.manta.com/C/nm/49c6l.

Pinkepanik, Jerry A. "How the Diesel Changed Railroading." Special edition, *Diesel Victory*. *Classic Trains* no. 4 (2006): 8–19.

Pirsig, Robert M. *Zen and the Art of Motorcycle Maintenance: An Inquiry into Values*. New York: HarperTorch, 1999.

Pitel, Mike. "New Mexico's Route 66 Corridor." *New Mexico: Enchanting New Mexico Calendar*. Santa Fe: New Mexico Magazine, 2001.

Platonov, Andrei. "Among Animals and Plants." Translated by Robert and Elizabeth Chandler and Olga Meerson. *New Yorker* (October 22, 2007): 123.

Poling-Kempes, Lesley. *The Harvey Girls: Women Who Opened the West*. Boston: Da Capo, 1994.

Port Terminal Railroad Association. *Port Terminal Railroad Infrastructure*. Houston, TX, n.d. https://houstontx.gov/events/.

QC Sun. *Sunscape: Visitor's Guide to Tucumcari & Quay County*. Spring–Summer 1993.

Railway Age. "Cheap Oil." (November 15, 1901): 555.

———. "Rock Island Bridge over the Canadian River in New Mexico." (December 8, 1901).

———. "The Rock Island's New Line to El Paso." (November 8, 1901).

Ranger, Dan. "There's a Difference Between Engineers and Truck Drivers." *Trains* (August 2007): 20–21.

"Recollections of Roy H. Smith." *Tucumcari Daily News*, February 13, 1940.

Regular Army Retired List. January 1, 1963, vol. 1, p. 738, https://www.archives.gov/military/part-1-notes.

Remley, David A. *Bell Ranch: Cattle Ranching in the Southwest, 1824–1947*. Albuquerque: University of New Mexico Press, 1993.

Richards, Fenton. "Vanishing Depots: Vintage Railroad Stations on an Uncertain Track." *New Mexico* (January 1996): 51–59.

Richardson, Bill, with Michael Ruby. *Between Worlds: The Making of an American Life*. New York: G. P. Putnam's Sons, 2005.

Rischin, Moses, and John Livingston, eds. *Jews of the American West*. Detroit: Wayne State University Press, 1991.

RoadKing. "More and More Couples Are Trucking Together—and Loving It." (January–February 2015).

Robbins, L. H. "America Hobnobs at the Tourist Camp." *New York Times Magazine* (August 12, 1934): 9, 19.

Roberts, Steven M. "Ode to a Freeway." *New York Times Magazine* (April 18, 1973): 21.

Rock Island Railroad. *1964 Annual Report*, 5.

Rodden, Robert G. *The Fighting Machinists: A Century of Struggle*. Washington, DC: Kelly Press, 1984.

Rogers, Jedediah S. *Tucumcari Project*. Historic Reclamation Projects, US Bureau of Reclamation, Washington, DC, 2009. Reformatted, edited, and reprinted by Andrew H. Gahan, June 2013.

Roper, James L. "Steel Rails to the Sunbelt: The Golden State and Sunset Routes." *Passenger Train Journal* (July 1991): 28.

Rosin, James. *Route 66: The Television Series*. Rev. ed. Philadelphia, PA: Autumn Road, 2006.

Rothman, Hal. *Neon Metropolis: How Las Vegas Started the Twenty-First Century*. New York: Routledge, 2002.

Roush, Andrew. "In Alien Territory." *New Mexico* (July 2017): 52–56, 58.

Route 66 News. "Route 66 Museum Likely will be in Tucumcari Convention Center." August 23, 2012. https://www.route66news.com/2012/08/23/route-66-museum-tucumcari-convention-center/.

Sanchez, Joseph P., Robert L. Spude, and Arthur R. Gomez. *New Mexico: A History.* Norman: University of Oklahoma Press, 2014.

Sartain, Pauline. Interview by Mary Grooms. *Tucumcari News,* July 25, 1975.

Saunders Jr., Richard. *Main Lines: Rebirth of the North American Railroads, 1970–2002.* DeKalb: Northern Illinois University Press, 2003.

Scharff, Virginia. *Twenty-Thousand Roads: Women, Movement, and the West.* Berkeley: University of California Press, 2003.

Schisgall, Oscar. *The Greyhound Story: From Hibbing to Everywhere.* Chicago: J. G. Ferguson/Doubleday, 1985.

Schneider, Gregory L. *Rock Island Requiem: The Collapse of a Mighty Fine Line.* Lawrence: University Press of Kansas, 2013.

Schwantes, Carlos A. *Going Places: Transportation Redefines the Twentieth-Century West.* Bloomington: University of Indiana Press, 2003.

———. *The Pacific Northwest: An Interpretive History.* Lincoln: University of Nebraska Press, 1989.

———. *Vision and Enterprise: Exploring the History of Phelps Dodge Corporation.* Tucson: University of Arizona Press & Phelps Dodge Corporation, 2000.

Schwantes, Carlos A., and James P. Ronda. *The West the Railroads Made.* Seattle: University of Washington Press in association with Washington State Historical Society, Tacoma, WA, and James W. Barringer III National Railroad Library at the St. Louis Mercantile Library, University of Missouri–St. Louis, 2008.

Schwieterman, Joseph P. *When the Railroad Leaves Town.* Kirksville, MO: Truman State University Press, 2004.

Shelburg, John D. "Conchas Dam." New Mexico Office of the State Historian, Santa Fe, NM.

Sloane, Arthur A. *Hoffa.* Cambridge, MA: MIT Press, 1991.

Smith, Toby. *Coal Town: The Life and Times of Dawson, New Mexico.* Santa Fe, NM: Ancient City, 1994.

———. "Recollections of a Golden God." *Albuquerque Journal,* November 21, 1995.

Smith-Peterson, Ted. "The Spigot: How Commerce Flows from Southern California Ports onto US Rails, Pt. 2." *Trains* (September 2013): 33–40, 54.

Snyder, Logan Thomas. "President Dwight Eisenhower and America's Interstate Highway System." *American History* (June 2006): 33–39.

Sonderman, Joe. *Images of America: Route 66 in New Mexico.* Charleston, SC: Arcadia, 2010.

———. *Route 66: Roadside Signs and Advertisements.* Minneapolis: Voyageur, 2016.

Sopronyi, Judy P. "Watching the Radio." *America in WWII* (April 2006): 44–49.

Southern Pacific Railroad Collection, Special Collections, University of Texas at El Paso Library, El Paso, TX.

————, *Annual Report, 1960*. SP Collection, UTEP.

————, *Annual Report, 1964*, 8. Department of Archives and Special Collections, Arizona State University (ASU) Libraries.

————, *Annual Report, 1967*, 3, ASU Libraries.

————, *Annual Report, 1982*, 2–3. ASU Libraries.

————, *Southern Pacific Bulletin* (March–April 1988): 36. SP Collection UTEP.

Spence, R. D. "A Message from the President." *Conrail*, company publication (April–May 1976).

Spencer, Leon B., comp. *U.S. Army Air Force, CG-4A, Combat Glider: A Brief History, in World War II*. https://ww2gliderpilot.blogspot.com/2012/06/us-army-air-force-cg-4a-combat-glider.html.

Steinbeck, John. *The Grapes of Wrath*. New York: Bantam Books, 1946.

Stillwell, Paul, ed. *Air Raid: Pearl Harbor! Recollections of a Day of Infamy*. Annapolis, MD: Naval Institute Press, 1981.

Stindt, Fred A. "The Last Days of Southern Pacific Steam." *Railroad History Bulletin* 149, (Autumn 1983): 101–13.

Stone, David L. "Fields of Hope: How Portales Won the Battle for Eastern New Mexico University." *New Mexico* 9November 2006): 72–74.

Stratton, David H. "The Jewish Founding Fathers of Tucumcari." *New Mexico Historical Review* 89 (Winter 2014): 25–62.

————, *Tempest over Teapot Dome: The Story of Albert B. Fall*. Norman: University of Oklahoma Press, 1998.

Stratton, Porter A. *The Territorial Press of New Mexico, 1834–1912*. Albuquerque: University of New Mexico Press, 1969.

Suttle, Howard. *Greyhound Tales from Route 66*. Raton, NM: Data Plus!, 2004.

Sutton, Horace. "Way Back When: Frisky, Risky Birth of the Auto Age." *Smithsonian* (September 1980): 135–48.

Sweeney, Steve. "Explaining the Surface Transformation Board." *Trains* (May 2016): 7.

Sweet, A. E. "All Employees of the Mechanical Department, Who Voluntarily Left the Service at 10:00 A.M., July 1st." Memorandum, July 5, 1922.

Tarter, Maria. "Truck Drivers, Families [*sic*] Lives Aren't Easy." *QC Sun*, February 11, 1995.

Taylor, William Carl. *Route 66: A Trail of Tears*. 90th anniversary ed. Carthage, MO: privately published, 2016.

Tennant, Tim. "Tucumcari Depot: Honoring the Past, Conducting the Future." Museum Interpretive Plan Presentation, Tucumcari MainStreet Program, Tucumcari, NM, August 11, 2011.

Theroux, Paul. *The Great Railway Bazaar: By Train Through Asia*. Boston: Houghton Mifflin, 1975.

Thompson, Fritz. "Return to Glory: Railroad Towns Turn Neglected Depots into Cultural and Economic Investments." *Albuquerque Sunday Journal*, August 27, 2000.

Thompson, William. "Murals Celebrate Tucumcari." *Route 66 Guide* (2005): 6.

Thornton, Linda. "Bettie Ditto: Tucumcari Businesswoman Plies Her Trade on Route 66." *New Mexico* (February 2001): 24.

Tobias, Henry Jack. *A History of the Jews in New Mexico*. Albuquerque: University of New Mexico Press, 2000.

Tobias, Henry, and Sarah R. Payne. *Jewish Pioneers of New Mexico: The Ilfeld and Nordhaus Families*. Albuquerque: New Mexico Jewish Historical Society, 2003.

Trains of the 1950s: Railroading's Decade of Change. 2013.

Trains. Special 75th Anniversary Edition. "75 People You Should Know." (November 2015): 58.

Trains. "Commentary: Inside the mind of Michael Ward." (July 2016): 14–15.

———. "Fantrip: Dots and Dashes Forever?" (May 2006): 76.

———. "Getting the Mail Back on Track." (March 2015): 6.

Trans World Airlines (TWA) Records. Collection No. K0453, State Historical Society of Missouri, Research Center, Kansas City.

Trauger, F. D., and F. X. Bushman. *Geology and Ground Water in the Vicinity of Tucumcari, Quay County, New Mexico*. New Mexico Bureau of Mines and Mineral Resources, in cooperation with the City of Tucumcari and the US Geological Survey, 1964.

Turnbeaugh, Billy Jack. *Tucumcari High School Rattler Football Greats through the Decades, 1920s–1990s*. Upland, CA: Dragonflyer, 2004.

Tuttle Jr., William M. *"Daddy's Gone to War": The Second World War in the Lives of America's Children*. New York: Oxford University Press, 1993.

Twitchell, Ralph Emerson. *The Leading Facts of New Mexican History*. 5 vols. Cedar Rapids, IA: Torch, 1912–1917.

US Census Bureau. Current Hispanic or Latino Population, Tucumcari, New Mexico, 2016, 2015 with Demographics and Stats by Age and Gender.

US Census Bureau. Quay County, NM, 1994.

US Census Reports, 1920 and 1930.

US Congress, Senate. Rock Island Transition Act, Hearing Before the Subcommittee on Surface Transportation of the Committee on Commerce, Science, and Transportation, S 2246, S2253, SJ Res. 139, 96th Cong., February 20, 1980.

US Department of the Interior, National Park Service. National Register of Historic Places Registration Form, "Metropolitan Park Bathhouse and Pool Historic District," Tucumcari, New Mexico, September 30, 1995.

US Interstate Commerce Commission. *Decisions of the Interstate Commerce Commission of the United States* (Finance Reports), vol. 328, August 1966–March 1967. Washington, DC: Government Printing Office, 1967.

US Interstate Commerce Commission. *Decisions of the Interstate Commerce Commission of the United States* (Finance Reports), vol. 331, September 1967–April 1968. Washington, DC: US Government Printing Office, 1970.

Visitor Guide: Tucumcari/Quay County, New Mexico. Tucumcari/Quay County Chamber of Commerce. Tucumcari, NM, ca. 2015.

Walker, Mike. *SPV's Comprehensive Railroad Atlas of North America: Arizona & New Mexico*. Upper Harbledown, Canterbury, Kent, UK: Stuart Andrews, 2006.

Wallis, Michael. "Mother Road Journey." *New Mexico* (February 1989): 42–43.

———. "Route 66: Cruising Down America's Mother Road." *New Mexico* (February 1989): 25–27.

———. *Route 66: The Mother Road*. New York: St. Martin's Press, 1990.

Walsh, Larry. "Why the Southern Pacific Failed." An Opinion Piece, Texas Transportation Museum, San Antonio, n.d.

Ward, James A. "On Time: Railroads and the Tempo of American Life." *Railroad History* 151 (Autumn 1984): 89.

Watts, Steven. *The People's Tycoon: Henry Ford and the American Century*. New York: Knopf, 2005.

Weingroff, Richard F. "Federal-Aid Highway Act of 1956: Creating the Interstate System." *Public Roads* (Summer 1996): 1–12, https://www.highways.dot.gov/public-roads-magazine.

Welsh, Michael E. *A Mission in the Desert: The US Army Corps of Engineers, Albuquerque District, 1985–2010*. Washington, DC: Government Printing Office, 2015.

Whipple, A. W. "Report of Explorations for a Railway Route, Near the Thirty-fifth Parallel of North Latitude from the Mississippi River to the Pacific Ocean. . . ." In *Reports of Explorations and Surveys . . . to Ascertain the Most Practical and Economic Route for a Railroad from the Mississippi River to the Pacific Ocean*. 11 vols., 33 Cong., 2 Sess., Senate Ex. Doc. 78. Washington, DC: Beverly Tucker, 1856.

Whisenhunt, Donald W. *New Mexico Courthouses*. Monograph No. 57, Southwest Studies. El Paso: Texas Western Press, University of Texas at El Paso.

Whitehead, Don. *The FBI Story: A Report to the People*. New York: Random House, 1956.

Whittington, Debra Ann. *In the Shadow of the Mountain: Living in Tucumcari*. Tucumcari: Copperhead, 1997.

Williams, J. W. *The Big Ranch Country*. Wichita Falls, TX: Terry Brothers, 1954.

Wilner, Frank N. "Railroads in the 20th Century." *Railway Age* (December 1999), https://www.issuu.com/railwayage/docs.

Wilson, Kemmons, and Robert Kerr. *Half Luck and Half Brains: The Kemmons Wilson, Holiday Inn Story*. Nashville: Hambleton-Hill, 1996.

Wilson, Neill C., and Frank J. Taylor. *Southern Pacific: The Roaring Story of a Fighting Railroad*. New York: McGraw-Hill, 1952.

Winston, Steve. "Tucumcari Born with a Railroad Boom." *Albuquerque Journal*, March 11, 1979.

Worobiec, Tony, and Eva Worobiec. *Icons of the Highway: A Celebration of Small-Town America*. London: AAPPL, 2008.

WPA Writers' Program of New Mexico, ed. *New Mexico: A Guide to the Colorful State*. American Guide Series, 2nd ed. Albuquerque: University of New Mexico Press, 1945.

Wyckoff, William. "Life on the Margin: The Evolution of the Waning West." *Montana: Magazine of Western History* 52 (Autumn 2002): 35.

Zaga, Michael E. "The Best on Wheels." *Trains* (April 2006): 70–71.

INDEX